ISBN 978-1-334-95087-2
PIBN 10779935

FB &c Ltd, Dalton House, 60 Windsor Avenue, London, SW19 2RR.
Company number 08720141. Registered in England and Wales.

POLITICAL ESSAYS,

WITH

Sketches of Public Characters.

BY

WILLIAM HAZLITT.

"Come, draw the curtain, shew the picture."

LONDON:

PRINTED FOR WILLIAM HONE,

45, LUDGATE HILL.

1819.

To JOHN HUNT, Esq.

THE tried, steady, zealous, and conscientious advocate of the liberty of his country, and the rights of mankind;——

One of those few persons who are what they would be thought to be; sincere without offence, firm but temperate; uniting private worth to public principle; a friend in need, a patriot without an eye to himself; who never betrayed an individual or a cause he pretended to serve—in short, that rare character, a man of common sense and common honesty,

This volume is respectfully and gratefully inscribed by

THE AUTHOR.

PREFACE.

I AM no politician, and still less can I be said to be a party-man: but I have a hatred of tyranny, and a contempt for its tools; and this feeling I have expressed as often and as strongly as I could. I cannot sit quietly down under the claims of barefaced power, and I have tried to expose the little arts of sophistry by which they are defended. I have no mind to have my person made a property of, nor my understanding made a dupe of. I deny that liberty and slavery are convertible terms, that right and wrong, truth and falsehood, plenty and famine, the comforts or wretchedness of a people, are matters of perfect indifference. That is all I know of the matter; but on these points I am likely to remain incorrigible, in spite of any arguments that I have seen used to the contrary. It needs no sagacity to discover that two and two make four; but to persist in maintaining this obvious position, if all the fashion, authority, hypocrisy, and venality of mankind were arrayed against it, would require a considerable effort of personal courage, and would soon leave a man in a very formidable minority. Again, I am no believer in the doctrine of *divine right*, either as it regards the Stuarts or the Bourbons; nor can I bring myself to approve of the enormous waste of blood and treasure wilfully incurred by a family that supplanted the one in this country to restore the others in France. It is to my mind a piece of sheer impudence. The question between natural liberty and hereditary slavery, whether men are born free or slaves, whether kings are the servants of the people, or the people the property of kings (whatever we may think of it in the abstract, or debate about it in the schools)—in this country, in Old England, and under the succession of the House of Hanover, is not a question of theory, but has been long since decided by certain facts and feelings, to call which in question would be equally inconsistent with proper respect to the people, or common decency towards the throne. An English subject cannot call this principle in question without renouncing his country; an English prince cannot call it in question without disclaiming his title to the crown, which was placed by our ancestors on the head of his ancestors, on no other ground and for no other possible purpose than to vindicate this sacred principle in their own persons, and to hold it out as an example to posterity and to the world. An Elector of Hanover, called over here to be made king of England, in contempt and to the exclusion of the claims of the old, hereditary possessors and pretenders to the throne, on any other plea except that of his being the chosen representative and appointed guardian of the rights and liberties of the people (the consequent pledge and guarantee of the rights and liberties of other nations) would indeed be a solecism more absurd and contemptible than any to be found in history. What! Send for a petty Elector of a petty foreign state to reign over us from respect to *his* right to the throne of these realms, in defiance of the legitimate heir to the crown, and "in contempt of the choice of the people!" Oh monstrous fiction! Miss Flora Mac Ivor would not have heard of such a thing: the author of Waverley has well answered Mr. Burke's "Appeal from the New to the Old Whigs."*

* Mr. Burke pretends in this Jesuitical Appeal, that a nation has a right to insist upon and revert to old establishments and prescriptive privileges, but not to lay claim to new ones; in a word, to change its governors, if refractory, but not its form of government, however bad. Thus he says we had a right to cashier James II., because he wished to alter the laws and religion as they were then established. By what right did we emancipate ourselves from popery and arbitrary power a century before? He defends his consistency in advocating the American Revolution, though the rebels, in getting rid of the reigning branch of the Royal Family, did not send for the next of kin to rule over them "in contempt of their choice," but prevented all such equivocations by passing at once from a viceroyalty to a republic. He also extols the Polish Revolution as a monument of wisdom and virtue (I suppose because it had not succeeded), though this also was a total and absolute change in the frame and principles of the government, to which the people were in this case bound by no feudal tenure or divine right. But he insists that the French Revolution was stark-naught, because the people here did the same thing, passed from slavery to liberty, from an arbitrary to a constitutional government, to which they had, it seems, no prescriptive right, and therefore, according to the appellant, no right at all. Oh

Let not our respect for our ancestors, who fought and bled for their own freedom, and to aid (not to stifle) the cause of freedom in other nations, suffer us to believe this poor ideot calumny of them. Let not our shame at having been inveigled into crusades and Holy Alliances against the freedom of mankind, suffer us to be made the dupes of it ourselves, in thought, in word, or deed. The question of genuine liberty or of naked slavery, if put in words, should be answered by Englishmen with scorn: if put in any other shape than words, it must be answered in a different way, unless they would lose the name of Englishmen! An Englishman has no distinguishing virtue but honesty: he has and can have no privilege or advantage over other nations but liberty. If he is not free, he is the worst of slaves, for he is nothing else. If he feels that he has wrongs and dare not say so, he is the meanest of hypocrites; for it is certain that he cannot be contented under them.—This was once a free, a proud, and happy country, when under a constitutional monarchy and a Whig king, it had just broken the chains of tyranny that were prepared for it, and successfully set at defiance the menaces

nice professor of humanity! We had a right to turn off James II. because he broke a compact with the people. The French had no right to turn off Louis XVI. because he broke no compact with them, for he had none to break; in other words, because he was an arbitrary despot, tied to no laws, and they a herd of slaves, and therefore they were bound, by every law divine and human, always to remain so, in perpetuity and by the grace of God! Oh unanswerable logician!

of an hereditary pretender; when the monarch still felt what he owed to himself and the people, and in the opposite claims which were set up to it, saw the real tenure on which he held his crown; when civil and religious liberty were the watch-words by which good men and true subjects were known to one another, not by the cant of legitimacy; when the reigning sovereign stood between you and the polluted touch of a bigot and a despot who stood ready to seize upon you and yours as his lawful prey; when liberty and loyalty went hand in hand, and the Tory principles of passive obedience and non-resistance were more unfashionable at court than in the country; when to uphold the authority of the throne, it was not thought necessary to undermine the privileges or break the spirit of the nation; when an Englishman felt that his name was another name for independence, "the envy of less happier lands," when it was his pride to be born, and his wish that other nations might become free; before a sophist and an apostate had dared to tell him that he had no share, no merit, no free agency, in the glorious Revolution of 1688, and that he was bound to lend a helping hand to crush all others, that implied a right in the people to chuse their own form of government; before he was become sworn brother to the Pope, familiar to the Holy Inquisition, an encourager of the massacres of his Protestant brethren, a patron of the Bourbons, and jailor to the liberties of mankind! Ah, John Bull! John Bull! thou art not what thou wert in the days of thy friend, Arbuthnot! Thou wert an honest fellow then: now thou art turned bully and coward.

This is the only politics I know; the only patriotism I feel. The question with me is, whether I and all mankind are born slaves or free. That is the one thing necessary to know and to make good: the rest is *flocci, nauci, nihili, pili*. Secure this point, and all is safe: lose this, and all is lost. There are people who cannot understand a principle; nor perceive how a cause can be connected with an individual, even in spite of himself, nor how the salvation of mankind can be bound up with the success of one man. It is in vain that I address to them what follows.—" One fate attends the altar and the throne." So sings Mr. Southey. I say, that one fate attends the people and the assertor of the people's rights against those who say they have no rights, that they are their property, their goods, their chattels, the live-stock on the estate of Legitimacy. This is what kings at present tell us with their swords, and poets with their pens. He who tells me this deprives me not only of the right, but of the very heart and will to be free, takes the breath out of the body of liberty, and leaves it a dead and helpless corse, destroys " at one fell swoop" the dearest hopes, and blasts the fairest prospects of mankind through all ages and nations, sanctifies slavery, binds it as a spell on the understanding, and makes freedom a mockery, and the name a bye-word. The poor wretch immured in the dungeons of the Inquisition may breathe a sigh to liberty, may repeat its name, may think of it as a blessing, if not to himself, to others; but the wretch imprisoned in the dungeon of Legitimacy, the very tomb of free dom, that "painted sepulchre, white without, but full of ravening and all uncleanness within," must not even think of it, must not so much as dream of it, but as a thing forbid: it is a profanation to his lips, an impiety to his thoughts; his very imagination is enthralled, and he can only look forward to the never-ending flight of future years, and see the same gloomy prospect of abject wretchedness and hopeless desolation spread out for himself and his species. They who bow to thrones and hate mankind may here feast their eyes with blight, mildew, the blue pestilence and glittering poison of slavery, "bogs, dens, and shades of death—a universe of death." This is that true moral atheism, the equal blasphemy against God and man, the sin against the Holy Ghost, that lowest deep of debasement and despair to which there is no lower deep. He who saves me from this conclusion, who makes a mock of this doctrine, and sets at nought its power, is to me not less than the God of my idolatry, for he has left one drop of comfort in my soul. The plague-spot has not tainted me quite; I am not leprous all over, the lie of Legitimacy does not fix its mortal sting in my inmost soul, nor, like an ugly spider, entangle me in its slimy folds; but is kept off from me, and broods on its own poison. He who did this for me, and for the rest of the world, and who alone could do it, was Buonaparte. He withstood the inroads of this new Jaggernaut, this foul Blatant Beast, as it strode forward to its prey over the bodies and minds of a whole people, and put a ring in its nostrils, breathing flame and blood, and led it in triumph, and played with its crowns and sceptres, and wore them in its stead, and tamed its crested pride, and made it a laughing-stock and a mockery to the nations. He, one man, did this, and as long as he did this, (how, or for what end, is nothing to the magnitude of this mighty question) he saved the human race from the last ignominy, and that foul stain that had so long been intended, and was at last, in an evil hour and by evil hands, inflicted on it. He put his foot upon the neck of kings, who would have put their yoke upon the necks of the people: he scattered before him with fiery execution, millions of hired slaves, who came at the bidding of their masters to deny the right of others to be free. The monument of greatness and of glory he erected, was raised on ground forfeited again and again to humanity—it reared its majestic front on the ruins of the shattered hopes and broken faith of the common enemies of mankind. If he could not secure the freedom, peace, and happiness of his country, he made her a terror to those who by sowing civil dissension and exciting foreign wars, would not let her enjoy those blessings. They who had trampled upon Liberty could not at least triumph in her shame and her despair, but themselves became objects of pity and derision. Their determination to persist in extremity of wrong only brought on themselves repeated defeat, disaster, and dismay: the accumulated aggressions their infuriated pride and disappointed malice meditated against others, returned in just and aggravated punishment upon themselves: they heaped coals of fire upon their own heads; they drank deep and long, in gall and bitterness, of the poisoned chalice they had prepared for others: the destruction with which they had threatened a people daring to call itself free, hung suspended over their heads, like a precipice, ready to fall upon and crush them. "Awhile they stood abashed," abstracted from their evil purposes, and felt how awful freedom is, its power how dreadful. Shrunk from the boasted pomp of royal state into their littleness as men, defeated of their revenge, baulked of their prey, their schemes stripped of their bloated pride, and with nothing left but the deformity of their malice, not daring to utter a syllable or move a finger, the lords of the earth, who had looked upon men as of an inferior species, born for their use, and devoted to be their slaves, turned an imploring eye to the people, and with coward hearts and hollow tongues invoked the name of Liberty, thus to get the people once more within their unhallowed gripe, and to stifle the name of Liberty for ever. I never joined the vile and treacherous cry of spurious humanity in favour of those who have from the beginning of time, and will to the end of it, make a butt of humanity, and its distresses their sport. I knew that shameful was this new alliance between kings and people; fatal this pretended league: that "never can true reconcilement grow where wounds of deadly hate have pierced so deep." I was right in this respect. I knew my friends from my foes. So did Lord Castlereagh: so did not Benjamin Constant. Did any of the Princes of Europe ever regard Buonaparte as any thing more than the child and champion of Jacobinism? Why then should I: for on that point I bow to their judgments as infallible. Passion speaks truer than reason. If Buonaparte was a conqueror, he conquered the grand conspiracy of kings against the abstract right of the human race to be free; and I, as a man, could not be indifferent which side to take. If he was ambitious, his greatness was not founded on the unconditional, avowed surrender of the rights of human nature. But with him, the state of man rose exalted too. If he was arbitrary and a tyrant, first, France as a country was in a state of military blockade, on garrison-duty, and not to be defended by mere paper bullets of the brain; secondly, but chief, he was not, nor he could not become, a tyrant by right divine. Tyranny in him was not sacred: it was not eternal: it was not instinctively bound in league of amity with other tyrannies; it was not sanctioned by all the laws of religion and morality. There was an end of it with the individual: there was an end of it with the temporary causes, which gave it birth, and of which it was only the too necessary reaction. But there are persons of that low and inordinate appetite for servility, that they cannot be satisfied with any thing short of that sort of tyranny that has lasted for ever, and is likely to last for ever; that is strengthened and made desperate by the superstitions and prejudices of ages; that is enshrined in traditions, in laws, in usages, in the outward symbols of power, in the very idioms of language; that has struck its roots into the human heart, and clung round the human understanding like a nightshade; that overawes the imagination, and disarms the will to resist it, by the very enormity of the evil; that is cemented with gold and blood; guarded by reverence, guarded by power; linked in endless succession to the principle by which life is transmitted to the generations of tyrants and slaves, and destroying liberty with the first breath of life; that is absolute, unceasing, unerring, fatal, unutterable, abominable, monstrous. These true devotees of superstition and despotism cried out Liberty and Humanity in their desperate phrenzy at Buonaparte's sudden elevation and incredible successes against their favourite idol, "that Harlot old, the same that is, that was, and is to be," but we have heard no more of their triumph of Liberty and their *douce humanité*, since they clapped down the hatches upon us again, like wretches in a slave-ship who have had their chains struck off and pardon promised them to fight the common enemy; and the poor Reformers who were taken in to join the cry, because they are as fastidious in their love of liberty as their opponents are inveterate in their devotion to despotism, continue in vain to reproach them with their temporary professions, woeful grimaces, and vows made in pain, which ease has recanted; but to these reproaches the legitimate professors of Liberty and Humanity do not even deign to return the answer of a smile at their credulity and folly. Those who did not see this result at the time were, I think, weak; those who do not acknowledge it now are, I am sure, hypocrites.—To this pass have we been brought by the joint endeavours of Tories, Whigs, and Reformers; and as they have all had a hand in it, I shall here endeavour to ascribe to each their share of merit in this goodly piece of work. It is, perhaps, a delicate point, but it is of no inconsiderable importance, that the friends of Freedom should know the strength of their enemies, and their own weakness as well; for

> ——— "At this day,
> When a Tartarean darkness overspreads
> The groaning nations; when the impious rule,
> By will or by established ordinance,
> Their own dire agents, and constrain the good
> To acts which they abhor; though I bewail
> This triumph, yet the pity of my heart
> Prevents me not from owning that the law
> By which mankind now suffers, is most just.
> For by superior energies; more strict
> Affiance to each other; faith more firm
> In their unhallowed principles; the bad
> Have fairly earned a victory o'er the weak,
> The vacillating, inconsistent good."

A Reformer is not a gregarious animal. Speculative opinion leads men different ways, each according to his particular fancy :—it is prejudice or interest that drives before it the herd of mankind. That *which is*, with all its confirmed abuses and "tickling commodities," is alone solid and certain: that *which may be* or *ought to be*, has a thousand shapes and colours, according to the eye that sees it, is infinitely variable and evanescent in its effects. Talk of mobs as we will, the only true mob is that incorrigible mass of knaves and fools in every country, who never think at all, and who never feel for any one but themselves. I call any assembly of people a mob (be it the House of Lords or House of Commons) where each person's opinion on any question is governed by what others say of it, and by what he can get by it. The only instance of successful resistance in the House of Commons to Ministers for many years was in the case of the Income-Tax; which touched their own pockets nearly. This was "a feeling disputation," in which selfishness got the better of servility, while reason and humanity might have pleaded in vain. The exception proved the rule; and this evidence was alone wanting to establish their character for independence and disinterestedness. When some years ago Mr. Robson brought forward in the House the case of an Exchequer Bill for 3*l.* 16*s.* which had been refused payment at the Bank, the Chancellor of the Exchequer (then Mr. Addington, now Lord Sidmouth) rose, and in a tone of indignation, severely reprimanded Mr. Robson for having prematurely brought forward a fact which he knew to be impossible; and the House cheered the Minister, and scouted Mr. Robson and his motion for inquiry. The next day, Mr. Robson repeated his charge, and Mr. Addington rose, and in the same tone of official authority, brow-beat Mr. Robson for having brought forward, as something reprehensible and extraordinary, what he said happened every day, though the day before he had undertaken of his own accord to pronounce it impossible; and the House cheered the Minister, and scouted Mr. Robson and his motion for inquiry. What was it to them whether Mr. Robson was right or wrong? It was their cue (I speak this of the House of Commons of 1803) to support the Minister, whether right or wrong! Every corporate body, or casual concourse of people, is nothing more than a collection of prejudices, and the only arguments current with them, a collection of watch-words. You may ring the changes for ever on the terms Bribery and Corruption with the people in Palace-yard, as they do in the Room over the way on Religion, Loyalty, Public Credit, and Social Order. There is no difference whatever in this respect between the Great Vulgar and the Small, who are managed just in the same way by their different leaders. To procure unanimity, to get men to act in *corps*, we must appeal for the most part to gross and obvious motives, to authority and passion, to their vices, not their virtues: we must discard plain truth and abstract justice as doubtful and inefficient pleas, retaining only the names and the pretext as a convenient salvo for hypocrisy! He is the best leader of a party who can find out the greatest number of common-places faced with the public good; and he will be the stoutest partisan who can best turn the lining to account.—Tory sticks to Tory: Whig sticks to Whig: the Reformer sticks neither to himself nor to any body else. It is no wonder he comes to the ground with all his schemes and castle-building. A house divided against itself cannot stand. It is a pity, but it cannot be helped. A Reformer is necessarily and naturally a Marplot, for the foregoing and the following reasons. First, he does not very well know what he would be at. Secondly, if he did, he does not care very much about it. Thirdly, he is governed habitually by a spirit of contradiction, and is always wise beyond what is practicable. He is a bad tool to work with; a part of a machine that never fits its place; he cannot be trained to discipline, for he follows his own idle humours, or drilled into an obedience to orders, for the first principle of his mind is the supremacy of conscience, and the independent right of private judgment. A man to be a Reformer must be more influenced by imagination and reason than by received opinions or sensible impressions. With him ideas bear sway over things; the possible is of more value than the real; that which is not, is better than that which is. He is by the supposition a speculative (and somewhat fantastical) character; but there is no end of possible speculations, of imaginary questions, and nice distinctions; or if there were, he would not willingly come to it; he would still prefer living in the world of his own ideas, be for raising some new objection, and starting some new chimera, and never be satisfied with any plan that he found he could realise. Bring him to a fixed point, and his occupation would be gone. A Reformer never is—but always to be blest, in the accomplishment of his airy hopes and shifting schemes of progressive perfectibility. Let him have the plaything of his fancy, and he will spoil it, like the child that makes a hole in its drum: set some brilliant illusion before his streaming eyes, and he will lay violent hands upon it, like little wanton boys that play with air-bubbles. Give him one thing, and he asks for another; like the dog in the fable, he loses the substance for the shadow: offer him a great good, and he will not stretch out his hand to take it, unless it were the greatest possible good. And then who is to determine what is the greatest possible good? Among a thousand pragmatical speculators, there will be a thousand opinions on this subject; and the more they differ, the less will they be inclined to give way or compromise the matter. With each of these, his self-opinion is the first thing to be attended to; his understanding must be satisfied in the first place, or he will not budge an inch; he cannot for the world give up a principle to a party. He would rather have slavery than liberty, unless it is a liberty precisely after his own fashion: he would sooner have the Bourbons than Buonaparte; for he truly is for a

Republic, and if he cannot have that, is indifferent about the rest. So (to compare great things with small) Mr. Place, of Charing-Cross, chose rather that Mr. Hobhouse should lose his Election than that it should not be accompanied with his Resolutions; so he published his Resolutions, and lost Mr. Hobhouse his Election. That is, a patriot of this stamp is really indifferent about every thing but what he cannot have; instead of making his option between two things, a good or an evil, within his reach, our exquisite Sir sets up a third thing as the object of his choice, with some impossible condition annexed to it,—to dream, to talk, to write, to be meddlesome and troublesome about, to serve him for a topic of captious discontent or vague declamation, and which if he saw any hopes of cordial agreement or practical co-operation to carry it into effect, he would instantly contrive to mar, and split it into a thousand fractions, doubts, and scruples, to make it an impossibility for any thing ever to be done for the good of mankind, which is merely the plaything of his theoretical imbecility and active impertinence! The Goddess of his idolatry is and will always remain a cloud, instead of a Juno. One of these virtuosos, these Nicolas Gimcracks of Reform, full of intolerable and vain conceit, sits smiling in the baby-house of his imagination, "pleased with a feather, tickled with a straw," trimming the balance of power in the looking-glass of his own self-complacency, having every thing his own way at a word's speaking, making the "giant-mass" of things only a reflection of his personal pretensions, approving every thing that is right, condemning every thing that is wrong, in compliment to his own character, considering how what he says will affect not the cause, but himself; keeping himself aloof from party-spirit, and from every thing that can cast a shade on the fancied delicacy of his own breast, and thus letting the cause of Liberty slip through his fingers, and be spilt like water on the ground:—while another, more bold than he, in a spirit of envy and ignorance, quarrels with all those who are labouring at the same oar, lays about him like mad, runs a-muck at every one who has done, or is likely to do, any thing to promote the common object, and with his desperate club dashes out his neighbour's brains, and thinks he has done a good piece of service to the cause, because he has glutted his own ill-humour and self-will, which he mistakes for the love of liberty and a zeal for truth! Others, not able to do mischief enough singly, club their senseless contradictions and unmanageable humours together, turn their attention to cabal and chicane, get into committees, make speeches, move or second resolutions, dictate to their followers, set up for the heads of a party, in opposition to another party; abuse, vilify, expose, betray, counteract and undermine each other in every way, and throw the game into the hands of the common enemy, who laughs in his sleeve, and watches them and their little perverse, pettifogging passions at work for him, from the high tower of his pride and strength! If an honest and able man arises among them, they grow jealous of him, and would rather, in the petty ostracism of their minds, that their cause should fail, than that another should have the credit of bringing it to a triumphant conclusion. They criticise his conduct, carp at his talents, denounce his friends, suspect his motives, and do not rest, till by completely disgusting him with the name of Reform and Reformers, they have made him what they wish, a traitor and deserter from a cause that no man can serve! This is just what they like—they satisfy their malice, they have to find out a new leader, and the cause is to begin again! So it was, and so it will be, while man remains the little, busy, mischievous animal described in Gulliver's Travels!—A pretty hopeful set to make head against their opponents—a rope of sand against a rock of marble—with no centre of gravity, but a collection of atoms whirled about in empty space by their own levity, or jostling together by numberless points of repulsion, and tossed with all their officious projects and airy predictions, by the first breath of caprice or shock of power, into that Limbo of Vanity, where embryo statesmen and drivelling legislators dance the hays of Reform, "perpetual circle, multiform and mix, and hinder all things," proud of the exclusive purity of their own motives, and the unattainable perfection of their own plans!—How different from the self-centred, well-knit, inseparable phalanx of power and authority opposed to their impotent and abortive designs! A Tory is one who is governed by sense and habit alone. He considers not what is possible, but what is real; he gives might the preference over right. He cries Long Life to the conqueror, and is ever strong upon the stronger side—the side of corruption and prerogative. He says what others say; he does as he is prompted by his own advantage. He knows on which side his bread is buttered, and that St. Peter is well at Rome. He is for going with Sancho to Camacho's wedding, and not for wandering with Don Quixote in the desert, after the mad lover. Strait is the gate and narrow is the way that leadeth to Reform, but broad is the way that leadeth to Corruption, and multitudes there are that walk therein. The Tory is sure to be in the thickest of them. His principle is to follow the leader; and this is the infallible rule to have numbers and success on your side, to be on the side of success and numbers. Power is the rock of his salvation; priestcraft is the second article of his implicit creed. He does not trouble himself to inquire which is the best form of government—but he knows that the reigning monarch is "the best of kings." He does not, like a fool, contest for modes of faith; but like a wise man, swears by that which is by law established. He has no principles himself, nor does he profess to have any, but will cut your throat for differing with any of his bigotted dogmas, or for objecting to any act of power that he supposes necessary to his interest. He will take his Bible-oath that black is white, and that whatever is, is right, if it is for his convenience. He is for having a slice in the loan, a share in a borough, a situation in the church or state, or for standing well with those who have. He is not for empty speculations, but for full pockets. He is for having plenty of beef and pudding, a good coat to his back, a good house over his head, and for cutting a respectable figure in the world. He is *Epicuri de grege porcus*—not a man but a beast. He is styed in his prejudices—he wallows in the mire of his senses—he cannot get beyond the trough of his sordid appetites, whether it is of gold or wood. Truth and falsehood are, to him, something to buy and sell; principle and conscience, something to eat and drink. He tramples on the plea of Humanity, and lives, like a caterpillar, on the decay of public good. Beast as he is, he knows that the King is the fountain of honour, that there are good things to be had in the Church, treats the cloth with respect, bows to a magistrate, lies to the tax-gatherer, nicknames the Reformers, and "blesses the Regent and the Duke of York." He treads the primrose path of preferment; "when a great wheel goes up a hill, holds fast by it, and when it rolls down, lets it go." He is not an enthusiast, a Utopian philosopher or a Theophilanthropist, but a man of business and the world, who minds the main chance, does as other people do, and takes his wife's advice to get on in the world, and set up a coach for her to ride in, as fast as possible. This fellow is in the right, and

" wiser in his generation than the children of the light " The " servile slaves" of wealth and power have a considerable advantage over the independent and the free. How much easier is it to smell out a job than to hit upon a scheme for the good of mankind! How much safer is it to be the tool of the oppressor than the advocate of the oppressed! How much more fashionable to fall in with the opinion of the world, to bow the knee to Baal, than to seek for obscure and obnoxious truth! How strong are the ties that bind men together for their own advantage, compared with those that bind them to the good of their country or of their kind! For as the Reformer has no guide to his conclusions but speculative reason, which is a source not of unanimity or certainty, but of endless doubt and disagreement, so he has no ground of attachment to them but a speculative interest, which is too often liable to be warped by sinister motives, and is a flimsy barrier against the whole weight of worldly and practical interests opposed to it. He either tires and grows lukewarm after the first gloss of novelty is over, and is thrown into the hands of the adverse party, or to keep alive an interest in it, he makes it the stalking-horse of his ambition, of his personal enmity, of his conceit or love of gossipping; as we have seen. An opinion backed by power and prejudice, rivetted and mortised to the throne, is of more force and validity than all the abstract reason in the world, without power and prejudice. A cause centred in an individual, which is strengthened by all the ties of passion and self-interest, as in the case of a king against a whole people, is more likely to prevail than that of a scattered multitude, who have only a common and divided interest to hold them together, and "screw their courage to the sticking-place," against an influence, that is never distracted or dissipated; that neither slumbers nor sleeps; that is never lulled into security, nor tamed by adversity; that is intoxicated with the insolence of success, and infuriated with the rage of disappointment; that eyes its one sole object of personal aggrandisement, moves unremittingly to it, and carries after it millions of its slaves and train-bearers. Can you persuade a king to hear reason, to submit his pretensions to the tribunal of the people, to give up the most absurd and mischievous of his prerogatives? No: he is always true to himself, he grasps at power and hugs it close, as it is exorbitant or invidious, or likely to be torn from him; and his followers stick to him, and never boggle at any lengths they are forced to go, because they know what they have to trust to in the good faith of kings to themselves and one another. Power then is fixed and immoveable, for this reason, because it is lodged in an individual who is driven to madness by the undisputed possession, or apprehended loss of it; his self-will is the key-stone that supports the tottering arch of corruption, steadfast as it leans on him:—liberty is vacillating, transient, and hunted through the world, because it is entrusted to the breasts of many, who care little about it, and quarrel in the execution of their trust. Too many cooks spoil the broth. The principle of tyranny is in fact identified with a man's pride and the servility of others in the highest degree; the principle of liberty abstracts him from himself, and has to contend in its feeble course with all his own passions, prejudices, interests, and those of the world and of his own party; the cavils of Reformers, the threats of Tories, and the sneers of Whigs.*

A modern Whig is but the fag-end of a Tory. The old Whigs were in principle what the modern Jacobins are, Anti-Jacobites, that is, opposers of the doctrine of divine right, the one in the soil of England, the other by parity of reasoning in the soil of France. But the Opposition have pressed so long against the Ministry without effect, that being the

* There is none of this perplexity and jarring of different objects in the tools of power. Their jealousies, heart-burnings, love of precedence, or scruples of conscience, are made subservient to the great cause in which they are embarked; they leave the amicable division of the spoil to the powers that be; all angry disputes are hushed in the presence of the throne, and the corrosive, fretful particles of human nature fly off, and are softened by the influence of a court atmosphere. Courtiers hang together like a swarm of bees about a honeycomb. Not so the Reformers; for they have no honey-comb to attract them. It has been said that Reformers are often indifferent characters. The reason is, that the ties which bind most men to their duties—habit, example, regard to appearances—are relaxed in them; and other and better principles are, as yet, weak and unconfirmed.

softer substance, and made of more yielding materials, they have been moulded into their image and superscription, spelt backwards, or they differ as concave and convex, or they go together like substantive and adjective, or like man and wife, they two have become one flesh. A Tory is the indispensable prop to the doubtful sense of self-importance, and peevish irritability of negative success, which mark the life of a Whig leader or underling. They "are subdued even to the very quality" of the Lords of the Treasury Bench, and have quarrelled so long that they would be quite at a loss without the ordinary food of political contention. To interfere between them is as dangerous as to interfere in a matrimonial squabble. To overturn the one is to trip up the heels of the other. Their hostility is not directed against things at all, nor to effectual and decisive opposition to men, but to that sort of petty warfare and parliamentary *tracasserie*, of which there is neither end nor use, except making the parties concerned of consequence in their own eyes, and contemptible in those of the nation. They will not allow Ministers to be severely handled by any one but themselves, nor even that: but they say civil things of them in the House of Commons, and whisper scandal against them at Holland House. This shews gentlemanly refinement and good breeding; while my Lord Erskine "calls us untaught knaves, unmannerly to come betwixt the wind and his nobility." But the leaden bullets and steel bayonets, the *ultima ratio regum*, by which these questions are practically decided, do their business in another-guess manner; they do not stand on the same ceremony. Soft words and hard blows are a losing game to play at: and this, one would think, the Opposition, if they were sincere, must have found out long ago. But they rather wish to screen the Ministry, as their *locum tenens* in the receipt of the perquisites of office and the abuse of power, of which they themselves expect the reversion.

> "Strange that such difference should be
> Twixt Tweedledum and Tweedledee."

The distinction between a great Whig and Tory Lord is laughable. For Whigs to Tories "nearly are allied, and thin partitions do their bounds divide." So I cannot find out the different drift (as far as politics are concerned) of the ********* and ********* Reviews, which remind one of Opposition coaches, that raise a great dust or spatter one another with mud, but both travel the same road and arrive at the same destination. When the Editor of a respectable Morning Paper reproached me with having called Mr. Gifford a cat's-paw, I did not tell him that he was a glove upon that cat's-paw. I might have done so. There is a difference between a sword and a foil. The Whigs do not at all relish that ugly thing, a knock-down blow; which is so different from their endless see-saw way of going about a question. They are alarmed, "lest the courtiers offended should be:" for they are so afraid of their adversaries, that they dread the reaction even of successful opposition to them, and will neither attempt it themselves, nor stand by any one that does. Any writer who is not agreeable to the Tories, becomes obnoxious to the Whigs; he is disclaimed by them as a dangerous colleague, merely for having " done the cause some service;" is considered as having the malicious design to make a breach of the peace, and to interrupt with most admired disorder the harmony and mutual good understanding which subsists between Ministers and the Opposition, and on the adherence to which they are alone suffered to exist, or to have a shadow of importance in the state. They are, in fact, a convenient medium to break the force of popular feeling, and to transmit the rays of popular indignation against the influence and power of the crown, blunted and neutralized by as many qualifications and refractions as possible. A Whig is properly what is called a Trimmer—that is, a coward to both sides of a question, who dare not be a knave nor an honest man, but is a sort of whiffling, shuffling, cunning, silly, contemptible, unmeaning negation of the two. He is a poor purblind creature, who halts between two opinions, and complains that he cannot get any two people to think alike. He is a cloak for corruption, and a mar-plot to freedom. He will neither do any thing himself, nor let any one else do it. He is on bad terms with the Government, and not on good ones with the people. He is an impertinence and a contradiction in the state. If he has a casting weight, for fear of overdoing the mark, he throws it into the wrong scale. He is a person of equally feeble understanding and passions. He has some notion of what is right, just enough to hinder him from pursuing his own interest: he has selfish and worldly prudence enough, not to let him embark in any bold or decided measure for the advancement of truth and justice. He is afraid of his own conscience, which will not let him lend his unqualified support to arbitrary measures; he stands in awe of the opinion of the world, which will not let him express his opposition to those measures with warmth and effect. His politics are a strange mixture of cross-purposes. He is wedded to forms and appearances, impeded by every petty obstacle and pretext of difficulty, more tenacious of the means than the end—anxious to secure all suffrages, by which he secures none—hampered not only by the ties of friendship to his actual associates, but to all those that he thinks may become so; and unwilling to offer arguments to convince the reason of his opponents lest he should offend their prejudices, by shewing them how much they are in the wrong; "letting I dare not wait upon I would, like the poor cat in the adage;" stickling for the letter of the Constitution, with the affectation of a prude, and abandoning its principles with the effrontery of a prostitute to any shabby Coalition he can patch up with its deadly enemies. This is very pitiful work; and, I believe, the public with me are tolerably sick of the character. At the same time, he hurls up his cap with a foolish face of wonder and incredulity at the restoration of the Bourbons, and affects to chuckle with secret satisfaction over the last act of the Revolution, which reduced him to perfect insignificance. We need not wonder at the results, when it comes to the push between parties so differently constituted and unequally matched. We have seen what those results are. I cannot do justice to the picture, but I find it done to my hands in those prophetic lines of Pope, where he describes the last Triumph of Corruption:—

" But 'tis the fall degrades her to a whore:
Let greatness own her, and she's mean no more.
Her birth, her beauty, crowds and courts confess;
Chaste matrons praise her, and grave bishops bless:
In golden chains the willing world she draws,
And her's the Gospel is, and her's the Laws;
Mounts the tribunal, lifts her scarlet head,
And sees pale virtue carted in her stead.
Lo! at the wheels of her triumphal car,
Old England's genius, rough with many a scar,
Dragg'd in the dust! his arms hang idly round,
His flag inverted trails along the ground;
Our youth, all liveried o'er with foreign gold,
Before her dance, behind her crawl the old!
See thronging millions to the Pagod run,
And offer country, parent, wife, or son!
Hear her black trumpet thro' the land proclaim,
That *not to be corrupted is the shame.*
In soldier, churchman, patriot, man in power,
'Tis avarice all, ambition is no more!
See all our nobles begging to be slaves!
See all our fools aspiring to be knaves!

All, all look up with reverential awe
At crimes that 'scape or triumph o'er the law;
While truth, worth, wisdom daily they decry:
'Nothing is sacred now but villainy.'
Yet may this verse (if such a verse remain)
Shew there was one who held it in disdain."

POLITICAL ESSAYS, &c.

THE MARQUIS WELLESLEY.

"And such other gambol faculties he hath, as shew a weak mind, and an able body."

April 13, 1813.

THE Marquis Wellesley's opening speech on India affairs was chiefly remarkable for its length, and the manner in which it was delivered. This nobleman seems to have formed himself on those lines in Pope:—

> "All hail him victor in both gifts of song,
> "Who sings so loudly, and who sings so long."

He aspires with infinite alacrity to the character of a great orator; and, if we were disposed to take the will for the deed, we should give him full credit for it. We confess, those of his speeches which we have heard, appear to us prodigies of physical prowess and intellectual imbecility. The ardour of his natural temperament, stimulating and irritating the ordinary faculties of his mind, the exuberance of his animal spirits, contending with the barrenness of his genius, produce a degree of dull vivacity, of pointed insignificance, and impotent energy, which is without any parallel but itself. It is curious, though somewhat painful, to see this lively little lord always in the full career of his subject, and never advancing a jot the nearer; seeming to utter volumes in every word, and yet saying nothing; retaining the same unabated vehemence of voice and action without any thing to excite it; still keeping alive the promise and the expectation of genius without once satisfying it—soaring into mediocrity with adventurous enthusiasm, harrowed up by some plain matter-of-fact, writhing with agony under a truism, and launching a common-place with all the fury of a thunderbolt!*

MR. SOUTHEY, POET LAUREAT.

Sept. 18, 1813.

The laurel is at length destined, unexpectedly, to circle the brows of this gentleman, where it will look almost like a civic crown. The patriot and the poet (two venerable names, which we should wish never to see disunited) is said to owe his intended elevation to the intercession of Mr. Croker, to whom, it will be recollected, he has dedicated his Life of Lord Nelson, with an appropriate motto in the title-page, from the poem of Ulm and Trafalgar. Mr. Croker having applied to the Regent in favour of his friend, the Prince is understood to have given his ready assent, observing, that Mr. Southey's efforts in the Spanish cause alone, rendered him highly worthy of the situation. As Mr. Croker, however, was taking his leave, he was met by Lord

* The above criticism first appeared in the *Courier* newspaper, and was copied the next day in the *Chronicle* with the following remarks:—"The treasury journals complain of the harsh treatment shewn to ministers,—let us see how they treat their opponents. If the following does not come from the poetical pen of the Admiralty *Creaker*, it is a close imitation of his style."

'Strange that such difference should be
'Twixt Tweedledum and Tweedledee!'"

Whether it was from the fear of this supposed formidable critic, the noble Marquis ceased from this time nightly to "fillip the ears of his auditors with a three-man beetle!"

Liverpool and the Marquis of Hertford, the latter of whom, as chamberlain, had, it seems, made an offer of the place to Mr. Walter Scott, who had signified his acceptance of it. Some little difficulty naturally arose on the occasion, but it was agreed that the two poets should settle the point of precedence between themselves. A friendly altercation, unlike that of the shepherds in Virgil, now took place between Mr. Scott and Mr. Southey, each waving his own pretensions, and giving the palm of victory to the other. But it was finally determined, that as Mr. Scott, though he would not allow himself to be the greatest, was at least the richest poet of the two, Mr. Southey, who had most need of this post of honour and of profit, should have it. So ends this important affair; and, without any ill-will to Mr. Southey, we should not have been disappointed if it had ended differently. Whatever may be the balance of poetical merit, Mr. Scott, we are quite sure, has always been a much better courtier than Mr. Southey; and we are of opinion that the honours of a Court can no where be so gracefully or deservedly bestowed as on its followers. His acceptance of this mark of court favour would not have broken in upon that uniformity of character, which we think no less beautiful and becoming in life than in a poem. But, perhaps, a passion for new faces extends to the intrigues of politics as well as of love; and a triumph over the scruples of delicacy enhances the value of the conquest in both cases. To *have been* the poet of the people, may not render Mr. Southey less a court favourite; and one of his old Sonnets to Liberty must give a peculiar zest to his new Birth-day Odes. His flaming patriotism will easily subside into the gentle glow of grateful loyalty; and the most extravagant of his plans of reform end in building castles in Spain!

MR. SOUTHEY'S NEW-YEAR'S ODE.

Jan. 8, 1814.

MR. SOUTHEY'S Ode has at length appeared—not as was announced, under the title of "Carmen Annuum," but under that of "CARMEN TRIUMPHALE, *for the Commencement of the Year* 1814." We see no reason why the author might not have adopted the title of Horace's Ode entire, and have called it *Carmen Seculare*, which would have been the best account he could give of it. We fear Mr. Southey will not form a splendid exception to the numberless instances which prove that there is something in the air of a court, not favourable to the genius of poetry. He has not deprived himself of the excuse made by one of his predecessors, of versatile memory, in extenuation of the degeneracy of his courtly lays,—"That poets succeed best in fiction." The Ode is in the ballad style, peculiar to Mr. Southey and his poetical friends. It has something of the rustic simplicity of a country virgin on her first introduction at Duke's Place, or of Pamela on the day of her marriage with Mr. B. Or rather it resembles a *fancy* birth-day suit, a fashionable livery worn inside out, a prince's feather with a sprig of the tree of liberty added to it,—the academy of compliments turned into quaint Pindarics,—is a sort of methodistical rhapsody, chaunted by a gentleman-usher, and exhibits the irregular vigour of Jacobin enthusiasm suffering strange emasculation under the hands of a finical lord-chamberlain. It is romantic without interest, and tame without elegance. It is exactly such an ode as we expected Mr. Southey to compose on this occasion. We say this from our respect for the talents and character of this eminent writer. He is the last man whom we should expect to see graceful in fetters, or from whom we should look for the soul of freedom within the *liberties of a court!*—The commencement of the Ode is as follows, and it continues throughout much as it begins:—

> "In happy hour *doth* he receive
> The Laurel, meed of famous bards of *yore*,
> Which Dryden and diviner Spenser wore,
> *In happy hour*, and well may he rejoice,
> Whose earliest task *must be*
> To raise the *exultant* hymn for *victory*,
> And *join* a nation's *joy* with harp and voice,
> Pouring the strain of triumph on the wind,
> Glory to God, his song—deliverance to mankind!
> Wake, lute and harp! &c. &c."

Mr. Southey has not exactly followed the suggestion of an ingenious friend, to begin his poem with the appropriate allusion,

> "Awake, my sack-but!"

The following rhymes are the lamest we observed. He says, speaking of the conflict between the Moors and Spaniards,

> "Age after age, from sire to *son*,
> The hallowed sword was handed *down*;
> Nor did they from that warfare cease,
> And sheath that hallowed sword in peace,
> Until the work was *done*."

Indeed, if Mr. S. can do no better than this, in his drawing-room verses, he should get some contributor to the Lady's Magazine to polish them for him.

We have turned over the Ode again, which extends to twenty pages, in the hope of finding some one vigorous or striking passage for selection, but in vain. The following is the most likely to please in a certain quarter:—

> "Open thy gates, O Hanover! display
> Thy loyal banners to the day!
> Receive thy old illustrious line once more!
> Beneath an upstart's yoke oppress'd,
> Long has it been thy fortune to deplore
> That line, whose fostering and paternal sway
> So many an age thy grateful children blest.

The yoke is broken now!—a mightier hand
Hath dash'd—in pieces dash'd—the iron rod.
To meet her princes, the delivered land
Pours her rejoicing multitudes abroad;
The happy bells, from every town and tower,
Roll their glad peals upon the joyful wind;
And from all hearts and tongues, with one consent,
The high thanksgiving strain is sent—
Glory to God! Deliverance to mankind!"

In various stanzas, Bonaparte is called an upstart, a ruffian, &c. We confess, we wish to see Mr. Southey, like Virgil, in his Georgics, " scatter his dung with a grace."

We do not intend to quarrel with our Laureat's poetical politics, but the conclusion is one which we did not anticipate from the author. We have always understood that the Muses were the daughters of Memory!

" And France, *restored* and shaking off her chain,
Shall join the Avengers in the joyful strain—
Glory to God! Deliverance for mankind!"

The poem has a few notes added to it, the object of which seems to be to criticise the political opinions of the Edinburgh Reviewers with respect to Spain, and to prove that the author is wiser after the event than they were before it, in which he has very nearly succeeded.

Mr. Southey announces a new volume of Inscriptions, which must furnish some curious *parallelisms*.

DOTTREL-CATCHING.

TO THE EDITOR OF THE MORNING CHRONICLE.

SIR, *Jan.* 27, 1814.

THE method of taking this bird is somewhat singular, and is described in an old book in the following terms:

" The Dottrel is a foolish bird of the crane species, very tall, awkward, and conceited. The Dottrel-catcher, when he has got near enough, turns his head round sideways, and *makes a leg* towards him: the bird, seeing this, returns the civility, and makes the same sidelong movement. These advances are repeated with mutual satisfaction, till the man approaches near enough, and then the bird is taken."

A poet-laureat or a treasury sophist is often taken much in the same way. Your Opposionist, Sir, was ever a true *gull.* From the general want of sympathy, he sets more store by it than it is worth; and for the smallest concession, is prevailed upon to give up every principle, and to surrender himself, bound hand and foot, the slave of a party, who get all they want of him, and then —"Spunge, you are dry again!"

A striking illustration of the common treatment of political drudges has lately occurred in the instance of a celebrated writer, whose lucubrations are withheld from the public, because he has declared against the project of restoring the Bourbons. As the court and city politicians have spoken out on this subject, permit me, Sir, to say a word in behalf of the country. I have no dislike whatever, private or public, to the Bourbons, except as they may be made the pretext for mischievous and impracticable schemes. At the same time I have not the slightest enthusiasm in their favour. I would not sacrifice the life or limb of a single individual to restore them. I have very nearly the same feelings towards them which Swift has expressed in his account of the ancient and venerable race of the Struldbruggs. It is true, they might in some respects present a direct contrast to Bonaparte. A tortoise placed on the throne of France would do the same thing. The literary sycophants of the day, Sir, are greatly enamoured (from some cause or other) with hereditary imbecility and native want of talent. They are angry, not without reason, that a Corsican upstart has made the princes of Europe look like wax-work figures, and given a shock to the still life of kings. They wish to punish this unpardonable presumption, by establishing an artificial balance of *weakness* throughout Europe, and by reducing humanity to the level of thrones. We may perhaps in time improve this principle of ricketty admiration to Eastern perfection, where every changeling is held sacred, and that which is the disgrace of human intellect is hailed as the image of the Divinity!

It is said that in France the old royalists and the revolutionary republicans are agreed in the same point. Bonaparte is the point of union between these opposite extremes, the common object of their hate and fear. I can conceive this very possible from what I have observed among ourselves. He has certainly done a great deal to mortify the pride of birth in the one, and the vanity of personal talents in the others. This is a very sufficient ground of private pique and resentment, but not of national calamity or eternal war. I am, Sir, your humble servant,

EICONOCLASTES SATYRANE.

THE BOURBONS AND BONAPARTE.

Dec. 6, 1813.

The following paragraph in a daily paper is equally worthy of notice for magnificence of expression and magnanimity of sentiment:—

"When or under what circumstances the great Commander may think fit to carry his forces against the large military or commercial depôts of the south of France, we do not pretend to form conjectures. We are confident, that as nothing will disturb the calm and meditative prudence of his plans, so nothing will arrest the rapidity of their execution. We trust alike in his caution and in his resolution: but, perhaps, there may be in store for him a higher destination than the capture of a town or the reduction of a province. What if the army opposed to him should resolve to avenge the cause of humanity, and to exchange the bloody and brutal tyranny of a Bonaparte for the mild paternal sway of a Bourbon? Could a popular French general open to himself a more glorious career at the present moment, than that which Providence seemed to have destined to the virtuous Moreau? Or is it possible that any power now existing in France could stop such a general and such an army, supported by the unconquered Wellington and his formidable legions, if they were to resolve boldly to march to Paris, and bring the usurper to the block! Every disposable soldier in France is on the Adour, or on the Rhine. In the case we are supposing, there would be no enemy to encounter, unless the northern frontier were at once denuded of troops, and the road to Paris on that side laid open to the allies. This is no question of the attachment of the French nation to one dynasty or to another: it is a question of military enterprise, in the minds of military adventurers. The simple possibility, not to say the high moral probability, that in a moment of general defection, an army which has so much in its hands may run with the stream of popular feeling throughout Europe, is enough to make the Tyrant tremble on his throne. Lord Wellington is doubtless prepared to take advantage of so desirable an occurrence, in case it should happen without his previous interference: but we wish him to interfere; we wish that he were authorised plainly and openly to offer his mighty co-operation to any body of men who would shake off the Tyrant's yoke in France, as has been done in Italy, in Germany, and in Holland!"

This is a fair specimen of that kind of declamation which has for a long time swayed the affairs of Europe, and which, if the powers of Europe are wise by experience, will not influence them much longer. It is this spirit of treating the French people as of a different species from ourselves—as a monster or a non-entity—of disposing of their government at the will of every paragraph-monger—of arming our hatred against them by ridiculous menaces and incessant reproaches—of supposing that their power was either so tremendous as to threaten the existence of all nations, or so contemptible that we could crush it by a word,—it is this uniform system, practised by the incendiaries of the press, of inflaming our prejudices and irritating our passions, that has so often made us rush upon disaster, and submit to every extremity rather than forego the rancorous and headstrong desire of revenge.

The writer of the paragraph talks familiarly of marching to Paris, and bringing Bonaparte to the block. He seems to wonder at the delay which has already taken place. This is the very style of ancient Pistol, " Bid him prepare, for I will cut his throat." This high tone of impotent menace and premature triumph always " reverbs its own hollowness." It is the echo of fear. Instead of a proud repose on our own strength and courage, these writers only feel secure in the destruction of an adversary. The natural intoxication of success is heightened into a sort of delirium by the recollection of the panic into which they had been thrown. *The Times'* editor thinks that nothing can be so easy as for an army " to run with the stream of popular feeling" from one end of Europe to the other. Strange that these persons, like desperate adventurers, are incorrigible to experience. They are always setting out on the same forlorn hope. The tide of fortune, while it sets in strong against us, they prove to be the most variable of all things; but it no sooner changes in our favour, than it straight

> " Flows on to the Propontic,
> And knows no ebb."

To encourage themselves in the extravagance of their voluntary delusions, they are as prodigal of titles of honour as the college of heralds, and erect a standard of military fame, with all the authority, but not with the impartiality of history. Lord Wellington is " the great commander," and " the unconquered general," while " the little captain," and " the hero" or " the deserter of Smorgonne," are the only qualifications of Bonaparte. If such are the true denominations and relative proportions of these two generals, then it is quite right to give to each of them the honour due;—if they are not, then it is quite wrong to stake the welfare of nations on a turn of expression—to put little equivocal scraps of paper into false scales, and decide the fate of Europe by nicknames. The scales in which Sir Humphrey Davy weighs the 500th part of a drachm, are not so slight nor insignificant as those in which his vilifiers, *The Times*, balance the destinies of the world.

"What," it is asked with a certain air of profundity and mystery, "What if the army opposed to him [Lord Wellington] should resolve to exchange the bloody tyranny of Bonaparte for the paternal sway of a Bourbon!"

Why, if the French wish to shake off the galling yoke of a military Usurper, we say, let them do it in God's name. Let them, whenever they please, imitate us in our recal of the Stuarts; and, whenever they please, in our banishment of them thirty years afterwards. But let them not, in the name of honour or of manhood, receive the royal boon of liberty at the point of the bayonet. It would be setting a bad precedent—it would be breaking in upon a great principle—it would be making a gap in the general feeling of national independence. For we are to observe, that this rational, popular, patriotic preference of the mild paternal sway of the Bourbons is to be enforced upon them by the powerful co-operation of the unconquered Wellington and his formidable legions. This is, in fact, returning to the original ground of the whole quarrel, and the question for them to consider, is whether all the evils and miseries which they may have endured in resisting these forcible appeals from foreign powers, are the strongest reasons why they should at length gratefully resign themselves to that tender concern for their sufferings, which so much persevering kindness, and disinterested preference of their interests to our own unequivocally proves. The impression produced by these formidable emissaries of mild paternity must, indeed, be only that of filial love and reverence. The constant *role* of these same Bourbons, now recognized, now disowned by the surrounding states, now held up as bugbears to frighten, and now brought forward as decoys to allure them, for awhile kept entirely in the back-ground, and then again set over them like puppets, in every reverse of fortune, must excite, one would suppose, some very pleasant associations, and give them some little insight into the nature of the machinery which is played off against them. In other nations, at least, these sort of *tentatives* would lead not to submission, but to indignation. It cannot be denied, however, that the French character has peculiar susceptibilities. France, like a modern coquet, may be fascinated once more by the courtly graces of discarded royalty; or, on the other hand, recollecting the malice and the impotence of which she was so long the victim, like Hellenore, entertained by the jolly satyrs, may wisely refuse to return to the cold and irksome embraces of the drivelling Malbecco. But our politician wishes all this not to be left to their own free will, but that we should interfere. We can easily believe it; "it was ever the fault of our English nation" to wish to interfere with what did not concern them, for the very reason that they could interfere with comparative impunity. What is sport to them is death to others. The writer also draws a parallel, as if it were a feasible case, between Holland, Spain, and Germany throwing off a foreign yoke, and the French throwing off their own; in other words, submitting to a foreign one. We beg pardon of these acute discriminators. We know they have an answer. We leave them in possession of the nice distinction—between a foreign yoke, and a yoke imposed by foreigners!

"This," says the writer in *The Times*, "is not a question of attachment to one dynasty or another, but a question of military enterprize between military adventurers." Does our speculator mean by this to confer the privileges of military adventurers, *en plein droit*, on the Emperor Alexander and the Crown Prince of Sweden? But whatever he means, it is clear that he is not consistent in what he says; for he has said just before, that the object of this so often repeated march to Paris is "to bring the Usurper to the block!" Here, then, it is a question, not between contending generals, but between a usurper and a lawful monarch. So true it is that those who have most need of their assistance have the worst memories! "What," exclaims our enthusiast, "would there be to oppose such a general and such an army, aided by the unconquered Wellington," &c. First, "this is the very coinage of his brain." There's no such general and no such army.

But granting the supposition to be true, the patriotic general, who should open to himself a glorious passage through the heart of his country, and attempt to make it the vassal of England, under the monstrous pretence of allegiance to his Sovereign, might perhaps meet the fate which Providence destined for the virtuous Moreau. Perhaps the French may think that as their affected loyalty could be only a cover for the most dastardly submission, so their hypocrisy and treachery to themselves might be justly retaliated upon them, by making the restoration of thrones a mask for the dismemberment of kingdoms. They may have acquired by experience some knowledge of that enlargement of view and boldness of nerve, which is inspired by the elevation of success. They may consider, that "when the wild and savage passions are set afloat, they are not so easily regulated" according to the dictates of justice or generosity. Some of them may even go so far as to think that all the respect of the Emperor of Russia for the talents and virtues of Moreau might be insufficient to deter him from memorizing another Warsaw at Paris! Of this we are tolerably certain, that there are not wanting staunch friends of order and civilization in this country who would advise and applaud such a catastrophe "to the very echo," as a masterpiece of political justice, chaunt *Te Deum* over the ruins, and very seriously invite the good people of France to join in the chorus! But we are not "the echo that shall applaud again." We shall not hail such a catastrophe, nor such a triumph. For out of the desolation would arise a poisoned stench that would choak almost the breath of life, and one low, creeping fog of universal despotism, that would confound the Eastern and the Western world together *in darkness that might be felt*. We do not wish for this final consummation, because we do not wish the pulse of liberty to be quite destroyed, or that the mass of our common nature should become a lifeless corpse, unable to rouse itself against never-ending wrongs, or that the last spark of generous enthusiasm should be extinguished in that moral atheism, which defaces and mangles the image of God in man. We do not wish that liberty should ever have a deer's heart given her, to live in constant fear of the fatal, inevitable venal pack behind her; but that she may still have the heart of a lioness, whose mighty roar keeps the hunters at bay, and whose whelps revenge their parent's death!

Rather than such an event should take place, if such an extremity were possible, we should even wish that a general and an army of our own, devoted by *The Times* to a far different service, might be empowered to make a firm stand against it: to stop the tide of barbarous despotism as they had already rolled back that of ungovernable ambition, and to say, Hitherto shalt thou come, and no further. Such an interference in such a cause would indeed give to Great Britain the character which she claims of being the Vindicator of the World. It would be to assume an attitude and a port indeed, loftier than she ever yet presented to the admiration of mankind; and would create a bulwark of strength round her, that would encircle her as with "impaling fire!"

VETUS.

Nov. 19, 1813.

THIS patriot and logician in a letter in *The Times* of Friday, labours to stifle the most distant hope of peace in its birth. He lays down certain general principles which must for ever render all attempts to restore it vain and abortive. With the watch-word of *Eternal war with Bonaparte* blazoned on his forehead, in the piety of his pacific zeal, he challenges Bonaparte as the wanton, unprovoked, implacable enemy of the peace of mankind. We will also venture to lay down a maxim, which is—That from the moment that one party declares and acts upon the avowed principle that peace can never be made with an enemy, it renders war on the part of that enemy a matter of necessary self-defence, and holds out a plea for every excess of ambition or revenge. If we are to limit our hostility to others only with their destruction, we impose the adoption of the same principle on them as their only means of safety. There is no alternative. But this is probably the issue to which Vetus wishes to bring the question. This writer not only outlaws Bonaparte, but in a summary way, disfranchises the French nation at large of the right of making peace or war. "Who," he exclaims in wanton defiance of common sense, "are the French nation? To us a rank non-entity. We have only to do with Napoleon Bonaparte—with his rights, his interests, his honour. Who are to be the sole judges of his rights? We and our Allies!" Admirable politician!

The events which have lately taken place on the Continent, and the moderate and manly tone in which those events have been received by Ministers, have excited the utmost degree of uneasiness and alarm in the minds of certain persons, who redouble the eagerness of their cries for war. The cold blooded fury and mercenary malice of these panders to mischief, can only be appeased by the prospect of lasting desolation. They rave, foam at the mouth, and make frantic gestures at the name of peace. These high-priests of Moloch daily offer up to their grim idol the same nauseous banquet of abuse and lies. Round them "a cry of hell-hounds never ceasing bark," that with greedy appetite devour the offal. Every day they act over the same foul imposture, and repeat their monstrous masque. These mighty soothsayers look forward to another restoration of Europe after another twenty years of havoc and destruction. After urging her to the very edge of the precipice from which she has only just recovered, breathless and affrighted, they wish to goad her on once more to the same mad career. The storm is for the moment over-past, but they will not suffer the vessel of the state to enter the harbour; in the hope that they may still plunder the wreck, and prey upon the carcases. The serpent's hiss, the assassin's yell, the mowing and chattering of apes, drown the voice of peace; and Vetus, like the solemn owl, joins in the distance, and prolongs the dreary note of death!

ON THE COURIER AND TIMES NEWSPAPERS.

Jan. 21, 1814.

THE following passage, among others of the same *calibre*, has lately appeared in *The Courier*:—

"The party call upon us to speak out. We thought it not very easy for any charge of not speaking out to be urged against us. However, we obey their call most willingly. 'Does *The Courier*, they ask, mean to insinuate, that because the South of France is more inclined to favour their pretensions, the Bourbons ought to have frigates allotted them to traverse the Bay of Biscay, and join the standard of Lord Wellington?' To this we reply, yes; decisively yes!—We say we would have a Bourbon proceed to the South of France. We hope we have spoken out on this point. One more remains;—Would we 'set up some new obstacle to the progress of the negociation that is on foot?' *Yes, if we thought there was any negociation on foot with Bonaparte. But we trust there is not—we trust there never will be.*"

And this at a time when it has been formally signified from the throne that there was no objection on the part of England to treat with the French Ruler; when Lord Liverpool has said publicly that no conditions of peace would be insisted on, which we, placed in the situation of France, should not think it reasonable to grant; when we, in concert with the Allies, have announced to France, that it is neither our intention nor our wish to interfere with their internal government, but to secure the independence and safety of the continent; and when Lord Castlereagh has gone from this country for the purpose, avowed and understood, of giving effect to that declaration, and of fixing the basis of a peace to be recognized by the common powers of Europe. To produce such a passage, at such a moment, required that union of impudence and folly which has no parallel elsewhere. From the quarter from which it comes, it could not surprize us; it is consistent; it is in keeping; it is of a piece with the rest. It is worthy of those harpies of the press, whose business is to scare away the approach of peace by their obscene and dissonant noises, and to tear asunder the olive-branch, whenever it is held out to us, with their well-practised beaks; who fill their hearts with malice, and their mouths with falsehood; who strive to soothe the dastard passion of their employers by inflaming those of the multitude; creatures that would sell the lives of millions for a nod of greatness, and make their country a by-word in history, to please some punk of quality.

We are to understand from no less an authority than that of *The Courier,* that Lord Castlereagh is sent out professedly to make peace, but in reality to hinder it: and we learn from an authority equally respectable (*The Times*) that nothing can prevent the destruction of Bonaparte but this country's untimely consenting to make peace with him. And yet we are told in the same breath, that the charge of eternal war which we bring against these writers, is the echo of the French war-faction, who, at the commencement of every series of hostilities, and at the conclusion of every treaty, have accused this country of a want of good faith and sincere disposition to peace. We are told, that if the French do not force Bonaparte to make peace now, which yet these writers are determined to prevent him from doing, "they are sunk beneath the worshippers of cats and onions." These "knavish but keen" politicians tell the French people in so many words—"We will not make peace with your government, and yet, if it does not make peace with us, we will force what Government we please upon you." What effect this monstrous and palpable insult must have upon the French nation, will depend upon the degree of sense and spirit they have left among them. But with respect to ourselves, if the line of policy pointed out by these juggling fiends is really meant to be pursued, if a pretended proposal to treat for peace on certain grounds is only to be converted into an insidious ground of renewed war for other purposes, *if* this offensive and unmanly imposture is to be avowed and *practised* upon us in the face of day, then we know what *will be* the duty of Parliament and of the country. The wars, in which the Governments of Europe have been engaged, have not succeeded the worse when the people took an effective share in them. We should hope that the interference of the people will not be necessary to effect the restoration of peace.

It is curious to hear these systematic opponents of peace, (with infuriate and insensate looks scattering firebrands and death,) at the same time affecting the most tender concern for the miseries of war; or like that good-natured reconciler of differences, *Iago*, hypocritically shifting the blame from themselves—" What, stab men in the dark!" They ask with grave faces, with *very* grave faces, " Who are the authors, the propagators, and practisers of this dreadful war system? who the aggressors? who the unrelenting persecutors of peace?" War is their everlasting cry, " one note day and night;" during war, during peace, during negociation, in success, in adversity; and yet they dare to tax others as the *sole* authors of the calamities which they would render eternal, sooner than abate one jot of their rancorous prejudices. One of these writers (the Editor of *The Times)* asserts with an air of great confidence, while he himself is hallooing as loud as he can among the indefatigable war-pack, that Bonaparte is the cause, the *sole author* of all the calamities of Europe for the last fourteen years; and what is remarkable, he brings as a proof of this sweeping assertion, a state paper, written under the Pitt Administration of *pacific memory,* deprecating *all* conciliation with the French at the very period from which the writer dates the wanton, unprovoked aggressions of Bonaparte, and which paper he quotes at length, as an admirable description of the mode by which we are to avert the calamities of Europe for the next fourteen years, as we have done for the last. Better late than never. So industrious an inquirer need not despair of effectually averting our future miseries, and pacifying the world, if it is to be done by referring back to state papers of this description, or by resuming the principles of those good old anti-jacobin times, or by finishing the war as it was begun. There would be no end of precedents and documents for prosecuting the war with vigour under every variety of circumstances, in order never to bring it to a conclusion. As a proof of the aggressions and implacable hatred of France, he might cite that monument of romantic and disinterested generosity "of heroic sentiment and manly enterprise," on the part of the Allies, the treaty of Pilnitz.* He might proceed to those pacific manifestations—Lord Hawkesbury's march to Paris—the *Bellum internecinum* of Mr. Windham, and his consistent phrenzy at the treaty of Amiens—Mr. Pitt's abstract impossibility of maintaining the relations of peace and amity with the French Republic, or with the child and champion of Jacobinism—Mr. Burke's Regicide Peace—the project of starving France in 1796—of hurling her down the gulph of bankruptcy in 1797—the coalitions of different periods in which England saved herself and Europe *from peace* by her energy, or her example—the contemptuous rejection of every offer of negociation in every situation, the unwearied prosecution of the war on the avowed principle that we were never to leave it off as long as we could carry it on, or get any one to carry it on for us, or till we had buried ourselves under the ruins of the civilized world (a prediction which we narrowly escaped verifying)—all these undeniable proofs and substantial demonstrations of our fond desires, our longings after peace, and of the determination of France to aggrandize herself by war and conquest, would, indeed, with the ingenious glosses of our well-meaning commentator form a very entertaining volume, and would at least teach us, if not what to follow, what we ought to shun, in our future advances to this first of earthly blessings, so long and studiously and systematically

* As he is fond of the good old times before the Revolution, the writer might go still farther back to that magnanimous undertaking, concerted and executed by the same persons of honour, the partition of Poland.

withheld from us—only to render its attainment more certain and more precious!

To the other solid grounds of an indefinite prolongation of this war, religious, moral, political, commercial, constitutional, continental, Jacobinical, Revolutionary, Corsican, foreign or domestic—our apologist, in the true spirit of the French *petit maitre* in *Roderic Random*, has now added a ground of his own, of equal efficacy and validity with the former, viz. that we are to carry it on in the character of gentlemen and men of honour. We are to fight for the restoration of the Bourbons, say *The Times*, "that we may have gentlemen and men of honour to fight with." There is some prudence in this resolution; it goes on the old principle, that we are not to fight except with our *match*. Don Quixote, after he had been soundly drubbed by the Yanguesian carriers, recollected that he ought not to have engaged with plebeians. The writer whom we have here quoted, told us, some time ago, from a greater authority certainly than that of *The Times*, the true grounds of war, or "that we might spill our blood for our country, for our liberty, for our friends, for our kind;" but we do not remember, among these legitimate sources of the waste of human blood, that we were to shed it for a punctilio. If war were to be decided by the breaking of white and black sticks among gentlemen-ushers, or even by the effusion of courtly phrases in *The Courier* and *The Times*, we should have no objection to this fastidious refinement; but we cannot consent to shed the best blood of Europe, nor that of "the meanest peasant in this our native land," in order that the delicate honour of the Carlton House Minority may not be stained, nor the purity of their moral taste perverted, by an intercourse with any but gentlemen and men of honour. And thou, Carl John, what hast thou to say to this new plea of the old school?—Or why, not being clad with the inherent right to "monarchize, be feared, and kill with looks,"—dost thou insult over the King of Denmark, menace Holstein, and seize upon Norway, and yet tellest thy little son, that the time is coming, when conquerors shall be no more?—*The Times'* editor scornfully rejects our practical opinion on the probability of restoring the Bourbons, because it seems we always reject every proposition that makes the continuance of war necessary. Be it so. But do not these persons also attach the highest degree of probability, or, when they are so inclined, moral certainty, to every thing that tends to make peace unattainable? It is true we did not, as they say, anticipate the reverses of the French Emperor before they happened. If we did not anticipate them before, it was because we had nothing in past experience to guide us to such a conclusion, except, indeed, the constant unverified predictions of *The Times* and *The Courier*. If these inspired writers had the slightest intimation of them one moment before they happened, we are willing to bow down to them, and they shall be our Gods. But of this we are sure, from all experience, that the way to render the fruits of those reverses uncertain, or to defeat them altogether, is the very mode of proceeding recommended by the ceaseless partizans of interminable hostilities. If the French are a nation of men—if they have the common faculties of memory, of understanding, and foresight; if they are, as they have been pronounced by one no ways favourable to them, "the most civilized, and with one exception, the most enlightened people in Europe," surely, if any thing can kindle in their minds "the flame of sacred vehemence, and move the very stones to mutiny," it is the letting loose upon them the mohawks of Europe, the Cossacks, with General Blucher's manifesto in their hands. It is restoring to Bonaparte the very weapon which we had wrested from him, the mighty plea of the independence of nations; it is reclothing his power with those adamantine scales "which fear no discipline of human hands," the hearts and wills of a whole people, threatened with emasculation of their moral and physical powers, by half a dozen libellers of the human species, and a horde of barbarians scarcely human. Even the writer in *The Times* acknowledges that the Cossacks entering France as a sort of masters of the ceremonies to the Bourbons, is only better, and less likely to excite horror and dismay, than their entering it in their own rights and persons. It may be so. The bear bringing in the monkey on his back may be more inviting than the bear alone. But we should think that either portent must be fatal, that neither hieroglyphic will be favourably interpreted.

ILLUSTRATIONS OF VETUS.

"Those nauseous harlequins in farce may pass,
"But there goes more to a substantial ass;
"Our modern wits such monstrous fools have shewn,
"They seem not of Heaven's making but their own."—DRYDEN.

Dec. 2, 1813.

THERE is a degree of shameless effrontery which disarms and baffles contempt by the shock which it gives to every feeling of moral rectitude or common decency; as there is a daring extravagance in absurdity which almost challenges our assent by confounding and setting at defiance every principle of human reasoning. The ribald paragraphs, which fill the columns of our daily papers, and disgrace the English language, afford too many examples of the former assertion; the Letters of Vetus are a striking instance of the latter.

It would have been some satisfaction to us, in the ungrateful task which we have imposed upon ourselves, if, in combating the conclusions of Vetus, we could have done justice to the ingenuity of his arguments, or the force of his illustrations. But his extreme dogmatism is as destitute of proofs, as it is violent in itself. His profound axioms are in general flat contradictions; and he scarcely makes a single statement in support of any proposition which does not subvert it. In the Parliamentary phrase, he constantly *stultifies* himself. The glaring and almost deliberate incongruity of his conclusions is such as to imply a morbid defect of comprehension, a warped or overstrained understanding. Absorbed in an inveterate purpose, bent on expanding some vapid sophism into a cumbrous system, he is insensible to the most obvious consequences of things; and his reason is made the blind pander to his prejudices.

We are not converts to this author's style, any more than to his reasoning. Indeed the defects of the one very much assist those of the other, and both have the same character. There is a perpetual effort to make something out of nothing, and to elevate a common-place into sublimity. The style of Vetus is not very different from that of Don Adriano de Armado; every word is as who should say, "I am Sir Oracle." Like the hero of Cervantes, haranguing the shepherds, he assaults the very vault of Heaven with the arrogance of his tone, and the loudness of his pretensions. Nothing can exceed the pompous quaintness, and laborious foolery of many of his letters. He unfolds the book of fate, assumes the prophet or historian, by virtue of alliteration and antithesis;—sustains the balance of power by well-poised periods, or crushes a people under a ponderous epithet. The set style of Vetus does not conform easily to the march of human affairs; and he is often forced to torture the sense to "hitch it" in a metaphor. While he is marshalling his words, he neglects his arguments, which require all his attention to connect them together; and in his eagerness to give additional significance to his sentences, he loses his own meaning.

We shall proceed to the task we at first proposed, viz. that of supplying marginal notes to the voluminous effusions of Vetus, and shall continue our comments as often as he furnishes us with the text.

We agree with the sentiment with which he commences his last Letter, that it is "particularly desirable to follow up the question of peace" at the present crisis, but not with the reason which he assigns for his extreme anxiety to enter upon the question, "because this is just the moment to dread the entertainment of a pacific overture." We can readily believe that at no other moment than when he dreads its approach, would Vetus ever breathe a syllable on the subject of peace, and then only to avert it. Whenever "a spurious and mawkish beneficence" gives an alarm of peace, the dogs of war stand ready on the slip to hunt it down.

"I have stated to you" (*To the Editor of the Times*) "as the only legitimate basis of a treaty, if not on the part of the continental Allies, at least for England herself, that *she should conquer all she can, and keep all she conquers.* This is not by way of retaliation, *however just,* upon so obdurate and rapacious an enemy—but as an indispensable condition of her own safety and existence."

That which is here said to be the *only* legitimate basis of a treaty is one, which if admitted and acted upon, would make it impossible that any treaty should ever be formed. It is a basis, not of lasting peace, but of endless war. To call that the basis of a treaty which precludes the possibility of any concession or compensation, of every consideration either of the right or power of each party to retain its actual acquisitions, is one of those misnomers which the gravity of Vetus's manner makes his readers overlook. After the imposing and guarded exordium which ushers in the definition of our only legitimate basis of a treaty, we are not prepared to expect Vetus's burlesque solution of the difficulty—"that we are not to treat at all." The human mind is naturally credulous of sounding professions, and reluctantly admits the existence of what is very common, and common for that reason—*pompous nonsense.* It seems, however, that this basis of a treaty is to apply only to one of the contracting powers, namely, England, it is equivocal as to the Allies, and with respect to France, it is, we suppose, meant to be altogether null. For in a former letter, after asking, "Who are to be the judges of his (Bonaparte's) rights?" he answers emphatically, "We and our Allies!" Bobadil did not come up to this exquisite pacificator of the world! To make common sense of Vetus's axiom with reference to any state whatever, "that it should keep all it conquers," it seems necessary to add this trifling condition, "if it can." And with respect to Great Britain in particular, if from her peculiar situation she has the power to keep all she conquers without being amenable to any other tribunal than her own will, this very circumstance proves that the exercise of that power is not *necessary to her safety and existence.* Again, if England has an interest of her own, quite independent on and separate from that of the continent, what has she to do with continental Allies? If her interests may be and are interwoven with those of the rest of Europe, is it too much to expect from her a common sacrifice to the common cause? We quarrel with France on continental grounds; we strip her of her colonies to support the quarrel; and yet we refuse to restore any part of them, in order to secure peace. If so, we are only ostensible parties in the contest, and in reality robbers.

"The first policy of a wise people is to make rival nations afraid to disturb them, to impress their enemies with a *terrific sense,*" (how magnificent is this epic mode of expression) "that to attack them is to suffer not only transient defeats, but deep, grievous, and *irrecoverable losses;* and to hold in abhorrence any peace which shall not be a living record of *their own superiority,* and a monument worthy of those warriors, through whose noble blood it was obtained."

If the losses sustained in war were to be irrecoverable, it is easy to foresee that the seat of empires would be very soon changed in almost all cases whatever. But Vetus here, as is customary with him when it tends to enforce the hyperbolical effect of his style, assumes as a broad ground of national wisdom, a physical impossibility. It is not in the nature of things that the losses of rival States should be irrecoverable. Vetus would do better to decree at once that the possessions of nations are *unassailable* as well as *irrecoverable,* which would prevent war altogether. But still more preposterous is the madness or malice of the assertion, that no peace can be made by a wise nation, which is not a living record of *their own superiority.* "This is the key-stone which makes up the arch" of Vetus's indestructible war-system. Can it have escaped even the short-sighted logic of this writer, that to make superiority an indispensable condition of a wise peace is to proscribe peace altogether, because certainly this superiority cannot belong at the same time to both parties, and yet we conceive that the consent of both parties is necessary to a peace? Any other peace, we are told, than that which is at all times impracticable between rival states, ought not only never to be made, but it ought to be held in abhorrence, we ought to shudder at its approach as the last of evils, and throw it to an immeasurable distance from us. This is indeed closing up the avenues to peace, and shutting the gates of mercy on mankind, in a most consummate and scientific manner. Our philosophic rhetorician appears also to forget, in that high tone in which he speaks of the *monuments raised by the noble blood of warriors*, that these sort of monuments are cemented by the blood of others as well as by our own, and tell the survivors a double story. His heated imagination seems to have been worked up into a literal belief of his own assertion, that the French nation are a rank non-entity; or he supposes that there is some celestial ichor in our veins, which we alone shed for our country, while other nations neither bleed nor suffer from war, nor have a right to profit by peace. This may be very well in poetry, or on the stage, but it will not pass current in diplomacy. Vetus, indeed, strains hard to reconcile inconsistencies, and to found the laws of nations on the sentiments of exclusive patriotism. But we should think that the common rules of peace and war, which necessarily involve the rights, interests, and feelings of different nations, cannot be dictated by the heroic caprices of a few hair-brained egotists, on either side of the question.

ILLUSTRATIONS OF VETUS.

(CONTINUED.)

" He is indeed a person of great acquired follies."
SIR FOPLING FLUTTER.

Dec. 10, 1813.

" NOTHING," continues Vetus, " can be more opposite to this great policy, than to fight and to render back the fruits of our successes. We may be assured, that those with whom we contend are ready enough to improve *their* victories. If we are not equally so, *we shall never be at rest.* If the enemy beats us, he wins our provinces.—[*What provinces of ours?*]—If we beat him, we restore all. What more profitable game could he desire! Truly, at this rate, our neighbours must be arrant fools if they leave us one week's repose !"

There is a spirit of Machiavelian policy in this paragraph which is very commendable. It reminds us of the satirist's description of " fools aspiring to be knaves." It is, in fact, this fear of being outwitted by the French, that constantly makes us the dupes of our suspicions of them, as it is a want of confidence in our own strength or firmness, that leads us to shew our courage by defiance. True courage, as well as true wisdom, is not distrustful of itself. Vetus recommends it to us to act upon the maxims of the common disturbers of mankind, of " this obdurate and rapacious foe," as the only means to secure general tranquillity. He wishes to embody the pretended spirit and principles of French diplomacy in a code,—the acknowledged basis of which should be either universal conquest, or endless hostility. We have, it seems, no chance of repelling the aggressions of the French, but by retaliating them not only on themselves, but on other states. At least, the author gives a pretty broad hint of what he means by the improvement of *our* victories, when he talks of annexing Holland and Danish Zealand to Hanover, as " her natural prey," *instead* of their being the dependencies of

France. This is certainly one way of trimming the balance of power in Europe, and placing the independence of nations in a most happy dilemma. The inventor of this new and short way with foreign states only laments that Hanover, "under British auspices," has not been beforehand with France in imitating Prussia in her seizure of the Austrian provinces on one side, and her partition of Poland on the other. He can scarcely express his astonishment and regret, that Holland and Denmark should so long have escaped falling into our grasp, after the brilliant example of "rapacity and obduracy" set to our phlegmatic, plodding, insipid, *commercial* spirit by Prussia and Russia. But now that we have rescued "our natural prey" from the French, it is to be hoped, that we shall make sure of it. Vetus's great principles of morality seem to be borrowed from those of Peacham, and his acknowledgments of merit to flow much in the same channel:—"A good clever lad, this Nimming Ned—there's not a handier in the whole gang, nor one more industrious to save goods from the fire!"—His chief objection to that "revolutionist," Bonaparte, (Vetus too is a projector of revolutions) is not, evidently, to his being a robber, but because he is at the head of a different gang; and we are only required to bestir ourselves as effectually as he does, *for the good of mankind!* But Vetus, whose real defect is a contraction of intellectual vision, sees no alternative between this rapacious and obdurate policy, and unconditional submission, between "restoring all" or none. This is not sound logic. He wishes by a *coup sur* to prevent an unfair and dishonourable peace, by laying down such rules as must make peace impossible, under any circumstances, or on any grounds that can enter into human calculation. According to him, our only security against the most wild and extravagant concessions, is the obstinate determination to make none; our only defence against the fascinations of our own folly, is to take refuge from the exercise of our discretion in his impregnable paradoxes.—"The same argument which goes to justify a war, prescribes war measures of the most determined and active character." Good;

because the nature and essence of war is *a trial of strength;* and, therefore, to make it as advantageous to ourselves as possible, we ought to exert all the strength that we possess. "The very object," continues Vetus, "that of weakening the enemy, for which we pursue those vigorous measures, and strip him of his possessions, renders it *necessary* to keep him in that state of weakness by which he will be deterred from repeating his attack; and, *therefore, to hold inflexibly* what we have acquired." Here again Vetus confounds himself, and, involving a plain principle in the mazes of a period, represents war not as a trial of strength between contending states, each exerting himself to the utmost, but as a voluntary assumption of superiority on the part of one of them. He talks of stripping the enemy of his possessions, and holding them inflexibly—as matters of course, as questions of will, and not of power.

It is neither the actual possession, nor *the will* to keep certain acquisitions, but the *power* to keep them, and, *at the same time,* to extort other concessions from an enemy, that must determine the basis of all negociations, that are not founded on verbal chimeras.

"We are taught, indeed, to take for granted, that a peace, whose conditions bear hard on either party, will be the sooner broken by that party; and, therefore, that we have an indirect interest in sacrificing a portion of our conquests." The general principle here stated is self-evident, and one would think indisputable. For the very ground of war is a peace whose conditions are thought to *bear hard* on one of the parties, and yet, according to Vetus, the only way to make peace durable, to prevent the recurrence of an appeal to force, is to impose such hard conditions on an enemy, as it is his interest, and must be his inclination, to break *by force.* An opinion of the disproportion between our general strength, and our actual advantages, seems to be the necessary ground of war, but it is here converted into the permanent source of peace. The origin of the common prejudice is, however, very satisfactorily illustrated in the remainder of the paragraph. "This language is in favour with the two extremes of English faction. The blind opponents of every minister *who happens to be engaged in conducting a war*" [*Is war then a mere affair of accident?*] "can see no danger in national dishonour; and cry out for peace with double vehemence, whenever it is least likely to be concluded well. The dependents, on the other hand, of any feeble government, will strive to lower the expectations of the country—to exclaim against *immoderate* exertion—to depreciate her powers in war, and her pretensions at a peace:—thus preparing an oblique defence for their employers, and undermining the honest disappointment" [*Quere expectations*] "of the people when they reflect how little has been done by war, and how much" [of that little] "undone by negociation. But besides being a factious expedient, it is a principle of action equally false and absurd. I deny that we effect any thing more by granting an enemy what are *called favourable terms*, than convince him that he may go to war with England, gratis. The conditions he obtains will encourage him to try the chance of another war, in the hope of a still more advantageous treaty." Here Vetus entirely shifts the state of the question. The terms of a peace, if *not hard*, must be immediately *favourable!* Because we grant an enemy such terms as he has a right to expect, it is made a conclusion that we are also to grant him such as he has no right to expect, and which will be so decidedly advantageous as to induce him to try his fortune still farther against so generous an adversary. That is, Vetus has no idea of the possibility of a just, fair, or honourable peace; his mind refuses to dwell for a moment on any arrangement of terms, which, by bearing hard on one party or another, will not be sure to end speedily, from the desire on one side to retrieve its affairs, and on the other to improve its advantages, in a renewal of war. "The only valid security for peace is the accession to our own strength, and the diminution of our rival's, by the resources and dominions we have wrested from him." First, this security can be good only on one side: secondly, it is not good at all: the only security for peace is not in the actual losses or distresses incurred by states, but in the settled conviction that they cannot *better* themselves by war. But all these contradictions are nothing to Vetus, who alone does not fluctuate between the extremes of faction, but is still true to war—and himself.

But there is, in our opinion, a third extreme of English faction (if Vetus will spare us the anomaly) not less absurd, and more mischievous than either of the others: we mean those who are the blind adherents of every minister who happens to be engaged in a war, however unnecessarily or wantonly it may have been begun, or however weakly and wickedly carried on: who see no danger in repeated disgraces, and impending ruin, provided we are obstinately bent on pursuing the same dreadful career which has led to them; who, when our losses come thronging in upon us, urge us to persist till we recover the advantages we have lost, and, when we recover them, force us on till we lose all again: with whom peace, in a time of adverse fortune, is dishonour, and in the pride of success, madness: who only exaggerate "our pretensions at a peace," that they may never be complied with: who assume a settled unrelenting purpose in our adversary to destroy us, in order to inspire us with the same principle of never-ending hostility against him: who leave us no alternative but eternal war, or inevitable ruin: who irritate the hatred and the fears of both parties, by spreading abroad incessantly a spirit of defiance, suspicion, and the most galling contempt: who, adapting every aspect of affairs to their own purposes, constantly return in the same circle to the point from which they set out: with whom peace is always unattainable, war always necessary!

We shall pass over Vetus's historic researches, the wars of the Romans and Carthaginians (the formal latitude of Vetus's pen delights in these great divisions of human affairs), and come to what is more to our purpose.

In modern times he first comes to the treaty of 1763, only (as far as we can find) to affix the epithet "American rebels" as a sort of Pragmatic Sanction to our colonists, with whom, he says,

France joined a few years afterwards, and, " in spite of her ruined finances and her peaceful king, aimed a mortal blow at the British monarchy." Yet, notwithstanding this long-standing and inveterate animosity of the French court to this country, we find the same France, in the next paragraph but one, stigmatized as *republican* and *Corsican*, " with centric and eccentric scribbled o'er," as if these were important distinctions, though Vetus himself " would prefer for France the scourge of Bonaparte, to the *healthier*, and to England *not less hostile*, sovereignty of the banished house of Bourbon." Why then pertinaciously affix these obnoxious epithets? They are bad ornaments of style—they are worse interpreters of truth.

To prove his general axiom, that in order to be stable, " the conditions of peace must bear hard on one of the parties," Vetus asks, " Were the powers that partitioned unhappy Poland so conciliated by her acquiescence in their first encroachments, as to abstain from offering her any second wrong?" Now this is an instance precisely in point to prove the direct reverse of Vetus's doctrine: for here was a treaty in which the terms bore exceedingly hard on one of the parties, and yet this only led to accumulated wrongs by a renewal of war. We say that hard conditions of peace, in all cases, will lead to a rupture. If the parties are nearly equal, they will lead to resistance to unfounded claims; if quite unequal—to an aggravation of oppression. But would Russia and Prussia have been more lenient or deterred from their encroachments, if Poland had pretended to impose hard conditions of peace on them? These governments partitioned Poland, not in consequence of any treaty good or bad, but because they had the will and the power to do so. Vetus would terrify the French into moderation by hard conditions of peace, and yet he supposes us to be in the same relation to France as Poland to its implacable enemies.

" Did the wretched complaisance of the leading continental courts in their several treaties with France, ensure their tranquillity even for a moment?" This is still altering the record. The question is not about submitting to hard conditions, but about imposing them. Besides, "the aggravated and multiplied molestations, injuries, and insults, which these courts were doomed to suffer," might be accounted for from those which they had in vain attempted to inflict on France, and from their still more wretched complaisance in being made the tools of a court which was not continental.

"Then comes the peace of Amiens, our peace of Amiens—a peace born, educated, nourished, and matured in this very philanthropic spirit of gentleness and forgiveness. In the war which preceded *the truce* of which I am speaking, *the French government* involved *us* in considerably more than two hundred millions of debt." Vetus then proceeds to state that we made peace without any liquidation of this claim, without satisfaction, without a bond, *(what else?)* without a promise, without a single guinea! "I will have ransom, most egregious ransom." Why was it ever heard of that one government paid the debts in which another had involved itself in making war upon it?

"The language of England," says our author, "was correctly what follows:—You, Monsieur, have loaded *me* with unspeakable distresses and embarrassments," *(all this while, be it recollected, our affairs were going on most prosperously and gloriously in the cant of The Times)* "you have robbed me of half my fortune, and reduced me to the brink of beggary," *(the French by all accounts were in the gulph of bankruptcy)* "you have torn away and made slaves of my friends and kindred," *(indeed)* "you have dangerously wounded me, and murdered my beloved children, who armed to defend their parent."—This is too much, even for the dupes of England. Stick, Vetus, to your statistics, and do not make the pathetic ridiculous! Sophistry and affectation may confound common sense to a certain degree, but there is a point at which our feelings revolt against them.

We have already remarked on what Vetus says of Hanover; he probably will not wish us to go farther into it. Of Bonaparte he says, of course, that nothing short of unconditional submission will ever satisfy that revolutionist, and that he will convert the smallest concession made to him into a weapon for our destruction. That is, we have it in our power to set him at defiance, to insult him, to " bring him to the block," &c. whenever we please; and yet we are so completely in his power, so dependent on him, that the smallest concession must be fatal to us, will be made the instrument of our inevitable destruction. Thus is the public mind agitated and distracted by incredible contradictions, and made to feel at once " the fierce extremes" of terror and triumph, of rashness and despair. " Our safety lies in his weakness, not in his will." If so, or if it depends on either of the conditions here stated, we are in no very pleasant situation. But our real safety depends on our own strength, and steady reliance on it, and not on the arguments of Vetus.

ILLUSTRATIONS OF VETUS.

(CONTINUED.)

" Madmen's epistles are no gospels."

Dec. 16, 1813.

THE last Letter of Vetus begins with an allusion to the events which have lately taken place in Holland. He then proceeds— " What final effect this popular movement by the Dutch may have upon the future interests and prosperity of England is a question to be discussed with deliberate caution—with extreme solicitude—and with the chance, I trust, the distant chance, of its conducting us to no very gratifying conclusion!" There is something in this passage truly characteristic, and well worthy of our notice. Vetus is, it seems, already jealous of the Dutch. The subtle venom of his officious zeal is instantly put in motion by the prospect of their national independence and commercial prosperity; and his pen is, no doubt, prepared, on the slightest provocation of circumstances, to convert them from an ally to be saved, into a rival and an enemy to be crushed. He, however, waives for the present the solemn discussion, till he can find some farther grounds to confirm him in his extreme solicitude and mysterious apprehensions. The perverse readiness of Vetus to pick a quarrel out of every thing, or out of nothing, is exactly described in Spenser's Allegory of *Furor* and *Occasion*, which if we thought him "made of penetrable stuff," we would recommend to his perusal.

The introductory comment on the Revolution in Holland is a clue to the whole of our author's political system, which we shall here endeavour to explain. He looks askance with "leer malign" on the remotest prospect of good to other nations. Every addition to the general stock of liberty or happiness, is to him so much taken from our own. He sees nothing gratifying in that prosperity or independence, which is shared (or any part of it) with foreign nations. He trembles with needless apprehension at the advantages in store for them, which he anticipates only to prevent, and is indifferent to our own welfare, interests, honour—except as they result from the privations, distress, and degradation of the rest of the world. Hatred, suspicion, and contempt for other nations are the first and last principles of the love which "an upright Englishman" bears to his country. To prevent their enjoying a moment's repose, or indulging even in a dream of future comfort, he would involve his own country in incessant distraction and wretchedness, and risk its final ruin on the cast of a die!—Vetus professes, with some reason, not to be enamoured of quotation: but he may, perhaps, allow us to refer to an author, who, though not so deep read in Vattel and the writings of the jurists, had just and penetrating views of human nature. "Think, there's livers out of England. What's England in the world's map? In a great pool a swan's nest." Now this "swan's nest" is indeed to us more than all the world besides—to cherish, to protect, to love, and honour it. But if we expect it to be so to the rest of the world—if we do not allow them to cultivate their own affections, to improve their own advantages, to respect their own rights, to maintain their own independence—if in the blindness of our ignorance, our pride, and our presumption, we think of setting up our partial and local attachments as the law of nature and nations—if we practise, or so much as tolerate in theory that "exclusive patriotism" which is inconsistent with the common privileges of humanity, and attempt to dictate our individual caprices, as paramount and binding obligations on those, to whose exaction of the same claims from us we should return only loud scórn, indignation, and defiance—if we are ever so lost to reason, as Vetus would have us, who supposes that we cannot serve our country truly and faithfully but by making others the vassals of her avarice or insolence; we shall then indeed richly deserve, if we do not meet with, the natural punishment of such disgraceful and drivelling hypocrisy.

Vetus, who is extremely dissatisfied with our application of the term "exclusive patriotism" to him, is nevertheless "at a loss to understand the patriotism which is not exclusive. The word *implies* a preference of the rights and welfare of our own country to those of other (and above all other) of rival countries. This is not indeed the philanthropy of Anacharsis Cloots—it is not the dreary jargon of metaphysics, nor the shop-boy philosophy of a printer's devil—nor the *sans-culotterie* of scholastic virtue." We will tell Vetus what we mean by exclusive patriotism, such as (we say) his is. We mean by it then, not that patriotism which implies a preference of the rights and welfare of our own country, but that which professes to annihilate and proscribe the rights of others—not that patriotism which supposes us to be the creatures of circumstance, habit, and affection, but that which divests us of the character of reasonable beings—which fantastically makes our interests or prejudices the sole measure of right and wrong to other nations, and constitutes us sole arbiters of the empire of the world—in short, which, under the affectation of an overweening anxiety for the welfare of our own country, *excludes* even the shadow of a pretension to common sense, justice, and humanity. It is this wretched solecism which Vetus would fain bolster up into a system, with all the logic and rhetoric he is master of. It is true, this kind of patriotism is not the philanthropy of Anacharsis Cloots; it has nothing to do with philanthropy in any shape, but it is a vile compound of "the jargon of metaphysics, with the vulgar notions of a printer's devil." It is an intense union of the grossness and narrowness of ignorance with the dangerous refinement of the most abstracted speculation. It is passion and prejudice, inflamed by philosophy, and philosophy distorted by passion and prejudice.

After his cold exordium on the Revolution in Holland, our consistent politician enters with warmth on Lord Castlereagh's speech on the subsidiary treaties, in which he finds a *But* before the word *Peace*, which has a most happy efficacy in healing the wounds inflicted on his tortured apprehensions, by the explicit, unqualified declaration of Lord Liverpool in the other House. "After describing the laudable solicitude of Ministers for the attainment of that *first* of earthly goods, peace," (we thought it had ranked last in the mind of Vetus) "his Lordship added *what was worth all the rest*—BUT we must have a *secure* peace. We must not only recollect with whom we contend, but with whom we negociate, and never grant to *such* an enemy conditions, which under the name of peace, would disarm this nation, and expose her to *contingent* dangers." (To place any nation out of the reach of contingent dangers in peace or war is, we imagine, an undertaking beyond even the *calibre* of Lord Castlereagh's talents as a statesman.) "These," proceeds Vetus, "were nearly the words; they certainly do not compromise his meaning." (Our author cannot be much mistaken in attributing to his Lordship any words which seeming to have some meaning, in reality have none.) "Here then the noble Secretary has *chased away every doubtful expression* of his colleague." ("Why so,—this horrible shadow" of peace "being gone," Vetus "is himself again.")

"The sentiment delivered by the sovereign on the throne is now given to us with a construction, at which we need no longer be alarmed. *I* ask only that *secure* peace,—a peace consistent with English safety—*void of the shadow of regard or indulgence to the pretensions and honour, otherwise the ambition and arrogance of Bonaparte,* which, as compared with *the relief of one day's hunger to the meanest peasant in this our native land,* are baubles not worth a name!"—This is undoubtedly one of the most remarkable specimens we ever met with of that figure in rhetoric, designated by an excellent writer as "the figure of *encroachment.*"* Vetus, by a series of equations (certainly not mathematical ones) at length arrives at a construction of peace at which he is no longer alarmed; at the identical peace which he wants, and the only one he will admit,—a peace preposterous in its very terms, and in its nature impracticable,—a peace "void of the shadow of regard or indulgence to the pretensions and honour" of the enemy, which are to pass with them as well as with us, for so much "arrogance and ambition." This is the only peace consistent with English safety—this is the secure peace of Lord Castlereagh—the fair and honourable peace announced from the throne—the very peace which Lord Liverpool meant to describe when he startled Vetus by the doubtful expression of a peace "consistent with the honour, rights, and interests of France"—"of such a peace as we in her situation should be disposed to grant." To the mind of Vetus, which is indeed the very receptacle for contradictions "to knot and gender in," these two sorts of peace appear to be perfectly compatible, and the one a most happy explanation of the other, viz. a peace void of every shadow of regard to the rights and honour of a rival nation, and a peace consistent with those rights and that honour. If this is not "mere midsummer madness," we do not know what is. Or if any thing can surpass it ("for in this lowest deep of absurdity, a lower deep still opens to receive us, gaping wide") it is the forlorn piece of sentimental mummery by which it is attempted to protract this endless war of proscription against the pretensions of France, under the mask of relieving the wants and distresses of

* See Remarks on Judge Eyre's Charge to the Jury, 1794, by W. Godwin.

the meanest peasant of this our native land! Compared with the tears and blood of our countrymen, all the sophistries of Vetus by which he would make them victims of his own vanity and egotism, not less than of the arrogance and ambition of Bonaparte, are indeed contemptible and mischievous baubles.

" What means the impious cry raised by degenerate Englishmen against the mere chance—nay, the remotest possibility of a peace, whose terms should be honourable to their country? Whence arises this profligate and abandoned yell with which these traitors insult us? *Are they still in pay? Is their patron still rich enough to bribe them?* When we demand compensation for our *dreadful sufferings*, it is but what justice grants. When we call for security, it is what our existence requires. Yet, when these undoubted rights and essential safeguards of an injured people are asserted, it is nothing less than blaspheming the holy supremacy of Bonaparte!"

First, when Vetus demands compensation for our sufferings, it would perhaps hardly be sufficient to refer him to the satisfaction which the patriotic contributors to *The Times, The Courier, The Morning Post, The Sun* and *The Star*, must have had in writing, and their admirers in reading the daily paragraphs, of which those sufferings were the dreadful price, and the inevitable result. When we demand compensation for what we have suffered, it is but *justice*, if we can at the same time make compensation for what we have made others suffer; but at all events, it is no compensation for past sufferings, to make them perpetual. When we call for security, we are right; but when we tell the enemy that our only security is in his destruction, and call upon him for this pledge and safeguard of our undoubted rights, we shew, by asking for what we know we cannot have, that not security, but defiance is our object. As to the terms of abuse which are introduced in this paragraph (we suppose, to vary the general gravity and decorum of Vetus's style) we shall answer them by a very short statement of what we conceive to be the truth. Europe has been for the last twenty years engaged in a desperate and (for some reason or other) an unequal struggle against France;—by playing at double or quits, she has just recovered from the very brink of destruction; and the keepers of our political E. O. tables treat us as traitors and miscreants, who would dissuade her from sitting down once more to finish the game, and ruin her adversary.

"—It is asked,—' Do we propose to humble France? Do we propose to destroy her? If so, we breathe *eternal* war; if so, we convert the aggressor into the sufferer, and transfer all the dignity and authority of justice to the enemy against whom we arm!" Yes, against whom we arm for the avowed purpose of his destruction. From the moment that we make the destruction of an enemy (be he who he may) the indispensable condition of our safety, our destruction from that moment *becomes* necessary to his, and an act of self-defence. Not much liking this dilemma from which our author has more than once " struggled to get free," he in the next passage makes a wide career indeed, in order, no doubt, to return to the charge with better effect hereafter. " The question of peace or eternal war is not *a naked question* of right and wrong. It is a question, whose morality is determined by its reference to our preservation as a people. To such interrogatories I answer without reserve, that we ought to exact *precisely* that measure of humiliation from France, and that we do recommend *that critical advance towards her destruction*, that may combine the utmost *attinaable* satisfaction for our past grievances with a solid protection to our future interest and welfare. From France, since the *fatal* battle of Hastings, what has *this nation of Saxon warriors*"—(We hardly know ourselves in the learned livery of Vetus's style. He himself is doubtless descended from some very old family settled here before the Conquest)—" What has this nation of Saxon warriors ever yet endured from France but injury and affliction?" Yet we have made a shift to exist as a nation under all this load of calamity. We still breathe and live notwithstanding some intervals of repose, some short resting places afforded us, before this morbid inspector of health, like another Doctor Pedro Positive) injoined his preposterous regimen of incessant war as necessary to lasting peace, and to our preservation as a people!

"Modern France" continues Vetus, rising in his argument, "has no principle so deeply rooted as that of everlasting enmity to England. I confess for this reason that in my uncorrupted judgment *the best security* for Great Britain, and therefore, *if practicable, her most imperious duty,* would be *the absolute conquest of France.* But since that, *unfortunately,* is an event which *at present* we are not likely to accomplish, *the second best security* is" (one would think not to attempt it at all; no, but) "to reduce her, *if we can,* to a degree of weakness consistent *with our immediate repose.*" After thus modestly postponing the absolute conquest of France to a more convenient opportunity, he adds the following incredible sentence. "If the enemy should be so far borne away by *his hatred,* as to command *his emissaries* in London to announce that he prefers waging eternal war to the acceptance of conditions, which *his own persevering and atrocious outrages* have rendered in the mind of every Englishman indispensable to the safety of these islands, the woeful alternative of perpetual war very plainly originates not with Great Britain but with Bonaparte!" That is to say, *The Times* not long ago laid it down as a fixed, unalterable maxim, without reference to terms of one sort or another, that we were never to make peace with Bonaparte; Vetus in this very letter enters into an elaborate apology, for that multitude of wise, honest, and virtuous persons who think his existence as a sovereign *at all times* threatens our existence as a nation, and it is because we entered our protest against this "frantic outcry raised by degenerate Englishmen," that Bonaparte is here made to charge his emissaries in London to announce that he prefers eternal war to the acceptance of conditions, the moderation of which conditions or of *our second best security* may be judged of when we are told that the best, and indeed only real security for Great Britain, and therefore her most imperious duty, would be the absolute conquest of France.

Vetus is, however, contented with such terms of peace as will imply only *a critical advance to her destruction*, and if Bonaparte is not contented with the same terms, the alternative of eternal war, it seems, originates with him and not with Vetus.*

But we deny that though this best security for Great Britain, the absolute conquest of France, were in her power, that it would be her most imperious duty to effect it. And we deny it, because on the same ground a better security still for Great Britain would be the conquest or destruction of Europe and the world; and yet we do not think it her imperious duty, even if she could, to accomplish the one, or to make a *critical* advance to the other. For if it is once laid down and acted upon as a maxim in national morality, that the best and most desirable security of a state is in the destruction of its neighbours, or that there is to be an unrelenting ever watchful critical approximation to this object as far as possible, there is an end of civil society. The same principle of not stopping short of this *maximum* of selfish security will impose the same imperious duty of rankling jealousy, and inexorable hostility on others. Our speculator's "best possible security" for the independence of states, is nothing but a watchword for mutual havoc, and wide-spreading desolation. Terrified with the phantom of imaginary danger, he would have us rush headlong on the reality. We are obstinately to refuse the enjoyment of a moment's repose, and proceed to commit wilful dilapidation on the estate of our happiness, because it is not secured to us by an everlasting tenure. Placed at the mercy of the malice or hypocrisy of every venal alarmist, our only resource must be to seek a refuge from our fears in our own destruction, or to find the gratification of our revenge in that of others. But a whole nation is no more justified in obtaining this best of all possible securities for itself, by the immediate subversion of other states, than the assassin is justified in taking the life of another, to pre-

* Observe that these critically destructive terms of peace are not strictly called for by Bonaparte's persevering and atrocious outrages, but are at all times rendered necessary by the everlasting enmity of France.

vent the possibility of any future attempt upon his own. For in proportion as a state is weak and incapable of subjugating us, is the manifest injustice of any such precaution;—and in proportion as a state is formidable, and likely to excite serious apprehension for our own safety, is the danger and folly of setting an example which may be retaliated with so much greater effect, and "like a devilish engine, recoil upon ourselves." That exclusive patriotism which claims for our country an exemption from "contingent danger," which would place its wealth, its power, or even its safety beyond the reach of chance and the fluctuation of human affairs, claims for it an exemption from the common lot of human nature. That exclusive patriotism which seeks to enforce this claim (equally impious and unwise) by the absolute conquest of rival states, tempts the very ruin it professes to avert.

But Vetus mistakes the nature of patriotism altogether. He would transform that principle which was intended for the tutelary genius of nations, into the destroying demon of the world. He ransacks past history to revive old grudges; he anticipates the future to invent new ones. In his whole system, there is not room for "so small a drop of pity as a wren's eye." His patriotism is the worm that dies not; a viper gnawing at the heart. He would strip this feeling of every thing but the low cunning, and brutal ferocity of the savage state, and then arm it with all the refinements of scholastic virtue, and the most rigid logic. The diverging rays of human reason which should be diffused to cheer and enlighten the moral world, are in him collected into a focus of raging zeal to burn and destroy. It is well for mankind that in the order of the universe, our passions naturally circumscribe themselves, and contain their own antidote within them. The only justification of our narrow, selfish passions, is their shortsightedness:—were it not for this, the jealousies of individuals and of nations would not leave them the smallest interval of rest. It is well that the ungovernable impulses of fear and hatred are excited only by gross, palpable objects; and are therefore transient, and limited in their operation. It is well that those motives which do not owe their birth to reason, should not afterwards receive their nourishment and support from it. If in their present desultory state, they produce so many mischiefs, what would be the case, if they were to be organized into systems, and elevated into abstract principles of right and wrong?

The whole of Vetus's reasoning is founded on the false notions of patriotism which we have here pointed out, and which we conceive to be totally inconsistent with "the just principles of negociation." The remainder of his letter, which unfolds his motives for a pacific arrangement with Bonaparte, is founded entirely on the same jaundiced and distempered views. Many wise, many honest, many virtuous persons, he says, have maintained, not without reason, "the incompetency of *this Corsican* under any circumstances to discharge the obligations of a state of peace." But he, more wise, more honest, more virtuous, sees a hope, a shadow of peace, rising like a cloudy speck out of a quarter where it was least expected. "The stone which the builders rejected, is become the corner-stone of his Temple of Peace."— "It does not appear to Vetus, that a peace with Bonaparte is now unattainable on terms sufficient for our safety." He thinks there is no man so proper to make peace with as this Corsican, this Revolutionist,—no one so proper to govern France—to the complete exclusion of the Bourbons, whose pretensions he scouts analytically, logically, and chronologically, and who, it seems, had always the same implacable animosity against this country as Bonaparte, *without a tythe of his ability*. [Surely this circumstance might plead a little in their favour with Vetus.] And why so? Whence arises this unexpected partiality shewn to Bonaparte? Why it is "from the strong conviction that by no other means so decisive as the existence of this man, with his consuming, depressing and degrading system of government, can we hope to see France *crushed and ground down below the capacity of contending for ages to come* with the force of the British Empire, *moved by the spirit of freedom!* Regarding France under every known form of government as the irreconcileable foe of England, *I have beheld with almost unmingled joy the growth and accumulation of this savage despotism!*" To be sure "while there appeared to some persons," [Vetus was not one of them] "a *chance* of his enslaving the Continent, and hurling the mass of subjugated nations against our shores—then, indeed, those who entertained such fears were justified in seeking his *personal* and political destruction. But once released from the terror of his arm, *what genuine Englishman* can fail to rejoice in the privilege of consigning Bonaparte and the French people, for better for worse, to the paradise of each other's embraces?" Vetus then proceeds to inveigh at great length against the persons and pretensions of the Bourbons. Leaving them to the mercy of this good-natured remembrancer, we shall only observe, that he decides the impolicy of restoring the Bourbons, by asking, whether their restoration would not be advantageous to France, and consequently (he infers very consistently with himself) *injurious to this country*. Looking forward but half a century, he sees France gradually regain under the old regime "her natural ascendancy over Great Britain, from which she falls, and must fall every hour more rapidly from the necessary operation of those principles on which the Corsican dynasty is founded." Nay, looking on farther than the expiration of the same half century, he sees "sloth, weakness, and poverty, worse than ever sprung from Turkish policy, proceeding from this odious, self-dissolving power, and a gulph of irretrievable destruction, already yawning for our eternal foe."

It is not long ago since Vetus drew an historical parallel between this country and Carthage, encouraging us to expect the same fate from France which Carthage received from Rome, and to act upon this fanciful comparison as a solid ground of wisdom. Now all at once "this mendicant in argument, this perfect juggler in politics," inverts the perspective, takes a prophetic view of the events of the next fifty years, and France is seen dwindling into another Turkey, which the genius of British freedom grinds to powder, and crushes beneath her feet! These great statesmen-like views of things, "this large discourse of reason, looking before and after," are, we confess, beyond us. We recollect indeed a similar prophecy to that of Vetus, couched in nearly the same terms, when in the year 1797, the French were said to be "on the verge, nay, in the very gulph of bankruptcy," and that their finances could not hold out six months longer. Vetus, however, taught by the failure of past prognostics, constructs his political calculations for the ensuing century, instead of the ensuing year, and puts off the day of reckoning to a period when he and his predictions will be forgotten.

Such are the charitable grounds on which our author wishes to secure Bonaparte on the throne of France, and thinks that peace may at present be made with him, on terms consistent with our safety. He is not, like others, "ready to shake hands with the Usurper over the tomb of the murdered D'Enghien, provided he will *return to the paths of religion and virtue*;" but he will shake hands with him over the ruins of the liberty and happiness of France, on the express condition that "he never returns to the paths of religion and morality." Vetus is willing to forget the injuries which Bonaparte may have done to England, for the sake of the greater mischiefs he may do to France. These are the "obligations" which Vetus owes to him—this the source of his gratitude, the sacred pledge that reconciles him to "that monster whom England detests." He is for making peace with the "tyrant," to give him an opportunity to rivet on the chains of France, and fix her final doom. But is Vetus sincere in all this? His reasoning comes in a very questionable shape; and we the more doubt it, because he has no sooner (under the auspices of Bonaparte) hurled France down the gulf of irretrievable destruction, than he immediately resumes the old topic of eternal war or perpetual bondage, as the only alternative which this country can look to. Why, if he is in earnest, insist with Lord Castlereagh on the caution with which we must grant terms to "such an enemy," to this disabled and paralyzed foe? Why assert, as Vetus did in his very last letter, that "nothing short of unconditional submission will ever satisfy that revolutionist, and that any concession made to him will be instantly converted into a weapon for our destruction?" Why not grant to him such terms as might be granted to the Bourbons, since they would be granted to a much less dangerous and powerful rival? Why not subsist, as we have hitherto done, without the fear of perpetual war or perpetual bondage before our eyes, now that the crown of France has lost its original brightness, and is shorn of those beams which would again sparkle round it, if fixed on the head of a Bourbon? We suspect that our author is not quite in earnest in his professions, because he is not consistent with himself. Is it possible that his anxiety to keep out the Bourbons arises from his fear that peace might creep in with them, at least as a sort of compliment of the season? Is our veteran politician aware, in his own mind, that the single epithets, Corsican, republican, revolutionary, will have more effect in stirring up the embers of war, than all the arguments which he might use to demonstrate the accumulating dangers to be apprehended from the mild paternal sway of the ancient dynasty?

We cannot help saying, however, that we think the elaborate attempt of Vetus to prove the necessary extinction of the power of France under the government of Bonaparte, a total failure. What is the amount of his argument? That in a period when the French were to owe their existence and their power to war, Bonaparte has made them a warlike people, and that they did not sit down quietly to "the cultivation of arts, luxuries, and letters," when the world was beleaguered against them. Is it for Vetus, who reprobates the peace of Amiens, *that hollow truce* (as he justly calls it), that intermission of war but for a moment, to say of Bonaparte, "His application of public industry is only to the arts of death—all other perishes for want of wholesome nourishment?" What then becomes of the long-resounded charge against him on his exclamation "for ships, colonies, and commerce?" We suspect, that energy in war is not an absolute proof of weakness in peace. He lays down, indeed, a general principle (true enough in itself) that a government, in its nature and character at variance with the people, must be comparatively weak and insecure; yet, in applying this maxim, he proves not that the French people and government are at irreconcileable variance, but that the one has become entirely subdued and assimilated to the other. But hear him speak for himself. "The causes of the overthrow of the old government are foreign to our present purpose. The consequence has been the birth of *this bloody and scorching despotism*,—this giant, armed from his mother's womb with sweeping scimitar and consuming fire. Can such a government be fit for such a people? Can a tyranny, operating by direct violence and characteristic of the earliest periods in the most barbarous condition of mankind, have any quality adapted to the wants or feelings of a nation, grown *old in arts*, luxuries, and letters? Is it not plain to the least acute observer, that where the principles of such a government, and such a stage of society, are so vehemently contrasted, there can be no immediate alliance; but that an incessant counteraction must ensue—that the government or the people must change their character before a just harmony and co-operation can exist between them; *in other words, that one of them must yield!*"

[Well, this is the very thing which, in the next sentence, he shews has actually taken place.] "And *from whom* are we to infer this ultimate submission to its rival? Has the tyrant loosed his chains?—has he relaxed his hold, or flung aside the whip of scorpions? No! it is *France herself which has given way.* It is the French nation who gradually recede from the rest of the civilized world." That is, it is France who, contrary to Vetus's argument, in receding gradually from the rest of the civilized world, has been identified with the government, and become that whip of scorpions in the hands of Bonaparte, which has been the scourge and dread of all Europe. It is thus that our author always defeats himself. He is fond of abstruse reasoning and deep investigation in exact proportion to his incapacity for them—as eunuchs are amorous through impotence!

But though he fails in his argument, the moral is not less instructive. He teaches us on what grounds a genuine English patriot goes to war, and on what terms he will make peace. A patriot of this exclusive stamp, who is troubled with none of the symptoms of a "spurious and mawkish beneficence," threatens France with the restoration of the Bourbons, only to throw her into the convulsions of anarchy, and withdraws that kindly interference, only that she may sink into the more fatal lethargy of despotism. It is the same consistent patriot who kindles the fires of La Vendée, and whenever it suits his purpose, is no longer borne away by the "torrent of royal, flaming, unreflecting sympathies!" It is the same tried friend of his country, who carries on a twenty years' war for the preservation of our trade and manufactures, and when they are mentioned as inducements for peace, disdains "all gross, commercial calculations." It is the same conscientious politician, who at one time makes war for the support of social order, and the defence of our holy religion;—who, at another, hails the disappearance of "the last glimmering of education among a people grown old in arts and letters," and who rejoices "to see the Christian religion made studiously contemptible by the poverty and debasement of its professors!" It is the same true patriot, the same Vetus, who "beholds with unmingled joy, the growth and accumulation of a savage despotism, which is to crush and bow down France under our feet;"—who holds "the whip of scorpions over her head;"—who "arms a scorching tyranny with sweeping scimeter and consuming fire" against her;—who pushes her headlong down "the yawning gulf of irretrievable destruction;"—it is the same Vetus, who, suddenly recovering all the severity of justice, and all the tenderness of humanity, makes a piteous outcry about "the dreadful sufferings we have endured," in attempting to heap coals of fire on our adversary, demands the payment of "two hundred millions of debt, in which her government have wantonly involved us," complains of our being "driven to beggary and want" in this unnatural conflict, calls for the release of our countrymen, "sent into hopeless captivity," and invokes the murdered names of those children of the state, who "armed to defend a beloved parent, and an injured country!" Even Vetus shrinks from the enormity of such inconsistencies, and excuses himself by saying, "Do I feel the spontaneous and unprovoked desire that such a mass of evil should be perpetuated for any portion of mankind? *God forbid.* But it is, *I conscientiously* believe, a question, *which of these countries shall destroy the other.* In that case, my part is taken—France must be ruined, to save our native country from being ruined. If this be perpetual war, I cannot help it. *Perpetual war has little terror, when perpetual bondage threatens us.*" Here then our bane and antidote are both before us: perpetual war or perpetual bondage;—a pleasant alternative!—but it is an alternative of Vetus's making, and we shall not, *if we can help it,* submit to either of his indispensable conditions. We shall not learn of him, for "his yoke is not easy, nor his burden light." If this be our inevitable lot, "he cannot help it." No; but he can help laying the blame of his own irritable and mischievous conclusions on Nature and Providence; or at least we think it our duty to guard ourselves and others against the fatal delusion.

ILLUSTRATIONS OF VETUS.

"Take him, and cut him out in little stars."

Jan. 3, 1814.

WE undertook, some time ago, the task of ascertaining the true value of this writer's reasoning, by removing the cumbrous load of words which oppress his understanding, as well as that of his readers; and we find that "our occupation is not yet gone." His last letter, indeed, furnishes us with comparatively slender materials. His style is considerably abated. With Bottom in the play, he may be said to "aggravate his voice so, that he roars you an 'twere any sucking dove." His swaggering paradoxes dwindle into unmeaning common-places; his violent dogmas into tame equivocations. There is scarcely an attempt made to defend his own extreme opinions, or to repel the charge of gross and glaring inconsistency which we brought against them. He makes indeed a faint effort to screen certain general positions from the odium and contempt they deserve, by explaining them away, and to *shift* off the responsibility of others, by directly denying them. Vetus has, in fact, marched boldly on in a fog of splendid words, till he unexpectedly finds himself on the edge of a precipice, and he seems willing to retreat from it as well as his accustomed solemnity, and the incumbrances of his style will permit. It may, perhaps, be some consolation, if we remind him that he is not the first enthusiast on record, who mistook a cloud for a goddess. His present situation is certainly no very pleasant one: it a good deal resembles that of Parolles, when he undertook the recovery of his drum.

The most striking part of Vetus's last letter is his gratuitous *tirade* against what has been called the modern philosophy, as if this were the only alternative (whereas it is in truth the antithesis or converse) of his system of exclusive patriotism. Our contradiction of his first principle, that the basis of a peace with France is to be one which does not leave a shadow of regard to her honour, rights, or interest, and that the terms of peace to which she is in duty bound to accede, must be such as to imply a *critical advance* to her destruction—our utter rejection of this new-fangled theory of negociation he considers as "a sucker from the root of that poisonous vegetable, the doctrine of universal benevolence;" and deprecates our reasoning on the subject as "a blossom which threatens the desolation of the moral world!" We really cannot attribute to our opinions any such power or any such tendency as the morbid imagination of our political hypochondriac lends to them. The arguments of Vetus on this question seem a sort of transcript of Dr. Parr's Spital Sermon, or of one of Sir James Mackintosh's lectures at Lincoln's Inn; and are very tolerable, dull, common-place declamation—a little bordering on fustian. But, as is the invariable fate of Vetus's arguments, they contain a flat contradiction to the principle he is aiming to establish. Though the passage has little to do with the immediate question, we shall give it as a literary curiosity. It is an instance of one of those lapses of thought, of that epilepsy of the mind, which we have already pointed out as the distinguishing characteristic of this author's understanding. His object is to exclude all general reasoning, or the seeds of what he absurdly calls "theo-philanthropy" from the feelings of patriotism; and in his eagerness to do this, he effectually explodes and laughs to scorn all patriotism, as a branch of the same theo-philanthropy, as impracticable and romantic folly. His words are these:—

"One of these patriots enacts the part of a drawling hypocritical projector, whom no natural affection can move, nor individual happiness enliven. He is a regular brother of a well known sect, which we of this generation have had the misfortune to behold in high activity—and which, having seen, it is but wisdom to remember. The men I speak of were those who in some degree precipitated the French revolution, and who entirely perverted its possible uses, the mongrel race of metaphysical enthusiasts, who undertook to change the objects of human feeling, that they might disappoint more effectually the ends for which it was bestowed. Such were the worshippers of the strumpet goddess Reason; a deity, in herself, and in the prostitute who represented her, convertible to purposes equally abandoned. The next step, after acknowledging this divinity, was to make a display of her power. Mankind were to be *reasoned* out of *all* human sensibilities; but the loss was to be supplied by reasoning them into a new assortment of human sensibilities, on a larger and nobler scale. Brotherly regard was a puny sentiment; what was a single brother to him who felt that millions of freemen were his brothers! Marriage, too, that holy and heavenly* and heart-sustaining institution,

* "In heaven they neither marry nor are given in marriage." There is nothing so provoking as these matter-of-fact Utopia-mongers.

what with its graceful and beautiful assemblage of bland obligations and virtuous sympathies—how stood the fixed relation of husband and wife? Why, treason to natural liberty!—'exclusive tenderness'—a bar to the performance of those unconfined embraces, which spoke the reign of universal love. Parental affection, and filial piety, also, were still less worthy to escape the blight of this ruthless philosophical reform. How narrow was the father's mansion! How diminutive the mind that could look with reverence to the beings that gave it birth, when the republic, sole heiress of philanthropy and freedom—the great republic, offered herself as the fond and universal parent. Nor could the sire, who argued logically, bewail the sacrifice of his devoted offspring. His children—not his, but their country's children—were to be educated by and for that country. His paternal feelings were not to be extinguished—no, nothing more than transferred to the state, and ennobled by the magnitude of the object. This same republic was a perfect 'Scrub.' She was to play the sister, husband, wife, son, and mother—confiscating and appropriating the individual duties, rights, and charities of mankind—ransacking the deepest recesses of the heart, and seizing as prizes to her sovereign will the royalties and wrecks of human nature.

"*But the phrenzy did not terminate here.* It was not enough that all the relations of life should merge in that of citizen: even 'exclusive patriotism' was a vulgar thought. In the paroxysms of disorder, it was sometimes proposed, that the citizen himself should evaporate into a citizen of the world. The universal republic—the vast family of mankind—the deputations from the human race—became instruments with the knaves who led, and visions for the dupes who admired. There can really be no objection to this superfine theory, but that it is inconsistent with the order of Providence, and destructive of the nature of man—that it unfixes our moral land-marks—melts into air every practical virtue and definite duty—substitutes words for salutary deeds—and by directing our most natural and useful passions to objects indistinct or unattainable, leaves these powerful agents afloat, and ends by abusing them to the production of crime and misery. Such were the results of that system of speculation, which assumed for its basis the existence of a species of beings far above the pitch of humanity, and which, in its application to human affairs, reduces them to the level of brutes.

" A sucker from the root of this poisonous vegetable is again in blossom, and threatens the desolation of the moral world. We are called upon to abdicate the right and obligation of preferring and protecting our native country, that is, of enjoying our proper advantages, and of discharging our specific trusts—and for what? Why, that we may undertake the preposterous office, and execute the factitious duty of handing over to a mortal enemy the greatness to which we have waded through blood and fire, and raising his empire on the ruins of our own. Beware, we are warned, of neglecting the rights of the adversary. It is our peculiar business to guard the rights of France."*

The whole of this pompous episode is a mere diversion to the question. Vetus, some time ago, asked, in a tone which could not be mistaken, " Who are the French nation? A rank nonentity. Who are to be the sole judges of the rights and pretensions of what once was France? We, and our allies!"—and when we protest against this unheard-of basis of a negociation between rival states, he answers with a tedious prize-dissertation on the doctrine of universal benevolence, and the perfectibility of man. Vetus insists on a peace (the only peace fit for a wise nation) that shall remain a proud monument of its own superiority,—that is, a peace which can never be made between any two states, a peace that does not admit of the shadow of regard to the rights, interests, or honour of the enemy, a peace that implies a critical advance to the destruction of France. But it seems, that all this proud display of pedantic phraseology, by which he attempted to " confound the ignorant, and amaze indeed the very faculties of eyes

* The style of Vetus bears the same relation to eloquence that gilded lead does to gold;—it glitters, and is heavy.

and ears," now means nothing more than that we are to guard and protect our native country, and not surrender our own rights to the enemy. There needed no oracle to tell us that. But Vetus, having set out on the forlorn hope of political paradox, is himself ashamed to turn back to a trite truism, and contends that there is no safety for this country but in the destruction of the enemy, and no patriotism which is not inconsistent with the rights, liberties, and even existence of other countries. We deny it. We say there is a patriotism consistent with the claims of reason, justice, and humanity; and another *exclusive* of them. The latter is Vetus's patriotism; the former is ours. This we have stated before. We do not wonder that Vetus has not answered it; for it does not admit of an answer.

It seems, however, that the view we have taken (in common with all civilized nations) of this subject, is "a sucker from the poisonous root of universal benevolence;" and Vetus's prejudices, coupling with that *strumpet* Reason, beget in his mind a sort of "mongrel metaphysical enthusiasm," in which he sees visions, and has revelations of the general nature of man. He tells us, we are regular adepts in that school which, under the direction of the goddess, or the strumpet, Reason, (for with him they are both the same) trampled on all human sensibilities, and the charities of private life, to offer them up as a sacrifice to that *monstrous fiction*, their country, and then to that *more monstrous fiction*, their kind. This is the most curious defence of patriotism we ever met with, and a striking instance of the pains which this laborious reasoner takes to confute himself. Our country, according to this patriotic writer, is "a perfect Scrub," a kind of Sin and Death business, a contradiction, and a dire chimera, "confiscating and appropriating the individual duties, rights, and charities of mankind—ransacking the deepest recesses of the heart, and seizing as prizes to her sovereign will the royalties and wrecks of human nature." It is "a superfine theory, inconsistent with the order of Providence, and destructive of the nature of man, and which, by pretending to raise us far above the pitch of humanity, degrades us below the level of brutes." But then "there is a phrenzy still greater" than this, which is the love of mankind. This is the consummation of enormity, and the triumph of the strumpet-goddess. Vetus has here fallen into a more desperate dilemma than any he has yet encountered in his perilous way. We present him with the choice of a pair of alternatives: either he must mean that the love of the republic, or our country, which he treats with such profound contempt and abhorrence, is only bad when it destroys the private and natural affections, or he must exclude at once every shadow of regard to the rights, liberties, and happiness of mankind, and then the same thing will follow of patriotism itself, which, as he says truly, is an emanation from the same impure source, human reason, and so to establish his favourite principle of *exclusive* patriotism, he gets rid of it altogether. "The latter end of this writer's reasoning always forgets the beginning." We will tell Vetus the hinge on which this whole controversy turns, and what is the radical error of the system of general philanthropy, which he has attempted to expose. It is, that it is an *exclusive* system, and is therefore unfitted for the nature of man, who is a mixed being, made up of various principles, faculties, and feelings. All these are good in their place and degree, as well as the affections that spring from them—natural affection, patriotism, benevolence: it is only *exclusive* selfishness, *exclusive* patriotism, *exclusive* philanthropy, that are inconsistent with the order of Providence, and destructive of the nature of man: Vetus in avoiding one extreme has fallen into another, for the extremes not only "of faction" but of folly meet; though we should be loth to compare the splendid dreams of the philosophical enthusiast, who wished to raise man above the pitch of his common nature, to the groveling, sordid, shuffling paradoxes of Vetus, who would degrade him below the level of the brutes, and whose maxims are as repugnant to common sense, and the practical rules of life, as they are devoid of every thing elegant in imagination, or consistent in reasoning.

ILLUSTRATIONS OF VETUS.

(CONCLUDED.)

" What do you read, my lord?—Words, words, words.
What is the matter?——*Nothing*."

Jan. 5, 1814.

We gave in our last article Vetus's quaint denunciation of the principles of patriotism and philanthropy. It appears by this, that the same "jargon of metaphysics," and the same vapid rhetoric may be employed against both these sacred and inviolable feelings, by any one who is weak and vain enough to suppose that language was given us, not to communicate truth to others, but to impose falsehood on ourselves. Does Vetus mean to assert, that his *topics* are fatal to all patriotism, as well as all philanthropy? Or (which is the alternative) that they are fatal to neither, properly understood,—that there is a true and a false patriotism, a true and a false philanthropy? What will " the acknowledged saviours of Europe, the magnanimous defenders of the commonwealth of nations, the liberators of Spain, the recreators of Portugal, the regenerators of Germany," say to Vetus's exclusive patriotism? Or, we would ask, whether the abuse of reason, of which he complains in certain moderns, is a sufficient cause that we should explode it altogether? In the dialect of Don Quixotte's books of chivalry, must " the unreasonableness of their reason so unreason our reason," that we are to reject the faculty, both root and branch? Shall we impiously renounce the goddess, because she has been personated by a strumpet? Reason is the queen of the moral world, the soul of the universe, the lamp of human life, the pillar of society, the foundation of law, the beacon of nations, the golden chain, let down from heaven, which links all animated and all intelligent natures in one common system—and in the vain strife between fanatic innovation, and fanatic prejudice, we are exhorted to dethrone this queen of the world, to blot out this light of the mind, to deface this fair column, to break in pieces this golden chain! We are to discard and throw from us, with loud taunts and bitter imprecations, that reason, which has been the lofty theme of the philosopher, the poet, the moralist, and the divine, whose name was not first named to be abused by the enthusiasts of the French revolution, or to be blasphemed by the madder enthusiasts, their opponents, but is co-eval with, and inseparable from the nature and faculties of man,—is the image of his Maker stamped upon him at his birth, the understanding breathed into him with the breath of life, and in the participation of which alone he is raised above the brute creation, and his own physical nature!—Vetus labours hard to persuade us, that the goddess and the strumpet are really *one* person, equally " convertible to the same abandoned purposes;" that reason and sophistry are the same thing. He may find his account in endeavouring to confound them; but his indifference betrays the hollowness of his claims to true reason, as the false mother was detected by her willingness to compromise her own pretensions, only to be revenged on her rival.

Vetus has, however, without knowing it, stumbled on an important truth, which is, that patriotism, in modern times, and in great states, is and must be the creature of reason and reflection, rather than the offspring of physical or local attachment. Our country is a complex abstract existence, known only to the understanding. It is an immense riddle, containing numberless modifications of reason and prejudice, of thought and passion. Patriotism is not, in a strict or exclusive sense, a natural or personal affection, but a law of our rational and moral nature, strengthened and determined by particular circumstances and associations, but not born of them, nor wholly nourished by them. It is not possible that we should have an individual attachment to sixteen millions of men, any more than to sixty millions. We cannot be attached, except rationally and "logically," to places we never saw, and people we never heard of. Is not the name of Englishman a general term, as well as that of man? How many varieties does it not combine within it? Are the opposite extremities of the globe our native place, because they are a part of that geographical and political denomination, our country? Does natural affection expand in circles of latitude and longitude? What personal or instinctive sympathy has the English peasant with the African slave-driver, or East India nabob? None but the most "drawling hypocritical" sophist will say that there is any. These wretched bunglers in metaphysics would fain persuade us to discard all public principle, and all sense of abstract justice, as a violation of natural affection, and yet do not see that the love of our country is itself in the order of our general affections, except, indeed, that exclusive sort which consists in a mere negation of humanity and justice. The common notions of patriotism are, in fact, transmitted to us from the savage tribes, or from the states of Greece and Rome, where the fate and condition of all was the same, or where the country of the citizen was the town in which he was born. Where this is no longer the case, where our country is no longer contained within the narrow circle of the same walls, where we can no longer behold its glimmering horizon from the top of our native mountains—beyond these limits it is not a natural but an artificial idea, and our love of it either an habitual dictate of reason, or a cant term. It was said by an acute observer, and eloquent writer, that the love of mankind was nothing but the love of justice: the same might be said, with considerable truth, of the love of our country. It is little more than another name for the love of liberty, of independence, of peace, and social happiness. We do not say, that other indirect and collateral circumstances do not go to the superstructure of this sentiment, (as language,* literature, manners, national customs,) but this is the broad and firm basis. All other patriotism, not founded on, or not consistent with truth, justice, and hu-

* He who speaks two languages has no country. The French, when they made their language the common language of the courts of Europe, gained more than by all their other conquests put together.

manity, is a painted sepulchre, fair without, but full of ravening and all uncleanness within. "It leaves our passions afloat, and ends with abusing them to crime and misery." It is the watchword of faction, the base pander of avarice and pride, the ready tool in the hands of those who, having no sense of public duty, and disclaiming all pretensions to common humanity, sacrifice the lives of millions to the madness of one, and are eager to offer up their country a devoted victim at the shrine of power, as the miserable slave is yoked to the foul Eastern idol,* and crushed beneath its chariot wheels! Thus the hired scribbler of a profligate newspaper sits secure and self-satisfied at his desk—with a venomed word, or a lie that looks like truth, sends thousands of his countrymen to death,—receives his pay, and scribbles on, regardless of the dying and the dead!—And this is patriotism.

The *tempora mollia fandi* do not belong to Vetus any more than to ourselves. He is, like us, but an uncouth courtier, a rough, sturdy, independent politician, who thinks and speaks for himself. He complains of "the soft nonsense whispered in the higher circles," and gossipped in *The Morning Post*, in favour of peace. Be it so, for once, that these soft whispers are fraught with ruin, dishonour, and slavery to this country. Yet, if the effeminate and dastard sound once floats through the air, borne on the downy wing of fashion—if it is whispered from the prince to the peer, and from lords to ladies, from ministers to their clerks, from their clerks to the treasury-prints, and from the knaves who write to the dupes who read—even the warning voice of Vetus will not be able to prevent the Syren sound from spreading in gentle murmurs, and "smoothing the raven down of dis-

* See Mr. Canning's speech on the Jaggernaut.—They manage these things better in the East (it is to be hoped we shall do so in time here); otherwise, if there had been any occasion, what pretty Anti-Jacobin sonnets might not Mr. Canning have written in praise of this Jaggernaut? Or Mr. Southey, after in vain attempting its overthrow, might have "spun his brains" into a CARMEN ANNUUM to celebrate his own defeat. Or Vetus might play off his discovery of the identity of the strumpet and the goddess Reason, against any disposition to disarm its power or arrest its progress.

cord, till it smiles." And will Vetus pretend such ignorance both of the court and of the country, as not to know, that whether the word is war or peace, the same effect will follow—that whether the breath of kings breathe "airs from heaven or blasts from hell," the same well-attuned system of undulating sounds will disperse them wide in eddying circles, and the same round of smiles and whispers and significant shrugs will be repeated, whether the country bleeds or starves, is enslaved within, or conquered without? All those who do not catch the soft whisper, and mimic the gracious smile, and join the magic circle, are no better than hypocrites, madmen, and traitors to *their country!* We know it well.

Vetus in vain attempts to repel the charge which we brought against *The Times*, whose profession of eternal war with Bonaparte we said was incompatible with the possibility of his making peace with us, by asserting that this doctrine is "an audacious plagiarism, from the portfolio of the French Minister." We have not such near access to the port-folio of the French Government as this writer; but we have access to *The Times*, and there we find this audacious plagiarism written in large letters in almost every page. We say that wherever the doctrine is found (whoever invented or whoever adopted it), there is an insuperable bar to peace. If it is found on one side, that is the responsible side; if it is found on both, neither can reproach the other with the continuance of hostilities. This statement is plain and unanswerable. Does Vetus think to "thrust us from a level consideration by a confident brow, and the throng of words which come with such affected gravity from him?" He disclaims the doctrine for himself. Why then is he so eager to justify it in *The Times*? They are caught in the fact; they are taken with the *manner;* and Vetus would divert us from executing summary justice on them, by offering himself as security that they are only the receivers of the stolen goods; "the audacious plagiarists," instead of the atrocious inventors of this mischievous doctrine. Besides, the answer is a wretched evasion, and makes the assertion itself senseless and nugatory. The principle of *The Times* was and is (if they have not retracted it) that we are never to make peace with Bonaparte at all, that is, though he would make peace with us, (otherwise the words have no meaning) and then comes the gloss of Vetus, which is, that we will not make peace with him, only because he will not make peace with us. Ridiculous!—*Vetus* asks, "Who has been the founder of this shocking creed—who the aggressor—who the unrelenting enemies of peace?" May we not answer—"The incessant war-faction of England?" Why would Vetus strip "these acknowledged saviours of Europe" of the praise which is so justly due to them, or degrade them from that proud eminence which they have maintained with so much persevering fortitude? We cannot withhold from these persons our sincere and conscientious thanks for all the benefits which this war has conferred on our country, on Europe, and the world. While France strove insidiously to ruin us by peace, these firm patriots have always been determined to save us by war—from "England's" greatest and most magnanimous politician," down to the last desperate incendiary of *The Times*, who is only willing to conclude "a Regicide Peace" by celebrating "the condign and solemn punishment of Bonaparte!"*

Vetus says, that "eternal war is no expression of his, and that it is a deliberate falsehood in us who assert that he has used it, or that this country has no alternative between eternal war and eternal bondage" "It is not England," he says, "but France—not Vetus, but the French government—who has broached the

* Of the facility of realising this devout aspiration of the writer in *The Times*, we have no exact means of judging by his own statements, for he one day tells us that "there is *nothing* to hinder Lord Wellington from marching to Paris, and bringing the Usurper to the block," and the next endeavours to excite the panic fears of his readers, by telling them, in a tone of equal horror and dismay, "That the *monster* wields at will the force of forty millions of men." The assertions of these writers have no connection with the real state of things, but depend entirely on their variable passions, and the purpose they have in view.

creed, that one of the two countries must in the end destroy the other."

If it is a falsehood, it is a deliberate one, for we do deliberately assert that he uses these words, and inculcates this doctrine incessantly. But instead of contradicting Vetus, it is better to let him contradict himself; no one else can do it so effectually. In his last letter but one he has these words:—" It is, I conscientiously believe, a question, *which of these two countries shall destroy the other*. In that case my part is taken.—France must be ruined to save our native country from being ruined.—If this be perpetual war, I cannot help it.—Perpetual war has little terror, when perpetual bondage threatens us." Either the interpretation of this passage is that which we have given to it, or, as Vetus says, " the English language must be constructed anew."

He now, indeed, mitigates the dread sentence he had passed upon us, by saying, not that we have no alternative but either war, or slavery, but that we have no alternative but either war, or slavery, or *peace*. We are glad that Vetus has introduced this new clause in our favour into the codicil; it was not in the original will, or expressed in such faint characters, that we, with the rest of the public, missed the intended benefaction. Just in the same manner, that profound politician and humane writer, the author of the Essay on Population, found out that the only possible checks to excessive population, were vice and misery, which were, therefore, to be considered as the greatest blessings of mankind, and having gained a vast reputation by this singular discovery, he then recollected what every one knew before, that there was another check to this principle, viz. *moral restraint*, and that consequently vice and misery were not the greatest blessings of society.

We did not state it as an inconsistency in Vetus, that he held out *France* as an object of terror, and yet recommended a negociation with Bonaparte, because his government tended to weaken France, but we did state it as a rank inconsistency in Vetus to hold up *Bonaparte* as an object of peculiar terror to this country, and yet to represent his government as tottering on the brink of deplorable weakness and unavoidable ruin. Vetus could not meet the objection, and he has altered the terms.

Vetus concludes his letter with the following note:—

"*The stupid impertinence*" (charged on the attacks made upon him) "has no relation to *The Morning Chronicle*, with which I am disposed to part in peace. One feels a tolerance towards that paper, for the talents which once adorned it; and of the continuance of which I should rejoice to see more proof in its late attacks on Vetus. We have little common faith in politics, but we have, I trust, a common stake in the spirit and dignity of the press."

We are obliged to Vetus for this amicable offer, of the sincerity of which we entertain no doubt. As to the talent shown in our attacks on him, we are ready to admit that it is little enough; but we at the same time think that if it had been greater, it would have been more than the occasion required. We have no enmity to Vetus, but to his extravagance, and if he will correct that, he will save us the trouble of correcting it for him. We are ready to believe that this writer has talents and acquirements which might be made useful to the public, if he would forego his mistaken pretensions to extraordinary wisdom and eloquence. The qualities of profound thought and splendid imagery are seldom found singly in the same person, and the union of both together is an undertaking much beyond the capacity of Vetus. And now we leave him to return to his indigestions with "what appetite he may."*

* We only wish to add one thing, which is, to protest against the self-importance of such expressions as the following, which occur often in Vetus's letters:—"*The men I speak of were*" those, &c. "This sentiment never prevailed with *the better sort*." This is an affectation of the worst part of Burke's style, his assumption of a parliamentary tone, and of the representation of the voice of some corporate body. It was bad enough in him; in Vetus it is intolerable.

ON THE LATE WAR.

April 3, 1814.

THE systematic patrons of eternal war are always returning, when they dare, to the point from which they set out twenty years ago; the war with them has not yet lost its original character: they have long memories: they never lose sight of their objects and principles. We cannot but admire their candour as well as their consistency, and would wish to imitate it. It is deemed necessary by the everlasting war-faction to prove in their own justification, "that the march to Paris was not chimerical in 1793," by carrying it into effect now, and to blot France out of the map of Europe, three-and-twenty years after the event had been announced by that great prophet and politician, Mr. Burke. This splendid reverie is not yet accomplished. The triumph of the Pitt-school over the peace-faction is not yet complete; but we are put in complete possession of what is required to make it so. As the war with them was a war of extermination, so the peace, not to fix a lasting stigma on their school and principles, must be a peace of extermination. This is what we always said and thought of those principles and that school. This is their triumph, their *only* triumph—the true crown of their hopes, the consummation of their utmost wishes, nothing short of which can satisfy their proud pretensions, or finish this just and necessary war, as it was begun. Otherwise, no peace for them; otherwise, they will have failed in both branches of that happy dilemma, hit upon by the beneficent genius of "the great statesman, now no more," the necessity of destroying France, or being ourselves destroyed in the attempt. If they succeed in neither experiment, all that they have done is surely lost labour. They have then a right to their revenge, "their pound of carrion-flesh"—"'tis theirs, 'tis dearly bought, and they will have it." Be it so. But we shall let them feast alone: we are not *man-eaters*. We shall not join the barbarous yell of this worse than Thracian rout, nor figure in at the close of their dance of death, nor applaud the catastrophe of their twenty years' tragedy. We did not approve it in its commencement or progress; nor will we hail its threatened conclusion. We have had, and we will have, no hand in the plot, the execution, the scene-shifting, or the decoration. We leave the full credit of it to the original authors; and, in spite of all the puffing of the Bayes's of the Pitt-school, the only answer they will get from us is, "'Tis an indifferent piece of work: would 'twere done!" Though the torch of *The Times* blazes over Paris, "fierce as a comet;" though *The Sun* sees the lilied banner of the Bourbons floating before Lord Wellington in the plains of Normandy; though *The Courier* is setting out post-haste to break up the negociations at Chatillon; and *The Morning Herald* sheds tears of joy over the fashionable virtues of the rising generation, and finds that we shall make better man-milliners, better lacqueys, and better courtiers than ever—we remain sceptical as to the success, and more than sceptical as to the necessity of this last cast of our political dicers, and desperate venture of our licenced dealers and chapmen in morality and massacre. In our opinion, lives enough have been thrown away to prove, that the survivors are only born to *bear fardels*. This is the moral of the piece, if it succeeds on the principles of the Pitt-school, and all short of that is mere gratuitous mischief. The war, conducted on those principles and for those purposes, "was not, and it cannot come to good." Its failure, or its success, must be fatal.

The war, as it was carried on from the first by the Pitt-school, and as they would now revive it, was not a national quarrel, but a question about a political principle. It had no more to do with France or England as geographical denominations, than the wars between the Guelphs and Gibelines. It was not a war of mercantile advantage, or a trial of strength between two countries. which must be decided by the turn of events, by the probable calculation of loss and profit, but a war against an opinion, which could, therefore, never cease, but with the extirpation of that opinion. Hence there could be neither safety, nor honour, nor justice, in any terms of peace with the French government, because, by the supposition, it was not with its power or its conduct, but with its existence, that we were at war. Hence the impossibility of maintaining the relations of peace and amity with France. Hence Mr. Burke's regicide war. Hence the ridiculousness asserted by *The Courier*, of even attempting negociation with this hated power. Hence the various and contradictory aspects which the war assumed after its first out-set, and all of which answered the purpose equally well, because there was another pivot on which the whole turned, the sheet-anchor which never loosed its hold, and which enabled "the pilot to weather the storm." It was not a temporary or local question of the boundaries, the possessions, or particular rights of rival states, but a question, in which all states are at all times equally interested, of the internal right of any people to choose its own form of government. Whether this was a just ground of war or not, is another question; but it was the true one—that which gave its character to the war, and accounts for all its consequences. It was a war of proscription against a great and powerful state, for having set the example of a people ridding itself of an odious and despicable tyranny. It was the question of the balance of power between kings and people; a question, compared with which the balance of power in Europe is petty and insignificant. That what we have here stated, are the real and paramount grounds of this bloody and inveterate contest in the minds of the war-faction is, what we apprehend they will not, in their present state of frenzy, deny. They are the only ones that always survive the shock of accident and the fluctuation of circumstances, and which are always recurred to when all others fail, and are constantly avowed in the face of day, whenever the least probability of success attends them. It has been declared again and again, month after month, and year after year, that no peace should be made with France till the last remaining effort had been tried to attain this object. We were to bury ourselves with our great war-minister, under the ruins of the civilized world, sooner than relax in our exertions, or recede from our object. No sacrifices were to be held too dear—no sufferings too great in the prosecution of this sacred cause. No other than the last extremity was to force peace from us. Nothing short of the complete subjugation of France was to satisfy us—nothing short of our own ruin was to drive us to despair. We were like wrestlers, struggling on the edge of a precipice, one (or both) of whom must be certain of destruction. Such were the mad, mischievous, and unprincipled terms, on which a pampered crew of sycophants have played away the welfare, the repose, the liberties, and happiness of mankind, and on which they would now urge us to stake our all again, to realize their favourite scheme of the march to Paris, and the annihilation of the French people.

The consequences of the Pitt project were inevitable. From the moment that the existence of France as a nation was declared to be incompatible with that of the surrounding states—that she was denounced as a nuisance which must be abated, and set up as a mark for the vengeance of the rest of the world, the struggle necessarily became convulsive, and the re-action terrible. Is it then a matter of wonder, that in this unnatural strife, France, proscribed, hunted down, put out of the pale of nations, endeavoured rather to reduce others to the last extremity than to be reduced to it herself? Or are we entitled to wreak that vengeance upon her which we could not at first execute, because the engine which we had prepared to crush her has recoiled with the greatest violence upon ourselves? It has been said that we less easily forgive the injuries we do or meditate against others, than those we receive from them. There are, we know, persons to whom the celebrated line of the historian is, at all times, applicable: *Odia in longum jaciens, quæ conderet, auctaque promeret.* We are not surprised to find that the good intentions of these persons towards France, though she did not submit to the original tender made to her of their kind interference and paternal care, have not spoiled by keeping. If Titus complained with so much bitterness, that he had lost a day to virtue, what must not some modern friends to mankind feel, when they reflect that they have lost so many years in the execution of their just and beneficent plans!—In spite of Mr. Southey's reasoning in his *Carmen Triumphale*, about joining "the avengers of mankind," we conceive that the wheel has gone once round already, "full circle home," and that now it had better stand still.

But it may be said, do we mean to apply these remarks to Bonaparte? As far as relates to any merits of the war-faction. It was they who implicated him with the cause of the French people, as "the child and champion of Jacobinism." We cannot express our opinion better than in the words of Mr. Whitbread, "that England had made Bonaparte, and he had undone himself." He was the creature of the Pitt-school. Was the iron scourge which he has held over Europe put into his hands by the peace-party? Were the battles of Austerlitz and Jena—were the march to Vienna, the possession of Berlin, the invasion of Spain, the expedition to Russia, and the burning of Moscow, the consequences of the signing or of the breaking of the treaty of Amiens?

The author of the letters of Vetus, (who we suppose is silenced by *The Times*, for asserting that the Bourbons have no more a lawful right to the throne of France, at this moment, than the Stuarts had to the throne of England twenty years after the Revolution of 1688,) is of opinion, that this war is merely national, merely the old grudge between the two countries; and that the Bourbons, the Republic, and Bonaparte, are equally hostile to England, and we to them. In this, as in most things else, our opinion is the opposite of his. There is only one period of the history of the two countries, which, reversed, furnishes an exact counterpart to the present contest, both in its avowed principles and secret motives—we mean the war waged by Louis XIV. against this country and its allies, for nearly as long a period after the

English Revolution. The difference in the results of these two revolutions has been this: that from the insular situation of this country, which enables us to do either right or wrong, nearly with impunity, and which makes our means of defence greater, and our means of offence proportionably less—that from this collateral cause, the internal struggle, in proportion to the danger, was less bloody in our own case, and the re-action of our efforts to defend ourselves from the imposition of a foreign yoke and of hereditary slavery, less violent and fatal to other states. All the differences have arisen from the character of the two nations, and from local and accidental circumstances: there was none in the abstract political principle. We gave them the example of their Revolution; we also gave them an example of "national fortitude" in maintaining it. We—the people of England, (not an upstart jacobite faction in the Hanoverian line,) are proud of having imitators; and we think it not unlikely that the French, if forced upon it, may behave on this occasion as the English behaved, when an hereditary pretender came over to us, backed by the aid of foreign arms, to assert his lawful claim to the throne—that is, in other words, to be the natural proprietor of a whole people. We twice sent him back again with all his myrmidons; we would not be made a property of. We felt that in not doing so we should be traitors, not only to our country, but to our kind—the worst species of treason to our country. It is curious that the "deepest enmity which the French people have drawn down upon them by their early struggles in the same cause, should be shewn by that government who had long insulted the slavery of Europe by the loudness of its boasts of freedom." We do not know how it is, but so it has happened, that in the thirty years of war which have graced the annals of the present reign, there has been a considerable want of sympathy between the crown and the people, as if the quarrel were merely the cause of kings, in which the people had no concern. Has this circumstance arisen from any unpleasant sense of obligation, or consciousness of a little irregularity and deviation from the right line in the descent of the crown, no more accounted for in Mr. Burke's Reflections, than the declination of atoms in Epicurus's philosophy? The restoration of the Bourbons in France will be the re-establishment of the principles of the Stuarts in this country.*

PRINCE MAURICE'S PARROT;

Or, French Instructions to a British Plenipotentiary.

Sept. 18, 1814.

1. That the French people were so deeply implicated in the Slave Trade, as not even to know that it had been abolished by this country.

2. That the French press had been so long under the complete despotic control of Bonaparte, that the present government must despair of making any immediate impression on the independence of the political opinions, or the energetic firmness of the individual feelings of the people, lately consigned to their protection.

3. That such were their blind and rooted prejudices against the English, that we could only hope to convince them of our entire sincerity and disinterestedness in abolishing the Slave Trade ourselves, by lending a helping hand to its revival by others.

4. That if we consented to give up our colonial conquests to the French, on conditions dictated only by the general principles of humanity, this would be a proof that we intended to keep them in our own hands from the most base and mercenary motives.

5. That the French government simply wished to begin the Slave Trade again as the easiest way of leaving it off, that so they might combine the experiment of its gradual restoration with that of its gradual abolition, and, by giving the people an interest in it, more effectually wean their affections from it.

* Written originally for the Morning Chronicle.

6. That it is highly honourable in us to have proposed, and in the French to have agreed to, the abolition of the Slave Trade; at the end of five years, though it would have been insulting in us to have proposed, and degrading in them to have submitted to, any stipulation on the subject.

7. That to rob and murder on the coast of Africa is among the internal rights of legislation and domestic privileges of every European and Christian state.

8. That we are not to teach the French people religion and morality at the point of the sword, though this is what we have been professing to teach them for the last two and twenty years.

9. That his most Christian Majesty Louis XVIII. is so fully impressed with the humane and benevolent sentiments of Great Britain and the allies in favour of the abolition of the Slave Trade, that he was ready to have plunged all Europe into a war for its continuance.

10. That we could not possibly make the abolition, (though the French government would certainly have made the revival) of the Slave Trade a *sine qua non* in the treaty of peace, and that they would otherwise have gone to war to recover by force of arms what they can only owe to the credulity or complaisance of our negociators.

Lastly. That by consenting to the re-establishment of the Slave Trade in France, we were most effectually preparing the way for its abolition all over the world.

" With so little a web as this will I ensnare so great a fly as *Cassio!*"—Such were the formidable barriers, the intricate lines of circumvallation, drawn by the French round the abolition of the Slave Trade, as strong as those which they threw up to defend their capital: yet we think, that after our political missionary had overleaped the one, he might have broken through the other. Where there is a will, there is a way. But there are some minds to which every flimsy pretext presents an insurmountable obstacle, where only the interests of justice and humanity are at stake. These persons are always impotent to save—powerful only to oppress and to betray. Their torpid faculties and amiable apathy are never roused but by the calculations of self-interest, or the thirst of revenge. The glossy sleekness of the panther's skin does not blunt the sharpness of his fangs, and his fawning eye dooms his victim while it glitters. But to come to Lord Castlereagh. In the present instance, he appears to have been cajoled into acquiescence from his well-known indifference to the object. His speech contained nothing but a story of a cock and a bull, told by M. Talleyrand with great grace and gravity, assented to by his Lordship with equal affability and address, and repeated to the House of Commons with hesitating volubility and plausible negligence of manner. It is well to sacrifice to the graces; but it is too much to have sacrificed a whole continent to the graces of M. Talleyrand's person, or the purity of his French accent. We can imagine how the scene took place. This question of Africa, being considered as an idle question, in which neither courts nor ministers were concerned, would be naturally left as a sort of *carte-blanche* for all the flourishes of national *politesse,* as a kind of *noman's ground* for a trial of diplomatic skill and complaisance. So Lord Castlereagh, drawing on his gloves, hemmed once or twice, while the French minister carelessly took snuff: he then introduced the question with a smile, which was answered by a more gracious smile from M. Talleyrand: his Lordship then bowed, as if to bespeak attention; but the Prince of Benevento bowing still lower, prevented what he had to say; and the cries of Africa were lost amidst the nods and smile and shrugs of these demi-puppets. The Ex-bishop of Autun may in future hope to find a successful representative in the English ambassador from Paris; for the noble secretary *mistified* the house, as he had himself been *mistified* by his highness of Benevento.—Count Fathom, after his defeat by the French abbé, practised in this his adopted country with great applause! We may take this opportunity of remarking, that we do not think his Lordship at all improved during his stay in France. He performs the arc of his oscillation from the treasury bench to the table, and from the table back again, in a second less time than he used to do. He commits dulness with greater vivacity, and flounders more briskly in an argument. He has enhanced the loose dangling slip-shod manner which so well accords with his person and understanding, into something positive and dogmatical; and is even grown tenacious of the immaculateness of his maiden treaty, which he will not have so much as suspected: In this alteration of tone we think him wrong. We have always looked upon Lord Castlereagh as an excellent taffeta lining to a court dress; but he should leave the buckram of office to his friend the secretary of the Admiralty.

WHETHER THE FRIENDS OF FREEDOM CAN ENTERTAIN ANY SANGUINE HOPES OF THE FAVOURABLE RESULTS OF THE ENSUING CONGRESS?

Oct. 23, 1814.

An excellent article appeared in the Examiner of last week, giving a general outline of the views and principles which ought to actuate the allied powers at the approaching Congress, and of the leading arrangements with respect to the different subjects to be brought under consideration, which ought to follow from those principles. Cordially as we agree with this respectable writer in the several points which he has stated, we are, we confess, far from feeling any strong assurances that even any one of these points will be amicably adjusted. They are briefly these:— 1. That Poland should be restored to her independence. 2. That the other powers of Europe should no longer co-operate with Sweden in the subjugation of Norway. 3. That the Slave Trade should be immediately and generally abolished. 4. That Saxony should not share a fate similar to that of Poland. 5. That Austria should relinquish her views of unjust aggrandisement in Italy. 6. and last, That some concessions should probably be made by England as to her exclusive claims to maritime supremacy, as far as those claims are found to be rather galling to the feelings of other nations, than essential to her own security. All of the objects here recommended are, we should imagine, every way practicable as well as desirable, if there were any thing like a hearty good-will to avail themselves of the present favourable situation of the world in those who have the power to decide its fate. Armed with sovereign authority, seconded by public opinion, with every obstacle removed from their dread of the overwhelming power of France, they have all the means at their disposal to rear a splendid, lofty, and lasting monument to justice, liberty, and humanity. Are the views then of the allied sovereigns solely directed to these objects? That is the simple question; and we are afraid it would be great presumption to answer it in the affirmative. It would be supposing that the late events have purified the hearts of princes and nations; that they have been taught wisdom by experience, and the love of justice from the sense of injury; that mutual confidence and good-will have succeeded to narrow prejudices and rankling jealousy; that the race of ambitious and unprincipled monarchs, of crafty politicians, and self-interested speculators is at an end; that the destructive rivalry between states has given way to liberal and enlightened views of general safety and advantage; and that the powers of Europe will in future unite with the same zeal and magnanimity for the common good, as when they were bound in a common cause against the common enemy. All this appears to us quite as Utopian as any other scheme which supposes that the human mind can change. Happy should we be, if instead of those magnificent and beneficial projects in which some persons seem still to indulge their imaginations as the results of this meeting, the whole should not turn out to be no better than a compromise of petty interests, of shallow policy, and flagrant injustice.

We forbore for a long time from saying any thing on this ungrateful subject: but our forbearance has not hitherto, at least, been rewarded. We shall therefore speak out plainly on the subject; as we should be sorry to be thought accomplices in a delusion, which can only end in disappointment. The professions of justice, moderation, and the love of liberty, made by the powers of Europe at the end of the last, and at the beginning of the present year, were certainly admirable: they were called for at the time, and were possibly sincere. But we are all of us apt to forego those good resolutions which are extorted from us by circumstances rather than from reason or habit, and to recant "vows made in pain as violent and void." Without meaning any indirect allusion to the person into whose mouth these words are put, we believe this, that princes are princes, and that men are men; and that to expect any great sacrifices of interest or passion from either in consequence of certain well-timed and well-sounding professions, drawn from them by necessity, when that necessity no longer exists, is to belie all our experience of human nature. We remember what modern courts and ministers were before the dreaded power of Bonaparte arose; and we conceive this to be the best and only ground to argue what they will be, now that that power has ceased. "Why so, being gone, they are themselves again." It appears to us, that some very romantic and extravagant expectations were entertained from the destruction of the tyranny of Bonaparte. It is true, his violence and ambition for a while suspended all other projects of the same kind. "The right divine of kings to govern wrong" was wrested from the puny hands of its legitimate possessors, and strangely monopolized by one man. The regular professors of the regal art were set aside by the superior skill and prowess of an adventurer. They became in turn the tools, or the victims of the machinations of the maker and puller-down of kings. Instead of their customary employment of annoying their neighbours, or harrassing their subjects, they had enough to do to defend their territories and their titles. The aggressions which they had securely meditated against the independence of nations, and their haughty contempt for the liberties of mankind, were retorted on their own heads. The poisoned chalice was returned to their own lips. They then first felt the sting of injustice, and the bitterness of scorn. They saw how weak and little they were in themselves. They were roused from the still life of courts, and forced to assume the rank of men. They appealed to their people to defend their thrones; they called on them to rally round the altar of their country; they invoked the name of liberty, and in that name they conquered. Plans of national aggrandisement or private revenge were forgotten in the intoxication of triumph, as they had been in the agony of despair. This sudden usurpation had so overpowered the imaginations of men, that they began to consider it as the only evil that had ever existed in the world, and that with it, all tyranny and ambition would cease. War was talked of as if it had been an invention of the modern Charlemagne, and the Golden age was to be restored with the Bourbons. But it is hard for the great and mighty to learn in the school of adversity: emperors and kings bow reluctantly to the yoke of necessity. When the panic is over, they will be glad to drink of the cup of oblivion. The false idols which had been set up to Liberty and Nature, to Genius and Fortune, are thrown down, and they have once more " all power given them upon earth." How they are likely to use it, whether for the benefit and happiness of mankind, or to gratify their own prejudices and passions, we have, in one or two instances, seen already. No one will in future look for " the milk of human kindness" in the Crown Prince of Sweden, who is a monarch of the new school; nor for examples of romantic generosity and gratitude in Ferdinand of Spain, who is one of the old. A jackall or baboon, dandled in the paws of a royal Bengal tiger, may not be very formidable; but it would be idle to suppose, if they should providentially escape, that they would become tame, useful, domestic animals.

The King of Prussia has recovered the sword of the Great Frederick, his humane, religious, moral, and unambitious predecessor, only, as it appears, to unsheath it against the King of Saxony, his old companion in arms. The Emperor of Austria seems eager to catch at the iron crown of Italy, which has just fallen from the brows of his son-in-law. The King of France, our King of France, Louis the Desired, and who by the "all hail hereafter," is to receive the addition of Louis the Wise, has improved his reflections during a twenty years' exile, into a humane and amiable sanction of the renewal of the Slave Trade for five years only. His Holiness the Pope, happy to have escaped from the clutches of the arch-tyrant and impostor, employs his leisure hours in restoring the order of the Jesuits, and persecuting the Freemasons. Ferdinand, the grateful and the enlightened, who has passed through the same discipline of humanity with the same effect, shuts up the doors of the Cortes, (as it is scandalously asserted, at the instigation of Lord Wellington), and throws open those of the Inquisition. At all this, the romantic admirers of patriot kings, who fondly imagined that the hatred of the oppressor was the same thing as the hatred of oppression, (among these we presume we may reckon the poet-laureat,) hang their heads, and live in hope of better times. To us it is all natural, and in order. From this grand goal-delivery of princes and potentates, we could expect nothing else than a recurrence to their old habits and favourite principles. These observations have not been hastily or gratuitously obtruded: they have been provoked by a succession of disgusting and profligate acts of inconsistency and treachery, unredeemed by a single effort of heroic virtue or generous enthusiasm. Almost every principle, almost every profession, almost every obligation, has been broken. If any proof is wanting, look at Norway, look at Italy, look at Spain, look at the Inquisition, look at the Slave Trade. The mask of liberty has been taken off by most of the principal performers; the whining cant of humanity is no longer heard in *The Courier* and *The Times*. What then remains for us to build a hope upon, but the Whig principles of the Prince Regent, inherited from his ancestors, and the good nature of the Emperor of Russia, the merit of which is entirely his own? Of the former of these personages, our opinion is so well known, that we need not repeat it here. Again, of the good intentions of the last-mentioned sovereign, we declare that we have as full a persuasion. We believe him to be docile to instruction, inquisitive after knowledge, and inclined to good. But it has been said by those who have better means of information than ourselves, that he is too open to the suggestions of those about him; that, like other learners, he thinks the newest opinion the best, and that his real good-nature and want of duplicity render him not sufficiently proof against the selfish or sinister designs of others. He has certainly a character for disinterestedness and magnanimity to support in history: but history is a glass in which few minds fashion themselves. If in his late conduct there was any additional impulse given to the natural simplicity of his character, it probably arose from an obvious desire to furnish a contrast to the character of Bonaparte, and also to redeem the Russian character, hitherto almost another name for barbarity and ferociousness, in the eyes of civilized Europe. In this point of view, we should not despair that something may be attempted, at least with respect to Poland, by the present autocrat of all the Russias, to blot out certain stains on the reputation of his grand-mother, the Empress Catharine.

With regard to Norway, the only hope of the suspension of its fate seems to arise out of a very natural, if not laudable jealousy and distaste, which have been conceived by some of the old-standing sovereigns of Europe against the latest occupier and most forward pretender to thrones. An adventurer who has made a fortune by gaining a prize in the lottery, or by laying *qui tam* informations against his accomplices, cannot expect to be admitted, on an equality, into the company of persons of regular character and family estates. The Emperor of Austria, in particular, may have additional motives of dislike to Bernadotte, connected with late events; and we agree with the *Examiner*, that he may, in the end, "have to regret the length to which he was hurried against a man, who was the key-stone of all the new power which had been built on the ruin of thrones."

As to any immediate adjustment of the maritime rights of this country, on general principles, satisfactory to all parties, we see no reason to expect it. We think the following paragraph justifies us in this opinion. "We are told," says the *Morning Chronicle*, "that on the day when the capture of the city of Washington, and the demolition of its public buildings reached Paris, the Duke of Wellington had a ball: not one public ambassador of the potentates of Europe, our good allies, presented himself to congratulate his grace on the event." We here see, on one side, the most absurd expectations of disinterested sympathy with our national feelings, and as little disposition to enter into them on the other. It is strange that the above paragraph should have found its way into a paper which makes an almost exclusive profession of liberal and comprehensive views

Nor can we indulge in any serious expectations of "the immediate and general abolition of the Slave Trade." Africa has little to hope from "the prevailing gentle arts" of Lord Castlereagh. However sturdy he may be in asserting our maritime rights, he will, we imagine, go to sleep over those of humanity, and waking from his *doux sommeil*, find that the dexterous prince of political jugglers has picked his pocket of his African petitions, if, indeed, he chuses to carry the credentials of his own disgrace about with him. There are two obstacles to the success of this measure. In the first place, France has received such forcible lessons from this country on the old virtues of patriotism and loyalty, that she must feel particularly unwilling to be dictated to on the new doctrines of liberality and humanity. Secondly, the abolition of the Slave Trade, on our part, was itself the act of Mr. Fox's administration—an administration which we should suppose there is no very strong inclination to relieve from any part of the contempt or obloquy which it has been the fashion to pour upon it, by extending the benefit of its measures, or recommending the adoption of its principles.

There is another point, on which, though our doubts are by no means strong or lasting, we do not at all times feel the same absolute confidence—the continuance of the present order of things in France. The principles adhered to, in the determination of some of the preceding arrangements, and the permanent views which shall appear to actuate the other powers of Europe, may have no inconsiderable influence on this great question. Whatever tends to allay the ferment in men's minds, and to take away just causes of recrimination and complaint, must, of course, lessen the pretexts for change. We should not, however, be more disposed to augur such a change from the remaining attachment of individuals, or of the army, to Bonaparte, than from the general versatility and restlessness of the French character, and their total want of settled opinion, which might oppose a check to military enthusiasm. Even their present unqualified zeal, in the cause of the Bourbons, is ominous. How long this sudden fit of gratitude, for deliverance from evils certainly brought upon them by their slowness to admit the remedy, may continue, it is impossible to say. A want of *keeping* is the distinguishing quality of the French character. A people of this sort cannot be depended on for a moment. They are blown about like a weathercock, with every breath of caprice or accident, and would cry *vive l'empereur* to-morrow, with as much vivacity and as little feeling, as they do *vive le roi* to-day. They have no fixed principle of action. They are alike indifferent to every thing: their self-complacency supplies the place of all other advantages—of virtue, liberty, honour, and even of outward appearances. They are the only people who are vain of being cuckolded and being conquered.—A people who, after trampling over the face of Europe so long, fell down before their assailants without striking a blow, and who boast of their submission as a fine thing, are not a nation of men, but of women. The spirit of liberty, at the Revolution, gave them an impulse common to humanity; the genius of Bonaparte gave them the spirit of military ambition. Both of these gave an energy and consistency to their character, by concentrating their natural volatility on one great object. But when both of these causes failed, the Allies found that France consisted of nothing but ladies' toilettes. The army are the muscular part of the state; mere patriotism is a pasteboard visor, which opposes no resistance to the sword. Whatever they determine will be done; an effeminate public is a nonentity. They will not relish the Bourbons long, if they remain at peace; and if they go to war, they will want a monarch who is also a general.

THE LAY OF THE LAUREATE, CARMEN NUPTIALE, *by Robert Southey, Esq. Poet-Laureate, Member of the Royal Spanish Academy, and of the Royal Spanish Academy of History.*—London: Longmans, 1816.

Examiner, July 7, 1816.

THE dog which his friend Launce brought as a present to Madam Silvia in lieu of a lap-dog, was something like "The Lay of the Laureate," which Mr. Southey has here offered to the Princess Charlotte for a Nuptial Song. It is "a very currish performance, and deserves none but currish thanks." Launce thought his own dog, Crab, better than any other; and Mr. Southey thinks his own praises the fittest compliment for a lady's ear. His Lay is ten times as long, and he thinks it is therefore ten times better than an Ode of Mr. Pye's.

Mr. Southey in this poem takes a tone which was never heard before in a drawing-room. It is the first time that ever a Reformist was made Poet-laureate. Mr. Croker was wrong in introducing his old friend, the author of "Joan of Arc," at Carlton-House. He might have known how it would be. If we had doubted the good old adage before, "Once a Jacobin and always a Jacobin," since reading "The Lay of the Laureate," we are sure of it. A Jacobin is one who would have his single opinion govern the world, and overturn every thing in it. Such a one is Mr. Southey. Whether he is a Republican or a Royalist,—

whether he hurls up the red cap of liberty, or wears the lily, stained with the blood of all his old acquaintance, at his breast, —whether he glories in Robespierre or the Duke of Wellington, —whether he pays a visit to Old Sarum, or makes a pilgrimage to Waterloo,—whether he is praised by *The Courier*, or parodied by Mr. Canning,—whether he thinks a King the best or the worst man in his dominions,—whether he is a Theophilanthropist or a Methodist of the church of England,—whether he is a friend of Universal Suffrage and Catholic Emancipation, or a Quarterly Reviewer,—whether he insists on an equal division of lands, or of knowledge,—whether he is for converting infidels to Christianity, or Christians to infidelity,—whether he is for pulling down the kings of the East or those of the West,—whether he sharply sets his face against all establishments, or maintains that whatever is, is right,—whether he prefers what is old to what is new, or what is new to what is old,—whether he believes that all human evil is remediable by human means, or makes it out to himself that a Reformer is worse than a house-breaker,—whether he is in the right or the wrong, poet or prose-writer, courtier or patriot,—he is still the same pragmatical person—every sentiment or feeling that he has is nothing but the effervescence of incorrigible over-weening self-opinion. He not only thinks whatever opinion he may hold for the time infallible, but that no other is even to be tolerated, and that none but knaves and fools can differ with him. "The friendship of the good and wise is his." If any one is so unfortunate as to hold the same opinions that he himself formerly did, this but aggravates the offence by irritating the jealousy of his self-love, and he vents upon them a double portion of his spleen. Such is the constitutional slenderness of his understanding, its "glassy essence," that the slightest collision of sentiment gives an irrecoverable shock to him. He regards a Catholic or a Presbyterian, a Deist or an Atheist, with equal repugnance, and makes no difference between the Pope, the Turk, and the Devil. He thinks a rival poet a bad man, and would suspect the principles, moral, political, and religious, of any one who did not spell the word *laureate* with an *e* at the end of it.—If Mr. Southey were a bigot, it would be well; but he has only the intolerance of bigotry. His violence is not the effect of attachment to any principles, prejudices, or paradoxes of his own, but of antipathy to those of others. It is an impatience of contradiction, an unwillingness to share his opinions with others, a captious monopoly of wisdom, candour, and common sense. He is not an enthusiast in religion, but he is an enemy to philosophers; he does not respect old establishments, but he hates new ones; he has no objection to regicides, but he is inexorable against usurpers; he will tell you that "the re-risen cause of evil" in France yielded to "the Red Cross and Britain's arm of might," and shortly after, he denounces this Red Cross as the scarlet whore of Babylon, and warns Britain against her eternal malice and poisoned cup; he calls on the Princess Charlotte in the name of the souls of ten thousand little children, who are without knowledge in *this age of light*, "SAVE OR WE PERISH," and yet sooner than they should be saved by Joseph Fox or Joseph Lancaster, he would see them damned; he would go himself into Egypt and pull down "the barbarous kings" of the East, and yet his having gone there on this very errand is not among the least of Bonaparte's crimes; he would "abate the malice" of the Pope and the Inquisition, and yet he cannot contain the fulness of his satisfaction at the fall of the only person who had both the will and the power to do this. Mr. Southey began with a decent hatred of kings and priests, but it yielded to his greater hatred of the man who trampled them in the dust. He does not feel much affection to those who are born to thrones, but that any one should gain a crown as he has gained the laureate-wreath, by superior merit alone, was the unpardonable sin against Mr. Southey's levelling Muse!

The poetry of the Lay is beneath criticism; it has all sorts of obvious common-place defects, without any beauties either obvious or recondite. It is the Namby-Pamby of the Tabernacle;

a Methodist sermon turned into doggrel verse. It is a gossipping confession of Mr. Southey's political faith—the "Practice of Piety" or the "Whole Duty of Man" mixed up with the discordant slang of the metaphysical poets of the nineteenth century. Not only do his sentiments every where betray the old Jacobinical leaven, the same unimpaired desperate unprincipled spirit of partisanship, regardless of time, place, and circumstance, and of every thing but its own headstrong will; there is a gipsey jargon in the expression of his sentiments which is equally indecorous. Does our Laureate think it according to court-etiquette that he should be as old-fashioned in his language as in the cut of his clothes?— On the present occasion, when one might expect a truce with impertinence, he addresses the Princess neither with the fancy of the poet, the courtier's grace, nor the manners of a gentleman, but with the air of an inquisitor or father-confessor. Geo. Fox, the Quaker, did not wag his tongue more saucily against the Lord's Anointed in the person of Charles II., than our Laureate here assures the daughter of his Prince, that so shall she prosper in this world and the next, as she minds what he says to her. Would it be believed (yet so it is) that, in the excess of his unauthorized zeal, Mr. Southey in one place advises the Princess conditionally to rebel against her father? Here is the passage. The Angel of the English church thus addresses the Royal Bride:—

"Bear thou that great Eliza in thy mind,
Who from a wreck this fabric edified;
And HER who to a nation's voice resigned,
When Rome in hope its wiliest engines plied,
By her own heart and righteous Heaven approved,
Stood up against the Father whom she loved."

This is going a good way. Is it meant, that if the Prince Regent, "to a nation's voice resigned," should grant Catholic Emancipation in defiance of the "Quarterly Review," Mr. Southey would encourage the Princess in standing up against her father, in imitation of the pious and patriotic daughter of James II.?

This quaint effusion of poetical fanaticism is divided into four parts, the Proem, the Dream, the Epilogue, and L'Envoy. The Proem opens thus:—

> "There was a time when all my youthful thought
> Was of the Muse; and of the Poet's fame,
> How fair it flourisheth and fadeth not, ...
> Alone enduring, when the Monarch's name
> Is but an empty sound, the Conqueror's bust
> Moulders and is forgotten in the dust."

This may be very true, but not so proper to be spoken in this place. Mr. Southey may think himself a greater man than the Prince Regent, but he need not go to Carlton-House to tell him so. He endeavours to prove that the Prince Regent and the Duke of Wellington (put together) are greater than Bonaparte, but then he is by his own rule greater than all three of them. We have here perhaps the true secret of Mr. Southey's excessive anger at the late Usurper. If all his youthful thought was of his own inborn superiority to conquerors and kings, we can conceive that Bonaparte's fame must have appeared a very great injustice done to his pretensions: it is not impossible that the uneasiness with which he formerly heard the names of Marengo, of Austerlitz, of Jena, of Wagram, of Friedland, and of Borodino, may account for the industrious self-complacency with which he harps upon those of Busaço, Vimiera, Salamanca, Vittoria, Thoulouse, and Waterloo; and that the Iron Crown of Italy must have pressed upon his (Mr. Southey's) brows, with a weight most happily relieved by the light laureate-wreath! We are justified in supposing Mr. Southey capable of envying others, for he supposes others capable of envying him. Thus he sings of himself and his office:—

> "Yea in this now, while malice frets her hour,
> Is foretaste given me of that meed divine;
> Here undisturbed in this sequestered bower,
> The friendship of the good and wise is mine;

> And that green wreath which decks the Bard when dead,
> That laureate garland crowns my living head.
> That wreath which in Eliza's golden days
> My master dear, divinest Spenser, wore,
> That which rewarded Drayton's learned lays,
> Which thoughtful Ben and gentle Daniel* bore...
> Grin, Envy, through thy ragged mask of scorn!
> In honour it was given, with honour it is worn!"

Now we do assure Mr. Southey, that we do not envy him this honour. Many people laugh at him, some may blush for him, but nobody envies him. As to Spenser, whom he puts in the list of great men who have preceded him in his office, his laureateship has been bestowed on him by Mr. Southey; it did not "crown his living head." We all remember his being refused the hundred pounds for his "Fairy Queen." Poets were not wanted in those days to celebrate the triumphs of princes over the people. But why does he not bring his list down nearer to his own time—to Pye and Whitehead and Colley Cibber? Does Mr. Southey disdain to be considered as the successor even of Dryden? That green wreath which decks our author's living head, is so far from being, as he would insinuate, an anticipation of immortality, that it is no credit to any body, and least of all to Mr. Southey. He might well have declined the reward of exertions in a cause which throws a stigma of folly or something worse on the best part of his life. Mr. Southey ought not to have received what would not have been offered to the author of "Joan of Arc."

Mr. Southey himself maintains that his song has still been "to Truth and Freedom true;" that he has never changed his opinions; that it is the cause of French liberty that has left him, not he the cause. That may be so. But there is one person in the kingdom who has, we take it, been at least as consistent in

* The ignorant will suppose that these are two proper names.

his conduct and sentiments as Mr. Southey, and that person is the King. Thus the Laureate emphatically advises the Princess :—

> "Look to thy Sire, and in *his steady way*,
> *As in his Father's he*, learn thou to tread."

Now the question is, whether Mr. Southey agreed with his Majesty on the subject of the French Revolution when he published "Joan of Arc." Though Mr. Southey "as beseems him well" congratulates the successes of the son, we do not recollect that he condoled with the disappointments of the father in the same cause. The King has not changed, therefore Mr. Southey has. The sun does not turn to the sun-flower; but the sun-flower follows the sun. Our poet has thoughtlessly committed himself in the above lines. He may be right in applauding that one sole purpose of his Majesty's reign which he formerly condemned: that he can be consistent in applauding what he formerly condemned, is impossible. That his majesty King George III. should make a convert of Mr. Southey rather than Mr. Southey of George III. is probable for many reasons. The King by siding with the cause of the people could not, like King William, have gained a crown: Mr. Southey, by deserting it, has got a hundred pounds a-year. A certain English ambassador, who had a long time resided at the court of Rome, was on his return introduced at the levee of Queen Caroline. This lady, who was almost as great a prig as Mr. Southey, asked him why in his absence he did not try to make a convert of the Pope to the Protestant religion. He answered, "Madam, the reason was that I had nothing better to offer his Holiness than what he already has in his possession." The Pope would no doubt have been of the same way of thinking. This is the reason why kings, from sire to son, pursue "their steady way," and are less changeable than canting cosmopolites.

THE LAY OF THE LAUREATE, CARMEN NUPTIALE, *by Robert Southey, Esq. Poet-Laureate, Member of the Royal Spanish Academy, and of the Royal Spanish Academy of History.*—London: Longmans, 1816.

(CONCLUDED.)

"*Queen.* Hamlet, thou hast thy Father much offended.
"*Hamlet.* Madam, you have my Father much offended."

July 14, 1816.

THOUGH we do not think Mr. Southey has been quite consistent, we do not think him a hypocrite. This poem proves it. How should he maintain the same opinion all his life, when he cannot maintain it for two stanzas together? The weakness of his reasoning shews that he is the dupe of it. He has not the faculty of perceiving contradictions. He is not accountable for his mistakes. There is not a single sentiment advanced in any part of the *Lay*, which is not flatly denied in some other part of it. Let us see:—

"Proudly I raised the high thanksgiving strain
Of victory in a rightful cause achieved·
For which *I long had looked and not in vain,*
As one who with firm faith and undeceived,
In history and the heart of man could find
Sure presage of deliverance for mankind."

Mr. Southey does not inform us in what year he began to look for this deliverance, but if he had looked for it long, he must have looked for it long in vain. Does our poet then find no presage of deliverance for "conquered France" in the same principles that he found it for "injured Germany?" But he has no principles; or he does not himself know what they are. He praises Providence in this particular instance for having conformed to his hopes; and afterwards thus gives us the general results of his reading in history and the human heart. In the Dream he says, speaking of Charissa and Speranza—

"This lovely pair unrolled before the throne
"Earth's melancholy map," whereon to sight
Two broad divisions at a glance were shown,
The empires these of darkness and of light.
Well might the thoughtful bosom sigh to mark
How wide a portion of the map was dark.
Behold, Charissa cried, how large a space
Of earth lies unredeemed! Oh grief to think
That countless myriads of immortal race
In error born, in ignorance must sink,
Trained up in customs which corrupt the heart,
And following miserably the evil part!
Regard the expanded Orient from the shores
Of scorched Arabia and the Persian sea,
To where the inhospitable Ocean roars
Against the rocks of frozen Tartary;
Look next at those Australian isles which lie
Thick as the stars which stud the wintry sky.
Then let thy mind contemplative survey
That spacious region where in elder time
Earth's unremembered conquerors held the sway;
And Science trusting in her skill sublime,
With lore abstruse the sculptured walls o'erspread,
Its import now forgotten with the dead.
From Nile and Congo's undiscovered springs
To the four seas which gird the unhappy land,
Behold it left a prey to barbarous Kings,
The Robber and the Trader's ruthless hand;
Sinning and suffering, everywhere unblest,
Behold her wretched sons, oppressing and opprest!"

This is "a pretty picture" to be drawn by one who finds in the past history of the world the sure presage of deliverance for mankind. We grant indeed that Mr. Southey was right in one thing, viz. in expecting from it that sort of "deliverance of mankind," bound hand and foot, into the power of Kings and Priests, which has actually come to pass, and which he has celebrated with so much becoming pomp, both here and elsewhere.

The doctrine of "millions made for one" has to be sure got a tolerable footing in the East. It has attained a very venerable old age there—it is mature even to rottenness, but without decay. "Old, old, Master Shallow," but eternal. It is transmitted down in unimpaired succession from sire to son. Snug's the word. Legitimacy is not there militant, but triumphant, as the Editor of *The Times* would wish. It is long since the people had any thing to do with the laws but to obey them, or any laws to obey but the will of their task-masters. This is the necessary end of legitimacy. The Princes and Potentates cut one another's throats as they please; but the people have no hand in it. They have no French Revolutions there, no rights of man to terrify barbarous kings, no republicans or levellers, no weathercock deliverers and re-deliverers of mankind, no Mr. Southeys nor Mr. Wordsworths. In this they are happy. Things there are perfectly settled, in the state in which they should be,—still as death, and likely to remain so. Mr. Southey's exquisite reason for supposing that a crusade to pull down divine right would succeed in the East, is that a crusade to prop it up has just succeeded in the West. That will never do. Besides, what security can he give, if he goes on improving in wisdom for the next five and twenty years as he has done for the last, that he would not in the end be as glad to see these "barbarous kings" restored to their rightful thrones, as he is now anxious to see them tumbled from them? The doctrine of "divine right" is of longer standing and more firmly established in the East than in the West, because the Eastern world is older than ours. We might say of it,

> "The wars it well remembers of King Nine,
> "Of old Assaracus and Inachus divine."

It is fixed on the altar and the throne, safe, quite safe against Mr. Southey's enthusiasm in its second spring, his Missionary Societies, and his Schools for All. It overlays that vast continent, like an ugly incubus, sucking the blood and stopping up the breath of man's life. That detestable doctrine, which in

England first tottered and fell headless to the ground with the martyred Charles; which we kicked out with his son James, and kicked twice back with two Pretenders, to make room for "Brunswick's fated line," a line of our own chusing, and for that reason worth all Mr. Southey's lines put together; that detestable doctrine, which the French, in 1793, ousted from their soil, thenceforward sacred in the eyes of humanity, which they ousted from it again in 1815, making it doubly sacred; and which (oh grief, oh shame) was borne into it once more on English shoulders, and thrust down their throats with English bayonets; this detestable doctrine, which would, of right and with all the sanctions of religion and morality, sacrifice the blood of millions to the least of its prejudices; which would make the rights, the happiness, and liberty of nations, from the beginning to the end of time, dependent on the caprice of some of the lowest and vilest of the species; which rears its bloated hideous form to brave the will of a whole people; that claims mankind as its property, and allows hnman nature to exist only upon sufferance; that haunts the understanding like a frightful spectre, and oppresses the very air with a weight that is not to be borne; this doctrine meets with no rubs, no reverses, no ups and downs, in the East. It is there fixed, immutable. The Jaggernaut there passes on with its "satiate" scythe over the bleeding bodies of its victims, who are all as loyal, as pious, and as thankful as Mr. Southey. It meets with no opposition from any "re-risen cause of evil" or of good. Mankind have there been delivered once for all!

In the passage above quoted, Mr. Southey founds his hope of the emancipation of the Eastern world from "the Robber and the Trader's ruthless hand" on our growing empire in India. This is a conclusion which nobody would venture upon but himself. His last appeal is to scripture, and still he is unfortunate :—

> "Speed thou the work, Redeemer of the World!
> *That the long miseries of mankind may cease!*
> Where'er the Red Cross banner is unfurled,
> There let it carry truth, and light, and peace!

Did not the Angels who announced thy birth,
Proclaim it with the sound of Peace on Earth?

From the length of time that this prediction has remained unfulfilled, Mr. Southey thinks its accomplishment must be near. His Odes will not hasten the event.

Again, we do not understand the use which Mr. Southey makes of the Red Cross in this poem. For speaking of himself he says,

> "And when that last and most momentous hour
> Beheld the re-risen cause of evil yield
> To the Red Cross and England's arm of power,
> I sung of Waterloo's unrivalled field,
> Paying the tribute of a soul embued
> With deepest joy, devout and awful gratitude."

This passage occurs in the Proem. In the Dream the Angel of the English Church is made to warn the Princess—

> "Think not that lapse of ages shall abate
> The inveterate malice of that Harlot old;
> Fallen tho' thou deemest her from her high estate,
> She proffers still the envenomed cup of gold,
> And her fierce Beast, whose names are blasphemy,
> The same that was, is still, and still must be."

It is extraordinary that both these passages relate to one and the same thing, namely, Popery, which our author in the first identifies with the Christian religion, thus invoking to his aid every pure feeling or pious prejudice in the minds of his readers, and in the last denounces as that Harlot old, "whose names are blasphemy," with all the fury of plenary inspiration. This is a great effort of want of logic. Mr. Southey will hardly sing or say that it was to establish Protestantism in France that England's arm of power was extended on this occasion. Nor was it simply to establish Popery. That existed there already. It was to establish "the inveterate malice of that Harlot old," her "envenomed cup," to give her back her daggers and her fires, her mummeries, her holy oil, her power over the bodies and the minds of men, to restore her "the same that she was, is still, and still must be," that that celebrated fight was fought. The massacres of Nismes followed hard upon the triumph of Mr. Southey's Red Cross. The blood of French Protestants began to flow almost before the wounds of the dying and the dead in that memorable carnage had done festering. This was the most crying injustice, the most outrageous violation of principle, that ever was submitted to. What! has John Bull nothing better to do now-a-days than to turn bottle-holder to the Pope of Rome, to whet his daggers for him, to light his fires, and fill his poisoned bowl; and yet, out of pure complaisance (a quality John has learnt from his new friends the Bourbons) not venture a syllable to say that we did not mean him to use them? It seems Mr. Southey did not think this a fit occasion for the interference of his Red Cross Muse. Could he not trump up a speech either for "divine Speranza," or "Charissa dear," to lay at the foot of the throne? Was the Angel of the English Church dumb too—"quite chop-fallen?" Yet though our Laureate cannot muster resolution enough to advise the Prince to protect Protestants in France, he plucks up spirit enough to urge him to persecute Catholics in this country, and pretty broadly threatens him with the consequences, if he does not. "'Tis much," as Christopher Sly says.

There is another subject on which Mr. Southey's silence is still more inexcusable. It was understood to be for his exertions in the cause of Spanish liberty that he was made Poet-Laureate. It is then high time for him to resign. Why has he not written a single ode to a single Spanish patriot who has been hanged, banished, imprisoned, sent to the galleys, assassinated, tortured? It must be pleasant to those who are suffering under the thumb-screw to read Mr. Southey's thoughts upon that ingenious little instrument of royal gratitude. Has he discovered that the air of a Court does not very well agree with remonstrances against acts of oppression and tyranny, when exercised by those who are born for no other purpose? Is his patriotism only a false cover, a Carlton-House convenience? His silence on this subject is not equivocal. Whenever Mr. Southey shews the sincerity of his former professions of zeal in behalf of Spanish liberty, by writing an elegy on the death of Porlier, or a review of the conduct of Ferdinand VII. (he is a subject worthy of Mr. Southey's prose style), or by making the lame tailor of Madrid (we forget his name) the subject of an epic poem, we will retract all that we have said in disparagement of his consistency—*But not till then.*

We meant to have quoted several other passages, such as that in which old Praxis, that is, Experience, recommends it to the Princess to maintain the laws by keeping all that is old, and adding all that is new to them—that in which he regrets the piety and learning of former times, and then promises us a release from barbarism and brutishness by the modern invention of Sunday schools—that in which he speaks of his own virtues and the wisdom of his friends—that in which he undertakes to write a martyrology.—But we are very tired of the subject, and the verses are not worth quoting. There is a passage in Racine which is; and with that, we take our leave of the Laureate, to whom it may convey some useful hints in explanation of his ardent desire for the gibbeting of Bonaparte and the burning of Paris :—

> *Nabal.*—Que peut vous inspirer une haine si forte?
> Est-ce que de Baal le zèle vous transporte?
> Pour moi, vous le savez, descendu d'Ismaël,
> Je ne sers ni Baal ni le Dieu d'Israel.
> *Mathan.*—Ami, peux-tu penser que d'un zèle frivole
> Je me laisse aveugler pour une vaine idole!
> Né ministre du Dieu qu'en ce temple on adore,
> Peut-être que Mathan le serviroit encore,
> Si l'amour des grandeurs, la soif de commander,
> Avec son joug étroit pouvoient s'accommoder.
> Qu'est-il besoin, Nabal, qu'à tes yeux je rappelle
> De Joad et de moi la fameuse querelle?
> Vaincu par lui j'entrai dans une autre carrière,
> Et mon âme à la cour s'attacha tout entière.
> J'approchai par degrés l'oreille des rois;
> Et bientôt en oracle on érigea ma voix.
> J'étudiai leur cœur, je flattai leurs caprices,
> Je leur semai de fleurs le bord des précipices:

Près de leurs passions rien ne me fût sacré ;
De mesure et de poids je changeois à leur gré,
Autant que de Joad l'inflexible rudesse
De leur superbe oreille offensoit la mollesse ;
Autant je les charmois par ma dextérité,
Dérobant à leur yeux la triste vérité,
Prêtant à leur fureur des couleurs favourables,
Et prodigue sur-tout du sang des misérables.*
* * * * * * * * * *

Déserteur de leur loi, j'approvai l'entreprise,
Et par là de Baal méritai la prètrise ;
Par là je me rendis terrible à mon rival,
Je ceignis la tiare, et marchai son égal.
Toutefois, je l'avoue, en ce comble de gloire,
De Dieu que j'ai quitté l'importune mémoire
Jette encore en mon ame un reste de terreur ;
Et c'est ce qui redouble et nourrit ma fureur.
Heureux, si sur son temple achevant ma vengeance,
Je puis convaincre enfin sa haine d'impuissance,
Et parmi les débris, les ravages, et les morts,
A force d'attentats perdre tous mes remords.†

TO THE EDITOR OF THE EXAMINER.

SIR,—I hope you will not omit to notice two passages in Mr. Southey's poem, in which, to try his talent at natural de-

* "Carnage is her daughter."—*Mr. Wordsworth's Thanksgiving Ode.*

† This article falls somewhat short of its original destination, by our having been forced to omit two topics, the praise of Bonaparte, and the abuse of poetry. The former we leave to history: the latter we have been induced to omit from our regard to two poets of our acquaintance. We must say they have spoiled sport. One of them has tropical blood in his veins, which gives a gay, cordial, vinous spirit to his whole character. The other is a mad wag,—who ought to have lived at the Court of Horwendillus, with Yorick and Hamlet,—equally desperate in his mirth and his gravity, who would laugh at a funeral and weep at a wedding, who talks nonsense to prevent the head-ache, who would wag his finger at a skeleton, whose jests scald like tears, who makes a joke of a great man, and a hero of a cat's paw. The last is more than Mr. Garrard or Mr. Turnerelli can do. The busts which these gentlemen have made of a celebrated General are very bad. His head is worth nothing unless it is put on his men's shoulders.

scription, he gives an account of two of "the fearfullest wild-fowl living"—a British Lion and a Saxon one. Both are striking likenesses, and would do to hang on the outside of Exeter-'Change to invite the curious. The former (presumed not to be indigenous) is described to be in excellent case, well-fed, getting in years and corpulent, with a high collar buried in the fat of the neck, false mane, large haunches (for which this breed is remarkable), paws like a shin of beef, large rolling eyes, a lazy, lounging animal, sleeping all day and roaring all night, a great devourer of carcases and breaker of bones, pleased after a full meal, and his keepers not then afraid of him. Inclined to be uxorious. Visited by all persons of distinction, from the highest characters abroad down to the lowest at home.—The other portrait of the Saxon Lion is a contrast to this. It is a poor lean starved beast, lord neither of men nor lands, galled with its chain, which it has broken, but has not got off from its neck. This portrait is, we understand, to be dedicated to Lord Castlereagh.—Your constant reader,

NE QUID NIMIS.

"A NEW VIEW OF SOCIETY; or, *Essays on the Principle of the Formation of the Human Character, and the Application of the Principle to Practice.*" Murray, 1816.—"AN ADDRESS TO THE INHABITANTS OF NEW LANARK, *on opening an Institution for the Formation of Character.*" *By* Robert Owen, *one of his Majesty's Justices of the Peace for the County of Lanark.*"—Hatchard, 1816.

["Dedicated to those who have no Private Ends to accomplish, who are honestly in search of Truth, for the purpose of ameliorating the Condition of Society, and who have the firmness to follow the Truth wherever it may lead. without being turned aside from the Pursuit by the Prepossessions or Prejudices of any part of Mankind;—to Mr. Wilberforce, the Prince Regent," &c.]

August 4, 1816.

"A *NEW* View of Society"—No, Mr. Owen, that we deny. It may be true, but it is not new. It is not coeval, whatever the author and proprietor may think, with the New Lanark mills, but it is as old as the royal borough of Lanark, or as the county of Lanark itself. It is as old as the "Political Justice" of Mr. Godwin, as the "Oceana" of Harrington, as the "Utopia" of Sir Thomas More, as the "Republic" of Plato; it is as old as society itself, and as the attempts to reform it by shewing what it ought to be, or by teaching that the good of the whole is the good of the individual—an opinion by which fools and honest men have been sometimes deceived, but which has never yet taken in the knaves and knowing ones. The doctrine of Universal Benevolence, the belief in the Omnipotence of Truth, and in the Perfectibility of Human Nature, are not new, but "Old, old," Master Robert Owen;—why then do you say that they are new? They are not only old, they are superannuated, they are dead and buried, they are reduced to mummy, they are put into the catacombs at Paris, they are sealed up in patent coffins, they have been dug up again and anatomised, they have been drawn, quartered and gibbetted, they have become black, dry, parched in the sun, loose, and rotten, and are dispersed to all the winds of Heaven! The chain in which they hung up the murdered corse of human Liberty is all that remains of it, and my Lord Shallow keeps the key of it! If Mr. Owen will get it out of his hands, with the aid of Mr. Wilberforce and the recommendation of *The Courier*, we will "applaud him to the very echo, which shall applaud again." Till then, we must content ourselves with "chaunting remnants of old lauds" in the manner of Ophelia:—

> "No, no, he is gone, and we cast away moan,
> And will he not come again,
> And will he not come again?"

Perhaps, one of these days, he may .... "like a cloud over the Caspian:" then if ever, and never till then, human nature will hold up its head again, and the Holy and Triple Alliance will be dissolved. But as to this bald spectre of Liberty and Necessity conjured up by Mr. Owen from the falls of the Clyde, with a primer in one hand, and a spinning-jenny in the other, coming down from the Highlands in a Scotch mist, and discoverable only by second-sight, we may fairly say to it—

> "Thy bones are marrowless, thy blood is cold;
> Thou hast no speculation in those eyes,
> Which thou dost glare with."

Why does Mr. Owen put the word "New," in black-letter at the head of the advertisements of his plan of reform? In what does the New Lanark differ from the old Utopia? Is Scotland, after all, the true Lubber-land? Or must the whole world be converted into a cotton-factory? Does not Mr. Owen know that the same scheme, the same principles, the same philosophy of motives and actions, of causes and consequences, of knowledge and virtue, of virtue and happiness, were rife in the year 1793, were noised abroad then, were spoken on the house-tops, were whispered in secret, were published in quarto and duodecimo, in political treatises, in plays, poems, songs, and romances—made their way to the bar, crept into the church, ascended the rostrum, thinned the classes of the universities, and robbed "Durham's golden stalls" of their hoped-for ornaments, by sending our aspiring youth up to town to learn philosophy of the new teachers of philosophy; that these "New Views of Society" got into the hearts of poets and the brains of metaphysicians, took possession of the fancies of boys and women, and turned the heads of almost the whole kingdom: but that there was one head which they never got possession of, that turned the heads of the whole kingdom round again, stopped the progress of philosophy and necessity by wondrous fortitude, and that "thus repelled, *philosophy* fell into a sadness, then into a fast, thence to a watching, then into a weakness, thence to a lightness, and by this declension, to the lamentable state wherein it now lies,"—hooted by the boys, laughed at by the women, spit at by fools, trod upon by knaves, damned by poet-laureates, whined over by maudlin metaphysicians, rhymed upon by mincing ballad-makers, ridiculed in romances, belied in histories and travels, pelted by the mob, sneered at by the court, driven from the country, kicked out of society, and forced to take refuge and to lie snug for twenty years in the New Lanark mills, with the connivance of the worthy proprietor, among the tow and spindles; from whence he lets us understand that it is coming up again to Whitehall-stairs, like a spring-tide with the full of the moon, and floating on the blood that has flowed for the restoration of the Bourbons, under the patronage of the nobility, the gentry, Mr. Wilberforce, and the Prince Regent, and all those who are governed, like these great personages, by no other principle than truth, and no other wish than the good of mankind! This puff will not take with us: we are old birds, not to be caught with chaff: we shall not purchase in this new lottery, where there are all prizes and no blanks! We are inclined to throw Mr. Owen's "New View," behind the fire-place, as we believe most people do the letter they receive from the proprietors of the lucky lottery-office, informing them that their ticket was drawn a blank the first day, and in the postscript soliciting their future favours!

Mr. Owen may think that we have all this while been jesting, when we have been in sad and serious earnest. Well, then, we will give him the reason why we differ with him, out of "an old saw," as good as most "modern instances." It is contained in this sentence:—"If to do were as easy as to teach others what were good to be done, chapels had been churches, and poor men's cottages princes' palaces." Our author has discovered no new theory; he has advanced no new reasons. The former reasons were never answered, but the plan did not succeed. Why then does he think *his* must? All that he has done has been to leave out the reasons for his paradoxes, and to give his conclusions in capitals. This may take for a time with Mr. Wilberforce and the Methodists, who like hieroglyphics, but it cannot last. Here is a plan, strange as it may seem, "a new View of Society," published by two of our most loyal booksellers, and what is still more extraordinary, puffed in *The Courier* as an extremely practical, practicable, solid, useful, and good sort of work, which proposes no less than to govern the world without religion and without law, by the force of reason alone! This project is in one of its branches dedicated to the Prince Regent, by which (if carried into effect) he would be stuck up in his life-time as "a useless piece of antiquity;" and in another part is dedicated to Mr. Wilberforce, though it would by the same rule convert that little vital member of the community into "a monkey preacher," crying in the wilderness with no one to hear him, and sneaking about between his character and his conscience, in a state of ludicrous perplexity, as indeed he always appears to be at present! What is most remarkable is, that Mr. Owen is the first philosopher we ever heard of, who recommended himself to the great by telling them disagreeable truths. A man that comes all the way from the banks of the Clyde acquires a projectile force that renders him irresistible. He has access, we understand, to the men in office, to the members of parliament, to lords and gentlemen. He comes to "pull an old house about their ears," to batter down all their establishments, new or old, in church or in state, civil, political, and military, and he quietly walks into their houses with his credentials in his pocket, and reconciles them to the prospect of the innumerable Houses of Industry he is about to erect on the scite of their present sinecures, by assuring them of the certainty of his principles and the infallibility of his practice, in building up and pulling down. His predecessors were clumsy fellows; but he is an engineer, who will be sure to do their business for them. He is not the man to set the Thames on fire, but he will move the world, and New Lanark is the place he has fixed his lever upon for this purpose. To shew that he goes roundly to work with great people in developing his formidable system of the formation of character, he asks, p. 7 of the second Essay,—

"How much longer shall we continue to allow generation after generation to be taught crime from their infancy, and when so taught, hunt them like beasts of the forest, until they are entangled beyond escape in the toils and nets of the law? When, if the circumstances from youth of these poor unpitied sufferers had been reversed with those who are even surrounded with the pomp and dignity of justice, these latter would have been at the bar of the culprit, and the former would have been in the judgment-seat.

"Had the present Judges of these realms, whose conduct compels the admiration of surrounding states, been born and educated in St. Giles's, or some similar situation, is it not reasonable to conclude, as they possess native energies and abilities, that ere this they would have been at the head of their *then* profession, and in consequence of that superiority and proficiency, have already suffered imprisonment, transportation, or death? Or can we for a moment hesitate to decide, that if some of those men whom our laws, dispensed by the present Judges, have doomed to suffer capital punishment, had been born, trained, and surrounded as these Judges were born, trained, and surrounded; that some of those so imprisoned, transported, or hanged, would have been the identical individuals who would have passed the same awful sentences *on our present highly esteemed dignitaries of the law?*"

This is a delicate passage. So then according to the author of the "New View of Society," the Prince Regent of these realms, instead of being at the head of the allied sovereigns of Europe, might, in other circumstances, have been at the head of a gang of bravoes and assassins; Lord Castlereagh, on the same principle, and by parity of reasoning, without any alteration in his nature or understanding, but by the mere difference of situation, might have been a second *Count Fathom;* Mr. Vansittart, the chancellor of the exchequer, might, if he had turned his hand that way in time, have succeeded on *the snaffling lay*, or as a pick-pocket; Lord Wellington might have entered houses, instead of entering kingdoms, by force; the Lord-chancellor might have been a Jew-broker; the Marquis of ——— or Lord ——— a bawd, and their sons, tapsters and bullies at bagnios; the Queen

(God bless her) might have been an old washer-woman, taking her snuff and gin among her gossips, and her daughters, if they had not been princesses, might have turned out no better than they should be! Here's a levelling rogue for you! The world turned inside out, with a witness!—Such are Mr. Owen's general principles, to which we have nothing to say, and such his mode of illustrating them in his prefaces and dedications, which we do not think the most flattering to persons in power. We do not, however, wish him to alter his tone: he goes swimmingly on at present, "with cheerful and confident thoughts." His schemes thus far are tolerated, because they are remote, visionary, inapplicable. Neither the great world nor the world in general care any thing about New Lanark, nor trouble themselves whether the workmen there go to bed drunk or sober, or whether the wenches are got with child before or after the marriage ceremony. Lanark is distant, Lanark is insignificant. Our statesmen are not afraid of the perfect system of reform he talks of, and, in the meantime, his cant against reform in parliament, and about Bonaparte, serves as a practical diversion in their favour. But let the good which Mr. Owen says he has done in one poor village be in danger of becoming general,—let his plan for governing men by reason, without the assistance of the dignitaries of the church and the dignitaries of the law, but once get wind and be likely to be put in practice, and his dreams of elevated patronage will vanish. Long before he has done as much to overturn bigotry and superstition in this country, as he says Bonaparte did on the continent, (though he thinks the restoration of what was thus overturned also a great blessing) Mr. Wilberforce will have cut his connection. When we see Mr. Owen brought up for judgment before Lord Ellenborough, or standing in the pillory, we shall begin to think there is something in this *New Lanark Scheme* of his. On the other hand, if he confines himself to general principles, steering clear of practice, the result will be the same, if ever his principles become sufficiently known and admired. Let his "New View of Society" but make as many disciples as the "Enquiry concerning Political Justice," and we shall soon see how the tide will turn about. There will be a fine hue and cry raised by all *the good and wise,* by all "those acute minds" who, Mr. Owen tells us, have not been able to find a flaw in his reasonings, but who will soon discover a flaw in his reputation. Dr. Parr will preach a Spital sermon against him; lectures will be delivered in Lincoln's Inn Hall, to prove that a perfect man is such another chimera as a golden mountain; Mr. Malthus will set up his two checks of vice and misery as insuperable bars against him; Mr. Southey will put him into the "Quarterly Review;" his name will be up in the newspapers, *The Times, The Courier,* and *The Morning Post;* the three estates will set their faces against him; he will be marked as a Jacobin, a leveller, an incendiary, in all parts of the three kingdoms; he will be avoided by his friends, and become a bye-word to his enemies; his brother magistrates of the county of Lanark will refuse to sit on the bench with him; the spindles of his spinning-jennies will no longer turn on their soft axles; he will have gone out for wool, and will go home shorn; and he will find that it is not so easy or safe a task as he imagined to make fools wise, and knaves honest; in short, to make mankind understand their own interests, or those who govern them care for any interest but their own. Otherwise, all this matter would have been settled long ago. As it is, things will most probably go on as they have done, till some comet comes with its tail; and on the eve of some grand and radical reform, puts an end to the question.

THE SPEECH OF CHARLES C. WESTERN, Esq. M. P. *on the Distressed State of the Agriculture of the Country, delivered in the House of Commons, March* 7, 1816.

THE SPEECH OF HENRY BROUGHAM, Esq. M. P. *on the same subject, delivered in the same place, April* 9, 1816.

THIS is a sore subject; and it is here handled with much tenderness and delicacy. It puts one in mind of the traveller's nose, and the nuns of Strasburgh, in the tale of Slaukenbergius. "I will touch it, said one; I dare not touch it, said another; I wish I had touched it, said a third; let me touch it, said a fourth." While the gentlewomen were debating the point, the traveller with the great nose rode on. It would be no ungracious task to treat of the distresses of the country, if all were distressed alike; but that is not the case; nor is it possible to trace the necessities of one part of the community to their source, or to hint at a remedy, without glancing invidiously at the superfluities of others. "Aye, there's the rub, that makes calamity of so long life." The speeches before us are to the subject what a veil is to a lady's face, or a blind to a window. Almost all that has been said or written upon it is a palpable delusion—an attempt to speak out and say nothing; to oppose something that might be done, and propose something that cannot be done; to direct attention to the subject, and divert it from it; to do something and nothing; and to come to this potent conclusion, that while nothing *is done*, nothing *can be done*. "But have you then any remedy to propose instead?" What sort of a remedy do you mean? "Oh, one equally safe and efficacious, that shall set every thing to rights, and leave every thing just as it is, that does not touch either the tythes or the national debt, nor places and pensions, nor property of any kind, except the poor's fund; *that* you may take from them to make them independent of the rich, as you leave Lord Camden in possession of thirty thousand a year to make him independent of the poor."—Why, then, what if the Lord Chancellor and the Chancellor of the Exchequer were to play a game at push-pin on the top of St. Paul's; or if Mr. Brougham and Mr. Horner were to play at cat's-cradle on the top of the Monument; or if the little garden between the Speaker's house and the river-side were to be sown with pearls and cockle-shells? Or if—— Pshaw! Patience, and shuffle the cards.

The great problem of our great problem-finders appears to be, *to take nothing from the rich, and give it to the poor*. That will never do. We find them and their schemes of diversion well described in Rabelais, book v. chap. xxii.

"*How Queen Whim's Officers were employed, and how the said Lady retained us among her Abstractors.*

"I then saw a great number of the Queen's officers, who made blackamoors white, as fast as hops, just rubbing their bellies with the bottom of a pannier.

"Others, with three couples of foxes in one yoke, ploughed a sandy shore, and did not lose their seed.

"Others washed burnt tiles, and made them lose their colour.

"Others extracted water out of pumice-stones, braying them a good while in a mortar, and changed their substance.

"Others sheered asses, and thus got long fleece wool.

"Others gathered off of thorns grapes, and figs off of thistles.

"Others stroked he-goats by the dugs, and saved their milk, and much they got by it.

"Others washed asses' heads, without losing their soap.

"Others taught cows to dance, and did not lose their fiddling.

"Others pitched nets to catch the wind, and took cock lobsters in them.

"Others out of nothing made great things, and made great things return to nothing.

"Others made a virtue of necessity, and the best of a bad market; which seemed to me a very good piece of work.

"I saw two Gibroins by themselves, keeping watch on the top of a tower; and we were told they guarded the moon from the wolves."

The war has cost the country five or six hundred millions of money. This has not been a nominal expence, a playing at ducks and drakes with the King's picture on the water, or a manufacturing of bank-notes, and then lighting our pipes with them, but a real *bonâ fide* waste of the means, wealth, labour, produce, or resources of the country, in the carrying on of the war. About one hundred of these five or six hundred millions have been sent directly out of the country in loans to our Allies, from the year 1793 to the year 1815, inclusive, during which period there is not a single year in which we did not (from our desire of peace with the legitimate government of that country) subsidise one or all of the powers of Europe to carry on war against the rebels, regicides, republicans, and usurpers of France. Now the interest of this money alone would be five millions yearly, which would be nearly enough to pay the amount of the poor-rates of the whole country, which is seven millions of our yearly taxes, or might at least be applied to mitigate the mild severity of Mr. Malthus's sweeping clauses on that defenceless part of the subject. Here is a hundred millions then gone clean out of the country: there are four or five hundred millions more which have been sunk in the expenses of the war, and which might as well have been sunk in the sea; or what has been saved out of the wreck by those who have been most active in running the vessel aground, is in the hands of persons who are in no hurry that the public should go snacks with them in their excessive good fortune. In all three cases, and under each several head of loans, waste, or monopoly, John Bull pays the piper, or the interest of the whole money in taxes. He is just so many hundred millions the worse for the war, (whoever may be the better for it) not merely in paper, which would be nothing, nor in golden guineas, which would be something; but in what is better and more substantial than either, in goods and chattels, in the produce of the soil, and the work of his hands—in the difference between what the industry of man, left to itself, produces in time of peace for the benefit of man, and what the same industry, under the direction of government, produces in time of war for the destruction of others, without any benefit to himself, real, imaginary, or pretended; we mean in a physical and economical point of view, which is here the question—a question, which seems to last when the religion, politics, and morality of the affair are over. We have said that the expenses of the war might as well have been sunk in the sea; and so they might, for they have been sunk in unproductive labour, that is, in maintaining large establishments, and employing great numbers of men in doing nothing or mischief; for example, in making ships to destroy other ships, guns and gun-powder to blow out men's brains, pikes and swords to run them through the body, drums and fifes to drown the noise of cannon and the whizzing of bullets; in making caps and coats to deck the bodies of those who live by killing others; in buying up pork and beef, butter and cheese, to enable them to do this with more effect: in barracks, in transport-ships, in baggage and baggage-waggons, in horses, bridles and saddles, in suttlers and followers of the camp, in chaplains of the regiment, in common trulls, and the mistresses of generals and commanders in chief; in contractors, in army and navy agents, their partners, clerks, relations, dependants, wives, families, servants in and out of livery, their town and country houses, coaches, curricles, parks, gardens, grottos, hot-houses, green-houses, pictures, statues, libraries; in treasury scribes, in secretaries and under-secretaries of state, of the foreign, colonial, and war departments, with their swarms of underlings, all of whom are maintained out of the labour and sweat of the country, and for all of whom, and for all that they do (put together) the country is not one pin the better, or at least, one penny more in pocket, than if they were at the bottom of the Channel. The present may have been the most just and necessary war, in a political, moral, and religious point of view, that ever was engaged in; but it has also been the most expensive; and what is worse, the expense remains just the same, though it may have been the most unjust and unnecessary in the world. We have paid for it, and we must pay for it equally in either case, and wholly out of our own pockets. The price of restoring the Pope, the Inquisition, the Bourbons, and the doctrine of Divine Right, is half of our nine hundred millions of debt. That is the amount of the government bill of costs, presented to John Bull for payment, not of the principal but the interest; that is what he has got by the war; the load of taxes at his back, with which he comes out of his glorious five and twenty years' struggle, like Christian's load of sins, which whether it will not fall off from his back like Christian's, into the Slough of Despond, will be seen before long. The difference between the expense of a war or a peace establishment is just the difference between a state of productive and unproductive labour. Now this whole question, which from its complexity puzzles many people, and has given rise to a great deal of partly wilful and partly shallow sophistry,* may be explained in two words.—Suppose I give a man five shillings a day for going out in a boat and catching fish for me. This is paying for productive labour: that is, I give him so much for what he does, or a claim upon so much of the public stock: but in taking so much from the stock by laying out his five shillings, he adds so much to it by his labour, or the disposal of his time in catching fish. But if I, having the money to do what I please with, give him five shillings a day for shooting at crows, he is paid equally for his trouble, and accordingly takes so much from the public stock, while he adds nothing to it but so much carrion. So if the government pay him so much a-day for shooting at Frenchmen and Republicans, this is a tax, a loss, a burthen to the country, without any thing got by it; for we cannot, after all, eat Frenchmen and Republicans when we have killed them. War in itself is a thriving, sensible traffic only to cannibals! Again—if I give a man five shillings for making a pair of shoes, this is paying for productive labour, viz. for labour that is useful, and that must be performed by some one; but if I give the same man five shillings for standing on his head or behind my chair while I am picking my teeth, or for running up a hill and down again for a wager—this is unproductive labour, nothing comes of it, and though the man who is thus idly employed lives by it, others starve, upon whose pittance and whose labour he lives through me. Such is the nature and effect of war; all the energies of which tend to waste, and to throw an additional and

* See an article on this subject in Mr. Coleridge's *Friend*.

heavy burthen upon the country, in proportion to the extent and length of time that it is carried on. It creates so many useless members of the community: every man paid by the war out of the taxes paid by the people, is, in fact, a dead body fastened to a living one, that by its weight drags it to the earth. A five and twenty years' war, and nine hundred millions of debt, are really a couple of millstones round the neck of a country, that must naturally press her down a little in the scale of prosperity. That seems to be no riddle. We defy any sophist to answer this statement of the necessary tendency of war in its general principle to ruin and impoverish a country. We are not to wonder, when it does so; but when other causes operate to counteract or retard this tendency. What is extraordinary in our own case is, that the pernicious effects of war have been delayed so long, not that they have come upon us at last.*—That money laid out in war is thrown away is self-evident from this single circumstance, that government never refund. The reason is, because they never do any thing with their money that produces money again. They are the worst bankers in the world. The Exchequer is a true Sinking Fund. If you lend money to a farmer, a manufacturer, a merchant, he employs it in getting something done, for which others will pay, because it is useful; as in raising corn, in weaving cotton, in bringing home sugar or tobacco. But money sunk in a war brings in no returns—except of killed and wounded. What will any one give the government for the rotten bones that lie buried at Walcheren, or the dry ones at Waterloo? Not a six-pence. They cannot make a collection of wooden legs or dangling sleeves from the hospitals at Greenwich or Chelsea to set up a raffle or a lottery. They cannot bring the fruits of the war to auction, or put up the tottering throne of the Bourbons to the best bidder.

* We are somewhat in the situation of *Captain Macheath* in the "Beggar's Opera." "The road had done the Captain justice, but the gaming-table had been his ruin." We have been pretty successful on the high seas; but the Bank have swallowed it all up. The taxes have outlived the war, trade, and commerce. *They* are the soul, the immortal part of the Pitt system.

They can neither bring back a drop of the blood that has been shed, nor recover a shilling of the treasure that has been wasted. If the expenses of the war are not a burden to the people, which must sink it according to their weight, why do not government take the whole of this thriving concern into their own hands, and pay the national debt out of the Droits of Admiralty? In short, the way to ascertain this point is, by the old method of *reductio ad absurdum:* Suppose we had to pay the expenses of such another peace-establishment and such another war. Who does not see that they would eat up the whole resources of the country, as the present peace-establishment and actual debt do just one half?

Speeches in Parliament on the Distresses of the Country, *by* Mr. Western *and* Mr. Brougham.

(concluded.)

> "Come, let us leave off children's play, and go to push-pin."
>
> *Polite Conversation.*

Dec. 29, 1816.

The war has wasted the resources of the country in foolery, which the country has now to pay for in a load of taxes on its remaining resources, its actual produce and labour. The tax-gatherer is a government-machine that takes sixty-five millions a-year from the bankrupt pockets of the nation, to give to those who have brought it into that situation; who takes so much from the necessaries of life belonging to the poor, to add to the superfluities of the rich; who adds so much to the hard labour of the working part of the community, to "relieve the killing languor and over-laboured lassitude of those who have nothing to do;" who, in short, out of the grinding poverty and ceaseless toil of those who pay the taxes, enables those who receive them to live in luxury and idleness.

Mr. Burke, whom we have just quoted, has said, that "if the poor were to cut the throats of the rich, they would not have a meal the more for it." First, (for truth is the first thing in our thoughts, and not to give offence the second) this is a falsehood; a greater one than the answer of a Bond-street lounger, who coming out of a confectioner's shop, where he has had a couple of basons of turtle-soup, an ice, some jellies, and a quantity of pastry, as he saunters out picking his teeth and putting the change into his pocket, says to a beggar at the door, "I have nothing for you." We confess, we have always felt it an aukward circumstance to be accosted in this manner, when we have been caught in the act of indulging a sweet tooth, and it costs us an additional penny. The rich and poor may at present be compared to the two classes of frequenters of pastry-cooks' shops, those on the outside and those on the in. We would seriously advise the latter, who see the gaunt faces staring at them through the glass-door, to recollect, that though custard is nicer than bread, bread is the greatest necessary of the two.—We had forgot Mr. Burke's sophism, to which we reply in the second place, that the cutting of throats is a figure of speech, like the dagger which he produced in the House of Commons, not necessary to the speculative decision of the question. The most civil, peaceable, and complaisant way of putting it is this—whether if the rich were to give all that they are worth to the poor, the latter would be none the richer for it? If so, the rich would be none the poorer, and so far could be no losers on Mr. Burke's own hypothesis, which supposes, with that magnanimity of contempt for plain matter of fact which distinguished the author's theories, that the rich have nothing, and the poor have every thing? Had not Mr. Burke a pension of 4000*l*. a-year? Was this nothing? But even this is not the question neither. It is not, whether if the rich were to part with all they have to the poor (which is a mere absurdity) but whether if the rich do not take all they have left from the poor (which we humbly hope is a proposition that has common sense in it) the latter may not be the better off with something to live upon than with nothing? Whether, if the whole load of taxes could be taken off from them, it would not be a relief to them? Whether, if half the load of taxes were taken off from them, it would not be a relief to them? Whether, if any part of the load of taxes that can be taken off from them were taken off, it would not in the same proportion be a relief to them? We will venture to say, that no one will deny these propositions who does not receive so much a year for falsehood and impudence. The resistance which is made to the general or abstract principle is not intended to prevent the extreme sweeping application of that principle to the plundering or (as Mr. Burke will have it) to the cutting the throats of the rich, but it is a manœuvre, by getting rid of the general principle altogether, viz. that the extravagance and luxury of the rich, war, taxes, &c. have a tendency to increase the distresses of the poor, or measures of retrenchment and reform to lighten those distresses—to give *carte-blanche* to the government to squander the wealth, the blood, the happiness of the nation at pleasure; to grant jobs, places, pensions, sinecures, reversions without end, to grind down, to starve and impoverish the country with systematic impunity. It is a legerdemain trick played off by hireling politicians, to enable their patrons and employers to pick our pockets and laugh in our faces at the same time.

It has been said by such persons that taxes are not a burthen to the country; that the wealth collected in taxes returns through those who receive to those who pay them, only divided more equally and beneficially among all parties, just (they say) as the vapours and moisture of the earth collected in the clouds return to enrich the soil in soft and fertilizing showers. We shall set ourselves to shew that this is not true.

Suppose a society of ten persons, without taxes to pay, and who live on their own labour, on the produce of the ground, and the exchange of one commodity among themselves for another. Some of these persons will be naturally employed in tilling the ground, others in tending cattle, others in making instruments of husbandry, others in weaving cloth, others in making shoes, others in building houses, others in making roads, others in buying and selling, others in fetching and carrying what the others want. All will be employed in something that they want themselves, or that others want. In such a state of society, nothing will be given for nothing. If a man has a bushel of wheat, and only wants half of it, he will give the other half to some one, for making him a coat or a pair of shoes. As every one will be paid for what he does out of the earnings of the labour of others, no one will waste his time or his strength in doing any thing that is not wanted by some one else, that is not as useful and necessary to his subsistence and comfort, and more so, than the commodity which he gives in exchange for it. There will be no unproductive labour. What each person gets will be either in proportion to what he has done for himself, or what he has added to the comforts of others. Exchange there will be no robbery. The wealth of all will be the result of the exertions of each individual, and will circulate equally and beneficially, because those who produce that wealth will share it among themselves. This is an untaxed state of society, where wealth changes hands indeed, but finds its level, notwithstanding.—Now suppose two other individuals to be fastened upon this society of ten persons—a government-man and a fund-holder. They change the face of it in an instant. The equilibrium, the balance is upset. The amount of the wealth of the society before was a thousand pounds a-year, suppose. The two new-comers take a writ out of their pockets, by which they quietly lay hands on five hundred of it as their fair portion. Where are the ten persons now? Mr. Burke, Mr. Coleridge, Mr. Vansittart, *The Courier*, say—Just where they were before! We say, No such thing. For three reasons: 1. It cannot be denied that the interlopers, the government-man and his friend, the fund-holder, who has lent him money to sport with on all occasions, are substantial *bonâ fide* persons, like other men, who live by eating, drinking, &c. and who, if they only shared equally with the other ten what they had got amongst them, (for they add nothing to the common stock) must be a sufficient burthen upon the rest, that is, must diminish the comforts or increase the labour of each person one-fifth. To hear the other side talk, one would suppose that those who raise and are paid out of the taxes never touch a farthing of them, that they have no occasion for them, that they neither eat nor drink, nor buy clothing, or build houses with them; that they live upon air, or that harmless food, bank notes (a thing not to speak of), and that all the money they are so anxious to collect is distributed by them again for the sole benefit of others, or passes back through the Exchequer, as if it were a conduit-pipe or empty tunnel, into the hands of the original proprietors, without diminution or diversion. Now this is not so. 2. Not only do our government-man and his friend live like other people upon their means, but they live better than other people, for they have better means, that is, these two take half of what the other ten get. They would be fools if they gave it back to them; no, depend upon it, they lay out their five hundred a-year upon themselves, for their own sole use, benefit, pleasure, mirth, and pastime. For each of these gentlemen has just five times as much to spend as any of those that he lives upon at free cost, and he has nothing to do but to think how he shall spend it. He eats and drinks as much as he can, and always of the best and most costly. It is pretended that the difference in the consumption of the produce of the soil is little or nothing, for a poor man's belly will hold as much as a rich man's. But not if the one is full, and the other empty. The man who lives upon the taxes, feasts upon venison and turtle, and crams himself to the throat with fish, flesh, and fowl; the man who pays the taxes, upon a crust of mouldy bread, and fat rusty bacon: the man who receives the taxes drinks rich and sparkling wines, hock and canary; the man who pays them, sour small beer. If the poor man gets drunk and leads an idle life, his family starve: the rich man drinks his three bottles a day and does nothing, while his family live on the fat of the land. If the poor man dies of hard labour and poor living, his family comes to the parish; if the rich man dies of hard living and want of exercise, he leaves his family to be provided for by the state. But, 3. All that the government-man and the fund-holder do not spend upon their bellies, in revelling and gormandising, they lay out upon their backs, their houses, their carriages, &c. in inordinate demands upon the labour of the former ten persons, who are now employed, not in working for one another, but in pampering the pride, ostentation, vanity, folly, or vices, of our two gentlemen comers. After glutting their physical appetites, they take care to apply all the rest to the gratification of their factitious, arbitrary, and fantastic wants, which are unlimited, and which the universe could not supply. "They toil not, neither do they spin, and yet even Solomon in all his glory was not arrayed like one of these:"—while the poor are clothed in rags, and the dogs lick up their sores. The money that is taken from you and me, or the more industrious members of the community, and that we should have laid out in having snug, comfortable houses built for us all, or two bed-rooms for our families instead of one, is employed, now that it has got into the tax-gatherer's hands, in hiring the same persons to build two enormous houses for the government-man and the fund-holder, who live in palaces while we live in hovels. What are we, the people, the original ten men, the better for that? The taxes enable those who receive them to pay our masons, carpenters, &c. for working for them. If we had not been forced to pay the money in taxes, the same persons would have been employed by us for our common benefit. Suppose the government-man takes it into his head to build a colossus, a rotunda, a pyramid, or any thing else equally absurd and gigantic, it would, we say, be a nuisance in proportion to its size. It would be ten times as great a nuisance if it was ten times bigger. If it covered a whole county, it would ruin the landed interest. If it was spread over the whole country, the country must starve. When the government-man and the fund-holder have got their great houses built, they must next have them furnished with proportionable magnificence, and by the same means; with Persian and Turkey carpets, with Egyptian sofas, down beds, silk curtains, china vases, services of plate, tables, chairs, stoves, glasses, mirrors, chandeliers, paper hangings, pictures, busts, ornaments, kickshaws without number, while you and I live on a mud floor, with bare walls, stuck with a penny ballad, with a joint-stool to sit upon, a tea-pot without a tea-spout to drink out of, a truckle-bed or some straw and a blanket to lie upon! Yet Mr. Burke says, that if we were suddenly converted into state-pensioners with thirty-thousand a-year, we could not furnish our houses a bit the better for it, This is like Lord Peter, in the Tale of a Tub. Then the government-man and his friend must have their train of coaches, horses, dogs, footmen dressed in blue, green, yellow, and red, lazy rascals, making work for the taylor, the hatter, the shoemaker, the button-maker, the hair-dresser, the gold and silver laceman, to powder, dress, and trick them out, that they may lounge behind their mistresses' coaches, walk before their sedan chairs, help on their master's stockings, block up his doors, and perform a variety of little nameless offices, much to the ease and satisfaction of the great, but not of the smallest benefit to any one else. With respect to the article of dogs and horses, a word in Mr. Malthus's ear. They come under the head of consumption, and a swinging item they are. They eat up the food of the children of the poor. The pleasure and coach-horses kept in this kingdom consume as much of the produce of the soil as would maintain all the paupers in it. Let a tax be laid upon them directly, to defray the expense of the poor-rates, and to suspend the operation of Mr. Malthus's geometrical and arithmetical ratios. We see no physical necessity why that ingenious divine should put a stop to the propagation of the species, that he may keep two sleek geldings in his stable. We have lately read Swift's account of the Houynhyms and Yahoos. There is some truth in it; but still it has not reconciled us to Mr. Malthus's proposal of starving the children of the poor to feed the horses of the rich. But no more of that! We have said enough at present to shew how the taxes fly away with the money of a nation; how they go into the hands of the government-man and the fund-holder, and do not return into the pockets of the people, who pay them. For the future, Mr. Burke's assertion, that the taxes are like the vapours that ascend into the clouds and return to the earth in fertilizing showers, may pass for an agreeable metaphor, but for nothing more. A pretty joke truly, this, of the people's receiving their taxes back again in payment for what the rich want of them. It is as if I should buy a pound of beef in a butcher's shop, and take the money out of his own till to pay him! It is as if a bill is presented to me for payment, and I ask the notary for the money to take it up with! It is as if a Noble Earl was to win 50,000*l.* of a Noble Duke over-night, and offer to return it to him the next morning, for one of his estates! It is as if Mr. Burke had been robbed of a bond for 4000*l.* and the fortunate possessor had offered to restore it, on receiving in lieu his house and gardens at Beaconsfield! Having thus pointed out the nature of the distress, we need not inquire far for the remedy.

A Lay-Sermon on the Distresses of the Country, *addressed to the Middle and Higher Orders. By* S. T. Coleridge, *Esq.* Printed for Gale and Fenner, price 1s.*

——————" Function
Is smother'd in surmise, and nothing is
But what is not."
" Or in Franciscan think to pass disguis'd."

Sept. 8, 1816.

This Lay-Sermon puts us in mind of Mahomet's coffin, which was suspended between heaven and earth, or of the flying island at Laputa, which hovered over the head of Gulliver. The

* It may be proper to notice, that this article was written before the Discourse which it professes to criticise had appeared in print, or probably existed any where, but in repeated newspaper advertisements.

ingenious author, in a preface, which is a master-piece in its kind, having neither beginning, middle, nor end, apologizes for having published a work, not a line of which is written, or ever likely to be written. He has, it seems, resorted to this expedient as the only way of appearing before the public in a manner worthy of himself and his genius, and descants on the several advantages to be derived from this original mode of composition;—That as long as he does not put pen to paper, the first sentence cannot contradict the second; that neither his reasonings nor his conclusions can be liable to objection, *in the abstract;* that *omne ignotum pro magnifico est,* is an axiom laid down by some of the best and wisest men of antiquity; that hitherto his performance, in the opinion of his readers, has fallen short of the vastness of his designs, but that no one can find fault with what he does not write; that while he merely haunts the public imagination with obscure noises, or by announcing his spiritual appearance for the next week, and does not venture out *in propria persona* with his shroud and surplice on, the Cock-lane Ghost of mid-day, he may escape in a whole skin without being handled by the mob, or uncased by the critics; and he considers it the safest way to keep up the importance of his oracular communications, by letting them remain a profound secret both to himself and the world.

In this instance, we think the writer's modesty has led him into a degree of unnecessary precaution. We see no sort of difference between his published and his unpublished compositions. It is just as impossible to get at the meaning of the one as the other. No man ever yet gave Mr. Coleridge " a penny for his thoughts." His are all maiden ideas; immaculate conceptions. He is the " Secret Tattle " of the press. Each several work exists only in the imagination of the author, and is quite inaccessible to the understandings of his readers—" Yet virgin of Proserpina from Jove."—We can give just as good a guess at the design of this Lay-Sermon, which is not published, as of *the Friend,* the Preliminary Articles in *the Courier, the Watchman, the Con-*

ciones ad Populum; or any of the other courtly or popular publications of the same author. Let the experiment be tried, and if, on committing the manuscript to the press, the author is caught in the fact of a single intelligible passage, we will be answerable for Mr. Coleridge's loss of character. But we know the force of his genius too well. What is his *Friend* itself but an enormous title-page; the longest and most tiresome prospectus that ever was written; an endless preface to an imaginary work; a table of contents that fills the whole volume; a huge bill of fare of all possible subjects, with not an idea to be had for love or money? One number consists of a grave-faced promise to perform something impossible in the next; and the next is taken up with a long-faced apology for not having done it. Through the whole of this work, Mr. Coleridge appears in the character of the Unborn Doctor; the very Barmecide of knowledge; the Prince of preparatory authors!

"He never is—but always to be *wise*."

He is the Dog in the Manger of literature, an intellectual Mar-Plot, who will neither let any body else come to a conclusion, nor come to one himself.* This gentleman belongs to the class of eclectic philosophers; but whereas they professed to examine different systems, in order to select what was good in each, our perverse critic ransacks all past or present theories, to pick out their absurdities, and to abuse whatever is good in them. He takes his notions of religion from the "sublime piety" of Jordano Bruno, and considers a belief in a God as a very subordinate question to the worship of the Three Persons of the Trinity. The thirty-nine articles and St. Athanasius's creed are, upon the same principle, much more fundamental parts of the Christian

* This work is so obscure, that it has been supposed to be written in cypher, and that it is necessary to read it upwards and downwards, or backwards and forwards, as it happens, to make head or tail of it. The effect is exceedingly like the qualms produced by the heaving of a ship becalmed at sea; the motion is so tedious, improgressive, and sickening.

religion than the miracles or gospel of Christ. He makes the essence of devotion to consist in Atheism, the perfection of morality in a total disregard of consequences. He refers the great excellence of the British Constitution to the prerogative of the Crown, and conceives that the old French Constitution must have been admirably defended by the States-General, which never met, from the abuses of arbitrary power. He highly approves of *ex-officio* informations and special juries, as the great bulwarks of the liberty of the press; taxes he holds to be a providential relief to the distresses of the people, and war to be a state of greater security than peace. He defines Jacobinism to be an abstract attachment to liberty, truth, and justice; and finding that this principle has been abused or carried to excess, he argues that Anti-jacobinism, or the abstract principles of despotism, superstition, and oppression, are the safe, sure, and undeniable remedy for the former, and the only means of restoring liberty, truth, and justice in the world. Again, he places the seat of truth in *the heart*, of virtue in *the head*; damns a tragedy as shocking that draws tears from the audience, and pronounces a comedy to be inimitable, if nobody laughs at it; labours to unsettle the plainest things by far-fetched sophistry, and makes up for the want of proof in matters of fact by the mechanical operations of the spirit. He judges of men as he does of things. He would persuade you that Sir Isaac Newton was a money-scrivener, Voltaire dull, Bonaparte a poor creature, and the late Mr. Howard a misanthrope; while he pays a willing homage to the Illustrious Obscure, of whom he always carries a list in his pocket. His creed is formed not from a distrust and disavowal of the exploded errors of other systems, but from a determined rejection of their acknowledged excellences. It is a transposition of reason and common sense. He adopts all the vulnerable points of belief as the triumphs of his fastidious philosophy, and holds a general retainer for the defence of all contradictions in terms and impossibilities in practice. He is at cross-purposes with himself as well as others, and discards his own caprices if ever he suspects there is the least ground for them. Doubt succeeds to doubt, cloud rolls over cloud, one paradox is driven out by another still greater, in endless succession. He is equally averse to the prejudices of the vulgar, the paradoxes of the learned, or the habitual convictions of his own mind. He moves in an unaccountable diagonal between truth and falsehood, sense and nonsense, sophistry and common-place, and only assents to any opinion when he knows that all the reasons are against it. A matter of fact is abhorrent to his nature: the very *air* of truth repels him. He is only saved from the extremities of absurdity by combining them all in his own person. Two things are indispensable to him —to set out from no premises, and to arrive at no conclusion. The consciousness of a single certainty would be an insupportable weight upon his mind. He slides out of a logical deduction by the help of metaphysics: and if the labyrinths of metaphysics did not afford him "ample scope and verge enough," he would resort to necromancy and the cabbala. He only tolerates the science of astronomy for the sake of its connection with the dreams of judicial astrology, and escapes from the *Principia* of Newton to the jargon of Lily and Ashmole. All his notions are floating and unfixed, like what is feigned of the first forms of things flying about in search of bodies to attach themselves to; but *his* ideas seek to avoid all contact with solid substances. Innumerable evanescent thoughts dance before him, and dazzle his sight, like insects in the evening sun. Truth is to him a ceaseless round of contradictions: he lives in the belief of a perpetual lie, and in affecting to think what he pretends to say. His mind is in a constant estate of flux and reflux: he is like the Sea-horse in the Ocean; he is the Man in the Moon, the Wandering Jew.—The reason of all this is, that Mr. Coleridge has great powers of thought and fancy, without will or sense. He is without a strong feeling of the existence of any thing out of himself; and he has neither purposes nor passions of his own to make him wish it to be. All that he does or thinks is involuntary; even his perversity and self-will are so. They are nothing but a necessity of yielding to the slightest motive. Everlasting inconsequentiality marks all that he attempts. All his impulses are loose, airy, devious, casual. The strongest of his purposes is lighter than the gossamer, "that wantons in the idle summer-air:" the brightest of his schemes a bubble blown by an infant's breath, that rises, glitters, bursts in the same instant:—

> "Or like the Borealis race,
> That flit ere you can mark their place:
> Or like the snow falls in the river,
> A moment white, then gone for ever."

His mind has infinite activity, which only leads him into numberless chimeras; and infinite resources, which not being under the guidance of his will, only distract and perplex him. His genius has angel's wings; but neither hands nor feet. He soars up to heaven, circles the empyrean, or dives to the centre of the earth, but he neither lays his hands upon the treasures of the one, nor can find a resting place for his feet in the other. He is no sooner borne to the utmoſt point of his ambition, than he is hurried away from it again by the same fantastic impulse, or his own specific levity. He has all the faculties of the human mind but one, and yet without that one, the rest only impede and interfere with each other—"Like to a man on double business bound who both neglects." He would have done better if he had known less. His imagination thus becomes metaphysical, his metaphysics fantastical, his wit heavy, his arguments light, his poetry prose, his prose poetry, his politics turned—but not to account. He belongs to all parties and is of service to none. He gives up his independence of mind, and yet does not acquire independence of fortune. He offends others without satisfying himself, and equally by his servility and singularity, shocks the prejudices of all about him. If he had had but common moral principle, that is, sincerity, he would have been a great man; nor hardly, as it is, appears to us—

> "Less than arch-angel ruined, and the excess
> "Of glory obscur'd."

We lose our patience when we think of the powers that he has wasted, and compare them and their success with those, for instance, of such a fellow as the ———, all whose ideas, notions, apprehensions, comprehensions, feelings, virtues, genius, skill, are comprised in the two words which *Peachum* describes as necessary qualifications in his gang, "To stand himself and bid others stand!"

When his six Irish friends, the six Irish gentlemen, Mr. Makins, Mr. Dunkley, Mr. Monaghan, Mr. Gollogher, Mr. Gallaspy, and Mr. O'Keeffe, after an absence of several years, discovered their old acquaintance John Buncle, sitting in a mixed company at Harrowgate Wells, they exclaimed with one accord—"There he is—making love to the finest woman in the universe!" So we may say at a venture of Mr. Coleridge—"There he is, at this instant (no matter where) talking away among his gossips, as if he were at the Court of Semiramis, with the Sophi or Prestor John." The place can never reach the height of his argument. He should live in a world of enchantment, that things might answer to his descriptions. His talk would suit the miracle of the Conversion of Constantine, or Raphael's Assembly of the Just. It is not short of that. His face would cut no figure there, but his tongue would wag to some purpose. He is fit to take up the deep pauses of conversation between Cardinals and Angels—his cue would not be wanting in presence of the beatific vision. Let him talk on for ever in this world and the next; and both worlds will be the better for it. But let him not write, or pretend to write, nonsense. Nobody is the better for it. It was a fine thought in Mr. Wordsworth to represent Cervantes at the day of judgment and conflagration of the world carrying off the romance of Don Quixote under his arm. We hope that Mr. Coleridge, on the same occasion, will leave "the Friend" to take its chance, and his "Lay Sermon" to get up into the Limbo of Vanity, how it can.

. . . .

THE STATESMAN'S MANUAL; or *the Bible the best Guide to Political Skill and Foresight. A Lay Sermon, addressed to the Higher Classes of Society. By* S. T. Coleridge, *Esq.* Gale and Fenner.

Dec. 29, 1816.

HERE is the true Simon Pure. We have by anticipation given some account of this Sermon. We have only to proceed to specimens in illustration of what we have said.

It sets out with the following sentence:—

"If our own knowledge and information concerning the Bible had been confined to the one fact of its immediate derivation from God, we should still presume that it contained rules and assistances for all conditions of men under all circumstances; and therefore for communities no less than for individuals."

Now this is well said; "and 'tis a kind of good deed to say well." But why did not Mr. Coleridge keep on in the same strain to the end of the chapter, instead of himself disturbing the harmony and unanimity which he here very properly supposes to exist on this subject, or questioning the motives of its existence by such passages as the following, p. 23 of the Appendix:

"Thank heaven! notwithstanding the attempts of Mr. Thomas Paine and his compeers, it is not so bad with us. *Open infidelity* has ceased to be a means even of gratifying vanity; for the leaders of the gang themselves turned apostates to Satan, as soon as the number of their proselytes became *so large*, that Atheism ceased to give distinction. Nay, it became a mark of original thinking to defend the Belief and the Ten Commandments; so the *strong minds* veered round, and religion came again into fashion."

Now we confess we do not find in this statement much to thank heaven for; if religion has only come into fashion again with the strong minds—(it will hardly be denied that Mr. Coleridge is one of the number)—as a better mode of gratifying their vanity than "open infidelity." Be this as it may, Mr. Coleridge has here given a true and masterly delineation of that large class of Proselytes or their teachers, who believe any thing or nothing, just as their vanity prompts them. All that we have ever said of modern apostates is poor and feeble to it. There is however one error in his statement, inasmuch as Mr. Thomas Paine never openly professed Atheism, whatever some of his compeers might do.

It is a pity that with all that fund of "rules and assistances" which the Bible contains for our instruction and reproof, and which the author in this work proposes to recommend as the Statesman's Manual, or the best Guide to Political Skill and Foresight, in times like these, he has not brought forward a single illustration of his doctrine, nor referred to a single example in the Jewish history that bears at all, in the circumstances, or the inference, on our own, but one, and that one he has purposely omitted. Is this to be credited? Not without quoting the passage.

"But do you require some one or more particular passage from the Bible that may at once illustrate and exemplify its application to the changes and fortunes of empires? Of the numerous chapters that relate to the Jewish tribes, their enemies and allies, before and after their division into two kingdoms, it would be more difficult to state a single one, from which some guiding light might *not* be struck." [Oh, very well, we shall have a few of them. The passage goes on.] "And in nothing is Scriptural history more strongly contrasted with the histories of highest note in the present age, than in its freedom from the hollowness of abstractions." [Mr. Coleridge's admiration of the inspired writers seems to be very much mixed with a dislike of Hume and Gibbon.]—"While the latter present a shadow-fight of Things and Quantities, the former gives us the history of Men, and balances the important influence of individual minds with the previous state of national morals and manners, in which, as constituting a specific susceptibility, it presents to us the true cause, both of the influence itself, and of the Weal or Woe that were its consequents. *How should it be otherwise?* The histories and political economy of the present and preceding century partake in the general contagion of its mechanic philosophy," ['still harping on my daughter'] "and are the *product* of an unenlivened generalizing understanding. In the Scriptures they are the living *educts* of the Imagination; of that reconciling and mediatory power, which incorporating the reason in Images of the Sense, and organizing (as it were) the flux of the Senses by the permanence and self-circling energies of the Reason, gives birth to a system of symbols, harmonious in themselves, and consubstantial with the truths, of which they are the *conductors.* These are the Wheels which Ezekiel beheld when the hand of the Lord was upon him, and he saw visions of God as he sat among the captives by the river of Chebar. *Whither soever the Spirit was to go, the wheels went, and thither was their spirit to go; for the spirit of the living creature was in the wheels also.* The truths and the symbols that represent them move in conjunction, and form the living chariot that bears up (for us) the throne of the Divine Humanity. *Hence by a derivative, indeed, but not a divided influence, and though in a secondary, yet in more than a metaphorical sense, the Sacred Book* is worthily entitled the Word of God," p. 36.

So that, after all, the Bible is not the immediate word of God, except according to the German philosophy, and *in something between a literal and metaphorical sense.* Of all the cants that ever were canted in this canting world, this is the worst! The author goes on to add, that "it is among the miseries of the present age that it recognises no medium between *literal* and *metaphorical,*" and laments that "the mechanical understanding, in the blindness of its self-complacency, confounds SYMBOLS with ALLEGORIES."—This is certainly a sad mistake, which he labours very learnedly to set right, "in a diagonal sidelong movement between truth and falsehood."—We assure the reader that the passages which we have given above are given in the order in which they are strung together in the Sermon; and so he goes on for several pages, concluding his career where the Allies have concluded theirs, with the doctrine of Divine Right; which he does not however establish quite so successfully with the pen, as they have done with the sword. "Herein" (says this profound writer) "the Bible differs from all the books of Greek philosophy, and in a two-fold manner. It doth not affirm a Divine Nature only, but a God; and not a God only, but the living God. *Hence in the Scriptures alone is the* JUS DIVINUM *or direct Relation of the State and its Magistracy to the Supreme Being, taught as a vital and indispensable part of* ALL MORAL AND ALL POLITICAL WISDOM, *even as the Jewish alone was a true theocracy!*"

Now it does appear to us, that as the reason why the *Jus Divinum* was taught in the Jewish state was, that that alone was a true theocracy, this is so far from proving this doctrine to be a *part of all moral and all political wisdom,* that it proves just the contrary. This may perhaps be owing to our mechanical understanding. Wherever Mr. C. will shew us the theocracy, we will grant him the *Jus Divinum.* Where God really pulls down and sets up kings, the people need not do it. Under the true Jewish theocracy, the priests and prophets cashiered kings; but our lay-preacher will hardly take this office upon himself as a part of the *Jus Divinum,* without having any thing better to shew for it than his profound moral and political wisdom. Mr. Southey hints at something of the kind in verse, and we are not sure that Mr. Coleridge does not hint at it in prose. For after his extraordinary career and interminable circumnavigation through the heaven of heavens, after being rapt in the wheels of Ezekiel, and sitting with the captives by the river of Chebar, he lights once more on English ground, and you think you have him.

"But I refer to the demand. Were it my object to touch on the present state of public affairs in this kingdom, or on the prospective measures in agitation respecting our Sister Island, I would direct your most serious meditations to the latter period of the reign of Solomon, and the revolutions in the reign of Rehoboam his son. *But I tread on glowing embers.* I will turn to a subject on which all men of reflection are at length in agreement—the causes of the Revolution and fearful chastisement of France."—Here Mr. Coleridge is off again on the wings of fear as he was before on those of fancy.—This trifling can only be compared to that of the impertinent barber of Bagdad, who being sent for to shave the prince, spent the whole morning in preparing his razors, took the height of the sun with an astrolabe, sung the song of Zimri, and danced the dance of Zamtout, and concluded by declining to perform the operation at all, because the day was unfavourable to its success. As we are not so squeamish as Mr. Coleridge, and do not agree with him and all other men of reflection on the subject of the French Revolution, we shall turn back to the latter end of the reign of Solomon, and that of his successor Rehoboam, to find out the parallel to the present reign and regency which so particularly strikes and startles Mr. Coleridge.—Here it is for the edification of the curious, from the First Book of Kings :—

" And the time that Solomon reigned over all Israel was forty years. And Solomon slept with his fathers, and was buried in the city of David his father: and Rehoboam his son reigned in his stead. And Rehoboam went to Shechem: *for all Israel were come to Shechem to make him king.** And Jeroboam and all the congregation of Israel came and spake unto Rehoboam, saying, Thy father (Solomon) made our yoke grievous; now, therefore, make thou the grievous service of thy father, and his heavy yoke which he put upon us, lighter, *and we will serve thee.* And he said unto them, Depart yet for three days, then come again to me. And the people departed. And King Rehoboam consulted with the old men that stood before Solomon his father while he yet lived, and said, How do ye advise, that I may answer this people? And they spake unto him, saying, *If thou wilt be a*

* Does this verse come under Mr. C.'s version of *Jus Divinum?*

servant unto this people this day, and wilt serve them, and answer them, and speak good words unto them, *then* they will be thy servants for ever. But he forsook the counsel of the old men, which they had given him, *and consulted with the young men that were grown up with him, and which stood before him:* And he said unto them, What counsel give ye, that we may answer this people, who have spoken to me, saying, Make the yoke which thy father did put upon us lighter? And the young men that were grown up with him spake unto him, saying, Thus shalt thou speak unto this people that spake unto thee, saying, Thy father made our yoke heavy, but make thou it lighter unto us; thus shalt thou say unto them, *My little finger shall be thicker than my father's loins. And now, whereas my father did lade you with a heavy yoke, I will add to your yoke: my father hath chastised you with whips: but I will chastise you with scorpions.* So Jeroboam and all the people came to Rehoboam the third day, as the king had appointed, saying, come to me again the third day. And the king *answered the people roughly*, and forsook the old men's counsel that they gave him: And spake to them after the counsel of the young men, saying, *My father made your yoke heavy, and I will add to your yoke; my father also chastised you with whips, but I will chastise you with scorpions.* Wherefore the king hearkened not unto the people; *for the cause was from the Lord*, that he might perform his saying which the Lord spake by Ahijah, the Shilonite, unto Jeroboam the son of Nebat." [We here see pretty plainly how the principle of "a true theocracy" qualified the doctrine of *Jus Divinum* among the Jews; but let us mark the sequel.] "*So when all Israel saw that the King hearkened not unto them, the people answered the king, saying, What portion have we in David: neither have we inheritance in the son of Jesse: to your tents, O Israel: now see to thine own house, David. So Israel departed unto their tents.* Then king Rehoboam sent Adoram, who was over the tribute; and all Israel stoned him with stones that he died; therefore king Rehoboam made speed to get him up to his chariot to flee to Jerusalem. So Israel rebelled against the house of David unto this day. And it came to pass when all Israel heard that Jeroboam was come again, that they sent and called him unto the congregation, and made him king over all Israel."

Here is the doctrine and practice of divine right, with a vengeance. We do not wonder Mr. Coleridge was shy of instances from his Statesman's Manual, as the rest are like this. He does not say (neither shall we, for we are not salamanders any more than he, *to tread on glowing embers*) whether he approves of the conduct of all Israel in this case, or of the *grand, magnificent, and gracious* answer of the son of Solomon; but this we will say, that his bringing or alluding to a passage like this immediately after his *inuendo* (addressed to the higher classes) that the doctrine of divine right is contained *par excellence* in the Scriptures alone, is we should suppose, an instance of a power of voluntary self-delusion, and of a delight in exercising it on the most ticklish topics, greater than ever was or ever will be possessed by any other individual that ever did or ever will live upon the face of the earth. "Imposture, organized into a comprehensive and self-consistent whole, forms a world of its own, in which inversion becomes the order of nature." Compared with such powers of inconceivable mental refinement, hypocrisy is a great baby, a shallow dolt, a gross dunce, a clumsy devil!

Among other passages, unrivalled in style and matter by any other author, take the following:—

"When I named this Essay a Sermon, I sought to prepare the inquirers after it for the absence of all the usual softenings *suggested by worldly prudence*, of all compromise between truth and courtesy. But not even as a Sermon would I have addressed the present Discourse to a promiscuous audience: and for this reason I likewise announced it in the title-page, as exclusively *ad clerum*, i. e. (in the old and wide sense of the word*) to men of *clerkly* acquirements, of whatever profession." [All that we know is,

* That is, in a sense not used and without any intelligible meaning.

that there is no such title-page to our copy.] "I would that the greater part of our publications could be thus *directed*, each to its appropriate class of readers. But this cannot be! For among other odd burs and kecksies, the misgrowth of our luxuriant activity, we have a READING PUBLIC, as strange *a phrase*, methinks, as ever forced a splenetic smile on the staid countenance of meditation; and yet *no fiction!* For our readers have, in good truth, multiplied exceedingly, and have waxed proud. It would require the *intrepid accuracy* of a Colquhoun"—[Intrepid and accurate applied to a Colquhoun! It seems that whenever an objection in matter of fact occurs to our author's mind, he instinctively applies the flattering unction of words to smooth it over to his conscience, as you apply a salve to a sore]—"to venture at the precise number of that vast company only, whose heads and hearts are dieted at the two public *ordinaries* of literature, the circulating libraries and the periodical press. But what is the result? Does the *inward man* thrive on this regimen? Alas! if the average health of the consumers may be judged of by the articles of largest consumption"—[Is not this a side-blow at the *Times* and *Courier*?]—"if the secretions may be conjectured from the ingredients of the dishes that are found best suited to their palates; from all that I have seen, either of the banquet or the guests, I shall utter my *profaccia*"—['Oh thou particular fellow!']—"with a desponding sigh: From a popular philosophy, and philosophic populace, good sense deliver us!"

Why so, any more than from a popular religion or a religious populace, on Mr. Coleridge's own principle, p. 12, "Reason and religion are their own evidence?" We should suspect that our unread author, the "Secret Tattle" of the Press, is thus fastidious, because he keeps an ordinary himself which is not frequented. He professes to be select: but we all know the secret of "seminaries for a limited number of pupils." Mr. Coleridge addresses his Lay-Sermon "to the higher classes," in his printed title-page: in that which is not printed he has announced it to be *directed ad clerum*, which might imply the clergy, but no: he issues another EXTENT for the benefit of the Reading Public, and says he means by the annunciation *ad clerum*, all persons of clerkly acquirements, that is, who can read and write. What wretched stuff is all this! We well remember a friend of his and ours saying, many years ago, on seeing a little shabby volume of *Thomson's Seasons* lying in the window of a solitary ale-house, at the top of a rock hanging over the British Channel,—"*That is true fame!*" If he were to write fifty Lay-Sermons, he could not answer the inference from this one sentence, which is, that there are books that make their way wherever there are readers, and that there ought every where to be readers for such books!

To the words READING PUBLIC, in the above passage, is the following note, which in wit and humour does not fall short of Mr. Southey's "Tract on the Madras System:"—

"Some participle passive in the diminutive form, *eruditorum natio* for instance, might seem at first sight a fuller and more exact designation: but the superior force and humour of the former become evident whenever the phrase occurs, as a step or stair in the climax of irony....Among the revolutions worthy of notice, the change in the introductory sentences and prefatory matter in serious books is not the least striking. The same gross flattery, which disgusts us in the dedications to individuals, in the elder writers, is now transferred to the nation at large, or the READING PUBLIC; while the Jeremiads of our old moralists, and their angry denunciations against the ignorance, immorality, and irreligion of the *people* appear (*mutatis mutandis*, and with an appeal to the worst passions, envy, discontent, scorn, vindictiveness,* &c.) in the shape of bitter libels on ministers, parliament, the clergy; in short, on the state and church, and all persons employed in them. Likewise, I would point out to the reader's attention the marvellous predominance at present of the words, Idea and Demonstration. Every talker now-a-days has an *Idea*; aye, and he will demonstrate it too! A few days ago,

* If these are the worst passions, there is plenty of them in this Lay-Sermon.

I heard one of the READING PUBLIC, a thinking and independent smuggler, euphonise the latter word with much significance, in a tirade against the planners of the late African expedition: '*As to Algiers, any man that has half an* IDEA *in his scull must know, that it has been long ago dey-monstered, I should say, dey-monstrified,*' *&c.* But the phrase, which occasioned this note, brings to my mind the mistake of a lethargic Dutch traveller, who, returning highly gratified from a showman's caravan, which he had been tempted to enter by the words LEARNED PIG, gilt on the pannels, met another caravan of a similar shape, with the READING FLY on it, in letters of the same size and splendour. 'Why, dis is voonders above voonders,' exclaims the Dutchman, takes his seat as first comer, and soon fatigued by waiting, and by the very hush and intensity of his expectation, gives way to his constitutional somnolence, from which he is roused by the supposed showman at Hounslow, with a '*In what name, Sir, was your place taken? are you booked all the way for Reading?*' Now a Reading Public is (to my mind) more marvellous still, and in the third tier of 'Voonders above voonders.'"

A public that could read such stuff as this with any patience would indeed be so. We do not understand how, with this systematic antipathy to the Reading Public, it is consistent in Mr. Coleridge to declare of "Dr. Bell's original and unsophisticated plan," that he "himself regards it as an especial gift of Providence to the human race, as an incomparable machine, a vast moral steam-engine." Learning is an old University mistress, that he is not willing to part with, except for the use of the church of England; and he is sadly afraid she should be debauched by the "liberal ideas" of Joseph Lancaster! As to his aversion to the prostitution of the word *Idea* to common uses and in common minds, it is no wonder, from the very exalted *idea* which he has given us of this term.

"What other measures I had in contemplation it has been my endeavour to explain elsewhere.....O what treasures of practical wisdom would be once more brought into open day by the solution of this problem," to wit, "a thorough recasting of the moulds in which the minds of our gentry, the characters of our future land-owners, magistrates, and senators, are to receive their shape and fashion. Suffice it for the present to hint the master-thought. *The first man, on whom the light of an* IDEA *dawned, did in that same moment receive the spirit and the credentials of a Lawgiver*; and as long as man shall exist, so long will the possession of that antecedent knowledge which exists only in the power of an *idea*, be the one lawful qualification for all dominion in the world of the senses," p. 58. Now we do think this a shorter cut towards the undermining of the rotten boroughs, and ousting the present ministry, than any we have yet heard of. One of the most extraordinary ideas in this work is where the Author proves the doctrine of free will from the existence of property; and again, where he recommends the study of the Scriptures, from the example of Heraclitus and Horace. To conclude this most inconclusive piece of work, we find the distant hopes and doubtful expectations of the writer's mind summed up in the following rare rhapsody. "Oh what a mine of undiscovered treasures, what a new world of power and truth would the Bible promise to our future meditation, if *in some gracious moment one solitary text of all its inspired contents* should but dawn upon us in the pure untroubled brightness of an IDEA, that most glorious birth of the godlike within us, which even as the light, its material symbol, reflects itself from a thousand surfaces, and flies homeward to its parent mind, enriched with a thousand forms, itself above form, and still remaining in its own simplicity and identity! O for a flash of that same light, in which the first position of geometric science that ever loosed itself from the generalizations of a groping and insecure experience, did for the first time reveal itself to a human intellect in all its evidence and in all its fruitfulness, Transparence without Vacuum, and Plenitude without Opacity! O! that a single gleam of our own inward experience would make comprehensible to us the rapturous

EUREKA, and the grateful hecatomb of the philosopher of Samos: or that vision which, from the contemplation of an arithmetical harmony, rose to the eye of Kepler, presenting the planetary world, and all their orbits in the divine order of their ranks and distances; or which, in the falling of an apple, revealed to the ethereal intuition of our own Newton the constructive principle of the material universe. The promises which I have ventured to hold forth concerning the hidden treasures of the Law and the Prophets will neither be condemned as paradox, or as exaggeration, by the mind that has learnt to understand the possibility that the reduction of the sands of the sea to number should be found a less stupendous problem by Archimedes than the simple conception of the Parmenidean ONE. What, however, is achievable by the human understanding without this light may be comprised in the epithet κενοσπουδοι; and *a melancholy comment on that phrase would the history of the human Cabinets and Legislatures for the last thirty years furnish!* The excellent Barrow, the last of the disciples of Plato and Archimedes among our modern mathematicians, shall give the description and state the value; and, in his words, I shall conclude:—

"*Aliud agere, to be impertinently busy, doing that which conduceth to no good purpose, is, in some respect, worse than to do nothing. Of such industry we may understand that of the Preacher, 'The labour of the foolish wearieth every one of them.'*"

A better conclusion could not be found for this Lay-Sermon· for greater nonsense the author could not write, even though he were inspired expressly for the purpose.

MR. COLERIDGE'S LAY-SERMON.

TO THE EDITOR OF THE EXAMINER.

Jan. 12, 1817.

SIR,

YOUR last Sunday's "Literary Notice" has given me some uneasiness on two points.

It was in January, 1798, just 19 years ago, that I got up one morning before day-light to walk 10 miles in the mud, and went to hear a poet and a philosopher preach. It was the author of the "Lay-Sermon." Never, Sir, the longest day I have to live, shall I have such another walk as this cold, raw, comfortless one in the winter of the year 1798. Mr. Examiner, *Il y a des impressions que ni le tems ni les circonstances peuvent effacer. Dusse-je vivre des siècles entiers, le doux tems de ma jeunesse ne peut renaitre pour moi, ni s'effacer jamais dans ma mémoire.* When I got there, Sir, the organ was playing the 100th psalm, and when it was done, Mr. C. rose and gave out his text, "And he went up into the mountain to pray, HIMSELF, ALONE." As he gave out this text, his voice "rose like a steam of rich distill'd perfumes," and when he came to the last two words, which he pronounced loud, deep, and distinct, it seemed to me, Sir, who was then young, as if the sounds had echoed from the bottom of the human heart, and as if that prayer might have floated in solemn silence through the universe. The idea of St. John came into my mind, "of one crying in the wilderness, who had his loins girt about, and whose food was locusts and wild honey." The preacher then launched into his subject, like an eagle dallying with the wind. *That* sermon, like *this* Sermon, was upon peace and war; upon church and state—not their alliance, but their separation—on the spirit of the world and the spirit of Christianity, not as the same, but as opposed to one another. He talked of those who had "inscribed the cross of Christ on banners dripping with human gore." He made a poetical and pastoral excursion,—and to shew the fatal effects of war, drew a striking contrast between the simple shepherd boy, driving his team afield, or sitting under the hawthorn, piping to his flock, as though he should never be old, and the same poor country-lad, crimped, kidnapped, brought into town, made drunk at an alehouse, turned into a wretched drummer-boy, with his hair sticking on end with powder and pomatum, a long cue at his back, and tricked out in the loathsome finery of the profession of blood.

> "Such were the notes our once-lov'd poet sung."

And for myself, Sir, I could not have been more delighted if I had heard the music of the spheres. Poetry and Philosophy had met together, Truth and Genius had embraced, under the eye and with the sanction of Religion. This was even beyond my hopes. I returned home well satisfied. The sun that was still labouring pale and wan through the sky, obscured by thick mists, seemed an emblem of the *good cause:* and the cold dank drops of dew that hung half melted on the beard of the thistle, had something genial and refreshing in them; for there was a spirit of hope and youth in all nature, that turned every thing into good. The face of nature had not then the brand of JUS DIVINUM on it;

> "Like to that sanguine flower inscrib'd with woe."

Now, Sir, what I have to complain of is this, that from reading your account of the "Lay-Sermon," I begin to suspect that my notions formerly must have been little better than a deception: that my faith in Mr. Coleridge's great powers must have been a vision of my youth, that, like other such visions, must pass away from me; and that all his genius and eloquence is *vox et preterea nihil:* for otherwise how is it so lost to all common sense upon paper?

Again, Sir, I ask Mr. Coleridge, why, having preached such a sermon as I have described, he has published such a sermon as you have described? What right, Sir, has he or any man to make a fool of me or any man? I am naturally, Sir, a man of a plain, dull, dry understanding, without flights or fancies, and can just contrive to plod on, if left to myself: what right then has Mr. C., who is just going to ascend in a balloon, to offer me a seat in the parachute, only to throw me from the height of his career upon the ground, and dash me to pieces? Or again, what right has he to invite me to a feast of poets and philosophers, fruits and flowers intermixed,—immortal fruits and amaranthine flowers,—and then to tell me it is all vapour, and, like *Timon*, to throw his empty dishes in my face? No, Sir, I must and will say it is hard. I hope, between ourselves, there is no breach of confidence in all this; nor do I well understand how men's opinions on moral, political, or religious subjects can be kept a secret, except by putting them in *The Correspondent.**

SEMPER EGO AUDITOR.

BONAPARTE AND MULLER,

THE CELEBRATED HISTORIAN OF SWITZERLAND.

[*From Müller's Posthumous Works.*]

"ON the 19th May I was informed by the Minister Secretary of State, Maret, that at seven o'clock of the evening of the following day I must wait on the Emperor Napoleon. I waited accordingly on this Minister at the appointed hour, and was presented. The Emperor sat on a sofa: a few persons whom I did not know stood at some distance in the apartment. The Em-

* A paper set up about this time by Dr. Stoddart.

peror began to speak of the History of Switzerland; told me that I ought to complete it; that even the more recent times had their interest. He came to the work of mediation, discovered a very good will, if we do not meddle with any thing foreign, and remain quietly in the interior. He proceeded from the Swiss to the old Greek Constitution and History, to the Theory of Constitutions, to the complete diversity of those of Asia, (and the causes of this diversity in the climate, polygamy, &c.) the opposite characters of the Arabian (which the Emperor highly extolled), and the Tartarian Races (which led to the irruptions that all civilization had always to dread from that quarter, and the necessity of a bulwark): the peculiar value of European culture (never greater freedom, security of property, humanity, and better laws in general, than since the 15th century); then how every thing was linked together, and in the inscrutable guidance of an invisible hand; and how he himself had become great through his enemies: the great confederation of nations, the idea of which Henry the 4th. never had: the foundation of all religion, and its necessity; that man could not well bear completely clear truth, and required to be kept in order; the possibility, however, of a more happy condition, if the numerous feuds ceased, which were occasioned by too complicated constitutions (such as the German), and the intolerable burden suffered by States from excessive armies. A great deal more besides was said, and indeed we spoke of almost every country and nation. The Emperor spoke at first in his usual manner; but the more interesting our conversation became, he spoke in a lower and lower tone, so that I was obliged to bend myself quite down to his face; and no man can have understood what he said (and therefore many things I will not repeat).—I opposed him occasionally, and he entered into discussion. Quite impartially and truly, as before God, I must say, that the variety of his knowledge, the acuteness of his observations, the solidity of his understanding (not dazzling wit), his grand and comprehensive views, filled me with astonishment, and his manner of speaking to me, with love for him. A couple of Marshals, and also the Duke of Benevento, had entered in the mean time; he did not break off. After five quarters, or an hour and a half, he allowed the concert to begin; and I know not, whether accidentally or from goodness, he desired pieces, which, one of them especially, had reference to pastoral life and the Swiss *(Rans des Vaches)*. After this, he bowed in a friendly manner and left the room.—Since the audience with Frederick (1782), I never had a conversation on such a variety of subjects, at least with any Prince: if I can judge correctly from recollection, I must give the Emperor the preference in point of solidity and comprehension; Frederick was somewhat Voltairian. Besides, there is in his tone much firmness and vigour, but in his mouth something as attractive and fascinating as in Frederick. It was one of the most remarkable days of my life. By his genius and his disinterested goodness he has also conquered me."

ILLUSTRATIONS OF THE TIMES NEWSPAPER.

ON MODERN APOSTATES.

————————— " Out of these convertites
There is much matter to be heard and learnt."—*As you like it.*

Dec. 15, 1816.

THIS is an age in which, to hear some people talk, you would suppose there is no such thing as literary prostitution or political apostacy, in the sense in which those vices used formerly to be practised and condemned. We live in a liberal age; and a very different and much more liberal turn has been given to the whole matter. Men do indeed change sides, but then it is proper at present that they should. They go from one extreme to another, they proceed to the utmost lengths of violence and abuse, both against the principles they formerly held and the persons they formerly agreed with; but then this is entirely owing to the force of reason and honest conviction. "All honourable men"—no hypocrites amongst them—

"But all is conscience and tender heart."

They have deserted the cause of liberty in as far as it deserted them; but no farther. No sinister motives, no disappointed expectations from a new order of things, no places to be got under the old, no laureatships, no editorships, no popular odium to contend with, no court-smiles to inveigle, have had any weight with them, or can be supposed to have had any. They could not tolerate wrong on any side, on the side of kings, or of the people. That's all. They have changed sides to preserve the integrity of their principles and the consistency of their characters. They have gone over to the strong side of the question, merely to shew the conscious purity of their motives; and they chose the moment of the total failure of all hopes from the weaker side to desert to the stronger, to put the matter out of all doubt. They are not only above corruption, but above suspicion. They have never once been at fault, have neither sneaked nor shuffled, botched or boggled, in their politics. They who were loud against the abuses of a principle which they set out with considering as sacred, the right of a people to chuse their own form of government, have not turned round to flatter and to screen, with the closeness of their fulsome embraces, the abuses of a power which they set out with treating as monstrous, the right of a discarded family to reign over a nation in perpetuity by the grace of God. They "whose love of liberty was of that dignity that it went hand in hand even with the vow they made this virgin bride," have not stooped to "commit whoredom greedily" with that old harlot, Despotism. They "who struck the foremost man of all this world but for supporting robbers," have not contaminated their fingers with base bribes, nor turned receivers of stolen goods for paltry knaves and licensed freebooters. Nice, scrupulous, firm, inflexible, uncorrupted, incapable of injustice or disguise; patriots in 1793, and royalists in 1816; at all times extreme and at all times consistent in their opinions; converts to the cause of kings, only because kings were converts (unaccountable converts) to the cause of the people: they have not become, nor are they in danger of becoming, thorough-paced time-servers, regular-bred courtiers, trammelled tools of despotism, hired pimps and panders of power. Nothing of the sort. They have not been made (not they) the overweening dupes of their own conceit and cunning. These political innocents have not, like the two poor devils in the *Recruiting Officer*, been laid hold of, entrapped, kidnapped, by that fell serjeant, Necessity, and then, in the height of their admiration of "the wonderful works of nature" and the King's picture, been enlisted for life in his Majesty's service, by some Court crimp, some Treasury scout in the shape of a well-bred baronet or booby Lord. Our maiden poets, patriots, and philanthropists, have not, it is to be hoped, like *Miss Lucy Lockitt*, been bilked of their virtue, "bamboozled and bit." They have got into a house of ill fame in the neighbourhood of Pall-Mall, like *Miss Clarissa Harlowe*, but they will defend their honour to the last gasp with their pens against that old bawd, Legitimacy, as she did hers with a penknife against the old Lady in Duke's place; or if the opiates and provocatives unfairly administered, and almost unavoidable when people get into such company and such situations, should for an instant rob them of what they hold most dear, their immaculate purity, they will, like Richardson's heroine, die a lingering death of grief and shame for the trick that has been played upon their unsuspecting credulity!—See, here comes one of them to answer for himself. It is the same person who in the year 1800 was for making an example of the whole House of Commons (in spite of the humble petition and remonstrance of the writer of this article in favour of a small minority), for being the echoes of the King's speeches for carrying on the war against the French Revolution. What is that *thing* he has in his hand? It is not, nor it cannot be, a sonnet to the King, celebrating his "royal fortitude," in having brought that war to a successful close fourteen years after!

"Such recantation had no charms for him,
"Nor could he brook it."

Nor is it the same consistent person whose deep-toned voice rebellows among the mountain echoes with peals of ideot rage and demon laughter—

"Proud Glaramara northward caught the sound,
"And Kirkstone tossed it from his misty head,
"That there was strange commotion in the hills,"—

at the infamy and madness of Sir Robert Wilson's gallant conduct in having rescued one of its victims from the fangs of that Bourbon despotism which that royal fortitude had restored.—Is not *that* Mr. Southey, with something of the glow on his cheek which he had in writing *Joan of Arc,* and with the beaked curl of his nose which provoked him to write the *Inscription on Old Sarum,* returning in disgrace from the Prince's Levee, for having indignantly noticed in one of his Birth-day Odes, Ferdinand's treatment of the Spanish Patriots?—Just yonder, at the corner of Paternoster-row, you may see Mr. Coleridge, the author of the eclogue called FIRE, FAMINE, AND SLAUGHTER, who has been to his bookseller's to withdraw his "Lay Sermon," or Statesman's Manual in praise of Fire, Slaughter, and Famine! But who is he "whose grief

Bears such an emphasis, whose phrase of sorrow
"Conjures the wandering stars, and makes them stand
"Like wonder-wounded hearers?"

'Tis the editor of *The Times,* (poor man, his virtuous indignation must cost him a great deal of pains and trouble!) as hard at it as ever, about liberty and independence without respect of persons; in a most *woundy* passion, we warrant now, at finding legitimacy at some of its old tricks, caught *flagranti delicto,* so that the poor gentleman could not hush the matter up, if he would, and would not, if he could, he is a man of such a nice morality, and such high notions of honour;—thrown into daily and hourly cold sweats and convulsions at the mention of daily and hourly acts of tyranny and base submission to it; flying into the same heats and hysterics as ever, for he has all the reason now, that he used to say he had; laying it on, thick and threefold, upon the magnanimous deliverers of Europe; still in the old King Cambyses' vein, "horrors on horror's head accumulating;" heaping up epithets and compound epithets of abuse against his new friends, as he used to do against his old ones, till Mr. Koenig's new press groans under the weight of both together; ordering in a new set of types with a new set of unheard-of nicknames to be applied everlastingly to the present candidates for newspaper fame, as the worn-out, feeble, and now insignificant ones of Monster, Tyrant, Fiend, Upstart, Usurper, Rebel, Regicide, Traitor, Wretch, Villain, Knave, Fool, Madman, Coward, Impostor, Unnatural Monster, Bloody Tyrant, Hellish Fiend, Corsican Upstart, Military Usurper, Wicked Rebel, Impious Regicide, Perfidious Traitor, Vile Wretch, Base Villain, Low-born Knave, Rank Fool, Egregious Madman, Notorious Coward, Detestable Impostor, were applied to the old; swearing as he picks his way to court along the streets, (so that the people ask who the honest, angry gentleman is) that Ferdinand alone has done more acts of baseness, treachery, cruelty, oppression, infamy, and ingratitude, in one year, than Napoleon did in his whole reign; teaching a parrot to call jade and rogue to all legitimate princes and princesses that deserve it, as he used himself to rail at all the illegitimate ones, whether they deserved it or not; repeating over and over, till he is black in the face, Dr. Slop's curse upon the Allies and their proceedings; cursing them in Spain, cursing them in Italy, cursing them in Genoa, cursing them in Saxony, cursing them in Norway, cursing them in Finland, cursing them in Poland, cursing them in France, cursing them every where as they deserve, and as the people every where curse them; sending the Pope and the Inquisition to the Devil; swooning at the extinction of Spanish liberty under the beloved Ferdinand; going into a shivering fit at the roasting of Protestants under Louis the Desired; biting his lips at Lord Castlereagh's

Letter to *Mon Prince;* horror-struck at the transfer of so many thousand souls, like so many head of horned cattle, from one legitimate proprietor of the species to another, after all his vapouring about the liberties of the people and the independence of states; learned and lofty, sad and solemn, on the Convention of Paris; looking big at the imposing attitude of Russia, and going stark staring mad at the application of the torture and the thumb-screw to the brave Cortes; gnashing his teeth, rolling his eyes, and dashing his head against the wall, at the total falsification, and overthrow of every one of his hopes and his prognostics in every corner of Europe where the Allies have got footing, and there is no corner which they have not got under their feet, like a toad under a harrow; and roaring out like Perillus's bull against the partitions and repartitions of the coalesced Sovereigns, their invasions, conquests, seizures, transfers of men and lands; the murders, massacres, imprisonments, pillagings, frauds, treacheries, breaches of written treaties and of verbal promises; usurpations, pretensions, and overt acts of legitimacy, since it was restored to itself, to one and the self-same tune that he used to lift up his voice, "his most sweet voice," against Bonaparte's wars and conquests, till the Stock Exchange was stunned with the clamour, and Mr. Walter well-nigh fainted! The only fault of this account is, that not one word of it is true.

> "Thy stone, oh Sisyphus, stands still:
> "Ixion rests upon his wheel!"

Once a Jacobin and always a Jacobin, is a maxim, which, notwithstanding Mr. Coleridge's see-saw reasoning to the contrary, we hold to be true, even of him to this day. *Once an Apostate and always an Apostate,* we hold to be equally true; and the reason why the last is true, is that the first is so. A person who is what is called a Jacobin (and we apply this term in its vulgarest sense to the persons here meant) that is, who has shaken off certain well-known prejudices with respect to kings or priests, or nobles, cannot so easily resume them again, whenever his pleasure or his convenience may prompt him to attempt it. And it is because he cannot resume them again in good earnest, that he endeavours to make up for his want of sincerity by violence, either by canting till he makes your soul sicken, like the author of *The Friend*, or by raving like a Bedlamite, as does the Editor of *The Times*. Why does he abuse Bonaparte and call him an upstart? Because he is himself, if he is any thing at all, an upstart; and because Bonaparte having got the start of him one way, he turned back to gain the race another, by trying for a court-livery, and to recommend himself to the house of Brunswick, by proclaiming the principles of the house of Stuart. Why does he make such a route about Kings and Queens, and Dukes and Duchesses, and old women of all ages and both sexes? Because he cares no more for them in his heart than we do. How should he? "What's Hecuba to him or he to Hecuba?" What motive has he, or what ground of passion, that he should

"Cleave the general ear with horrid speech,
"And, like a whore, unpack his heart with words!"

None in the world, any more than the poor player in *Hamlet*, who tried to "work his soul to his conceit, tears in his eyes, distraction in his looks," because it was his cue to do so. He blusters and hectors, and makes a noise to hide his want of consistency, as cowards turn bullies to hide their want of courage. He is virulent and vulgar in proportion as he is insincere; and yet it is the only way in which he can seem himself not to be a hypocrite. He has no blind prejudices to repose on; no unshaken principles to refer to; no hearty attachment to altars or to thrones. You see the Jacobinical leaven working in every line that he writes, and making strange havoc with his present professions. He would cashier Louis and Ferdinand, Alexander and Frederick, to-morrow, and hurl them headlong from their thrones with a stroke of his pen, for not complying with any one of his favourite dogmas. He has no regard for any thing but his own will; no feeling of any thing but of hatred to the cause he has deserted, and of the necessity of keeping from his mind, by every demonstration of outward scorn and horror, whatever might recal his old, unprofitable, exploded errors. His hatred and dread of the principles of others, proceeds from his greater hatred and dread of his own. The spectre of his former opinions glares perpetually near him, and provokes his frantic zeal. For close behind him stalks the ghost of the French Revolution, *that unfortunate Miss Bailey* of modern politicians, their mistress and their saint, what time

> ——"Society became their glittering bride
> "And airy hopes their children,"—

which, if he was once to turn round, would stare him in the face with self-conviction, and make his pen drop from his hands. It is this morbid conflict with his own feelings that many persons do not know what to make of, and which gives such a tragic, and at the same time, ludicrous air to his writings. He is obliged to wink and shut his apprehension up, so that he is blind, stupidly blind to all that makes against him, and all that makes for him. His understanding seems to labour under a quinsy; and instead of the little *bonnet rouge* of 1793, wears a huge pair of Bourbon blinkers for 1816. Hence the endless inconsistencies in which he involves himself; and as it is his self-will that makes him insensible to all objections, it is the same headstrong obstinacy which makes him regardless of contradictions, and proof against conviction.

In a word, to conclude this part of the subject, the writer of *The Times* is governed entirely by his will; and this faculty is strong, and bears sway in him, as all other principles are weak. He asserts a fact the louder, as he suspects it to be without proof: and defends a measure the more lustily, as he feels it to be mischievous. He listens only to his passions and his prejudices, not to truth or reason. Prove to him that any thing is the most idle fiction that ever was invented, and he will swear to it: prove to him that it is fraught with destruction to the liberties of mankind in all places and in all time to come, and he is your own for ever. *Sed hæc hactenus.* Goethe has given to one of his heroes this motto—"Mad but wise." We would give the following to the hero of *The Times*—Mad but not wise.

ILLUSTRATIONS OF "THE TIMES" NEWSPAPER.

ON MODERN LAWYERS AND POETS.

> ——————"Facilis descensus Averni;
> Noctes atque dies patet atri janua Ditis;
> Sed revocare gradum superasque evadere ad auras,
> Hoc opus, hic labor est."

December 22, 1816.

THE meaning of which passage is, that it is easier to sail with the stream, than to strive against it. Our classical reformers should have known this passage in Virgil. They should have known themselves too; but they did not. "Let no man go about to cozen honesty," or to be a knave by halves. The man, as well as the woman, who deliberates between his principle and the price of its sacrifice, is lost. The same rule holds with respect to literary as to any other kind of prostitution. It is the first false step that always costs the most; and which is, for that reason, always fatal. It requires an effort of resolution, or at least obstinate prejudice, for a man to maintain his opinions at the expense of his interest. But it requires a much greater effort of resolution for a man to give up his interest to recover his independence; because, with the consistency of his character, he has lost the habitual energy of his mind, and the indirect aid of prejudice and obstinacy, which are sometimes as useful to virtue as they are to vice. A man, in adhering to his principles in contradiction to the decisions of the world, has many disadvantages. He has nothing to support him but the supposed sense of right;

and any defect in the justice of his cause, or the force of his conviction, must prey on his mind, in proportion to the delicacy and sensitiveness of its texture: he is left alone in his opinions; and, like *Sam Sharpset*, in Mr. Morton's new comedy (when he gets into solitary confinement in the spunging-house,) grows nervous, melancholy, fantastical, and would be glad of *somebody* or *anybody* to sympathize with him; but when he has once gone over to the strong side of the question (perhaps from these very scruples of conscience, suggested by weakness and melancholy, as "the Devil is very potent with such spirits, and abuses them to damn them") our wavering sceptic no longer finds the same scruples troublesome; the air of a court promotes their digestion wonderfully; the load on his conscience falls off at the foot of the throne. The poet-laureate, standing with his laurel-wreath amidst "Britain's warriors, her statesmen, and her fair," thinks no more or says no more about the patriots of Spain pining in dungeons or consigned to the torture, though it was his zeal, his virtuous, patriotic, romantic, disinterested zeal for them, which brought *them* there, and him to court. His Prince's smile soothes the involuntary pang of sympathy rising in his breast; and Mr. Croker's whispers drown their agonizing shrieks. When we are at Rome, we must do as the people at Rome do. A man in a crowd must go along with the crowd, and cannot stop to pick his way; nor need he be so particular about it. He has friends to back him: appearances are for him; the world is on his side; his interest becomes surety for his honour, his vanity makes him blind to objections, or overrules them, and he is not so much ashamed of being in the wrong in such good company. It requires some fortitude to oppose one's opinion, however right, to that of all the world besides; none at all to agree with it, however wrong. Nothing but the strongest and clearest conviction can support a man in a losing minority: any excuse or quibble is sufficient to salve his conscience, when he has made sure of the main chance, and his understanding has become the stalking-horse of his ambition. It is this single circumstance of not being answerable for one's opinions one's-self, but being able to put them off to other men's shoulders in all crowds and collections of men, that is the reason of the violence of mobs, the venality of courts, and the corruption of all corporate bodies. It is also the reason of the degeneracy of modern apostates and reformed Jacobins, who find the applause of their king and country doubly cheering after being so long without it, and who go all lengths in adulation and servility, to make up for their former awkward singularity.

Many of the persons we have known, who have deserted the cause of the people to take a high tone against those who did not chuse to desert it, have been lawyers or poets. The last took their leave of it by a poetic license; the first slunk out of it by some loop-hole of the law. We shall say a word of each.

"Our's is an honest employment," says *Peachum*; "and so is a lawyer's." It is a lawyer's business to confound truth and falsehood in the minds of his hearers; and the natural consequence is, that he confounds them in his own. He takes his opinion of right and wrong from his brief: his soul is in his fee. His understanding is *upon the town*, and at the service of any cause that is paid for beforehand. He is not a hired suborner of *facts*, but of *reasons;* and though he would not violate the sacred obligation of an oath, as Lord Ellenborough calls it, by swearing that black is white, he holds himself at all times in readiness and bound in duty, to prove it so. He will not swear to an untruth to get himself hanged, but he will assert it roundly by the hour together to hang other persons, however innocent,—if he finds it in his retainer. We do not wish to say any thing illiberal of any profession or set of men in the abstract. But we think it possible, that they who are employed to argue away men's lives at a venture in a court of justice, may be tempted to write them away deliberately in a newspaper. They who find it consistent with their honour to do this under the sanction of the court, may find it to their interest to do the same thing at the suggestion of a court. A lawyer is a sophist by profession; that is, a person who barters his opinion, and speaks what he knows to be false in defence of wrong, and to the prejudice of right. Not only the confirmed habit of looking at any side of a question with a view to make the worse appear the better reason, from a motive always foreign to the question itself, must make truth and falsehood sit loose upon him, and lead him to "look on both indifferently," as his convenience prompts; but the quibbles and quillets of the law give a handle to all that is petty and perverse in his understanding, and enable him to tamper with his principles with impunity. Thus the intricacy and verbal distinctions of the profession promote the practical duplicity of its professors; and folly and knavery become joint securities for one another. The bent of a lawyer's mind is to pervert his talents, if he has any, and to keep down his feelings, if they are at all in his way. He lives by forging and uttering counterfeit pretexts; he says not what he believes to be true, but any thing that by any trick or sleight he can make others believe; and the more petty, artificial, and far-fetched the contrivance, the more low, contemptible, and desperate the shift, the more is he admired and cried up in his profession. A perfect lawyer is one whose understanding always keeps pace with the inability of words to keep pace with ideas: who by natural conformation of mind cannot get beyond the letter to the spirit of any thing; who, by a happy infirmity of soul, is sure never to lose the form in grasping at the substance. Such a one is sure to arrive at the head of his profession! Look at the lawyers in the House of Commons (of course at the head of their profession)—look at Garrow. We have heard him stringing contradictions there with the fluency of water, every third sentence giving the lie to the two former; gabbling folly as if it were the last opportunity he might ever have, and as regularly put down as he rose up—not for false statements, not for false reasoning, not for common-place absurdities or vulgar prejudices, (there is enough of these to be found there without going to the bar), but for such things as nobody but a lawyer could utter, and as nobody (not even a lawyer) could believe. The only thing that ever gave us a good opinion of the House of Commons was to see the contempt with which they treat lawyers there. The reason is, that no one there but a lawyer fancies himself holding a brief in his hand as a *carte blanche* for vanity and impertinence—no one else thinks he has got an *ad libitum* right to express any absurd or nonsensical opinions he pleases, because he is not supposed to hold the opinions he expresses—no one else thinks it necessary to confound the distinctions of common-sense to subject them to those of the law (even Lord Castlereagh would never think of maintaining it to be lawful to detain a person kidnapped from France, on the special plea, that the law in that case *not provided* had *not declared* it lawful to detain persons so kidnapped, if not reclaimed by their own country)—no one else thinks of huddling contradictions into self-evident truths by legal volubility, or of sharpening nonsense into sense by legal acuteness, or of covering shallow assumptions under the solemn disguises of the long robe. The opinions of the gentlemen of the bar go for nothing in the House of Commons: but their votes tell; and are always sure—in the end! The want of principle makes up for the want of talent. What a tool in the hands of a minister is a whole profession, habitually callous to the distinctions of right and wrong, but perfectly alive to their own interest, with just ingenuity enough to be able to trump up some fib or sophistry for or against any measure, and with just understanding enough to see no more of the real nature or consequences of any measure than suits their own or their employer's convenience! What an acquisition to "the tried wisdom of parliament" in the approaching hard season!

But all this, though true, seems to fall short of the subject before us. The weak side of the professional character is rather an indifference to truth and justice, than an outrageous and inveterate hatred to them. They are chargeable, as a general class of men, with levity, servility, and selfishness; but it seems to be quite out of their character to commence furious and illiberal fanatics against those who have more principle than themselves. But not when this character is ingrafted on that of a true Jacobin renegado. Such a person (and no one else) would be fit to write the leading article in *The Times*. It is this union of rare accomplishments (there seems, after all, to be nothing contradictory in the coalition of the vices) that enables that non-descript person to blend the violence of the bravo with the subtlety of a pettifogging attorney—to interlard his furious appeals to the lowest passions of the middle and upper classes, with nice points of law, reserved for the opinion of the adepts in the profession—to appeal to the passions of his city readers when any thing wrong is to be done, and to their cooler and dispassionate judgments when any thing right is to be done—that makes him stick (spell-bound) to the letter of the law when it is in his favour, and set every principle of justice and humanity at defiance when it interferes with his pragmatical opinion—that makes him disregard all decency as well as reason out of "the lodged hatred" he bears to the cause he has deserted, and to all who have not, like himself, deserted it—that made him urge the foul death of the brave Marshal Ney, by putting a legal interpretation on a military convention—that tempted him to make out his sanguinary list of proscribed rebels and regicides (he was not for making out any such list in the year 1793, nor long after the event he now deplores with such well-timed indignation)—that makes him desperately bent on hanging wretches at home in cobweb chains spun from his own brains—that makes him stake the liberty of nations or the independence of states on a nickname or a law-quillet, as his irritable humour or professional habits prevail—that sets him free from all restraints or deference to others in forming his own opinions, and which would induce him to subject all the rest of the world to his unprincipled and frantic dogmas, by entangling them in the quirks and technicalities of the law! No one else would heroically consign a whole continent to the most odious and despicable slavery in the world, on the strength of a flaw in a proclamation: or call that piece of diplomatic atrocity, the declaration of the 25th of March, a *delicious* declaration. Such a man might sell his country, or enslave his species, and justify it to his conscience and the world by some law-term! Such men are very dangerous, unless when they are tied up in the forms of a profession, where form is opposed to form, where no-meaning baffles want of sense, and where no great harm is done, because there is not much to do: but when chicane and want of principle are let loose upon the world, " with famine, sword, and fire at their heels, leashed in like hounds," when they have their prey marked out for them by the passions, when they are backed by force—when the pen of the Editor of *The Times* is seconded by eleven hundred thousand bayonets—then such men are very mischievous.

" My soul, turn from them: turn we to survey" where poetry, joined hand in hand with liberty, renews the golden age in 1793, during the reign of Robespierre, which was hardly thought a blot in their escutcheon, by those who said and said truly, for what we know, that he destroyed the lives of hundreds, to save the lives of thousands: (Mark; then, as now, " Carnage was the daughter of Humanity." It is true, these men have changed sides, but not parted with their principles, that is, with their presumption and egotism)—let us turn where Pantisocracy's equal hills and vales arise in visionary pomp, where Peace and Truth have kissed each other " in Philarmonia's undivided dale;" and let us see whether the fictions and the forms of poetry give any better assurance of political consistency than the fictions and forms of law.

The spirit of poetry is in itself favourable to humanity and liberty: but, we suspect, not in times like these—not in the present reign. The spirit of poetry is not the spirit of mortification or of martyrdom. Poetry dwells in a perpetual Utopia of its own, and is, for that reason, very ill calculated to make a Paradise upon earth, by encountering the shocks and disappointments of the world. Poetry, like the law, is a fiction; only a more agreeable one. It does not create difficulties where they do not exist; but contrives to get rid of them, whether they exist or not. It is not entangled in cobwebs of its own making, but soars above all obstacles. It cannot be " constrained by mastery." It has the range of the universe; it traverses the empyreum, and looks down on nature from a higher sphere. When it lights upon the earth, it loses some of its dignity and its use. Its strength is in its wings; its element the air. Standing on its feet, jostling with the crowd, it is liable to be overthrown, trampled on, and defaced; for its wings are of a dazzling brightness, "heaven's own tinct," and the least soil upon them shews to disadvantage. Sunk, degraded as we have seen it, we shall not insult over it, but leave it to time to take out the stains, seeing it is a thing immortal as itself. "Being so majestical, we should do it wrong to offer it but the shew of violence." But the best things, in their abuse, often become the worst; and so it is with poetry when it is diverted from its proper end. Poets live in an ideal world, where they make every thing out according to their wishes and fancies. They either find things delightful, or make them so. They feign the beautiful and grand out of their own minds, and imagine all things to be, not what they are, but what they ought to be. They are naturally inventors, creators not of truth but beauty: and while they speak to us from the sacred shrine of their own hearts, while they pour out the pure treasures of thought to the world, they cannot be too much admired and applauded: but when, forgetting their high calling, and becoming tools and puppets in the hands of others, they would pass off the gewgaws of corruption and love-tokens of self-interest, as the gifts of the Muse, they cannot be too much despised and shunned. We do not like novels founded on facts, nor do we like poets turned courtiers. Poets, it has been said, succeed best in fiction: and they should for the most part stick to it. Invention, not upon an imaginary subject, is a lie: the varnishing over the vices or deformity of actual objects, is hypocrisy. Players leave their finery at the stage-door, or they would be hooted: poets come out into the world with all their bravery on, and yet they would pass for *bonâ fide* persons. They lend the colours of fancy to whatever they see: whatever they touch becomes gold, though it were lead. With them every Joan is a lady: and kings and queens are human. Matters of fact they embellish at their will, and reason is the plaything of their passions, their caprice, or interest. There is no practice so base of which they will not become the panders: no sophistry of which their understanding may not be made the voluntary dupe. Their only object is to please their fancy. Their souls are effeminate, half man and half woman: they want fortitude, and are without principle. If things do not turn out according to their wishes, they will make their wishes turn round to things. They can easily overlook whatever they do not approve, and make an idol of any thing they please. The object of poetry is to please: this art naturally gives pleasure, and excites admiration. Poets, therefore, cannot do well without sympathy and flattery. It is, accordingly, very much against the grain that they remain long on the unpopular side of the question. They do not like to be shut out when laurels are to be given away at court—or places under government to be disposed of, in romantic situations in the country. They are happy to be reconciled on the first opportunity to prince and people, and to exchange their principles for a pension. They have not always strength of mind to think for themselves; nor honesty enough to bear the unjust stigma of the opinions they have taken upon trust from others. Truth alone does not satisfy their pampered appetites, without the sauce of praise. To prefer truth to all other things, it requires that the mind should have been at some pains in finding it out, and that it should feel a severe delight in the contemplation of truth, seen by its own clear light, and not as it is reflected in the admiring eyes of the world. A philosopher may perhaps make a shift to be contented with the sober draughts of reason: a poet must have the applause of the world to intoxicate him. Milton was however a poet, and an honest man; he was Cromwell's secretary.

We have here described the spirit of poetry when it comes in contact with the spirit of the world. Let us see what results from it when it comes in contact with the spirit of Jacobinism. The spirit of Jacobinism is essentially at variance with the spirit of poetry: it has "no figures nor no fantasies," which the prejudices of superstition or the world draw in the brains of men: "no trivial fond records:" it levels all distinctions of art and nature: it has no pride, pomp, or circumstance, belonging to it; it converts the whole principle of admiration in the poet (which is the essence of poetry) into admiration of himself. The spirit of Jacobin poetry is rank egotism. We know an instance. It is of a person who founded a school of poetry on sheer humanity, on ideot boys and mad mothers, and on Simon Lee, the old huntsman. The secret of the Jacobin poetry and the anti-jacobin politics of this writer is the same. His lyrical poetry was a cant of humanity about the commonest people to level the great with the small; and his political poetry is a cant of loyalty to level Bonaparte with kings and hereditary imbecility. As he would put up the commonest of men against kings and nobles, to satisfy his levelling notions, so for the same reason, he would set up the meanest of kings against the greatest of men, reposing once more on the mediocrity of royalty. This person admires nothing that is admirable, feels no interest in any thing interesting, no grandeur in any thing grand, no beauty in any thing beautiful. He tolerates nothing but what he himself creates; he sympathizes only with what can enter into no competition with him, with "the bare earth and mountains bare, and grass in the green field." He sees nothing but himself and the universe. He hates all greatness, and all pretensions to it but his own. His egotism is in this respect a madness; for he scorns even the admiration of himself, thinking it a presumption in any one to suppose that he has taste or sense enough to understand him. He hates all science and all art; he hates chemistry, he hates conchology; he hates Sir Isaac Newton; he hates logic, he hates metaphysics, which he says are unintelligible, and yet he would be thought to understand them; he hates prose, he hates all poetry but his own; he hates Shakespeare, or what he calls "those interlocutions between Lucius and Caius," because he would have all the talk to himself, and considers the movements of passion in *Lear*, *Othello*, or *Macbeth*, as impertinent, compared with the Moods of his own

Mind; he thinks every thing good is contained in the "Lyrical Ballads," or, if it is not contained there, it is good for nothing; he hates music, dancing, and painting; he hates Rubens, he hates Rembrandt, he hates Raphael, he hates Titian, he hates Vandyke; he hates the antique; he hates the Apollo Belvidere; he hates the Venus de Medicis. He hates all that others love and admire but himself. He is glad that Bonaparte is sent to St. Helena, and that the Louvre is dispersed for the same reason —to get rid of the idea of any thing greater, or thought greater than himself. The Bourbons, and their processions of the Holy Ghost, give no disturbance to his vanity; and he therefore gives them none.

THE TIMES NEWSPAPER.

ON THE CONNEXION BETWEEN TOAD-EATERS AND TYRANTS.

"Doubtless, the pleasure is as great
"In being cheated as to cheat."

Jan. 12, 1817.

We some time ago promised our friend, Mr. Robert Owen, an explanation of some of the causes which impede the natural progress of liberty and human happiness. We have in part redeemed this pledge in what we said about *Coriolanus*, and we shall try in this article to redeem it still more. We grant to our ingenious and romantic friend, that the progress of knowledge and civilization is in itself favourable to liberty and equality, and that the general stream of thought and opinion constantly sets in this way, till power finds the tide of public feeling becoming too strong for it, ready to sap its rotten foundations, and "bore through its castle-walls;" and then it contrives to turn the tide of knowledge and sentiment clean the contrary way, and either bribes human reason to take part against human nature, or knocks it on the head by a more summary process. Thus, in the year

1792, Mr. Burke became a pensioner for writing his book against the French Revolution, and Mr. Thomas Paine was outlawed for his *Rights of Man*. Since that period, the press has been the great enemy of freedom, the whole weight of that immense engine (for the purposes of good or ill) having a fatal bias given to it by the two main springs of fear and favour.

The weak sides of human intellect, by which power effects its conversion to the worst purposes, when it finds the exercise of free opinion inconsistent with the existence and uncontrouled exercise of arbitrary power, are these four, *viz.* the grossness of the imagination, which is seduced by outward appearances from the pursuit of real ultimate good; the subtlety of the understanding itself, which palliates by flimsy sophistry the most flagrant abuses; interest and advancement in the world; and lastly, the feuds and jealousies of literary men among one another. There is no class of persons so little calculated to act in *corps* as literary men. All their views are recluse and separate (for the mind acts by individual energy, and not by numbers): their motives, whether good or bad, are personal to themselves, their vanity exclusive, their love of truth independent; they exist not by the preservation, but the destruction of their own species; they are governed not by the spirit of unanimity, but of contradiction. They will hardly allow any thing to be right or any thing to be wrong, unless they are the first to find out that it is so; and are ready to prove the best things in the world the worst, and the worst the best, from the pure impulse of splenetic over-weening self-opinion, much more if they are likely to be well paid for it—not that interest is their ruling passion, but still it operates, silent and unseen, with them as with other men, when it can make a compromise with their vanity. This part of the character of men of letters is so well known, that Shakespear makes *Brutus* protest against the fitness of *Cicero* to be included in their enterprize on this very principle:—

> "Oh, name him not: let us not break with him;
> For he will never follow any thing,
> That other men begin."

The whole of Mr. Burke's *Reflections on the French Revolution* *
is but an elaborate and damning comment on this short text.
He quarrelled with the French Revolution out of spite to Rousseau, the spark of whose genius had kindled the flame of liberty in a nation. He therefore endeavoured to extinguish the flame—to put out the light; and he succeeded, because there were others like himself, ready to sacrifice every manly and generous principle to the morbid, sickly, effeminate, little, selfish, irritable, dirty spirit of authorship. Not only did such persons, according to Mr. Coleridge's valuable and competent testimony (see his *Lay-Sermon*) make the distinction between Atheism and Religion a mere stalking-horse for the indulgence of their idle vanity, but they made the other questions of Liberty and Slavery, of the Rights of Man, or the Divine Right of Kings to rule millions of men as their Slaves for ever, they made these vital and paramount questions (which whoever wilfully and knowingly compromises, is a traitor to himself and his species), subordinate to the low, whiffling, contemptible gratification of their literary jealousy. We shall not go over the painful list of instances; neither can we forget them. But they all or almost all contrived to sneak over one by one to the side on which "empty praise or solid pudding" was to be got; they could not live without the smiles of the great (not they), nor provide for an increasing establishment without a loss of character; instead of going into some profitable business and exchanging their lyres for ledgers, their pens for the plough (the honest road to riches), they chose rather to prostitute their pens to the mock-heroic defence of the most bare-faced of all mummeries, the pretended alliance of kings and people! We told them how it would be, if they succeeded; it has turned out just as we said; and a pretty figure do these companions of Ulysses *(Compagnons du Lys)*, these gaping converts to despotism, these

* When this work was first published, the King had copies of it bound in Morocco, and gave them away to his favourite courtiers, saying, "It was a book which every gentleman ought to read."

well-fed victims of the charms of the Bourbons, now make, nestling under their laurels in the stye of Corruption, and sunk in torpid repose (from which they do not like to be disturbed by calling on their former names or professions), in lazy sinecures and good warm births! Such is the history and mystery of literary patriotism and prostitution for the last twenty years.—Power is subject to none of these disadvantages. It is one and indivisible; it is self-centered, self-willed, incorrigible, inaccessible to temptation or entreaty; interest is on its side, passion is on its side, prejudice is on its side, the name of religion is on its side; the qualms of conscience it is not subject to, for it is iron-nerved; humanity it is proof against, for it sets itself up above humanity; reason it does not hearken to, except that reason which panders to its will and flatters its pride. It pursues its steady way, its undeviating everlasting course, "unslacked of motion," like that foul Indian idol, the Jaggernaut, and crushes poor upstart poets, patriots, and philosophers (the beings of an hour) and the successive never-ending generations of fools and knaves, beneath its feet; and mankind bow their willing necks to the yoke, and eagerly consign their children and their children's children to be torn in pieces by its scythe, or trampled to death by the gay, gaudy, painted, blood-stained wheels of the grim idol of power!

Such is the state of the Eastern world, where the inherent baseness of man's nature, and his tendency to social order, to tyrannize and to be tyrannized over, has had full time to develope itself. Our turn seems next. We are but just setting out, it is true, in this bye-nook and corner of the world—but just recovering from the effects of the Revolution of 1688, and the defeated Rebellions of the years 1715 and 1745, but we need hardly despair under the auspices of the Editor of *The Times*, and with the example of the defeat "of the last successful instance of a democratic rebellion," by the second restoration of the Bourbons, before our eyes and close under our noses. Mr. Owen may think the example of New Lanark more inviting, but the persons to whom he has dedicated his work turn their eyes another way!*

Man is a toad-eating animal. The admiration of power in others is as common to man as the love of it in himself: the one makes him a tyrant, the other a slave. It is not he alone, who wears the golden crown, that is proud of it: the wretch who pines in a dungeon, and in chains, is dazzled with it; and if he could but shake off his own fetters, would care little about the wretches whom he left behind him, so that he might have an opportunity, on being set free himself, of gazing at this glittering gew-gaw "on some high holiday of once a year." The slave, who has no other hope or consolation, clings to the apparition of royal magnificence, which insults his misery and his despair; stares through the hollow eyes of famine at the insolence of pride and luxury which has occasioned it, and hugs his chains the closer, because he has nothing else left. The French, under the old regime, made the glory of their *Grand Monarque* a set-off against rags and hunger, equally satisfied with *shows or bread;* and the poor Spaniard, delivered from temporary to permanent oppression, looks up once more with pious awe, to the time-hallowed towers of the Holy Inquisition. As the herd of mankind are stripped of every thing, in body and mind, so are they thankful for what is left; as is the desolation of their hearts and the wreck of their little all, so is the pomp and pride which is built upon their ruin, and their fawning admiration of it.

"I've heard of hearts unkind, kind deeds
With coldness still returning:

* Our loyal Editor used to bluster a great deal some time ago about putting down James Madison, and "the last example of democratic rebellion in America." In this he was consistent and logical. Could he not, however, find out another example of this same principle, by going a little farther back in history, and coming a little nearer home? If he has forgotten this chapter in our history, others who have profited more by it have not. He may understand what we mean, by turning to the story of the two elder Blifils in *Tom Jones.*

Alas! the gratitude of men
Has oftener set me mourning." *

There is something in the human mind, which requires an object for it to repose on; and, driven from all other sources of pride or pleasure, it falls in love with misery, and grows enamoured of oppression. It gazes after the liberty, the happiness, the comfort, the knowledge, which have been torn from it by the unfeeling gripe of wealth and power, as the poor debtor gazes with envy and wonder at the Lord Mayor's show. Thus is the world by degrees reduced to a spital or lazar-house, where the people waste away with want and disease, and are thankful if they are only suffered to crawl forgotten to their graves. Just in proportion to the systematic tyranny exercised over a nation, to its loss of a sense of freedom and the spirit of resistance, will be its loyalty; the most abject submission will always be rendered to the most confirmed despotism. The most wretched slaves are the veriest sycophants. The lacquey, mounted behind his master's coach, looks down with contempt upon the mob, forgetting his own origin and his actual situation, and comparing them only with that standard of gentility which he has perpetually in his eye. The hireling of the press (a still meaner slave) wears his livery, and is proud of it. He measures the greatness of others by his own meanness; their lofty pretensions indemnify him for his servility; he magnifies the sacredness of their persons to cover the laxity of his own principles. He offers up his own humanity, and that of all men, at the shrine of royalty. He sneaks to court; and the bland accents of power close his ears to the voice of freedom ever after; its velvet touch makes his heart marble to a people's sufferings. He is the intellectual pimp of power, as

* *Simon Lee, the old Huntsman*, a tale by Mr. Wordsworth, of which he himself says,

"It is no tale, but if you think,
Perhaps a tale you'll make it."

In this view it is a tale indeed, not "of other times," but of these.

others are the practical ones of the pleasures of the great, and often on the same disinterested principle. For one tyrant, there are a thousand ready slaves. Man is naturally a worshipper of idols and a lover of kings. It is the excess of individual power, that strikes and gains over his imagination: the general misery and degradation which are the necessary consequences of it, are spread too wide, they lie too deep, their weight and import are too great, to appeal to any but the slow, inert, speculative, imperfect faculty of reason. The cause of liberty is lost in its own truth and magnitude; while the cause of despotism flourishes, triumphs, and is irresistible in the gross mixture, the *Belle Alliance*, of pride and ignorance.

Power is the grim idol that the world adore; that arms itself with destruction, and reigns by terror in the coward heart of man; that dazzles the senses, haunts the imagination, confounds the understanding, and tames the will, by the vastness of its pretensions, and the very hopelessness of resistance to them. Nay more, the more mischievous and extensive the tyranny—the longer it has lasted, and the longer it is likely to last—the stronger is the hold it takes of the minds of its victims, the devotion to it increasing with the dread. It does not satisfy the enormity of the appetite for servility, till it has slain the mind of a nation, and becomes like the evil principle of the universe, from which there is no escape. So in some countries, the most destructive animals are held sacred, despair and terror completely overpowering reason. The prejudices of superstition (religion is another name for fear) are always the strongest in favour of those forms of worship which require the most bloody sacrifices; the foulest idols are those which are approached with the greatest awe; for it should seem that those objects are the most sacred to passion and imagination, which are the most revolting to reason and common sense. No wonder that the Editor of *The Times* bows his head before the idol of Divine Right, or of Legitimacy, (as he calls it) which has had more lives sacrificed to its ridiculous and unintelligible pretensions, in the last twenty-five years, than were ever sacrificed to any other idol in all preceding ages. Never was there any thing so well contrived as this fiction of Legitimacy, to suit the fastidious delicacy of modern sycophants. It hits their grovelling servility and petulant egotism exactly between wind and water. The contrivers or re-modellers of this idol, beat all other idol-mongers, whether Jews, Gentiles or Christians, hollow. The principle of all idolatry is the same: it is the want of something to admire, without knowing what or why: it is the love of an effect without a cause; it is a voluntary tribute of admiration which does not compromise our vanity: it is setting something up over all the rest of the world, to which we feel ourselves to be superior, for it is our own handy-work; so that the more perverse the homage we pay to it, the more it pampers our self-will: the meaner the object, the more magnificent and pompous the attributes we bestow upon it; the greater the lie, the more enthusiastically it is believed and greedily swallowed:—

> " Of whatsoever race his godhead be,
> Stock, stone, or other homely pedigree,
> In his defence his servants are as bold
> As if he had been made of beaten gold."

In this inverted ratio, the bungling impostors of former times, and less refined countries, got no further than stocks and stones: their utmost stretch of refinement in absurdity went no further than to select the most mischievous animals or the most worthless objects for the adoration of their besotted votaries: but the framers of the new law-fiction of legitimacy have started a nonentity. The ancients sometimes worshipped the sun or stars, or deified heroes and great men: the moderns have found out the image of the divinity in Louis XVIII.! They have set up an object for their idolatry, which they themselves must laugh at, if hypocrisy were not with them the most serious thing in the world. They offer up thirty millions of men to it as its victims, and yet they know that it is nothing but a scare-crow to keep the world in subjection to their renegado whimsies and preposterous hatred of the liberty and happiness of mankind. They do not think kings gods, but they make believe that they do so, to degrade their fellows to the rank of brutes. Legitimacy answers every object of their meanness and malice—*omne tulit punctum.*—This mock-doctrine, this little Hunchback, which our resurrection-men, the Humane Society of Divine Right, have foisted on the altar of Liberty, is not only a phantom of the imagination, but a contradiction in terms; it is a prejudice, but an exploded prejudice; it is an imposture, that imposes on nobody; it is powerful only in impotence, safe in absurdity, courted from fear and hatred, a dead prejudice linked to the living mind; the sink of honour, the grave of liberty, a palsy in the heart of a nation; it claims the species as its property, and derives its right neither from God nor man; not from the authority of the Church, which it treats cavalierly, and yet in contempt of the will of the people, which it scouts as opposed to its own: its two chief supporters are, the sword of the Duke of Wellington and the pen of the Editor of *The Times!* The last of these props has, we understand, just failed it.

We formerly gave the Editor of *The Times* a definition of a true Jacobin, as one "who had seen the evening star set over a poor man's cottage, and connected it with the hope of human happiness." The city-politician laughed this pastoral definition to scorn, and nicknamed the person who had very innocently laid it down, "the true Jacobin who writes in the Chronicle,"—a nickname by which we profited as little as he has by our Illustrations. Since that time our imagination has grown a little less romantic: so we will give him another, which he may chew the cud upon at his leisure. A true Jacobin, then, is one who does not believe in the divine right of kings, or in any other *alias* for it, which implies that they reign "in contempt of the will of the people;" and he holds all such kings to be tyrants, and their subjects slaves. To be a true Jacobin, a man must be a good hater; but this is the most difficult and the least amiable of all the virtues: the most trying and the most thankless of all tasks. The love of liberty consists in the hatred of tyrants. The true Jacobin hates the enemies of liberty as they hate liberty, with all his strength and with all his might, and with all his heart and with all his soul. His memory is as long, and his will as strong as theirs, though his hands are shorter. He never forgets or forgives an injury done to the people, for tyrants never forget or forgive one done to themselves. There is no love lost between them. He does not leave them the sole benefit of their old motto, *Odia in longum jaciens quæ conderet auctaque promeret.* He makes neither peace nor truce with them. His hatred of wrong only ceases with the wrong. The sense of it, and of the barefaced assumption of the right to inflict it, deprives him of his rest. It stagnates in his blood. It loads his heart with aspics' tongues, deadly to venal pens. It settles in his brain—it puts him beside himself. Who will not feel all this for a girl, a toy, a turn of the dice, a word, a blow, for any thing relating to himself; and will not the friend of liberty feel as much for mankind? The love of truth is a passion in his mind, as the love of power is a passion in the minds of others. Abstract reason, unassisted by passion, is no match for power and prejudice, armed with force and cunning. The love of liberty is the love of others; the love of power is the love of ourselves. The one is real; the other often but an empty dream. Hence the defection of modern apostates. While they are looking about, wavering and distracted, in pursuit of universal good or universal fame, the eye of power is upon them, like the eye of Providence, that neither slumbers nor sleeps, and that watches but for one object, its own good. They take no notice of it at first, but it is still upon them, and never off them. It at length catches theirs, and they bow to its sacred light; and like the poor fluttering bird, quail beneath it, are seized with a vertigo, and drop senseless into its jaws, that close upon them for ever, and so we see no more of them, which is well.

"And we saw three poets in a dream, walking up and down on the face of the earth, and holding in their hands a human heart, which, as they raised their eyes to heaven, they kissed and worshipped; and a mighty shout arose and shook the air, for the towers of the Bastile had fallen, and a nation had become, of slaves, freemen; and the three poets, as they heard the sound, leaped and shouted, and made merry, and their voice was choaked with tears of joy, which they shed over the human heart, which they kissed and worshipped. And not long after, we saw the same three poets, the one with a receipt-stamp in his hand, the other with a laurel on his head, and the third with a symbol which we could make nothing of, for it was neither literal nor allegorical, following in the train of the Pope and the Inquisition and the Bourbons, and worshipping the mark of the Beast, with the emblem of the human heart thrown beneath their feet, which they trampled and spit upon!"—This apologue is not worth finishing, nor are the people to whom it relates worth talking of. We have done with them.

INTERESTING FACTS *relating to the Fall and Death of Joachim Murat, King of Naples; the Capitulation of Paris in* 1815; *and the Second Restoration of the Bourbons: Original Letters from King Joachim to the Author, with some Account of the Author, and of his Persecution by the French Government. By* Francis Macirone, *late Aid-de-camp to King Joachim; Knight of the Order of the Two Sicilies, &c. &c.* London: Ridgways, 1817.

"Come, draw the curtain; shew the picture."

February 2, 1817.

WE have here a pretty peep behind "the dark blanket" of Legitimacy. We thank Mr. Macirone for having introduced us once more to the old lady of that name in her dressing-room. What a tissue of patches and of paint! What a quantity of wrinkles and of proud flesh! What a collection of sickly perfumes and slow poisons, with her love-powders and the assassin's knife placed side by side! What treacheries and lies upon her tongue! What meanness and malice in her heart! What an old hypocritical hag it is! What a vile canting, mumbling, mischievous witch! "Pah! and smells so." The very wind that kisses all it meets, stops the nose at her. We wonder how any prince should take a fancy to such an old rotten demirep! Yet this is the heroine of all heroines (Mr. Southey will tell you in hobbling illegitimate verse), a greater heroine than even *his* Joan of Arc—the heroine of Leipsic, of Saragossa, and of Waterloo! It is indeed the same. Look at her again, look at her well, look at her closely, and you will find that it is "that harlot old,"

"The same that was, that is, and is to be;"—

the mother of abominations, the daughter of lies. Dig up the bones of a few of her wretched favourites you may, in Carmelite dresses or any other trumpery; but can you dig up the bones of the men that she has murdered, from the earliest time? can you collect the blood of the millions of men that she has sacrificed in the last twenty-five years alone, and pour it into the Thames, while our merchant-men ride freighted with gold upon the gory stream, and the Editor of *The Times* (without being called to account for it) applauds with the "sweet thunder" of his pen the proud balance of our exports and our imports, blood and gold? or can you collect the sighs and dried-up tears of wretches that she, Legitimacy, has doomed to pine without a cause in dungeons, to prove that she is the dread sovereign of the human heart? or the groans and shrieks of victims stretched on the rack, or consumed by slow fire, to prove that the minds of men belong to her? or the cries of hunger and pinching cold, the sweat, the rags, the diseases, the emaciated wan looks, by which she proves that the bodies of men are her's? or can you conjure up the wide spreading desolation which she breathes from her nostrils, the famine and pestilence which she scatters before her for her sport and wantonness, the ruins of cities and of countries which she makes her throne, and from which, amidst the groans of the dying and the dead, she utters, laughing, the sacred doctrine of "millions made for one!"—One thing contents us, and sits light upon our hearts, that we have always seen through her disguises: we have known her from first to last, though "she has changed shapes with Proteus," and now gone by the name of Religion, now of Social Order, now of Morality, now been personified at Guildhall as Trade and Commerce, or sat in the Speaker's chair as the English Constitution (the most impudent trick of all)—under none of these respectable alias's and swindling characters, nor when she towered above the conflagration of Moscow, *dressed in a robe of flame-coloured taffeta*, or sat perched as Victory on the crests of British soldiers, nor when she hovered over the frightened country as the harpy of Invasion; no, nor at any other time did we ever take her for any thing but what we knew she was, the patron-saint of tyrants and of slaves; an adulteress, an impostor, and a murderess. The world, whom she has juggled, begin to find her out too: it will hardly "stand now with her sorceries and her lies, and the blood of men, with which she has made herself drunk;" and we may yet live to see her carted for a bawd.

Having thus vented the overflowings of our gall against the old lady above-mentioned, we shall proceed to a detail of some of her fraudulent transactions, as they are stated with great clearness and command of temper, in Mr. Macirone's "Interesting Facts." Interesting indeed! But no more comments for the present. We have not time to grace our narrative or confirm our doctrine of "the uses of *legitimacy*," by giving Mr. Macirone's history of the treatment of his family by the Holy See, which brought his father to this country, and eventually led to his connexion with Murat. It appears that his grandfather, the head of a noble and wealthy family at Rome, was ruined in a large concern, and then robbed of his right by Monsignore Banchieri, treasurer to the Pope, a "gentleman and man of honour" in those times; and that, though the tribunals awarded him reparation, the decisions in his favour were constantly defeated by the interposition of the papal power. The consequence was, that the elder Macirone, after a fruitless struggle of several years with legitimate power and injustice, died of grief and chagrin, and his family were dispersed in various directions: his eldest son came to England and married an English lady, of which union our author was the issue. This short episode shews what Legitimacy, that is, *a power above the law, and accountable only to heaven for its exercise, its use or its abuse,* always was, and always will be. These tricks were played long before the French revolution, and with a million other tricks of the same legitimate, that is, lawless kind, produced it.—We have here an account of some of the tricks resorted to by the wielders and abettors of mild paternal sway to restore the old right to do wrong with impunity, and to put down the principles and partizans of the revolution, as an example of successful rebellion against power held in contempt of the people, and exercised in disregard of law. Mr. Macirone, a native of England, went to Italy at the age of fifteen, and remained there from 1803 till 1812. Part of this time he was detained as an English prisoner. He was afterwards employed as an *aid-de-camp* to Murat, and gives the following narrative of his transactions with the Allies:—

1. A Treaty of Alliance, offensive and defensive, was signed between Austria and Naples, on the 11th of Jan. 1814, and the Austrian Plenipotentiary declared that England was ready to accede to a similar Treaty with King Joachim.—2. A Convention was signed by Lord William Bentinck with the Neapolitan Government, which opened the ports of Italy to the British fleet, and placed affairs on a footing of perfect peace.—3. Murat, on the strength of these engagements, opened the campaign in concert with the Allies, when instantly objections were made to the ratification of the Treaty with Austria, not by Austria, but by England, on some pretence of the territorial indemnifications to be granted to Murat at the expense of the Pope.—4. Murat assented to the proposed modifications, and Lord W. Bentinck declared, that the English Government now agreed entirely to the Treaty

between Austria and Naples.—5. This declaration of Lord W. Bentinck was confirmed by a declaration of Lord Castlereagh, that it was only from motives of delicacy to the King of Sicily that the English Government delayed the conclusion of a special and separate Treaty with Naples, *that a Treaty of Indemnities to the King of Sicily and of Peace with King Joachim might go hand in hand.*—6. Murat now joined the campaign of 1814, and turned the scale against France and Napoleon.—In this state of things, Mr. Macirone observes,—

"A variety of circumstances had now combined to induce the King to doubt the sincerity of the Allies. *The Emperor of Austria had delayed for many days the transmission of the ratification of the Treaty of the 11th January. Ferdinand of Sicily had published an order of the day to some Sicilian troops about to land at Leghorn, in which they were informed that they were going to recover his kingdom of Naples, which he had never ceded, and never would cede. The English general, Lord William Bentinck, had landed with these troops, under instructions to excite a revolution in Italy, and had insisted on the maintenance of a position (Tuscany) which intercepted the communication between the Neapolitan army and Naples; propositions at the same time were made in a foreign camp to Neapolitan generals and other officers, for the expulsion of the then reigning dynasty from the throne of Naples.* The doubts which these circumstances had excited were removed by a declaration of General Sir Robert Wilson, at Bologna; *that he considered the letter of Lord Castlereagh, containing the promise of a formal treaty, as of equal value and force with a treaty already signed. And that neither the executive authority, nor the parliament, would hesitate to recognize the validity of such an engagement.* Indeed, it was in his opinion more imperative, if possible, than a regular treaty, *because it connected an appeal to honour with an obligation on good faith.* From that moment the King again made the most zealous efforts in the common cause."—p. 20.

Alas! Sir Robert, "How little knew'st thou of Calista!" as a body may say. But you have in part redeemed your errors, and revenged the trick that was thus put upon your *preux chevalier* notions of honour!—One would think there was shuffling and paltering and evasion and cant and cunning enough in the foregoing part of this transaction. What follows is worse. After the campaigns which so providentially delivered France and Europe from the hands of illegitimate into those of legitimate power *en plein droit*, and while the immortal congress was yet assembled at Vienna, "Prince Talleyrand, on the part of King Louis," says Mr. Macirone, "was indefatigable in his exertions to induce the Austrian government to withdraw their alliance from the King of Naples, from whom the allied powers had so recently received the most efficient support. The Austrian government being warmly urged to undertake the *holy war* of legitimacy against its ally, the King of Naples, at length expressed its willingness to comply, but alleged the exhausted state of the finances of the country. *This difficulty was, it is said, immediately removed by the British ministers, who offered to defray all the expense of the expedition*, and moreover to furnish a British fleet, in preference to a French fleet, as proposed by Talleyrand in his famous note, which fleet should act in concert with and assist the movements of the Austrian forces."

One would think that after this open and profligate breach of faith, the legitimates had made up their minds to keep no terms with illegitimacy. But, no: expediency turns round once more, and British honour, simplicity, and good faith, with it! Murat, in consequence of the preparations against him, attacked the Austrians "at the very moment, as it afterwards turned out, that the apprehensions of his union with Napoleon, who had just returned to France from Elba, had determined the British cabinet to attend to the invocations of justice in his favour. Lord Castlereagh had written to the Duke of Wellington, who was at that time the plenipotentiary of the British court at Vienna, and informed him, that *in consequence of the reappearance of Napoleon at the head of the French nation,* the British ministers thought it adviseable to unite all the force they could collect, and had consequently come to a determination immediately to conclude a treaty of alliance with the King of Naples."

Bravo, my Lord Castlereagh! you may one day find, after all, that honesty is the best policy; and we hope the Editor of *The Times,* in the next number of *The Correspondent,* will relieve his praises of the allies and his compliments to the Duke of Levis, by a criticism to prove that Jonathan Wild and Count Fathom were "gentlemen and men of honour!"

But the tale of blushing British honour is not ended. At the time when Murat was at the height of his success against the Austrians, "Colonel Dalrymple arrived at Bologna, King Joachim's head-quarters, commissioned by Lord William Bentinck, *to request that the territory of his Britannic majesty's ally, the King of Sardinia, might not be violated by the Neapolitan army.*"—In consequence of Murat's polite attention to this delicate request, he lost his campaign, his crown, and his life; for no sooner was he defeated in his attempts to force the passage of the Po, which he might easily have effected, by infringing upon a small corner of the Piedmontese territory, than "he was surprized at receiving a notification from Lord William Bentinck, *that his instructions were to join the Austrians against him.*"—We know the consequences of this exquisite simplicity of proceeding on both sides. Poor Murat! he well deserved his fate, but not at the hands from which he received it. Foolish fellow! He did not know that legitimacy keeps no faith with illegitimacy. At present, we suppose that point is pretty well settled.

Murat was senseless enough to believe that he, who had been made a king by Bonaparte, would be cordially received in the list of kings by those who were so *by divine right;* and he was base enough to turn against his benefactor, his country, and the human race; but in himself he appears to have been a gallant, generous, and heroic-minded man. The account of his escape from the Austrians, and of his landing in France, is interesting:—

" On the king's approach to Naples with a small remnant of his army, six thousand of the national guard, with General Macdonald, minister of war, at their head, marched forth to meet him. They greeted his return in the most loyal and affectionate manner, exhorting him still to hope for success in the love and devotedness of his subjects, swearing that they were all ready to perish in defence of their king and country; but in consequence of the part England had taken against him, he declined making any further efforts, which would only tend to involve the brave and loyal in his own catastrophe.

" He entered Naples unknown, in the evening of the 19th May, accompanied by his nephew, who was colonel of the 9th regiment of lancers, and four privates. He immediately proceeded to his palace, where he appeared before the queen, pale and emaciated, in the habit of a lancer; tenderly embracing her, he said, 'All is lost, madam, but my life; that I have not been able to lose.'*

" Having taken farewell of his children, he caused his hair, which he had hitherto worn in long ringlets, to be cut short, and habited in a plain grey suit, accompanied by his nephew, the colonel, he proceeded on foot to the sea-shore, opposite to the island of Nisida. He there embarked in a little boat, and proceeded to the neighbouring island of Ischia. There he remained three days without being known, and on the fourth, as he was walking on the sea-shore on the southern side of the island, in company with the colonel, consulting about the means of effecting their escape to France, they discovered a small vessel to the east, in full sail, approaching the spot where they were standing.

" The king immediately hailed the vessel, and getting into a fishing-boat which was on the shore, ordered the crew to row

* During the retreat, the king was ever seen where the danger was greatest. Foremost in the ranks, he continually charged the Austrians in person. When his affairs grew desperate, it became evident that he sought for death in the field. At the head of a few of his cavalry, whom he constantly preceded, he often charged the enemy to their very cannons' mouth. How he escaped amidst so many dangers appears miraculous. He might well say that "he had sought death, but had not been able to find it."

towards it, and, as soon as they were perceived, a boat was sent from the vessel to meet them. The feelings of all parties may easily be imagined, when, in one of the persons on board, the king recognized his attached and faithful servant the Duke of Roccaromana, to whom the vessel belonged, and who, in company with the Marquis Giuliano, the king's aid-de-camp, had escaped from Naples, and was proceeding in this vessel in search of the king, under the greatest anxiety and apprehension, lest some accident might have befallen him, although, previously to quitting the palace, the king had divided with the duke and marquis a considerable sum in gold, and acquainted them with his plan of going to Ischia, accompanied only by his nephew, and of embarking from thence to France.

"The duke could not succeed in effecting his escape from Naples until three days after the departure of the king. The enemy's flag had been hoisted in Ischia; and it appeared highly improbable, under all circumstances, that the king could have remained there concealed for those three days. It was unsafe for the duke to attempt landing on the island, and yet there appeared no other means of ascertaining whether the king was there or had proceeded on his voyage. In this embarrassment, it happened that the duke, who was most anxiously examining the shore of the island with a glass, perceived and recognized the king. The rest of their voyage proved most prosperous and expeditious. They landed at Cannes the 27th or 28th of May."—p. 30.

We shall in our next give the particulars of Mr. Macirone's interviews with the Duke of Wellington, relating to the convention of Paris; and we shall be cautious what we say of his Grace's observations and conduct on that occasion; for if we were to say what we think of that noble person, there might be some offence in it. But we cannot help having an opinion of him, which all that we hear of him confirms.

INTERESTING FACTS *relating to the Fall of Murat, &c.*

By F. Macirone, *&c.*

(CONCLUDED.)

Sta viator, heroem calcas.

Feb. 9, 1817.

WE proceed to Mr. Macirone's account of the surrender of Paris. Let it speak for itself:—

"Immediately after the battle of Waterloo, Napoleon returned to Paris, and abdicated the throne in *favour of his son, who would have been accepted and proclaimed by the French people*, but for the opposition of two celebrated individuals.

"On this abdication, a commission of government, as it was called, was formed, consisting of Fouché, the President, Caulincourt, Carnot, Quinette, and Grenier.

"On the 26th of June, I believe, the Duke of Wellington, at the head of his victorious army, reached Compeigne. In the course of the following night, a deputation of five persons was sent to him from Paris by the two Chambers, to solicit an armistice for a few days. The avowed purpose of this mission was to afford time for the return of another deputation, which had been dispatched to the Allied Sovereigns, to assert the right of the French people to choose their own government, in conformity to the Declaration of the Allies, *that they warred against the person of Napoleon only, and not against the French people, or to force upon them any particular government.*

"The Chamber of Deputies, the majority of the Commissioners of Government, and the Army, now in great strength in Paris, were *determined to resist any attempt to force the Bourbons upon them*; while the avowed opinion of Fouché and Caulincourt was, that such a determination could only lead to the destruction of Paris, and the loss of thousands of lives. They therefore sought the means of opening a communication with the Duke of Wellington, in which they might impart to him their views, and avert the calamity which they apprehended from the projects of the other parties. In the expediency of procuring an armistice for a few days, *all* parties concurred; and Fouché, who had become acquainted with me in my interviews with him respecting King Joachim, solicited me to undertake the task of carrying on a communication between him and the Duke of Wellington. It was sufficient for me to know that the service in which I was to be engaged had for its object the prevention of a sanguinary conflict, which an attempt to take Paris by force would have occasioned, and I therefore consented to be the bearer of Fouché's message to the Duke.

"My feelings as an Englishman entirely influenced my conduct in this instance. I exulted in the success of our army, and in the military glory which the English name had acquired; and it appeared to me, that whatever might tend to prevent the further effusion of blood, must be highly acceptable to my country; and to be selected as an instrument, by which so humane and desirable an object might be accomplished, was highly gratifying to my mind, and I should not have thought myself at liberty to refuse to engage in it, from any opinion I might entertain of the private views of the persons by whom I should be employed. Impressed with these sentiments, I left Paris at midnight. I proceeded to the Barriere de la Villette, where I found some difficulty in getting my carriage over the different entrenchments and *abattis*, but still more from the French officers, who evinced the greatest reluctance in permitting me to pass, observing that I was probably a person sent out to treat with the enemy, and to betray them; but on my assuring them that the purport of my mission was entirely analogous to their views and interests, I was suffered to proceed without a trumpet. Before I had got beyond the French lines, I was again stopped by a piquet of cuirassiers, who refused to let me pass without an order from the officer commanding the inner posts; and while I was asserting my right to proceed, a cuirassier fortunately happened to hold a light to my face, and very respectfully accosted me with the salutation of " bon voyage, Major:" his comrades immediately asked him who I was? he answered, " it's the Major of the 9th Hussars," for whom I suppose he had mistaken me. This was instantly believed; and, greeted by the salutations and good wishes of the whole troop, I was allowed to continue my journey.

" The Prussian advanced posts were at less than two miles distant, and I was consequently very soon stopped by a Prussian lancer, who, upon my telling him that I was an English officer, proceeding with dispatches to the Duke of Wellington, immediately accompanied me to the next post. Here I learnt with great pleasure, that this advanced guard of cavalry was commanded by Prince William of Prussia, whose first Aid-de-camp, Baron Rochow, was my particular friend.

" I soon arrived at the spot where Prince William and his Staff were sleeping in a field, before a large fire, under some trees. I inquired for my friend, Baron Rochow. His name was called, and I immediately had the pleasure of seeing him. After a few urgent questions, he proposed to introduce me to Prince William, who by this time had raised himself upon his mattrass. The Prince received me with the greatest politeness, and directed that I should be presented with refreshments. On my taking leave, he ordered me to be furnished with an escort to General Baron Bulow. I arrived at this General's quarters at break of day, and was soon after introduced to him. While I was at breakfast with him, he told me that he wished me to see Prince Blucher on my way to the Duke of Wellington; and added, that he would send his Aid-de-camp with me. He then ordered his servant to call his Aid-de-camp, Baron Echardstein, to whom I was also particularly known.

" On our arrival at Prince Blucher's, my companion, Baron Echardstein, informed him that I was going on a mission from the French Government to the Duke of Wellington: this did not seem to please the Prince, who immediately retired to rest, and left me to converse with his Chef-d'etat-Major. This gentleman, whose name I believe was Gneisenau, was very indignant on being informed of the desire of the French to treat with the Duke of Wellington; and he completely lost his temper when he observed the coolness with which I listened to his indiscreet and authoritative language.

" On my quitting this choleric soldier, my friend Echardstein thought it necessary to apologise to me for the indelicate behaviour of his countryman. I proceeded on my journey, and soon met numerous columns of English cavalry, and found the five French Deputies, waiting for the Duke's arrival, at a village called Fresnoy. I thought it expedient to endeavour to see the Duke before the Deputies, and therefore passed them on the road. I shortly after met the Duke, and imparted to him the purport of my mission, and delivered to him also a sealed dispatch from Fouché, upon which he desired me to accompany him to the village where the Deputies were. He asked me if I was acquainted with the nature of the mission. I told him that I knew that one part of it, at least, was to request an armistice of some days, until news could arrive from other Deputies, who had been sent to treat with the united Sovereigns.

" On the Duke's arrival at the village of Fresnoy, he conferred with the Deputies for five hours. They adduced, in support of their mission, the solemn Declaration of the British Ministers, " that it was not the intention of the Allies to force the Bourbons, or any other government, on the French people; that they had made war against Napoleon only, and not against the nation," &c. Their mission failed. They received for answer, that the only thing left for the Chambers to do was to proclaim Louis 18th.

" The Duke then proceeded to Plessis, the head-quarters for that day. The Deputies remained behind. I was desired by the Duke to accompany him to Plessis, where I dined with him, and during dinner conversed with him on the object I had to propose respecting an armistice. Before I took my leave of the Duke, I requested that he would give me some answer to the remonstrances of the Commission of Government, which stated, "*that as the Allies had declared their hostility to be directed against the person of Napoleon only, it would be but just to await the result of the mission to the Sovereigns, before his Grace undertook to replace Louis 18th on the throne.*" The Duke, in the presence of Lord March, Colonels Hervey, Freemantle, Abercromby, and several other officers, replied,—"I can give no other answer than that which you know *I have just given* to the Deputies. *Tell them (the Commission of Government) that they had better immediately proclaim the King (Louis 18th). I cannot treat till then, nor upon any other condition. Their King is here at hand: let them send their submission to him.*"

We are glad the Duke is not an Englishman? *

"The Duke was at this time in constant communication with King Louis and Talleyrand, who were together in the rear of the army; and I saw one of the messengers of Louis 18th at the Duke's head-quarters.—I returned to Paris the next morning. Davoust had taken the chief command of the French army, and had fixed his head-quarters at the Barriere de la Villette, by which I entered Paris. On my being introduced to him, he demanded to know the object of my mission to the enemy, and said, that as he then held the supreme command, I must communicate to him any dispatches of which I might be the bearer? I answered him, that I had no written message; that my mission had been nearly similar to that of the Deputies; that I had been sent out by the Commission, and therefore thought it my duty to

* Let no country go about to enslave another with impunity. For out of the very dregs of rottenness and debasement will arise a low creeping fog of servility, a stench of corruption to choak the life of liberty, wherever it comes—a race of fortune-hunting, dastard, busy, hungry, heartless slaves and bloodsuckers, eager to fawn upon power and trample upon weakness, with no other pretensions than want of principle, and a hatred of those who possess what they want. Ireland has given us Castlereagh, Wellington, Burke. Is she not even with us? Let her smile now from her hundred hills, let her shake with laughter through her thousand bogs! Ireland, last of the nations, repose in peace upon thy green western wave! Thou and the world are quits.

account with its members only for my proceedings. I could, however, inform him of the declaration, which, in common with the Deputies, I had received from the Duke of Wellington. Hereupon I reported to him the Duke's *sine qua non.* He immediately declared that my intelligence was incredible, and expressed his disbelief of it in the strongest terms. Then, with the greatest emotion, and with uplifted hands and eyes, *he called heaven to witness the perfidy and arrogant injustice of the English Ministry, and of the Allies.* "*The Duke of Wellington,*" said he, "*surely could never dare to make a declaration so directly contrary to the avowed and solemnly protested intentions of the British Ministry, and of the other Allies. Have not they sworn that they would not impose a sovereign on the French people? However, they will find to their cost, that we are unanimous in our resolution. Napoleon can no longer be the pretext for their hostilities. We will all perish rather than submit to the hateful yoke that Lord Castlereagh would impose upon us! ——— is a traitor! he was about to compromise with the enemy—I have taken his command from him—he shall never again command a corporal's guard—we are an independent nation—England should be the last power to tyrannise over us in our choice of a government.*"—He then desired me to proceed to lay before the Commission at the Thuilleries the result of my mission, adding, "they know very well that I have now with me more than 100,000 men, with 500 pieces of cannon, and 25,000 cavalry."

"I proceeded to the palace of the Thuilleries, where I was introduced to the Commission. Carnot immediately asked, what my errand to the enemy had been? Fouché quickly answered, that he had sent me. Quinette and Grenier looked as if they were not satisfied with this answer. Carnot continued to address me, and asked whether I had seen the Deputies at the Duke of Wellington's head-quarters? I answered in the affirmative, and that I could give him an account of the result of their mission: upon this they became attentive, and heard my account with dismay and indignation. Carnot expressed the same sentiments that Davoust had recently done; and added, rather roughly, that he could by no means give credit to my account, either as to the Duke of Wellington's *sine qua non,* or as to the force of the enemy in the vicinity of Paris: he further said, with a sneer, "we shall have, I hope, a very different account on the return of the Deputies." Fouché defended me, and reproved him for so uncivilly questioning my veracity, and assured him that he might put implicit confidence in me. Carnot and Grenier then took me to a topographical map, and questioned me as to the movements of the Duke of Wellington? I answered their interrogatories to the extent to which I thought myself warranted: and it appeared that I informed them of nothing with which they were not already acquainted. Carnot then, in a polite manner, told me I might retire.

"It would appear, that in consequence of having learned from me the nature of the communication which the Deputies would have to make to the Chambers, and dreading its discouraging effects on the members, and on the people at large, their return to Paris had been prevented. Some private orders seem to have been given to that effect; for on the same day that I entered Paris by the Barriere de la Villette, the Deputies approached that part, preceded by Colonel Latour Maubourg, who was attached to their mission, when the French out-posts fired, killed the Prussian trumpeter's horse, and a ball grazed the epaulette of the Colonel. The Deputies turned back, and attempted to enter by the Barriere de St. Dennis, but were refused. They there received fresh instructions to treat, and it was so managed, that they did not return to Paris till after the capitulation.

"In the mean time Fouché and his coadjutors, who opposed the views of the other parties, were in great personal danger. The three other Members of the Commission more than suspected them of duplicity and treachery; and in consequence impeached them before the Chamber of Deputies. The Duke of Wellington being acquainted with these proceedings, sent a message to the Members of the Commission, as I was informed, assuring them that if any harm befel Fouché or Caulincourt, he would infallibly *hang up the other three on his arrival in Paris.* *

"It was proposed in the Chamber of Deputies, that its Members should quit Paris with the army, and rally round them all those who would oppose the enemy and the Bourbons. But this measure Fouché was particularly anxious to thwart, whilst Davoust, feeling himself confident in the strength of his army, insisted on attacking Blucher and the Duke of Wellington before other reinforcements should arrive; but as I understood at the time, Fouché succeeded in somewhat softening and in giving a new direction to the policy of Carnot: and it is certain that he managed to gain over Davoust by urging the force of the enemy, and the dreadful consequences that would ensue if Paris should be taken by assault. He pleaded the reliance which might be placed *on the faith of the English* (for with the Prussians the French would not have treated on any terms). He therefore recommended Davoust to evacuate Paris, and not to listen to the desperate suggestions of the Chambers, observing, that so long as his army remained entire, he might obtain favourable terms for all parties.

"The day before the capitulation of Paris (2d July), I repaired to the British camp with the following memorandum, as my instructions, from Fouché to the Duke of Wellington:—

"'The army opposes, because uneasy—assure it, it will even become devoted.

"'The Chambers are counter for the same reason. *Assure every body, you will have every body.*

"'The army sent away, the Chambers will agree, on according them the guarantee, as added to the charter and promised by the king. In order to be well understood, it is necessary to explain; therefore not to enter Paris before three days, and in the meantime every thing may be arranged.

* Here the reader may, if he pleases, read over again the last note.

" 'The Chambers will be gained, will believe in their independence, and will agree to every thing. Persuasion, not force, must be used with the Chambers.'

" On my arrival at the British advanced posts, which, owing to the obstructions I met with from the French, I was not able to effect till early in the morning of the 3d July, I was informed that the most positive orders had been given by the duke, not to allow any messenger to pass from Paris without his special permission. I was therefore detained at the English advanced post of guards, commanded by Lord Saltown. I dined with the officers of the advanced piquet, among whom I well remember Captain Fairfield, of the foot guards. These gentlemen informed me that the Duke of Wellington was at Gonesse, with Sir C. Stuart, Pozzo di Borgo, and Talleyrand. I wrote a letter to the duke, which was forwarded by Lord Saltown. In my letter, I entered into a detail of the line of conduct recommended by Fouché, and contained in the foregoing memorandum. On the receipt of my dispatch, the duke immediately proceeded to St. Cloud, General Blucher's head-quarters; there the capitulation of Paris was signed. The duke returned to Gonnesse and dispatched Lord March to bring me to him: I arrived very early on the morning of the 4th, and found Sir C. Stuart, Talleyrand, and Pozzo di Borgo; they assembled in council, and my presence was required by the duke. Talleyrand observed to me, that *this was already settled*, and, turning to the Duke of Wellington, requested him to read to me *the capitulation that they had just concluded*. On my urging the adoption of the line of conduct which Fouché recommended towards the Chambers, the Duke of Wellington proceeded to give me his sentiments in writing, which were as follow :—

" '*Je pense, que les Allies ayant déclaré le Gouvernment de Napoleon une Usurpation et non légitime, toute autorité qui émane de lui, doit être regardée comme nulle et d'aucun pouvoir.* Ainsi, ce qui reste à faire aux Chambres et à la commis-*

* *Encore un coup*. This Duke is an Irishman. Pray, suppose the Allies were

sion, est, de donner de suite leur démission, et de déclarer, qu'ils n'ont pris sur eux les responsibilitès de gouvernement, que pour assurer la tranquilitè publique, et l'intégritè du royaume de S. M. Louis XVIII.'

"Talleyrand, Sir Charles Stuart, and Pozzo di Borgo, each took a copy of this document, and each, by way of memorandum, put their names and mine to the paper, by way of recording, as I suppose, the parties present at the discussion.

"I forthwith mounted my horse and returned to Paris; Lord March was appointed by the duke to accompany me. On our arrival at the Barriere de la Villette, we found the French soldiery perfectly frantic, and vociferating "*Vive l'Empereur!*" "*A bas les Anglais!*" "*A bas les Bourbons!*" They were on the point of firing at the Belgian trumpeter who preceded us: it was with the greatest difficulty that some French hussars, under whose escort we had approached the barriers, could prevent the soldiers from firing at Lord March as he was riding off. They were also obliged to exert themselves strenuously in my defence, as many of the infantry pointed their muskets at me, vociferating "*Vive l'Empereur!*" "*Vive Napoleon!*" "We are betrayed!" "We have been sold!" "We will fight to the last drop of our blood!" "Down with the Bourbons!" "Let us kill this traitor!" "He has assisted in selling us!" "We have seen him pass before!" The hussars took me between them, some of the infantry also assisted in parrying off the blows aimed at me, and turning aside the muzzles of the muskets. Thus, after great peril, I was fortunate enough to gain the quarters of a general officer, with only a sabre cut on my left leg. The general dispersed the men, and gave me a strong escort to conduct me to the Thuilleries.

"In consequence of my communicating the documents and assurances I had received from Talleyrand and the Duke of Wel-

to declare the Protestant succession illegitimate, and the King of Sardinia, not the Prince Regent, the hereditary proprietor of the English throne and people in perpetuity and in a right line, would this annul the validity of his Grace's grants?

lington, the commission of government abdicated its powers that evening; but the Chambers still refused to comply; they continued their sittings, which they declared should be permanent, till the morning of the 6th, when the doors of the Chamber were closed, and guarded by a party of the national guards.

"On this, above one hundred and fifty of the deputies proceeded to the house of M. Laujuinais, their president, and there framed a solemn protest against the arbitrary and illegal violence which had been used towards them, *in violation of the most solemn declarations.*

"I have now no doubt that some extraordinary scheme had been contrived to seduce Napoleon into the measure of abdicating the throne in favour of his son. His resources were at that moment immense. The regular army in Paris alone, amounted to more than 80,000 men, every individual of which was animated with the most enthusiastic ardour. The national guard, above 30,000 strong, displayed the firmest resolution to obey the directions of the constituted authorities; numerous volunteers of all classes had taken up arms in the defence of their country. In the departments, the spirit of opposition to the invaders was still greater, particularly in the north, west, and east: in fine, Napoleon, who could not possibly be ignorant of the state of his resources, would never, I am convinced, have sheathed his sword, and abdicated the crown *even in favour of his son,* had he not been most confidently assured of the validity of the measure, and its being approved and supported by the French senate and people, and by at least *some part* of the coalition.

"What were the precise representations by which Napoleon was influenced to take this step, is perhaps known only to its contrivers, and their victim. Some future historian may probably unfold this mystery. As far as regards the share I had in the negociations between the provisional government, the allied armies, and Talleyrand, as minister of Louis XVIII., I feel it due to myself to declare, that *I had no suspicion of any deception or intended breach of engagements.* I was requested to open a communication between Fouché and the Duke of Wellington, for the avowed purpose of negociating an armistice, as a preliminary measure to the capitulation of Paris; and it was obvious that such a negociation might save the lives of thousands of my countrymen."

THE PLAY IS OVER, NOW LET US GO TO SUPPER.

John Bull, John Bull, John Bull, read the above account twice over, think well of it, and then say why you should not wear the yoke, which you have put round the neck of others, round your own. Ah! John, thou art not a metaphysician: thou dost lack a concatenation of ideas!—We are not proud of the share which as Englishmen we had in the proceedings recorded by Mr. Macirone: but we have one consolation for our national pride, Fouché and Talleyrand are Frenchmen. These two pettifogging miscreants seem to have made themselves perfect in the advice of the fool in *Lear:* "Let go thy hold, when a great wheel runs down hill, lest it should break thy neck with following it: but the great one that goes upwards, let it draw thee after. When a wise man gives thee better counsel, give me mine again: I would have none but knaves follow it." The great wheel, however, in this instance, kicked off the two knaves, that followed the fool's advice. One of these famous persons now writes letters of apology to the Duke of Wellington, and the other to Lord Castlereagh. They are not so well off as Murat and Berthier, one of whom was legitimately shot through the head, and the other legitimately thrown out of a window, if we are to believe Mr. Macirone, that he might die in *the good cause*—"a master-leaver, and a fugitive."

WAT TYLER; A DRAMATIC POEM.
THE QUARTERLY REVIEW: Article, "ON PARLIAMENTARY REFORM."

> "So was it when my life began,
> So is it now I am a man:
> So shall it be when I grow old and die.
> The child's the father of the man:
> Our years flow on
> Link'd each to each by natural piety."—WORDSWORTH.

March 9, 1817.

ACCORDING to this theory of personal continuity, the author of the Dramatic Poem, to be here noticed, is the father of Parliamentary Reform in the Quarterly Review. It is said to be a wise child that knows its own father; and we understand Mr. Southey (who is in this case reputed father and son) utterly disclaims the hypostatical union between the Quarterly Reviewer and the Dramatic Poet, and means to enter an injunction against the latter, as a bastard and impostor. Appearances are somewhat staggering against the legitimacy of the descent, yet we perceive a strong family-likeness remaining, in spite of the lapse of years and alteration of circumstances. We should not, indeed, be able to predict that the author of *Wat Tyler* would ever write the article on Parliamentary Reform; nor should we, either at first or second sight, perceive that the Quarterly Reviewer had ever written a poem like that which is before us: but if we were told that both performances were literally and *bonâ fide* by the same person, we should have little hesitation in saying to Mr. Southey, "Thou art the man." We know no other person in whom "fierce extremes" meet with such mutual self-complacency: whose opinions change so much without any change in the author's mind; who lives so entirely in the "present ignorant thought," without the smallest "discourse of reason looking before or after." Mr. Southey is a man incapable of reasoning connectedly on any subject. He has not strength of mind to see the whole of any question; he has not modesty to suspend his judgment till he has examined the grounds of it. He can comprehend but one idea at a time, and that is always an extreme one; because he will neither listen to, nor tolerate any thing than can disturb or moderate the petulance of his self-opinion. *The woman that deliberates is lost.* So it is with the effeminate soul of Mr. Southey. Any concession is fatal to his consistency; and he can only keep out of one absurdity by the tenaciousness with which he stickles for another. He calls to the aid of his disjointed opinions a proportionate quantity of spleen; and regularly makes up for the weakness of his own *reasons*, by charging others with *bad motives*. The terms *knave and fool, wise and good*, have undergone a total change in the last twenty years: the former he applies to all those who agreed with him formerly—the latter to all those who agree with him now. His public spirit was then a prude and a scold; and "his poor virtue," turned into a literary prostitute, is grown more abusive than ever. Wat Tyler and the Quarterly Review are an illustration of these remarks. The author of Wat Tyler was an Ultra-jacobin; the author of Parliamentary Reform is an Ultra-royalist; the one was a frantic demagogue; the other is a servile court-tool: the one maintained second-hand paradoxes; the other repeats second-hand common-places: the one vented those opinions which gratified the vanity of youth; the other adopts those prejudices which are most conducive to the convenience of age: the one saw nothing but the abuses of power; the other sees nothing but the horrors of resistance to those abuses: the one did not stop short of general anarchy; the other goes the whole length of despotism: the one vilified kings, priests, and nobles; the other vilifies the people: the one was for universal suffrage and perfect equality; the other is for seat-selling, and the increasing influence of the Crown: the one admired the preaching of John Ball; the other recommends the Suspension of the Habeas Corpus, and the putting down of the *Examiner* by the sword, the dagger, or the thumb-screw; for the pen,

Mr. Southey tells us, is not sufficient. We wonder that in all this contempt which our prose-poet has felt at different times for different persons and things, he has never felt any dissatisfaction with himself, or distrust of his own infallibility. Our differing from others sometimes staggers our confidence in our own conclusions: if we had been chargeable with as many contradictions as Mr. Southey, we suppose we should have had the same senseless self-sufficiency. A changeling is your only oracle. Those who have undergone a total change of sentiment on important questions, ought certainly to learn modesty in themselves, and moderation towards others; on the contrary, they are generally the most violent in their own opinions, and the most intolerant towards others; the reason of which we have shewn elsewhere, to the satisfaction of the proprietor of the *Old Times*. Before we have done, we shall, perhaps, do the same thing to the satisfaction of the publisher of the Quarterly Review; for the Mr. Murrays and the Mr. Walters, the patrons of the band of gentlemen-pensioners and servile authors, have "a sort of squint" in their understanding, and look less to the dirty sacrifices of their drudges, or the dirtier they are ready to make, than to their standing well with that great keeper, the public, for purity and innocence. The band of gentlemen-pensioners and servile authors do not know what to make of this, and hardly believe it: we shall in time convince them.

But to proceed to our extracts:—

MORCEAU I.

Wat Tyler. Hob—I have only six groats in the world,
And they must soon by law be taken from me.
Hob. Curse on these taxes—one succeeds another—
Our ministers—panders of a king's will—
Drain all our wealth away—waste it in revels—
And lure or force away our boys, who should be
The props of our old age!—to fill their armies,
And feed the crows of France! Year follows year,
And still we madly prosecute the war;—
Draining our wealth—distressing our poor peasants—

Slaughtering our youths—and all to crown our Chiefs
With glory!—I detest the hell-sprung name.

Tyler. What matters me who wears the crown of France?
Whether a Richard or a Charles possess it?
They reap the glory—they enjoy the spoil—
We pay—we bleed! The sun would shine as cheerly,
The rains of heaven as seasonably fall,
Tho' neither of these royal pests existed.

Hob. Nay—as for that, we poor men should fare better!
No legal robbers then should force away
The hard-earn'd wages of our honest toil.
The Parliament for ever cries *more money,*
The service of the State demands more money.
Just Heaven! of what service is the State?

Tyler. Oh! 'tis of vast importance! Who should pay for
The luxuries and riots of the court?
Who should support the flaunting courtier's pride,
Pay for their midnight revels, their rich garments,
Did not the State enforce?—Think ye, my friend,
That I—a humble blacksmith, here at Deptford,
Would part with these six groats—earn'd by hard toil,
All that I have! to massacre the Frenchmen;
Murder as enemies men I never saw,
Did not the State compel me!
(*Tax-gatherers pass by.*) There they go,
Privileg'd r——s!

MORCEAU II.

Piers. Fare not the birds well, as from spray to spray
Blithsome they bound—yet find their simple food
Scattered abundantly?

Tyler. No fancied boundaries of mine and thine
Restrain their wanderings: Nature gives enough
For all; but Man, with arrogant selfishness,
Proud of his heaps, hoards up superfluous stores
Robb'd from his weaker fellows, starves the poor,
Or gives to pity what he owes to justice!

Piers. So I have heard our good friend John Ball preach.

Alice. My father, wherefore was John Ball imprisoned?
Was he not charitable, good, and pious?
I have heard him say that all mankind are brethren,
And that like brethren they should love each other;—
Was not that doctrine pious?
Tyler. Rank sedition—
High treason, every syllable, my child!
The priests cry out on him for heresy;
The nobles all detest him as a rebel;
And this good man, this minister of Christ,
This man, the friend and brother of mankind,
Lingers in the dark dungeon!

MORCEAU III.

Tyler. Piers, I have not been idle,
I never ate the bread of indolence—
Could Alice be more thrifty than her mother?
Yet but with one child, and that one, how good
Thou knowest; I scarcely can provide the wants
Of nature: look at these wolves of the law,
They come to drain me of my hard-earn'd wages.
I have already paid the heavy tax
Laid on the wool that clothes me—on my leather—
On all the needful articles of life!
And now three groats (and I work'd hard to earn them)
The Parliament demands—and I must pay them,
Forsooth, for liberty to wear my head.

Enter Tax-gatherers,

Collector. Three groats a-head for all your family.
Piers. Why is this money gathered?—'tis a hard tax
On the poor labourer!—it can never be
That government should thus distress the people.
Go to the rich for money—honest labour
Ought to enjoy its fruits.
Col. The State wants money.
War is expensive—'tis a glorious war,

A war of honour, and must be supported.—
Three groats a-head.

Tyler. There, three for my own head,
Three for my wife's!—what will the State tax next?

Col. You have a daughter.

Tyler. She is below the age—not yet fifteen.

Col. You would evade the tax.—

Tyler. Sir Officer,
I have paid you fairly what the law demands.

[*Alice and her Mother enter the Shop. The Tax-gatherers go to her. One of them lays hold of her. She screams. Tyler goes in.*]

Col. You say she's under age.

[*Alice screams again. Tyler knocks out the Tax-gatherer's brains. His Companions fly.*]

Piers. A just revenge.

Tyler. Most just indeed; but in the eye of the law
'Tis murder—and the murderer's lot is mine.

MORCEAU IV.—SONG.

" When Adam delv'd and Eve span,
" Who was then the gentleman?"
Wretched is the infant's lot,
Born within the straw-roof'd cot!
Be he generous, wise, or brave,
He must only be a slave,
Long, long labour, little rest,
Still to toil to be oppress'd;
Drain'd by taxes of his store,
Punish'd next for being poor:
This is the poor wretch's lot,
Born within the straw-roof'd cot.

While the peasant works—to sleep;
What the peasant sows—to reap;
On the couch of ease to lie,
Rioting in revelry;

Be he villain, be he fool,
Still to hold despotic rule,
Trampling on his slaves with scorn;
This is to be nobly born.
" When Adam delv'd and Eve span,
" Who was then the gentleman?"

MORCEAU V.

John Ball. Friends! Brethren! for ye are my brethren all;
Englishmen met in arms to advocate
The cause of freedom! hear me! pause awhile
In the career of vengeance; it is true
I am a priest; but, as these rags may speak,
Not one who riots in the poor man's spoil,
Or trades with his religion. I am one
Who preach the law of Christ, and in my life
Would practise what he taught. The Son of God
Came not to you in power:—humble in mien,
Lowly in heart, the man of Nazareth
Preach'd mercy, justice, love: " Woe unto ye,
Ye that are rich:—if that ye would be saved,
Sell that ye have, and give unto the poor."
So taught the Saviour: oh, my honest friends!
Have ye not felt the strong indignant throb
Of justice in your bosoms, to behold
The lordly baron feasting on your spoils?
Have you not in your hearts arraign'd the lot
That gave him on the couch of luxury
To pillow his head, and pass the festive day
In sportive feasts, and ease, and revelry?
Have you not often in your conscience ask'd
Why is the difference, wherefore should that man
No worthier than myself, thus lord it over me,
And bid me labour, and enjoy the fruits?
The God within your breasts has argued thus!
The voice of truth has murmur'd; came he not
As helpless to the world?—shines not the sun

With equal ray on both?—do ye not feel
The self-same winds of heaven as keenly parch ye?
Abundant is the earth—the Sire of all
Saw and pronounced that it was very good.
Look round: the vernal fields smile with new flowers,
The budding orchard perfumes the soft breeze,
And the green corn waves to the passing gale.
There is enough for all, but your proud baron
Stands up, and, arrogant of strength, exclaims,
" I am a lord—by nature I am noble:
These fields are mine, for I was born to them,
I was born in the castle—you, poor wretches,
Whelp'd in the cottage, are by birth my slaves."
Almighty God! such blasphemies are uttered!
Almighty God! such blasphemies believ'd!

Tom Miller. This is something like a sermon.

Jack Straw. Where's the bishop
Would tell you truths like these?

Hob. There was never a bishop among all the apostles.

John Ball. My brethren!

Piers. Silence, the good priest speaks.

John Ball. My brethren, these are truths, and weighty ones:
Ye are all equal; nature made ye so.
Equality is your birth-right;—when I gaze
On the proud palace, and behold one man
In the blood-purpled robes of royalty,
Feasting at ease, and lording over millions;
Then turn me to the hut of poverty,
And see the wretched labourer, worn with toil,
Divide his scanty morsel with his infants;
I sicken, and, indignant at the sight,
" Blush for the patience of humanity."

Jack Straw. We will assert our rights.

Morceau VI.

Tyler. King of England,
Petitioning for pity is most weak,
The sovereign people ought to *demand justice.*

I killed your officer, for his lewd hand
Insulted a maid's modesty; your subjects
I lead to rebel against the Lord's anointed,
Because his ministers have made him odious:
His yoke is heavy, and his burden grievous.
Why do we carry on this fatal war,
To force upon the French a king they hate;
Tearing our young men from their peaceful homes;
Forcing his hard-earn'd fruits from the honest peasant;
Distressing us to desolate our neighbours?
Why is this ruinous poll-tax imposed,
But to support your court's extravagance,
And your mad title to the crown of France?
Shall we sit tamely down beneath these evils,
Petitioning for pity?
King of England!
Why are we sold like cattle in your markets—
Deprived of every privilege of man?
Must we lie tamely at our tyrant's feet,
And, like your spaniels, lick the hand that beats us?
You sit at ease in your gay palaces,
The costly banquet courts your appetite,
Sweet music sooths your slumbers; we the while,
Scarce by hard toil can earn a little food,
And sleep scarce shelter'd from the cold night wind:
While your wild projects wrest the little from us
Which might have cheered the wintry hour of age:
The parliament for ever asks more money:
We toil and sweat for money for your taxes;
Where is the benefit, what food reap we
From all the councils of your government?
Think you that we should quarrel with the French?
What boots to us your victories, your glory?
We pay, we fight, you profit at your ease.
Do you not claim the country as your own?
Do you not call the venison of the forest,
The birds of heaven your own?—prohibiting us,
Even tho' in want of food, to seize the prey

Which nature offers?—King! is all this just?
Think you we do not feel the wrongs we suffer?
The hour of retribution is at hand,
And tyrants tremble—mark me, King of England.

MORCEAU VII.

Hob. 'Twas well order'd,
I place but little trust in courtly faith.
John Ball. We must remain embodied; else the king
Will plunge again in royal luxury;
And when the storm of danger is past over,
Forget his promises.
Hob. Aye, like an aguish sinner,
He'll promise to repent when the fit's on him;
When well recover'd, laugh at his own terrors.
Piers. Oh! I am griev'd that we must gain so little!
Why are not all these empty ranks abolish'd,
King, slave, and lord, "ennobl'd into MAN?"
Are we not equal all?—have you not told me,
Equality is the sacred right of man,
Inalienable, tho' by force withheld?
John Ball. Even so; but Piers, my frail and fallible judgment
Knows hardly to decide if it be right,
Peaceably to return, content with little,
With this half restitution of our rights,
Or boldly to proceed thro' blood and slaughter,
Till we should all be equal and all happy.
I chose the milder way:—perhaps I erred.
Piers. I fear me—by the mass, the unsteady people
Are flocking homewards! how the multitude
Diminishes!

MORCEAU THE LAST.

John Ball. Why, be it so. I can smile at your vengeance:
For I am arm'd with rectitude of soul.
The truth, which all my life I have divulg'd,
And am now doom'd in torment to expire for,
Shall still survive—the destin'd hour must come,

When it shall blaze with sun-surpassing splendor,
And the dark mists of prejudice and falsehood
Fade in its strong effulgence. Flattery's incense
No more shall shadow round the gore-dyed throne;
That altar of oppression, fed with rites
More savage than the priests of Moloch taught,
Shall be consumed amid the fire of Justice:
The ray of truth shall emanate around,
And the whole world be lighted!

This will do.

THE COURIER AND "THE WAT TYLER."

Doth not the appetite alter? A man loves the meat in his youth, that he cannot endure in his age. Shall quips and sentences, and these paper bullets of the brain awe a man from the career of his humour?—*Much Ado about Nothing*.

March 30, 1817.

INSTEAD of applying for an injunction against *Wat Tyler*, Mr. Southey would do well to apply for an injunction against Mr. Coleridge, who has undertaken his defence in *The Courier*. If he can escape from the ominous patronage of that gentleman's pen, he has nothing to fear from his own. "The *Wat Tyler*," as Mr. Coleridge has personified it, can do the author no great harm: it only proves that he was once a wild enthusiast: of the *two* characters, for which Mr. Southey is a candidate with the public, this is the most creditable for him to appear in. At present his reputation "somewhat smacks." A strong dose of the Jacobin spirit of *Wat Tyler* may be of use to get the sickly taste of the Poet-laureate and the Quarterly Reviewer out of our mouths.

The best thing for Mr. Southey (if we might be allowed to advise) would be for his friends to say nothing about him, and for him to say nothing about other people. We have nothing to do with Mr. Southey "the man," or even with Mr. Southey the apostate; but we have something to do with Mr. Southey the spy and informer. Is it not a little strange, that while this gentleman is getting an injunction against himself as the author of *Wat Tyler*, he is recommending gagging bills against us, and the making up by force for his deficiency in argument! There is a want of keeping in this; but Mr. Southey and his friends delight in practical and speculative contradictions. What are we to think of a man who is "now a flagitious incendiary," (to use the epithets which Mr. Southey applies to the Editor of the *Examiner*) "a palliater of murder, insurrection, and treason," and anon a pensioned scribbler of court poetry and court politics? If the writer of the article on Parliamentary Reform thinks the Editor of this Paper "a flagitious incendiary," "a palliater of murder, insurrection, and treason," what does the Quarterly Reviewer think of the author of *Wat Tyler*? What, on the other hand, does the author of *Wat Tyler* think of the Quarterly Reviewer? What does Mr. Southey, who certainly makes a very aukward figure between the two, think of himself? Mr. Coleridge indeed steps in to the assistance of his friend in this dilemma, and says (unsaying all that he says besides) that the ultra-jacobinical opinions advanced in *Wat Tyler* were "more an honour to the writer's heart than an imputation on his understanding?" Be it so. The Editor of this Paper will, we dare say, agree to this statement from disinterested motives, (for he is not answerable for any ultra-jacobinical opinions) as we suppose Mr. Southey will accede to it from pure self-love. He hardly thinks that he was "a knave and fool" formerly, as he calls all those who formerly agreed or now differ with him: he only thinks with Mr. Coleridge and *The Courier*, that he was not quite so "wise and virtuous" then, as he is at present! Why then not extend the same charitable interpretation to those who have held a middle course between his opposite extravagances? We are sure, that to be thought *a little less wise and virtuous* than that celebrated person thinks himself, would content the ambition of any moderate man.

Will he allow of nothing short of the utmost intolerance of jacobinism or anti-jacobinism? Or will he tolerate this intolerance in nobody but himself? This seems to be his feeling: and it also seems to be Mr. Coleridge's opinion, whose maudlin methodistical casuistry leads him to clothe Mr. Southey's political sins with apostacy as with a garment, and to plead one excess of folly and indecency as a competent set-off against another. To be a renegado, is, with him, to be virtuous. The greater the sinner the greater the saint, says *The Courier*. Mr. Southey's Muse is confessedly not a vestal; but then she is what is much better, a Magdalen. Now a Magdalen is a person who has returned to her first habits and notions of virtue: but Mr. Southey's laurelled Muse is at present in high court-keeping, and tosses up her nose at the very mention of reform. Nor do we think Mr. Southey has a fairer claim to the degree of respectability good-naturedly assigned him by his friends, that of a pickpocket or highwayman turned thief-taker or king's evidence; for he in fact belies his own character to blacken every honest principle, and takes the government reward for betraying better men than himself. There are, as *The Courier* observes, youthful indiscretions; but there are also riper and more deliberate errors. A woman is more liable to prostitute her person at nineteen—a man is more likely to prostitute his understanding at forty. We do not see the exact parallel which *The Courier* sets up between moral repentance and political profligacy. A man, says *The Courier*, may surely express an abhorrence of his past vices, as of drunkenness. Yes; and he may also express a great abhorrence of his present vices, because his own opinion, as well as that of all impartial persons, condemns his conduct; but it would be curious if a man were to express a great abhorrence of his present opinions, and it is only a less degree of absurdity for a man to express a great abhorrence of his past opinions; for if he was not a hypocrite, he must have held those opinions, as he holds his present ones, because he thought them right. A man is at liberty to condemn his errors in practice as much as he pleases: it is a point agreed upon.

But he is not at liberty to condemn his errors in theory at the same unmerciful rate, because many people still think them right; because it is the height of arrogance in him to assume his own forfeited opinion as the invariable standard of right and wrong, and the height of indecency to ascribe the conclusions of others to bad motives, by which he can only arraign his own. Certainly, all the presumption of indirect and dishonest motives lies against Mr. Southey's unlooked-for conversion, and not against his original principles. Will he deny this himself? He must then retract what he says in the Quarterly Review; for he there says, that "the late war was so popular for three and twenty years together, that for any one to be against it," (and much more, to be a Jacobin, as he was, half that time,) "exposed him to contempt, insult, persecution, the loss of property, and even of life." The odds, we grant, were against Mr. Southey's pure reason; they proved too much for it. According, however, to the new theory of political integrity, to be a steady, consistent, conscientious Whig or Tory, is nothing. It is the change of opinion that stamps its value on it; and the more outrageous the change, the more meritorious the stigma attached to it. It is the sacrifice of all principle, that is the triumph of corruption; it is the shameless effrontery of a desertion of the people, that is the chief recommendation to the panders of a court; it is the contempt, the grinning scorn and infamy, which is poured on all patriotism and independence, by shewing the radical baseness and fickleness of its professors in the most startling point of view, that strengthens the rotten foundations of power, by degrading human nature. Poor Bob Southey! how they laugh at him! What are the abuse and contumely which we are in the habit of bestowing upon him, compared with the cordial contempt, the flickering sneers, that play round the lips of his new-fangled friends, when they see "the Man of Humanity" decked out in the trappings of his prostitution, and feel the rankling venom of their hearts soothed by the flattering reflection that virtue and genius are mere marketable commodities! What a squeeze must that be which

Mr. Canning gives the hand that wrote the Sonnet to Old Sarum, and the Defence of Rotten Boroughs in the Quarterly Review! Mr. Canning was at first suspected of being the author of this last article: no one has attributed *Wat Tyler* to the classical pen of that glib orator and consistent anti-jacobin. Yet what are the pretensions of that gentleman's profligate consistency opposed to Mr. Southey's profligate versatility; what a pitiful spectacle does his sneaking, servile adherence to a party make, compared with Mr. Southey's barefaced and magnanimous desertion of one! Mr. Canning has indeed served a cause; Mr. Southey has betrayed one. Mr. Canning threw contempt on the cause of liberty by his wit; Mr. Southey has done it by his want of principle. "This, this is the unkindest blow of all." We should not mind any thing but that;—that is the reflection that stabs us:

> ———————— "That the law
> By which mankind now suffers, is most just.
> For by superior energies; more strict
> Affiance with each other; faith more firm
> In their unhallow'd principles; the bad
> Have fairly earned a victory o'er the weak,
> The vacillating, inconsistent good."

Mr. Coleridge thinks that this triumph over himself and the Poet-laureate is a triumph to us. God forbid! It shews that he knows as little about us as he does about himself. This question of apostacy may be summed up in a very few words:—First, if Mr. Southey is not an apostate, we should like to know who ever was? Secondly, whether the term, apostate, is a term of reproach? If it has ceased to be so, it is another among the triumphs of the present king's reign, and a greater proof than any brought forward in the Quarterly Review, of the progress of public spirit and political independence among us of late years! A man may change his opinion. Good. But if he changes his opinion as his interest or vanity would prompt, if he deserts the weak to go to the stronger side, the change is a suspicious one; and we shall have a right to impute it rather to a defect of moral principle than to an accession of intellectual strength. Again, no man, be he who he may, has a right to change his opinion, and to be violent on opposite sides of a question. For the only excuse for dogmatical intolerance is, that the person who holds an opinion is totally blinded by habit to all objections against it, so that he can see nothing wrong on his own side, and nothing right on the other; which cannot be the case with any person who has been sincere in the opposite opinion. No one, therefore, has a right to call another "the greatest of scoundrels" for holding the opinions which he himself once held, without first formally acknowledging that he himself was the greatest of hypocrites when he maintained those opinions. When Mr. Southey subscribes to these conditions, we will give him a license to rail on whom and as long as he pleases: but not—*till then!* Apostates are violent in their opinions, because they suspect their truth, even when they are most sincere: they are forward to vilify the motives of those who differ from them, because their own are more than suspected by the world! We proceed to notice the flabby defence of "the *Wat Tyler*," from the well-known pen of Mr. Coleridge, which, as far as we can understand it, proceeds upon the following assumptions:—

1. *That Mr. Southey was only* 19 *when he wrote it, and had forgotten, from that time to this, all the principles and sentiments contained in it.*

Answer. A person who forgets all the sentiments and principles to which he was most attached at nineteen, can have no sentiments ever after worth being attached to. Further, it is not true that Mr. Southey gave up the general principles of *Wat Tyler*, which he wrote at nineteen, till almost as many years after. He did not give them up till many years after he had received his Irish pension in 1800. He did not give them up till with this *leaning* to something beyond "the slides of his magic lanthorn," and "the pleasing fervour of his imagination," he was canted out of them by the misty metaphysics of Mr. Coleridge, Mr. Southey being no conjurer in such matters, and Mr. Coleridge being a great quack. The dates of his works will shew this: as it was indeed excellently well shewn in *The Morning Chronicle* the other day. His Joan of Arc, his Sonnets and Inscriptions, his Letters from Spain and Portugal, his Annual Anthology, in which was published Mr. Coleridge's "Fire, Famine, and Slaughter," are a series of invectives against Kings, Priests, and Nobles, in favour of the French Revolution, and against war and taxes, up to the year 1803. Why does he not get an injunction against all these? To set aside all Mr. Southey's jacobin publications, it would be necessary to erect a new court of Chancery. Mr. Coleridge's insinuation, that he had changed all his opinions the year after, when Mr. S. and Mr. C., in conjunction, wrote the Fall of Robespierre, is, therefore, not true. But Mr. Coleridge never troubles himself about facts or dates; he is only "watching the slides of his magic lanthorn," and indulging in "the pleasing fervour of poetical inspiration."

2. *That Mr. Southey was a mere boy when he wrote* Wat Tyler, *and entertained Jacobin opinions: that being a child, he felt as a child, and thought slavery, superstition, war, famine, bloodshed, taxes, bribery and corruption, rotten boroughs, places and pensions, shocking things; but that now he is become a man, he has put away childish things, and thinks there is nothing so delightful as slavery, superstition, war, famine, bloodshed, taxes, bribery and corruption, rotten boroughs, places and pensions, and particularly, his own.*

Answer. Yet Mr. Coleridge tells us that when he wrote *Wat Tyler*, he was a man of genius and learning. That Mr. Southey was a wise man when he wrote this poem, we do not pretend: that he has ever been so, is more than we know. This we do know, and it is worth attending to; that all that Mr. Southey has done best in poetry, he did before he changed his political creed; that *all* that Mr. Coleridge ever did in poetry, as the *Ancient Mariner*, *Christabel*, the *Three Graves*, his Poems and his Tragedy, he had written when, according to his own account, he must have been a very ignorant, idle, thoughtless person; that much the greater part of what Mr. Wordsworth has done best in poetry was done about the same period; and if what these persons have done in poetry, in indulging the "pleasing fervour of a lively imagination," gives no weight to their political opinions at the time they did it, what they have done since in science or philosophy to establish their authority, is more than we know. All the authority that they have as poets and men of genius must be thrown into the scale of Revolution and Reform. Their Jacobin principles indeed gave rise to their Jacobin poetry. Since they gave up the first, their poetical powers have flagged, and been comparatively or wholly "in a state of suspended animation." Their genius, their style, their versification, every thing down to their spelling, was revolutionary. Their poetical innovations unhappily did not answer any more than the French Revolution. As their ambition was baulked in this first favourite direction, it was necessary for these restless persons to do something to get into notice; as they could not change their style, they changed their principles; and instead of writing popular poetry, fell to scribbling venal prose.—Mr. Southey's opinion, like Mr. Wordsworth's or Mr. Coleridge's, is of no value, except as it is his own, the unbiassed, undepraved dictate of his own understanding and feelings; not as it is a wretched, canting, reluctant echo of the opinion of the world. Poet-laureates are courtiers by profession; but we say that poets are naturally Jacobins. All the poets of the present day have been so, with a single exception, which it would be invidious to mention. If they have not all continued so, this only shews the instability of their own characters, and that their natural generosity and romantic enthusiasm, "their lofty, imaginative, and innocent spirits," have not been proof against the incessant, unwearied importunities of vulgar ambition. The poets, we say then, are with us, while they are worth keeping. We take the sound part of their heads and hearts, and make Mr. Croker and the *Courier* a present of the rest. What the philosophers are, let the dreaded name of *modern philosophy* answer!

3. *Mr. Coleridge compares us to the long-eared virtuoso, the ass, that found Apollo's lute, "left behind by him when he ascended to his own natural place, to sit thenceforward with all the Muses around him, instead of the ragged cattle of Admetus."*

Answer. Now it seems that Mr. Coleridge and other common friends of his, such as the author of the Fall of Robespierre and of Democratic Lectures, or Lectures on Democracy, in the year 1794, knew a good deal of Mr. Southey before he dropped this lute. Were they the ragged cattle of Admetus that Mr. Southey was fain to associate with during his obscure metamorphosis and strange Jacobin disguise? Did the Coleridges, the Wordsworths, the Lloyds and Lambs and Co. precede the Hunts, the Hazlitts, and the Cobbetts, in listening to Mr. Southey "tuning his mystic harp to praise Lepaux," the Parisian Theophilanthropist? And is it only since Mr. Southey has sat "quiring to the young-eyed cherubim," with the Barrymores, the Crokers, the Giffords, and the Stroehlings, that his natural genius and moral purity of sentiment have found their proper level and reward? Be this as it may, we plead guilty to the charge of some little indiscreet admiration of the Apollo of Jacobinism. We did not however find his lute three and twenty years after he had dropped it "in a thistle." We saw it in his hands. We heard him with our own ears play upon it, loud and long; and we can swear he was as well satisfied with his own music as we could be. "*Asinos asinina decent,*"—a bad compliment, in the style of *Dogberry*, which Mr. C. pays to his friend and to himself, as one of his early ragged auditors. Now whether Mr. Southey has since that period ascended to heaven or descended to the earth, we shall leave it to Mr. Coleridge himself to decide. For he says, that at the time when the present poet-laureate wrote *Wat Tyler*, he (Mr. Southey) was "a young man full of glorious visions concerning the possibilities of human nature, because his lofty, imaginative, and innocent spirit, had mistaken its own virtues and powers for the average character of mankind."—

Since Mr. Southey went to court, he has changed his tone. *Asinos asinina decent.* Is that Mr. Coleridge's political logic?*

4. *That Mr. Southey did not express his real opinions, even at that time, in Wat Tyler, which is a dramatic poem, in which mob-orators and rioters figure, with appropriate sentiments, as Jack Cade may do in Shakespear.*

Answer. This allusion to the dramatic characters of Shakespear is certainly unfortunate, and Mr. Coleridge himself hints as much. Rioters and mob-preachers are not the only persons who appear in "the *Wat Tyler*." The King and the Archbishop come forward in their own persons, according to Mr. Coleridge, with appropriate sentiments, labelled and put into their mouths. For example:—

> *Philpot*. Every moment brings
> Fresh tidings of our peril.
> *King*. It were well
> To yield them what they ask.
> *Archbishop*, Aye, that my liege
> Were politic. Go boldly forth to meet them,
> Grant all they ask—however wild and ruinous;—
> Meantime, the troops you have already summoned
> Will gather round them. Then my Christian power
> Absolves you of your promise.
> *Walworth*. Were but their ringleaders cut off, the rabble
> Would soon disperse.

* Of the three persons that Mr. Coleridge, by a most preposterous anachronism, has selected to compose his asinine auditory, Mr. Hunt was at the time in question a boy at school, not *a stripling bard* of nineteen or nine and twenty, but a real school-boy "declaiming on the patriotism of Brutus." As to Mr. Cobbett, he would at that time, had they come in his way, with one kick of his hard hoofs, have made a terrible crash among "the green corn" of Mr. Southey's Jacobin Pan's-pipe, and gone near to knock out the musician's brains into the bargain. The second person in this absurd trinity, who certainly thinks it "a robbery to be made equal to the other two," was the only hearer present at the rehearsal of Mr. Southey's overtures to Liberty and Equality, and to that "long-continued asinine bravura," which rings in Mr. Coleridge's ears, but which certainly was not unaccompanied, for he himself was present;

The very burden of *The Courier* all last week, and for many weeks last past and to come.

5. Mr. Coleridge sums up his opinion of the ultimate design and secret origin of "the *Wat Tyler*" in these remarkable words:—"We should have seen that the vivid, yet indistinct images in which he had painted the evils of war and the hardships of the poor, proved that neither the forms nor the feelings were the result of real observation. The product of the poet's own fancy, they"—[*viz.* the evils of war and the hardships of the poor]—"were impregnated, therefore, with *that pleasurable fervour which is experienced in all energetic exertion of intellectual power.* But as to any serious wish, akin to reality," [that is, to remove these evils] "as to any real persons or events designed or expected, we should think it just as wise and just as charitable, to believe that Quevedo or Dante would have been glad to realise the horrid phantoms and torments of *imaginary* oppressors, whom they beheld in the infernal regions—*i. e.* on the slides of their own magic lanthorn."

Answer. The slides of the guillotine, excited (as we have been told) the same pleasurable fervour in Mr. Southey's mind: and Mr. Coleridge seems to insinuate, that the 5,800,000 lives which have been lost to prove mankind the property of kings, by divine right, have been lost "on the slides of a magic lanthorn;" the evils of war, like all other actual evils, being "the products of a fervid imagination." So much for the sincerity of poetry.

> *Audrey.* Is not poetry a true thing?
> *Touchstone.* No.

Would these gentlemen persuade us that there is nothing evil in the universe but what exists in their imagination, but what is the product of their fervid fancy? That the world is full of nothing but their egotism, their vanity, and their hypocrisy? The world is *sick* of them, their egotism, their vanity, and their hypocrisy.

and those who know this gentleman, know that on these occasions he performs the part of a whole chorus.

6th and lastly. " Mr. Southey's darling poet from his childhood was Edmund Spenser, from whom, next to the spotless purity of his own moral habits, he learned that reverence for

> ———————— " constant chastity,
> Unspotted faith, and comely womanhood,
> Regard of honour and mild modesty."

" And we are strongly persuaded that the indignation which, in his early perusal of our history, the outrage on *Wat Tyler's* Daughter had kindled within him, was the circumstance that recommended the story to his choice for the first powerful exercise of his dramatic powers. It is this, too, we doubt not, that coloured and shaped his feelings during the whole composition of the drama.

> " Through the allegiance and just fealty
> Which he did owe unto all womankind."

Mr. Coleridge might as well tell us that the Laureate wrote *Wat Tyler* as an Epithalamium on his own marriage. There is but one line on the subject from the beginning to the end. No; it is not Mr. Southey's way to say nothing on the subject on which he writes. If this were the main drift and secret spring of the poem, why does Mr. Southey wish to retract it now? Has he been taught by his present fashionable associates to laugh at Edmund Spenser, the darling of the *boy* Southey, to abjure " his allegiance and just fealty to all womankind," and to look upon " rapes and ravishments " as " exaggerated evils," the product of an idle imagination, exciting a pleasurable fervour at the time, and signifying nothing afterwards? Is the outrage upon *Wat Tyler's* Daughter the only evil in history, or in the poem itself, which ought to inflame the virtuous indignation of the full-grown stripling bard? Are all the other oppressions recorded in the annals of the world nothing but " horrible shadows, unreal mockeries," that this alone should live " within the book and volume of his brain unmixed with baser matter?" Or has Mr.

Southey, the historian and the politician, at last discovered, that even this evil, the greatest and the only evil in the world, and not a mere illusion of his boyish imagination, is itself a bagatelle, compared with the blessings of the poll-tax, feudal vassalage, popery, and slavery, the attempt to put down which by murder, insurrection, and treason, in the reign of Richard II. the poet-laureate once celebrated *con amore* in "the *Wat Tyler*?"—In courtly malice and servility Mr. Southey has outdone Herodias's daughter. He marches into Chancery "with his own head in a charger," as an offering to Royal delicacy. He plucks out the heart of Liberty within him, and mangles his own breast to stifle every natural sentiment left there: and yet Mr. Coleridge would persuade us that this stuffed figure, this wretched phantom, is the living man. The finery of birth-day suits has dazzled his senses, so that he has "no speculation in those eyes that he does glare with;" yet Mr. Coleridge would persuade us that this is the clear-sighted politician. Famine stares him in the face, and he looks upon her with lack-lustre eye. Despotism hovers over him, and he says, "Come, let me clutch thee." He drinks the cup of human misery, and thinks it is a cup of sack. He has no feeling left, but of "tickling commodity;" no ears but for court whispers; no understanding but of his interest; no passion but his vanity. And yet they would persuade us that this non-entity is somebody—"the chief dread of Jacobins and Jacobinism, of quacks and quackery." If so, Jacobins and Jacobinism have not much to fear; and Mr. Coleridge may publish as many Lay Sermons as he pleases.

There is but one statement in the article in *The Courier* to which we can heartily assent; it is Mr. Southey's prediction of the fate of the French Revolution. "The Temple of Despotism," he said, "would be rebuilt, like that of the Mexican God, with human skulls, and cemented with human blood." He has lived to see this; to assist in the accomplishment of his prophecy, and to consecrate the spectre-building with pensioned hands!

A LETTER TO WILLIAM SMITH, ESQ. M. P. *from* Robert Southey, *Esq.* John Murray, Albemarle-street. 1817. *Price 2s.*

May 4, 1817.

THIS is very unlike Mr. Burke's celebrated "Letter to the Duke of Bedford." The last is the only work of the Irish orator and patriot, in which he was in earnest, and all that he wanted was sincerity. The attack made upon his pension, by rousing his self-love, kindled his imagination, and made him blaze out in a torrent of fiery eloquence, in the course of which his tilting prose-Pegasus darted upon the titles of the noble duke like a thunder-bolt, reversed his ancestral honours, overturned the monstrous straddle-legged figure of that legitimate monarch, Henry VIII., exploded the mines of the French revolution, kicked down the Abbé Sieyes's pigeon-holes full of constitutions, and only reposed from his whirling career, in that fine retrospect on himself, and the affecting episode to Admiral Keppel. Mr. Burke was an apostate, "a malignant renegado," like Mr. Southey; but there the comparison ends. He would not have been content, on such an occasion as the present, with *Mistering* his opponent, and *Esquiring* himself, like the ladies in the Beggar's Opera, who express the height of their rankling envy and dislike, by calling each other—*Madam*. Mr. Southey's self-love, when challenged to the lists, does not launch out into the wide field of wit or argument: it retires into its own littleness, collects all its slender resources in one poor effort of pert, pettifogging spite, makes up by studied malice for conscious impotence, and attempts to mortify others by the angry sense of his own insignificance. He grows tenacious of his ridiculous pretensions, in proportion as they are given up by every body else. His self-complacency riots, with a peculiar and pointed gusto, in the universal contempt or compassion of friends and foes. In the last stage of a galloping consumption, while the last expiring puff of *The Courier* makes "a swan-like end," in a compliment to his opponents, he is sanguine of a deathless reputation—considers his soreness to the least touch as a proof of his being in a whole skin, and his uneasiness to repel every attack as a proof of his being invulnerable. In a word, he mistakes an excess of spleen and irritability for the consciousness of innocence, and sets up his own egotism, vanity, ill-humour, and intolerance, as an answer in full to all the objections which have been brought against him of vanity, egotism, malignity, and intolerance. His "Letter" is a concentrated essence of a want of self-knowledge. It is the picture of the author's mind in little. In this respect, it is "a psychological curiosity;" a study of human infirmity. As some persons bequeath their bodies to the surgeons to be dissected after their death, Mr. Southey publicly exposes his mind to be anatomized while he is living. He lays open his character to the scalping-knife, guides the philosophic hand in its painful researches, and on the bald crown of our *petit tondu*, in vain concealed under withered bay-leaves and a few contemptible grey hairs, you see the organ of vanity triumphant—sleek, smooth, round, perfect, polished, horned, and shining, as it were in a transparency. This is the handle of his intellect, the index of his mind; "the guide, the anchor of his purest thoughts, and soul of all his moral being;" the clue to the labyrinth of all his tergiversations and contradictions; the *medius terminus* of his political logic.

———"The ruling passion once express'd,
Wharton is plain, and Chartres stands confess'd."

Once admit that Mr. Southey is always in the right, and every one else in the wrong, and all the rest follows. This at once reconciles "Wat Tyler" and the "Quarterly Review," which Mr. William Smith took down to the House, in two different pockets for fear of a breach of the peace; identifies the poet of the "Joan of Arc" and of the "Annual Anthology" with the poet-laureate; and *jumps* the stripling into the man, whenever the latter has a mind to jump into a place or pension. Till you can deprive him of his personal identity, he will always be the same infallible person—in his own opinion. He is both judge and jury in his own cause; the sole standard of right and wrong. To differ with him is inexcusable; for "there is but one perfect, even himself." He is the central point of all moral and intellectual excellence; the way, the truth, and the life. There is no salvation out of his pale; and yet he makes the terms of communion so strict, that there is no hope that way. The crime of Mr. William Smith and others, against whom this high-priest of impertinence levels his anathemas, is *in not being* Mr. Southey. What is right in him, is wrong in them; what is the height of folly or wickedness in them, is, "as fortune and the flesh shall serve," the height of wisdom and virtue in him; for there is no medium in his reprobation of others and approbation of himself. Whatever he does, is proper: whatever he thinks, is true and profound: "I, Robert Shallow, Esquire, have said it." Whether Jacobin or Anti-jacobin, Theophilanthropist or Trinitarian, Spencean or Ex-Spencean, the patron of Universal Suffrage or of close Boroughs, of the reversion of sinecure places, and pensions, or of the abolition of all property,—however extreme in one opinion or another, he alone is in the right; and those who do not think as he does, and change their opinions as he does, and go the lengths that he does, first on one side and then on the other, are necessarily knaves and fools. Wherever he sits, is the head of the table. Truth and justice are always at his side. The wise and virtuous are always with him. How should it be otherwise? He calls those "wise and virtuous" who are of his way of thinking; the rest are "sciolists, profligates, and coxcombs." By a fiction of his own making, not by a fiction of the law, Mr. Southey can do no wrong; and to accuse him of it, is a libel on the face of it, and little short of high treason. It is not the poet-laureate, the author of "Wat Tyler" and of the "Quarterly Review," who is to blame for his violence and apostacy; with that portion of self-sufficiency which this author possesses, "these are most virtuous;" but it is the person who brings forward the contradictions and intemperance of these two performances who is never to be forgiven for questioning Mr. Southey's consistency and moderation. All this is strange, but not new to our readers. We have said it all before. Why does Mr. Southey oblige us to repeat the accusation, by furnishing us with fresh proofs of it? He is betrayed to his ruin by trusting to the dictates of his personal feelings and wounded pride; and yet he dare not look at his situation through any other medium. "To know my deed, 't were best not know myself." But does he expect all eyes as well as his to be "blind with the pin and web?" Does he pull his laurel-crown as a splendid film over his eyes, and expect us to join in a game of political blindman's-buff with him, with a "Hoop, do me no harm, good man?" Are we not to cry out while an impudent, hypocritical, malignant renegado is putting his gag in our mouths, and getting his thumbscrews ready? "Dost thou think, because thou art virtuous, there shall be no more cakes and ale," says *Sir Toby* to the fantastical steward *Malvolio?* Does Mr. Southey think, because he is a pensioner, that he is to make us willing slaves? While he goes on writing in the "Quarterly," shall we give over writing in *The Examiner?* Before he puts down the liberty of the press, the press shall put him down, with all his hireling and changeling crew. In the *servile war* which Mr. Southey tells us is approaching, the service we have proposed to ourselves to do is, to neutralize the servile intellect of the country. This we have already done in part, and hope to make clear work of it, before we have done.—For example:

This heroic epistle to William Smith, Esq., from Robert Southey, sets off in the following manner:—

"Sir,—You are represented in the newspapers as having entered, during an important discussion in parliament, into a comparison between certain passages in the "Quarterly Review," and the opinions which were held by the author of "Wat Tyler" three-and-twenty years ago. It appears farther, according to the same authority, that the introduction of so strange a criticism, in so strange a place, did not arise from the debate, but was a premeditated thing; that you had prepared yourself for it, by stowing the "Quarterly Review" in one pocket, and "Wat Tyler" in the other; and that you deliberately stood up for the purpose of reviling an individual who was not present to vindicate himself, and in a place which afforded you protection." p. 2.

So that for Mr. William Smith in a debate on a bill *for the suppression of all political opinions* (as we are told by Mr. Alderman Smith, a very different person, to be sure, and according to Mr. Southey, no doubt, a highly respectable character, and a true lover of liberty and the constitution) for Mr. William Smith on such an occasion to introduce the sentiments of a well-known writer in a public journal, that writer being a whiffling tool of the court, and that journal the avowed organ of the government-party, in confirmation of his apprehensions of the objects and probable results of the bill then pending, was quite irrelevant and unparliamentary; nor had Mr. William Smith any right to set an additional stigma on the unprincipled and barefaced lengths which this writer now goes in servility and intolerance, by shewing the equal lengths to which he went formerly in popular fanaticism and licentiousness. Yet neither Mr. Southey nor his friend Mr. Wynne complained of Mr. Canning's want of regularity, or disrespect of the House, in lugging out of his pocket THE SPENCEAN PLAN as an argument against Reform, and as decisive of the views of the Friends of Reform in parliament. Nay, Mr. Southey requoted Mr. Canning's quotation, for the purpose of reviling all Reform and all Reformers, in the "Quarterly Review;"—a place in which any one so reviled can no more defend himself than Mr. Southey can defend himself in parliament; and which it seems affords equal "protection" to those who avail themselves of it; for a Quarterly Reviewer, according to Mr. Southey, being anonymous, is not at all accountable for what he writes. He says,—

"As to the "Quarterly Review," you can have no other authority for ascribing any particular paper in that journal to one person or to another, than common report. The "Quarterly Review" stands upon its own merits." [Yet it was for what Mr. Southey wrote in that Review, that *The Courier* told us at the time that

Mr. Southey was made Poet-laureate.] "What I may have said or thought in any part of my life, no more concerns that journal than it does you or the House of Commons." [What Mr. Southey has said publicly any where in any part of his life, concerns the public and every man in it, unless Mr. Southey means to say that his opinions are utterly worthless and contemptible, a piece of modesty of which we cannot suspect him.] "What I have written in it is a question which you, Sir, have no right to ask, and which certainly I will not answer. As little right have you to take that for granted which you cannot possibly know." Now mark. In the very paragraph before the one in which he skulks from the responsibility of the "Quarterly Review," and with pert vapid assurance repels every insinuation implying a breach of his inviolability as an anonymous writer, he makes an impudent, unqualified, and virulent attack on Mr. Brougham as an Edinburgh Reviewer, "This was not necessary in regard to Mr. Brougham ... *he only carried the quarrels as well as the practices of the Edinburgh Review into the House of Commons. But as calumny, Sir, has not been your vocation,* it may be useful, even to yourself, if I comment upon your first attempt."—p. 3. Such a want of common logic is to our literal capacities quite inexplicable: it is "in the third tier of wonders above wonders."

In page 5, Mr. Southey calls the person who published "Wat Tyler" "a skulking scoundrel," with his characteristic delicacy and moderation in the use of epithets; and says that it was published, "for the avowed purpose of insulting him, and with the hope of injuring him if possible." Perhaps one object was to prevent Mr. Southey from insulting and injuring other people. It was supposed that "Wat Tyler" might prove an antidote to the "Quarterly Review:" that, "the healing might come from the same weapon that gave the wound;" and in this instance it has turned out so. He adds, "You knew that the transaction bore upon its face every character of baseness and malignity. You knew that it must have been effected either by robbery, or by breach of trust. *These things, Mr. William Smith, you knew!*" [Mr.

Southey at least knows no such thing, but he is here in his glory; putting a false statement into epigrammatic phraseology; bristling with horror at antithetical enormities of his own fabricating, and concluding with that formidable and significant repetition of the title, Christian and surname of *Mr. William Smith.*] The above paragraph concludes thus, with the author's usual logical precision and personal modesty. " And knowing them as you did, I verily believe, that if it were possible to revoke what is irrevocable, you would *at this moment* be far more desirous of blotting from remembrance the *disgraceful* speech which stands upon record in your name, than I should be of cancelling the boyish composition which gave rise to it. " Wat Tyler" is full of errors . . . . but they are the errors of youth and ignorance; they bear no indication of an ungenerous spirit, or of a malevolent heart." p. 6. It seems by this passage that any attempt to fix disgrace on Mr. Southey only recoils upon the head of his accuser. " Upon his brow shame is ashamed to sit." He says that Mr. W. Smith's *disgraceful* speech was occasioned by " Wat Tyler." That is not true. It was occasioned by " Wat Tyler" coupled with the " Quarterly Review." He says, " ' Wat Tyler' is full of errors." So is the article in the " Quarterly Review;" but *they* are not " the errors of youth and ignorance; they bear strong indications of an ungenerous spirit and a malignant heart." Let not Mr. Southey mistake. It is not the indiscreet and romantic extravagance of the boy which has brought the man into this predicament: it is the deliberate and rancorous servility of the man that has made those who were the marks of his slanderous and cowardly invectives, rake up the errors of his youth against him.

Mr. Southey next proceeds to a defence of himself for writing " the Wat Tyler." He argues that " it is not *seditious,* because it is *dramatic.*" We deny that it is dramatic. He acknowledges that it is mischievous, and particularly so, at the present time. To the last part of the proposition we cannot assent. When this poem was written, there was a rage of speculation which might be dangerous: the danger at present arises from the rage of hunger.

And the true reason why Mr. Southey was eager to suppress this publication was not what he pretends, a fear that it might inculcate notions of perfect equality and general licentiousness: but a feeling that it might prevent him from defending every abuse of excessive inequality, and every stretch of arbitrary power, the end of which must be to sink "the people" in an abyss of slavery, and to plunge "the populace" in the depths of famine, despair, and misery, or by a sudden and tremendous revulsion, to occasion all that confusion, anarchy, violence, and bloodshed, which Mr. Southey hypocritically affects to deprecate as the consequences of seditious and inflammatory publications. Now we contend in opposition to Mr. Southey and all that servile crew, that the only possible preventive of one or other of these impending evils, namely, lasting slavery, famine, and general misery on the one hand, or a sudden and dreadful convulsion on the other, is the liberty of the press, which Mr. Southey calls sedition, and the firm, manly, and independent expression of public opinion, which he calls rebellion. We detest despotism: we deprecate popular commotion: but if we are forced upon an alternative, we have a choice: we prefer temporary to lasting evils. Mr. Southey has indeed a new-acquired and therefore lively dread of the horrors of revolution. But his passion for despotism is greater than his dread of anarchy; and he runs all the risks of the one, rather than not glut his insatiable and unnatural appetite for the other. Such are his politics, and such are ours. He says, "The piece was written under the influence of opinions which I have long since outgrown, and repeatedly disclaimed, but for which I have never felt either shame or contrition. They were taken up conscientiously in early youth, they were acted upon in disregard of all worldly considerations, *and they were left behind in the same strait-forward course, as I advanced in years.*" The latter part of this statement is not self-evident. Mr. Southey says that while he adhered to his first principles, he acted with a total disregard of his worldly interest; and this is easily understood:—but that his desertion of those principles, so contrary to his worldly views, was equally independent, disinterested and free from sinister motives, is not so plain. Nor can we take Mr. Southey's word for it. And we will tell him the reason. If he had been *progressive*, as he calls it, in his course, up to the year 1814, we should not have found much fault with him: but why did he become stationary then? Has nothing happened in the three last years, —nothing—to make Mr. Southey retreat back to some of his old opinions, as he had advanced from them, guided, as he professes to be in his undeviating course, by facts and experience? Are the actual events of the last three years nothing in the scale of Mr. Southey's judgment? Is not their weight overpowering, irresistible? What, do not the names of Poland, Norway, Finland, Saxony, Italy, Spain and Portugal, the Pope, the Inquisition, and the Cortes (to say nothing of France, Nismes, and the Bourbons) thrown into the scale of common sense and common honesty, dash it down, with a startling sound, upon the counter, where Mr. Southey is reckoning his well-gotten gains, the price of his disinterested exertions in the cause of Spanish liberty and the deliverance of mankind, making his hair stand on end at his own folly and credulity, and forcing him indignantly to fling his last year's pension and the arrears of the Quarterly in the face of Mr. Murray's shopmen and the clerks of the Treasury, and swear, "in disregard of all worldly considerations," never to set his foot in Downing or Albemarle-street again? No such thing. In advocating the cause of the French people, Mr. Southey's principles and his interest were at variance, and therefore he quitted his principles when he saw a good opportunity: in taking up the cause of the Allies, his principles and his interest became united and thenceforth indissoluble. His engagement to his first love, the Republic, was only upon liking; his marriage to Legitimacy is *for better, for worse*, and nothing but death shall part them. Our simple Laureate was sharp upon his hoyden Jacobin mistress, who brought him no dowry, neither place nor pension, who "found him poor and kept him so," by her prudish notions of virtue. He divorced her, in short, for nothing but the spirit and success with which she resisted the fraud and force to which the old bawd Legitimacy was forever resorting to overpower her resolution and fidelity. He said she was a virago, a cunning gipsey, always in broils about her honour and the inviolability of her person, and always getting the better in them, furiously scratching the face or cruelly tearing off the hair of the said pimping old lady, who would never let her alone, night or day. But since her foot slipped one day on the ice, and the detestable old hag tripped up her heels, and gave her up to the kind keeping of the Allied Sovereigns, Mr. Southey has devoted himself to her more fortunate and wealthy rival: he is become uxorious in his second matrimonial connexion; and though his false Duessa has turned out a very witch, a foul, ugly witch, drunk with insolence, mad with power, a griping, rapacious wretch, bloody, luxurious, wanton, malicious, not sparing steel, or poison, or gold, to gain her ends—bringing famine, pestilence, and death in her train—infecting the air with her thoughts, killing the beholders with her looks, claiming mankind as her property, and using them as her slaves—driving every thing before her, and playing the devil wherever she comes, Mr. Southey sticks to her in spite of every thing, and for very shame lays his head in her lap, paddles with the palms of her hands, inhales her hateful breath, leers in her eyes and whispers in her ears, calls her little fondling names, Religion, Morality, and Social Order, takes for his motto,

> "Be to her faults a little blind,
> Be to her virtues very kind"—

sticks close to his filthy bargain, and will not give her up, because she keeps him, and he is down in her will. Faugh!

> "What's here?
> Gold! yellow, glittering, precious gold!
> ———————— The wappened widow,
> Whom the spittle-house and ulcerous sores
> Would heave the gorge at, this embalms and spices
> To the April day again."

The above passage is, we fear, written in the style of Aretin, which Mr. Southey condemns in the *Quarterly*. It is at least a very sincere style: Mr. Southey will never write so, till he can keep in the same mind for three and twenty years together. Why should not one make a sentence of a page long, out of the feelings of one's whole life? The early Protestant Divines wrote such prodigious long sentences from the sincerity of their religious and political opinions. Mr. Coleridge ought not to imitate them.

A LETTER TO WILLIAM SMITH, ESQ. M. P. *from* Robert Southey, *Esq.* John Murray, Albemarle-street. 1817. *Price 2s.*

"What word hath passed thy lips, Adam severe?"

May 11, 1817.

HAS Mr. Murray turned Quaker, that he styles himself John Murray ("Mark you his absolute John?") in the title-page? Or has Mr. Southey resigned his place and his pretensions, that he omits in the same page his honorary titles of Poet-Laureate and Member of the Royal Spanish Academy? We cannot tell; but we should think it some sign of grace, if, without a hint from the Lord Chamberlain, he had for a while laid by his tattered laurel and spattered birth-day suit: if, as the Commander in Chief retired after the droll affair of Mrs. Clarke (we are not such rigid moralists as Mr. Southey) the Poet Laureate had thought proper to veil his blushing court favours during the dramatic representation of *Wat Tyler*, and did not consider it either prudent or becoming to be seen going to or coming from Carlton-house with the mob, "the reading rabble," at his heels, and with a shower of two-penny pamphlets sticking to the skirts of his turned coat. Poor *Morgan*, the honest Welchman in *Roderic Random*, reeking with the fumes of tobacco and garlic, was not more offensive to the sensitive organs of *Captain Whiffle*, than Mr. Southey must be to the nice feelings of an exalted Personage, reeking with the fumes of Jacobinism, and rolled, as he has been, in the kennel of the newspaper press. A voyage to Italy, a classical quarantine of a year or two, with the Pope's blessing, seems absolutely necessary to wipe out the stains of his *Wat Tyler*, "as pure as sin with baptism;" and to restore him to the vows of Prince and People as smug as a young novice in a monastery, and sweet as any waiting-gentlewoman.

Mr. Southey says, in continuation of his Defence of *Wat Tyler*, p. 7, "It was written when republicanism was confined to a very small number of the educated classes:" [Is it more common now among the intended hearers of Mr. Coleridge's Second and Third Lay-Sermons?]—"when those who were known to entertain such opinions were exposed to personal danger from *the populace*;" [The populace of course were not set on by the higher classes, the clergy or gentry, nor can Mr. S. mean to include the Attorney-General of that day, my Lord Eldon, as one of *the populace*.] "And when a spirit of anti-jacobinism was predominant, which I cannot characterise more truly than by saying that it was as unjust and intolerant, though not quite as ferocious, *as the Jacobinism of the present day*."—Why not the *anti-jacobinism* of the present day? "The collusion holds in the exchange." The business is carried on to the present hour; and though it has changed hands, the principal of the firm is still the same. Mr. Gifford, the present Editor of the *Quarterly Review*, where Mr. Southey now writes, was formerly the Editor of the *Anti-jacobin* newspaper, where he was written at. The above passage is however a sly passing hit at Mr. Canning's parodies, who (shame to say it) was as wise and as witty three and twenty years ago as he is now, and has not been making that progressive improvement ever since, on which Mr. Southey compliments himself, congratulates his friends, and insults over his enemies! How nicely this gentleman *differences* himself from all his contemporaries, Jacobin or anti-Jacobin! No one can come up to him at all points. "The lovely Marcia towers above her sex!"

The Letter-writer goes on to say:—"When therefore Mr. Smith informed the House of Commons that the author of *Wat Tyler* thinks no longer upon certain points as he did in his youth, he informed that legislative assembly of nothing more than what the author has shown during very many years, *in the course of his writings* . . . . . that while events have been moving on upon the great theatre of human affairs, *his intellect has not been stationary*."—[Mr. S. here confounds a change of opinions with the progress of intellect, a mistake which we shall correct presently.] —"But when the Member for Norwich asserts that I impute evil motives to men merely for holding the same doctrines" [No, only a tenth part of the same doctrines] "which I myself formerly professed, and when he charges me with the malignity and baseness of a Renegade, the assertion and the charge are as false, as the language in which they are conveyed is coarse and insulting." p. 9.

Now we know of no writings of Mr. Southey's, in the course of which he had shewn for many years the change or progress of his opinions, but in the *Quarterly Review* and other anonymous publications. We suppose he will hardly say that his Birth-day Odes, the *Carmen Nuptiale*, &c. have shewn the progress of his intellect. But in the same anonymous writings, in which the public would find, to Mr. Southey's credit, that his intellect had not been stationary, the Member for Norwich would find what was not so much to his credit, but all that was wanting to make good the charge—that Mr. Southey's moderation and charity to those whose intellects had been stationary, did not keep pace with the progress of his own—for in the articles in the *Quarterly*, which he claims or disclaims as he pleases, he, the writer of the Inscription on Old Sarum, describes "a Reformer as no better than a housebreaker:" he, the writer of the Inscription at Chepstow Castle, calls all those who do not bow their necks to the doctrine of Divine Right, Rebels and Regicides: he, the author of *Wat Tyler*, calls those persons who think taxes, wars, the wanton waste of the resources of a country, and the unfeeling profligacy of the rich, likely to aggravate and rouse to madness the intolerable sufferings of the poor, " flagitious incendiaries, panders to insurrection, murder, and treason, and the worst of scoundrels"; he, the equalizer of all property and of popular representation, would protect the holders of rotten boroughs and of entailed sinecures, by shutting up all those who write against them in solitary confinement, without pen, ink, or paper, to answer the unanswerable arguments of Mr. Southey—in short, the author of the articles in the *Quarterly Review*, if he was not always a base and malignant sycophant, shews himself to be a base and malignant Renegade, by defending all the rotten, and undermining all the sound parts of the system to which he professes to be a convert, and by consigning over to a " vigour beyond the law" all those who expose his unprincipled, pragmatical tergiversations, or would maintain the system itself, without maintaining those corruptions and abuses, which were all that Mr. Southey at one time saw to hold up to execration in the English Constitution, and are all that he now sees to admire and revere in it. This is as natural in a Renegado, as it would be unaccountable in any one else.

We must get on a little faster, for to expose the absurdities of this Letter one by one would fill " a nice little book." In the pages immediately following, Mr. Southey glances at the Editor of the *Edinburgh Review*, whom he condemns " to bear a *gore sinister tenné* in his escutcheon," for saying that Mr. Southey does not form an exception to the *irritabile genus vatum*. He says, that he has often refrained from exposing the ignorance and inconsistency of his opponents, as well as " that moral turpitude," which, our readers must by this time perceive, can hardly fail to accompany any difference of opinion with him. He says that " he has a talent for satire, but that (good soul!) he has long since subdued the disposition." This must be since writing the last *Quarterly:* we thought there were some shrewd hits there, and we suspect Sir Richard Phillips, whom he laughs at for his dislike of war and of animal food, for pages together, will be of our opinion. He says that "he has been lately employed, while among the mountains of Cumberland, upon the Mines of Brazil and the War in the Peninsula."

> "Why man, he doth bestride the world
> Like a Colossus, and we, petty men, peep
> Under his huge legs."

"His *name*, in the mean time, has served in London for the very shuttlecock of discussion." Why should not his name be a shuttlecock, when he himself is no better?—"He has impeded the rising reputation of Toby, the Sapient Pig;"—has overlaid the posthumous birth of the young Shiloh, and perhaps prevented Mr. Coleridge's premature deliverance of his last *Lay Sermon*. After all these misfortunes, the author makes merry with Bonaparte's "having been exposed, like Bishop Hatto, to be devoured by the rats!" The levelling rogue cares neither for Bishops nor Emperors, but grows grave again in recounting the retrograde progress of his own mind.

"In my youth, when my stock of knowledge consisted of such an acquaintance with Greek and Roman history, as is acquired in the course of a regular scholastic education,"—[The Greek and Roman history is as good as the history of rotten boroughs or the reign of George III.]—"when my heart was full of poetry and romance,"—[Is it so no longer?]—"and Lucan and Akenside were at my tongue's end."—[Instead of the red book and the court calendar]—"*I fell into* the political opinions which the French Revolution was then scattering throughout Europe." [We have here a pretty fair account of the origin and genealogy of the opinions of the French Revolution, which opinions of liberty, truth, and justice, neither the French Revolution shall destroy, nor those who destroyed *it*, because it was produced by and gave birth to those opinions; and does Mr. Southey suppose that the suppression of *Wat Tyler* is to suppress those opinions; and that a lying article in the *Quarterly Review* is to persuade us that they who made war on those opinions from the beginning (and by so doing, produced all the evils of those opinions, produced them purposely, in the malice of their hearts and the darkness of their minds produced them to destroy all liberty, truth, and justice, and to keep mankind their slaves in perpetuity by right divine) were right from the beginning, that they deserved well of mankind, that their boasted triumph, the triumph of kings over the species, is ours and Mr. Southey's triumph? Or would he persuade us that the Greek and Roman History has become obsolete, because Mr. Southey left school three and twenty years ago; that poetry and romance were banished from the human heart when he took a place and pension; that Lucan and Akenside will not live as long as *Wat Tyler*, or the *Quarterly Review!* —We broke off in an interesting part. Mr. Southey proceeds:] " Following those opinions with ardour wherever they led." [This is an old trick of the author, he is a keen sportsman;] " I soon perceived that inequalities of rank were a light evil compared to the inequalities of property,* and those more

* A sarcastic writer, like Mr. Southey, might here ask, whether it was a disappointment in sharing the estate of some rich landed proprietor that made Mr. Southey turn short round to a defence of sinecures and pensions? We do not know, but here follows a passage, which " some skulking scoundrel " in the *Quarterly Review* appears to have aimed at Mr. Southey's early opinions and character:—" As long as the smatterer in philosophy confines himself to private practice, the mischief does not extend beyond his private circle—his neighbour's wife may be in some danger, and his neighbour's property also; if the distinctions between *meum* and *tuum* should be practically inconvenient to the man of free opinions. But when he commences professor of moral and political philosophy for the benefit of the public—the fables of old credulity are then verified, his very breath becomes venomous, and every page which he sends abroad carries with it poison to the unsuspicious reader." Such is the interpretation given by the anonymous writer to the motives of smatterers in philosophy; this writer could not be Mr. Southey, for " *he* never imputes evil motives to men merely for holding the opinions he formerly held," such as the evils of the inequality of property, &c.

fearful distinctions which the want of moral and intellectual culture occasions between man and man. At that time, and with those opinions or rather feelings (for their root was in the heart, and not in the understanding) I wrote *Wat Tyler* as one who was impatient of 'all the oppressions that are done under the sun.'" [Here we must make another full stop. Mr. Southey is incapable of forming any other opinions but from his feelings: he never had any other opinions, he never will have any others, worth a rush. When the opinions he professes ceased to be the dictates of his heart, they became the dictates of his vanity and interest; they became good for nothing. When the first ebullition of youthful ardour was over, his understanding was not competent to maintain its independence against the artifices of sophistry, aided by the accumulating force of "worldly considerations," showy or substantial, the long neglect of which he had felt to his cost. Mr. Southey's pure reason was not steady enough to contemplate the truth in an unprejudiced and unimpassioned point of view. His imagination first ran away with his understanding; and now, that he is getting old, his convenience, the influence of fashion, and the tide of opinion, rush in, and fill up all the void both of sense and imagination, driving him into the very vortex of court-sycophancy, the sinks and common sewers of corruption. Mr. Southey is not a man to hear reason at any time of his life. He thinks his change of opinion is owing to an increase of knowledge, because he has in fact no idea of any progress in intellect but exchanging one error for another. He has no idea that a man may grow wiser in the same opinion by discovering new reasons for the faith that is in him; for Mr. Southey has no reasons for the faith that is in him. He does not see how a man may devote his whole life to the discovery of the principle of the most common truth; for he has no principles of thought, either to guide, enlarge, or modify his knowledge. He has nothing to shew for the wisdom of his opinions but his own opinion of their wisdom: they are mere self-opinions: he considers his present notions as profound and solid, because his former ones were hasty and shallow; asserts them with pert, vapid assurance, because he does not see the objections against them; and thinks he must be right in his premises in proportion to the violence and extravagance of his conclusions. Because when he wrote *Wat Tyler*, he was "impatient of all the oppressions that are done under the sun," he now thinks it his bounden duty to justify them all, with equal impatience of contradiction. Mr. Southey does not know himself so well as we do; and a greater confirmation of his ignorance in this respect cannot well be given than the rest of the above passage. "The subject of *Wat Tyler* was injudiciously chosen; and it was treated as might be expected by a youth of twenty, in such times, who regarded only one side of the question." [It is Mr. Southey's fault or his misfortune that at all times he regards only one side of a question.]

"There is no other misrepresentation. The sentiments of the historical characters are correctly stated." [What, of the King, the Judge, and the Archbishop?] "Were I now to dramatize the same story, there would be much to add, but little to alter. I should not express those sentiments less strongly, but I should oppose to them more enlarged views of the nature of man and the progress of society. *I should set forth with equal force the oppressions of the feudal system, the excesses of the insurgents, and the treachery of the government,*" [Doctors doubt that] "and hold up the errors and crimes which were then committed, as a warning *for this* and for future generations. I should write *as a man; not as a stripling*; with the same heart, and the same desires, but with a ripened understanding and competent stores of knowledge," p. 15. Let him do it, but he dare not. He would shew by the attempt the hollowness of his boasted independence, the little time-serving meanness of his most enlarged views; in a word, that he has still the same understanding, but no longer the same heart. What are "the ripened discoveries and competent stores of knowledge" which Mr. Southey would bring to this task? Are they the barefaced self-evident sophistries, the wretched shuffling evasions of common sense and humanity which he contributes to the *Quarterly Review*, the cast-off, thread-bare, tattered excuses of Paley's Moral Philosophy, and Windham's hashed-up speeches? Why, all the prodigious discoveries which Mr. Southey there details with such dry significance, are familiar to every school-boy, are the common stock in trade of every spouter at a debating society, have been bandied about, hackneyed, exhausted any time these thirty years? And yet Mr. Southey was quite ignorant of them till very lately; they have broke upon him with a new and solemn light; they have come upon him by surprise, after three-and-twenty years; and at the last rebound, have overturned his tottering patriotism? Where is the use of Mr. Southey's *regular scholastic education*, if he is to be thus ignorant at twenty, thus versatile at forty? The object of such an education is to make men less astonished at their own successive discoveries, by putting them in possession beforehand of what has been discovered by others. Mr. Southey cannot, like Mr. Cobbett, plead in extenuation of his change of sentiment, that he was a self-taught man, who had to grope his way from error and prejudice to truth and reason; neither can he plead like Mr. Cobbett, in proof of the sincerity of his motives, that he has suffered the loss of liberty and property by his change of opinion: Mr. Southey has suffered nothing by his—but a loss of character!

A LETTER TO WILLIAM SMITH, ESQ. M. P. *from* Robert Southey, *Esq.* John Murray, Albemarle-street. 1817. Price 2s.

(CONCLUDED.)

May 18, 1817.

MR. SOUTHEY in the next paragraph says, that, "it is a nice question, in what degree he, as the author, partook of the sentiments expressed in the dramatic poem of *Wat Tyler*;—too nice a one for Mr. Wm. Smith to decide;" and yet he accuses him of excessive malice or total want of judgment for deciding wrong.

He then falls foul of the *Monthly*, and other Dissenting Reviews, for praising his *Joan of Arc*, and makes it the subject of a sneer at Mr. W. Smith, that his Minor Poems were praised by the same critical authorities on their first appearance. We might ask here, Did not Mr. Southey himself write in these Reviews at one time? But he might refuse to answer the question. "In these productions, *Joan of Arc*," &c. Mr. Southey observes, and observes truly, that Mr. W. Smith "might have seen expressed an enthusiastic love of liberty," (not a cold-blooded recommendation to extinguish the liberty of the press) "a detestation of tyranny in whatever form," (legitimate or illegitimate, not a palliation of all its most inveterate and lasting abuses) "an ardent abhorrence of all wicked ambition," (particularly of that most wicked ambition which would subject mankind, as a herd of cattle, to the power and pride of Kings) "and a sympathy not less ardent with those who were engaged in war for the defence of their country, and in a righteous cause"—to wit, the French!

Mr. Southey, however, vindicates with still more self-complacency and success, the purity of his religious and moral character. "For while I imbibed the Republican opinions of the day, I escaped the atheism and leprous immorality which generally accompanied them. I cannot, therefore, join with Beattie in blessing

> ——'The hour when I escap'd the wrangling crew,
> From Pyrrho's maze, and Epicurus' sty;'

for I was never lost in the one, nor defiled in the other. My progress was of a different kind." And Mr. Southey then tells a story, not so good as the story of Whittington and his Cat, how he was prevented from setting off for America to set up the Pantisocracy scheme, and turned back, "from building castles in the air, and founding Christian Commonwealths," to turn Poet Laureate, and write in the Quarterly Review. The above extract is a fine specimen of character. Mr. Southey there thanks God that he is not, and was not, *like other men*. He was proof against the worst infection of his time. Poor Doctors Price and Priestley, who were Republicans like Mr. Southey, were religious, moral men; but they were Dissenters, and this excites as much contempt in Mr. Southey, as if they had been atheists and profligates. Others again, among Mr. Southey's political compeers, were atheists and immoral; and for this, Mr. Southey expresses the same abhorrence of them, as if they had been Dissenters! He, indeed, contrives to make the defects of others so many perfections in himself; and by this mode of proceeding, abstracts himself into a *beau ideal* of moral and political egotism—a *Sir Charles Grandison*, calculated for the beginning of the nineteenth, and the latter end of the eighteenth century, upon the true infallible principles of intellectual coxcombry. It is well for Mr. Southey that he never was lost "in Pyrrho's maze," for he never would have found his way out of it:—that his tastes were not a little more Epicurean, perhaps is not so well for him. There is a monachism of the understanding in Mr. Southey, which may be traced to the over-severity, the prudery of his moral habits. He unites somewhat of the fanaticism and bigotry of the cloister with its penances and privations. A decent mixture of the pleasurable and the sensual, might relieve the morbid acrimony of his temper, and a little more indulgence of his appetites might make him a little less tenacious of his opinions. It is his not sympathising with the enjoyments of others, that makes him feel such an antipathy to every difference of sentiment. We hope Mr. Southey, when he was in town, went to see *Don Giovanni*, and heard him sing that fine song, "Women and wine are the sustainers and glory of life." We do not wish to see Mr. Southey quite a *Don Giovanni*, (that would be as great a change in his moral, as to see him Poet-laureate, is in his political character) but if he had fewer pretensions to virtue, he would, perhaps, be a better man,—"to relish all as sharply, passioned as we!" The author, in p. 21, informs Mr. W. Smith, that his early Poems, which contain all the political spirit, without the dramatic form, of *Wat Tyler*, are continually on sale, and that he has never attempted to withdraw them? Why does he not withdraw them, or why did he attempt to get an Injunction against poor *Wat?* Some one who does not know Mr. Southey—has suggested as an answer,—By not withdrawing the Poems, he pockets the receipts; and by getting an Injunction against *Wat Tyler*, he would have done the same thing. In p. 23, Mr. Southey states, that he is "in the same *rank in society*" as Mr. Smith, which we have yet to learn: and that he and Mr. Smith "were cast by nature in different moulds," which we think was lucky for the Member for Norwich. In p. 25, Mr. Southey rails at "the whole crew of ultra Whigs and Anarchists, from Messrs. Brougham and Clodius, down to Cobbett, Cethegus, and Co.;" and in pages 26, 27, he compliments himself: "I ask you, Sir, in which of my writings I have appealed to the base and malignant feelings of mankind;—and I ask you, whether the present race of revolutionary writers appeal to any other? What man's private character did I stab? Whom did I libel? Whom did I slander? Whom did I traduce? THESE MISCREANTS LIVE BY CALUMNY AND SEDITION: THEY ARE LIBELLERS AND LIARS BY TRADE."—After this, *Sir Anthony Absolute*'s "Damn you, can't you be cool, like me?" will hardly pass for a joke! "For a man to know another well, were to know himself."

But we must conclude, and shall do so, with some passages taken at a venture. "I did not fall into the error of those, who, having been the friends of France when they imagined that the cause of liberty was implicated in her success, transferred their attachment from the Republic to the military tyranny in which it ended, and regarded with complacency the progress of oppression, because France was the oppressor." What does Mr. Southey call that military establishment which is at present kept up in France to keep the Bourbons on the throne, and to keep down the French people? Mr. Southey has, it seems, transferred his attachment from the Republic, not to Bonaparte, but to the Bourbons. *They* stand Mr. Southey instead of the Republic; they are the true "children and champions of Jacobinism;" the legitimate heirs and successors of the Revolution. We have never fallen into that error—into the error of preferring the monstrous claim of hereditary and perpetual despotism over whole nations, to a power raised to whatever height, (a gigantic, but glorious height) in repelling that monstrous claim; a claim set up in contempt of human nature and human liberty, and never quitted for a single instant; the unwearied, implacable, systematic prosecution of which claim, to force the doctrine of Divine Right on the French people, caused all the calamities of the Revolution, all the horrors of anarchy, and all the evils of military despotism, with loss of liberty and independence; and the restoring and hallowing of which claim, to hold mankind as slaves in perpetuity, Mr. Southey hails as the deliverance of mankind, and "a consummation devoutly to be wished." "O fool, fool, fool!" He cannot go along with France when France becomes the oppressor; nor can he leave the Allies when they become the oppressors, when they return to the point from whence they set out in 1792. He could not accompany the march to Paris then, but he has run all the way by the side of it twice since, with his laurel wreath on his head, playing tricks and antics like a Jack-of-the Green. We explained this before. Mr. Southey was a revolutionary weathercock; he is become a court-fixture. "They (says he, meaning us*) had turned their faces towards the East in the morning, to worship the rising sun, and in the evening they were looking eastward still, obstinately affirming that still the sun was there. I, on the contrary, altered my position as the world went round." It is not always that a simile runs on all-fours; but this does. The sun, indeed, passes from the East to the West, but it rises in the East again: yet Mr. Southey is still looking in the West—for his pension. The world has gone round a second time, but he has not altered his position—at the Treasury door. Does the sun of Liberty still rise over the towers of the Inquisition? Is its glow kindled at the funeral pile of massacred Protestants? Does

* Not the Editor of this Paper, but the writer of this Article.

its breath issue in vain from French dungeons, in which all those are confined who cannot forget that for twenty-five years they have been counted men, not slaves to Louis XVIII., under God and the Prince Regent? The doctrine of Divine Right has been restored, and Mr. Southey is still dreaming of military usurpation. The Inquisition has been re-established, and Mr. Southey still talks of the deliverance of Spain and Portugal. The war was renewed to put down Bonaparte as a military usurper, and not, as it was stated, to force the Bourbons as the legitimate Sovereigns, back upon the French nation; and yet the moment he was put down, the Bourbons were forced back upon the French people; (he was the only barrier between them and the delicious doctrine of Divine Right) and yet Mr. Southey says nothing of this monstrous outrage and insult on them, on us, on all mankind: his spirits are frozen up by this word "legitimacy," as fish are in a pond: and yet he does say something—for he dotes, and raves, and drivels about national monuments to commemorate the final triumph over national independence and human rights.

Mr. Southey next gives us his succedaneum to the doctrine of Legitimacy; and a precious piece of quackery it is:—

"Slavery has long ceased to be tolerable in Europe: the remains of feudal oppression are disappearing even in those countries which have improved the least: nor can it be much longer endured, that the extremes of ignorance, wretchedness, and brutality, should exist in the very centre of civilized society. There can be no safety with a populace, *half Luddite, half Lazzaroni.* Let us not deceive ourselves. We are far from that state in which any thing resembling equality would be possible; but we are arrived at that state in which *the extremes of inequality* are become intolerable. *They are too dangerous, as well as too monstrous, to be borne much longer.* Plans which would have led to the utmost horrors of insurrection, have been prevented by the government, and by the enactment of strong, but necessary laws. Let it not however, be supposed that the disease is healed, because the ulcer may skin over. The remedies by which the body politic can be restored to health, must be slow in their operation. The condition of the populace, physical, moral, and intellectual, must be improved, or a *Jacquerie*, a *Bellum Servile*, sooner or later, will be the result. *It is the people at this time who stand in need of reformation, not the government.*"

We could not have said most of this better ourselves; and yet he adds—"The Government must better the condition of the populace; and the first thing necessary is"—to do what—to suppress the liberty of the press, and make Mr. Southey the keeper. That is, the Government must put a stop to the press, in order that they may continue, with perfect impunity, all the other evils complained of, which Mr. Southey says are too dangerous, as well as too monstrous to be borne. Put down the liberty of the press, and leave it to Mr. Southey and the Quarterly Review to remove "the extremes of inequality, ignorance, wretchedness, and brutality, existing in the very centre of civilized society," and they will remain there long enough. Remove them, and what will become of Mr. Southey and the Quarterly Review? This modest gentleman and mild reformer, proposes to destroy at once the freedom of discussion, to prevent its ultimate loss; to make us free by first making us slaves; to put a gag in the mouths of the people instead of bread; to increase the comforts of the poor by laying on more taxes; to spread abroad the spirit of liberty and independence, by teaching the doctrines of Passive Obedience and Non-resistance; and to encourage the love of peace by crying up the benefits of war, and deprecating the loss of a war-establishment. The borough-mongers will not object to such a helpmate in the cause of reform. In the midst of all this desultory jargon, the author somehow scrapes acquaintance with Mr. Owen, and we find them disputing about the erection of a chapel of ease on a piece of waste ground. "To build upon any other foundation than religion, is building upon sand," says Mr. Southey, with a sort of *Do-me-good* air, as if in giving his advice he had performed an act of charity. We did not hear Mr. Owen's answer, but we know that a nod is as good as a wink to that gentleman. Mr. Southey then talks of the Established Church, whom, as well as the Government, in his courtly way, he accuses of having for centuries "neglected its first and paramount duty," the bettering the condition of the people; of Saving Banks; of colonies of disbanded soldiers and sailors; of columns of Waterloo and Trafalgar; of diminishing the poor-rates, and improving the morals of the people, so that they may live without eating; of the glories of our war-expenditure, and of the necessity of keeping up the same expenditure in time of peace. "Never indeed," he exclaims, "was there a more senseless cry than that which is at this time raised for retrenchment in the public expenditure, as a means of alleviating the present distress." [This senseless cry, however, is either an echo of, or was echoed by, the Prince Regent in his Speech from the Throne. Is there no better understanding between Mr. Southey and the Prince Regent's advisers?]—"That distress arises from a great and sudden diminution of employment, occasioned by many coinciding causes, the chief of which is, that the war-expenditure of from forty to fifty millions yearly, has ceased."—[No, the chief is, that our war-expenses of from forty to fifty millions yearly and for ever, are continued, and that our war-monopoly of trade to pay them with has ceased.]—"Men are out of employ"—[True.] . . . . "the evil is, that too little is spent," [Because we have wasted too much.]—"and as a remedy, we are exhorted to spend less." [Yes, to waste less, or to spend what we have left in things useful to ourselves, and not in Government gimcracks, whether of peace or war. Is it better, does Mr. Southey think, that ten poor men should keep ten pounds a-piece in their pockets, which they would of course spend in food, clothing, fuel, &c. for themselves and families, or that this hundred pounds, that is, ten pounds a-piece, should be paid out of the pockets of these ten poor men in *taxes*, which, added to Mr. Croker's salary, would enable him to keep another horse, to pay for the feed, furniture, saddle, bridle, whip, and spurs? We ask Mr. Southey this question, and will put the issue of the whole argument upon the answer to it. The money would be spent equally in either case, say in agriculture, in raising corn for instance, wheat or oats: but the corn raised and paid for by it in the one instance would go into the belly of the poor man and his family: in the other, into the belly of Mr. Croker's horse. Does that make no difference to Mr. Southey? Answer, Man of Humanity! Or, if Mr. Southey, the Man of Humanity, will not answer, let Mr. Malthus, the Man of God, answer for him! Again, what would go to pay for a new saddle for the Secretary of the Admiralty, would buy the poor man and his family so many pair of shoes in the year; or what would pay for a straw litter for his sleek gelding, would stuff a flock-bed for the poor man's children! Does not Mr. Southey understand this question yet? We have given him a clue to the whole difference between productive and unproductive labour, between waste and economy, between taxes and no taxes, between a war-expenditure and what ought to be a peace-establishment, between money laid out and debts contracted in gunpowder, in cannon, in ships of war, in scattering death, and money laid out in paying for food, furniture, houses, the comforts, necessaries, and enjoyments of life. Let Mr. Southey take the problem and the solution with him to Italy, study it there amidst a population, half Lazzaroni, half Monks:* let him see his error, and return an honest man! But if he will not believe us, let him at least believe himself. In the career of his triumph about our national monuments, he has fallen into one of the most memorable lapses of memory we ever met with. "In proportion," says he, "to their magnificence, also, will be the present benefit, as well as the future good; for they are not like the Egyptian pyramids, to be raised by bondsmen under rigorous taskmasters: the wealth which is taken from the people returns to them again, like vapours which are drawn imperceptibly from the earth, but distributed to it in refreshing dews† and fertilizing

* Perhaps Mr. Southey will inform us some time or other, whether in Italy also it is the people, and not the Pope, who wants reforming.

† *Dues of Office*, we suppose.

showers. What bounds could imagination set to the welfare and glory of this island, if a tenth part, or even a twentieth of what the war expenditure has been, were annually applied in improving and creating harbours, in bringing our roads to the best possible state, in colonizing upon our waste lands, in reclaiming fens and conquering tracks from the sea, in encouraging the liberal arts, in erecting churches, in building and endowing schools and colleges, and making war upon physical and moral evil with the whole artillery of wisdom and righteousness, with all the resources of science, and all the ardour of enlightened and enlarged benevolence!"

Well done, Mr. Southey. No man can argue better, when he argues against himself. What! one-twentieth part of this enormous waste of money laid out in war, which has sunk the nation into the lowest state of wretchedness, would, if wisely and beneficially laid out in works of peace, have raised the country to the pinnacle of prosperity and happiness! Mr. Southey in his raptures forgets his war-whoop, and is ready to exclaim with *Sancho Panza*, when the exploits of knight-errantry are over, and he turns all his enthusiasm to a pastoral account, "Oh what delicate wooden spoons shall I carve! What crumbs and cream shall I devour!" Mr. Southey goes on to state, among other *items*, that "Government should reform its prisons." But Lord Castlereagh, soon after the war-addition to Mr. Croker's peace-salary, said that this was too expensive. In short, the author sums up all his hopes and views in the following sentences:—"Government must reform the populace, the people must reform themselves." The interpretation of which is, The Government must prevent the lower classes from reading any thing; the middle classes should read nothing but the Quarterly Review. "This is the true Reform, and compared with this, all else is *flocci, nauci, nihili, pili.*"

The last page of this performance is "as arrogant a piece of paper" as was ever scribbled. We give it as it stands. "It will be said of him, (Mr. S.) that in an age of personality, he abstained from satire: and that during the course of his literary life, often as he was assailed, the only occasion on which he ever *condescended* to reply, was, when *a certain Mr. William Smith*"—[What, was the only person worthy of Mr. Southey's notice a very insignificant person?] "insulted him in Parliament with the appellation of Renegade. On that occasion, it will be said, that he vindicated himself, *as it became him to do*: [How so? Mr. Southey is only a literary man, and neither a commoner nor a peer of the realm] "and treated his calumniator *with just and memorable severity*. Whether it shall be added, that Mr. William Smith redeemed his own character, by coming forward with honest manliness, and acknowledging that he had spoken rashly and unjustly, concerns himself, but is not of the slightest importance to me. ROBERT SOUTHEY."

We do not think this conclusion is very like what Mr. Southey somewhere wishes the conclusion of his life to resemble—"the high leaves upon the holly tree." Mr. Southey's asperities do not wear off, as he grows older. We are always disposed to quarrel with ourselves for quarrelling with him, and yet we cannot help it, whenever we come in contact with his writings. We met him unexpectedly the other day in St. Giles's, (it was odd we should meet *him* there) were sorry we had passed him without speaking to an old friend, turned and looked after him for some time, as to a tale of other times—sighing, as we walked on, *Alas poor Southey!* "We saw in him a painful hieroglyphic of humanity; a sad memento of departed independence; a striking instance of the rise and fall of patriot bards!" In the humour we were in, we could have written a better epitaph for him than he has done for himself. We went directly and bought his Letter to Mr. W. Smith, which appeared the same day as himself, and this at once put an end to our sentimentality.

Morning Chronicle, June 30, 1817.

LORD CASTLEREAGH, in the debate some evenings ago, appeared in a new character, and mingled with his usual stock of political common places, some lively moral paradoxes, after a new French pattern. According to his Lordship's comprehensive and liberal views, the liberty and independence of nations are best supported abroad by the point of the bayonet; and morality, religion, and social order, are best defended at home by spies and informers. It is a pretty system, and worthy of itself from first to last. The Noble Lord in the blue ribbon took the characters of Castles and Oliver under the protection of his blushing honours and elegant casuistry, and lamented that by the idle clamour raised against such characters, *Gentlemen* were deterred from entering into the honourable, useful, and profitable profession of Government Spies. Perhaps this piece of intellectual gallantry on the part of the Noble Lord, was not quite so disinterested as it at first appears. There might be something of fellow-feeling in it. The obloquy which lights on the underlings in such cases, sometimes glances indirectly on their principals and patrons; nor do they wipe it off by becoming their defenders. Lord Castlereagh may say with *Lingo* in the play, who boasts "that he is not a scholar, but a master of scholars," that he is not a spy, but a creator of spies and informers—not a receiver, but a distributor of blood-money—not a travelling companion and scurvy accomplice in the forging and uttering of sham treasons and accommodation plots, but head of the town-firm established for that purpose—not the dupe or agent of the treasons hatched by others, but chief mover and instigator of the grand plot for increasing the power of the Sovereign, by hazarding the safety of his person. Lord Castlereagh recommended the character of his accomplices, as spies and informers, to the respect and gratitude of the country and the House; he lamented the prejudice entertained against this species of patriotic service, as hindering *gentlemen* from resorting to it as a liberal and honourable profession. One of these delicious protegés of ministerial gratitude, was, it seems, at one time a distributor of forged notes, and gained the reward promised by act of Parliament, by hanging his accomplices. Could not his Lordship's nice notions of honour relax a little farther, and recommend the legal traffic in bank notes and blood-money, as a new opening to honourable ambition and profitable industry? Castles's wife was also the keeper of a house of ill fame. Could not his Lordship, with the hand of a master, have drawn a veil of delicacy over this slight stain in his character, and redeemed a profession, not without high example to justify it, from the vulgar obloquy that attends it? We are afraid his Lordship is but half an adept in these sort of lax paradoxes, and that Peachum, Jonathan Wild, and Count Fathom, are much honester teachers of that kind of transcendental morality than he. This kind of revolutionary jargon must have sounded oddly in the ears of some of his Lordship's hearers. Mr. Wynne, who dreads all re-action so much, must have looked particularly argute at this innovation in the parliamentary theory of moral sentiments. What would the country gentlemen say to it? One would think Lord Lascelles's hat, that broad brimmed monument of true old English respectability, must have cowered and doubled down in dog's ears at the sound! What will the ardent and superannuated zeal of that *preux Chevalier*, the Editor of *The Day* and *New Times*, say to this stain upon the innate honour and purity of legitimacy, to this new proof that "the age of chivalry is gone for ever, and that of sophisters, economists, and calculators, has succeeded!" What will John Bull, who has been crammed these twenty-five years with the draff and husks of concrete prejudices, unsifted, unbolted, in their rawest state, say to the analytical distinctions, to the refined *police*-morality of the Noble Lord? We might consider his harangue on the public services and private virtues of spies and informers, according to the utility-doctrine of modern philosophy, as forming an era in the history of English loyalty and Parliamentary pliability. What! Is it meant, after building up the present system of power and influence on the accumulated pile of our political prejudices, to extend and strengthen it, by undermining all our moral sentiments and national habits? Yet we are told, that there is no imputation on the *moral* character of Oliver! We wonder Mr. Wilberforce did not suggest that his *religious* character also remained unimpeached, except, indeed, that he had been guilty of subornation of treason on the Sabbath-day. According to our present catechism of legitimacy, to be a *cat's-paw* is to be virtuous—is to be moral—is to be pious—is to be loyal—is to be a patriot—is to be what Castles *is*, and Castlereagh *approves!*—This subject naturally leads us into low company and low allusions. As, after Fielding's Hero had finished his speech on *honour*, his friend the *Count* pronounced him a Great Prig, so, after Lord Castlereagh's speech of Monday evening, we can no longer refuse to consider him a Great Man, in the sense of the philosophical historian; that is to say, a man who has a very great regard for himself, and a very great contempt for the prejudices and feelings of the rest of mankind.

July 15, 1817.

The debate in the House of Commons on Mr. Brougham's motion took a very spirited, and rather personal turn. We do not think Lord Castlereagh was quite successful in rebutting the principal charges brought against his foreign and domestic policy. With respect to Genoa, for instance, and the late arbitrary contributions levied on British merchants there, his Lordship seemed to say that he had but one object, and that in this respect his conduct had been uniformly consistent while abroad, namely, to protect legitimacy, and that the rights and property of British subjects were accordingly left to shift for themselves, as things beneath his notice. This answer will hardly satisfy most of our readers. He considered it an illiberal and injurious policy to attempt to force our exclusive commercial interests upon foreign nations. But is there no alternative in his Lordship's mind between bullying and domineering over other nations, and tamely crouching under every species of insult or act of pillage they may wantonly exercise upon us? We have put down the colossal power of Bonaparte. Is every "petty tyrant" who has succeeded him, to brave us with impunity, lest a word of remonstrance, a whisper of complaint, should rouse their vengeance? Are we not to mention their names, lest these new Gods of the earth, these modern *Dii Minores*, should hear us? His Lordship also appears to despair of the restoration of peace in Spanish America. If he includes in the idea of *peace* the quiet re-establishment of the tyranny of the old Government, we are happy to agree with him.

With respect to the changes which have taken place at home, his Lordship failed in making the necessity for them clear to our understandings. We cannot assent to the accuracy of his statements, or the soundness of his logic. He has suspended the laws of the country to save us from the danger of anarchy! We deny the danger, and deprecate the remedy. If ministers could afford to fan the flame of insurrection, to *alarm* the country into a surrender of its liberties, we contend that a danger that could be thus tampered with, thus made a convenient pretence for seizing a power beyond the law to put it down, might have been put down *without a power beyond the law.* If a Government's conspiring against itself were a sufficient ground for arming it with arbitrary power, no country could for a moment be safe against ministerial treachery and encroachment, against real despotism founded on pretended disaffection. Government would be in perpetual convulsions and affected hysterics, like a fine lady who wants to domineer over her credulous husband. We deny that disaffection existed, except that kind which arose from extreme distress. Hunger is not disloyalty. Nor can we admit that a Government's having reduced a country to a state of unparalleled distress, and consequent desperation, is a reason for giving *carte blanche* to the Government, and putting the people under military execution. At this rate, the worse the Government, the more firmly it ought to be rooted: the greater the abuse of confidence, the more blind and unlimited the confidence ought to be: and any administration need only bring a nation to the brink of ruin, in order to have a right to plunge it into the depths of slavery. It is easy to keep the peace with the sword;—more flattering to the pride of power to crush resistance to oppression, than to remove the causes of it. To reduce a people to the alternative of rebellion or of arbitrary sway, does not require the talents of a great statesman. If Lord Castlereagh claims the merit of having reduced us to that alternative, we shall not dispute it with him: whatever may be the result, we cannot thank him.

His Lordship might, however, have made good his retreat, with a decent orderly appearance, if he had not chosen to go out of his way to take up a Spy behind him on his new metaphysical charger, and to ride the high horse over all those, who are not the fast friends and staunch admirers of that profession, as traitors and *no true men*. Sir Francis Burdett, not relishing this assault of the master and man, pulled off the Squire, and rolling him in the mud, pelted him so unmercifully with Irish evidence and musty affidavits of his friends and relations, that his gallant patron, seeing the plight he was in, dismounted, and was condescending enough to acknowledge, that "cruelty was in every species detestable," and that "he lamented to think that there were miscreants in human nature capable of committing crime for the love of reward;" sentiments not new indeed, but new in his Lordship's mouth. The country gentlemen must have felt relieved, and Lord Lascelles's hat have recovered its primitive shape! The House of Commons is no dupe: Lord Castlereagh no driveller. Would he then seriously persuade them, that the Spy hanged his old friends and accomplices out of pure love to his country, and disinterested friendship to his Lordship? We would advise the noble Lord in the blue ribbon to *cut* his parliamentary connexion with his police acquaintance at once. The thing cannot answer;

it is against decorum. He might as well introduce his scavenger as a person of fashion at Carlton-House, as attempt to pass off his *Spy* as a gentleman, and a man of honour, any where else! The gentlemen-ushers would turn up their noses at one of his Lordship's necessary appendages, and the moral sense of the English nation turns with disgust from the other, when forced upon it as a *beau morçeau* of morality, with the *sauce picquant* of ministerial panegyric! We were glad to find the former Secretary for Ireland reprobating the practice of flogging to extract evidence, as "a most wicked and unwarrantable piece of torture;" a confession which seemed to be extorted from his Lordship by the impression made by the reading of some of Mr. Finnerty's affidavits, as they are called, though they are no more Mr. Finnerty's affidavits, who procured them, than they are Mr. Bennet's, who read them. Every thing relating to this subject is particularly interesting at this moment, when the same power is vested in the same hands in this country, that was wielded twenty years ago in Ireland—not indeed as a precedent to the English government, but as a warning to the English people. We give no opinion on the truth or falsehood of the allegations contained in the affidavits, but we do say, that the noble Secretary reasoned very badly on the subject. He says that Mr. Finnerty is not a very loyal man, that is, he is not very strongly attached to his Lordship's person or government, and therefore neither Mr. Finnerty, nor any person taking an oath in an Irish court of justice, reflecting on his Lordship's administration, is to be believed. Mr. Finnerty published an account of the proceedings on Orr's trial, which was deemed a libel, and therefore the whole history of the Irish rebellion and of the year 1798 is a fable. Lord Castlereagh would not consent to quash his prosecution of Mr. Finnerty on this ground some years ago, because he would not shun inquiry, and yet the affidavits were not suffered to be read in court, and his Lordship deprecates their production in parliament. He thinks it hard that he must be called on to prove a negative, when others swear positively to the affirmative. Accusation against his Lordship is to pass not for a proof of guilt but innocence, and his inability to refute the charge only calls for a greater degree of candid interpretation and implicit faith in his Lordship's word. Insinuation only requires confidence to repel it—proof more confidence—conviction unlimited confidence. Whether the things ever happened or no, they are to be equally buried in eternal silence in Mr. Finnerty's "disloyal breast:" not a tittle of evidence is to be suffered to escape from the budget of affidavits which he has got together by forbidden means. His Lordship's Irish administration is to be inscrutable as another Providence, secret as another Inquisition; the English Parliament are to put the broad seal of their sanction upon it! It was certainly unlucky at this juncture of the debate, that Mr. W. Smith should have started up with the case of Mr. Judkin Fitzgerald, who (it seems, by his own account of his services, not from any affidavits against him) had been most active in inflicting this "cruel and unwarrantable species of torture," and was made a Baronet in consequence.

"And struts Sir Judkin, an exceeding knave!"

The unconsciousness of the Irish government exceeds every thing. They are not only "innocent of the knowledge, till they applaud the deed," but ignorant of it, after they have applauded it. It is no wonder that the fixed air and volatile spirit of Mr. Canning's wit frothed up at this indiscreet mention of Sir Judkin, and that he wished to "bury him quick," under the artificial flowers of his oratory. *The dead tell no tales*—of the dead or the living! Mr. Canning twitted Mr. W. Smith with attacking the dead, because "he had found that the absent could answer." Does this allude to the Laureate? If so, let Mr. Canning call for more flowers, and lay him by the side of Sir Judkin. This allusion to the answer to Mr. W. Smith is, however, remarkably candid, as Mr. Southey declares in it that he never thought Mr. Canning worth an answer. He may now return the compliment in kind, by inscribing the next edition of his "Inscriptions" to the author of the "Anti-Jacobin."

"O silly sheep, come ye to seek the lamb here of the wolf!"

July 17, 1817.

A WRITER in a Morning Paper, a few days ago, commented very wisely and wittily on the situation of the State Prisoners, under the Suspension of the Habeas Corpus, as a warning to the people of England not to meddle in politics. He seemed infinitely amused with the inability of these poor devils "to get out," though he seemed to know no reason why they should be kept in. "One of these gentlemen must have a flute, *forsooth!*" he exclaims with a very hysterical air, as if it was a good joke truly for a man to have a flute taken from him, and not to be able to get it back again.* Even Mr. Hiley Addington allows that Evans might have his flute again, if he did not use it. If this writer had himself been in the habit of blowing a great war-trumpet, and wished to make as much noise as ever with it in time of peace, he might not like to have it taken from him. He, however, consoles Mr. Evans for the loss of his flute, with the very old and original observation, "That the people bear the same relation to the Government, as the sheep to the shepherd, and that the sheep ought not to dictate to the shepherd, or remonstrate against what he does for their good." Now the sheep are not usually in the habit of dictating, or remonstrating on such occasions, except in that sort of language which *Lawyer Scout* advices *Sheep-face* to imitate before *Justice Mittimus*, and to which this Professional Gentleman seems to wish the State Prisoners to resort in their

* It is the making light of the distresses and complaints of our victims, because we have them in our power, that is the principle of all cruelty and tyranny. Our pride takes a pleasure in the sufferings our malice has inflicted; every aggravation of their case is a provocation to new injuries and insults; and their pretensions to justice or mercy become ridiculous in proportion to their hopelessness of redress. It was thus that Mother Brownrigg whipped her prentices to death; and in the same manner our facetious Editor would work himself up to apply the thumb-screw to any one who was unable to resist the application, with a few "forsooths," and other such "comfit-makers wives' oaths."

intercourse with the Home Department. The fleecy fools, whom the writer holds up as models of wisdom and spirit to his countrymen, do, to be sure, make a terrible noise at a sheep-shearing, and a short struggle when they feel the knife at their throats. But our allegorist, we suspect, would regard these as Jacobinical, or Ultra-Jacobinical symptoms. He would have the people stand still to be fleeced, and have their throats cut, whenever Government pleases. He has in his eye the sublimest example of self-devotion: "As a lamb, he was led to the slaughter: as a sheep before the shearers is dumb, so he opened not his mouth." We cannot understand the point of comparison in this *sheep-biting* argument. If the people are really to be as silly, and as submissive as sheep, they will be worse treated. A flock of sheep pass their time very comfortably on Salisbury plain, biting the short sweet grass, or lying with "meek mouths ruminant," till they are fit to send to market: we have sometimes heard them fill the air with a troublous cry, as they pass down Oxford-street, to Smithfield, and the next morning it is all over with them. But Governments have not the same reason for taking care of the people, "poor, poor dumb mouths," they do not ordinarily sell them or eat them. The comparison would be much nearer to beasts of burden, asses, or "camels in their war," who, as Shakspeare expresses it,—

> ——— "have their provender
> Only for bearing burthens, and sore blows
> For sinking under them."

However edifying and attractive these kind of examples of simplicity, patience, and good behaviour, taken from sheep, oxen, and asses, must be to the people, they are rather invidious, something worse than equivocal, as they relate to the designs and good-will of the Government towards them. This writer indeed commits himself very strangely on this subject, or, as the phrase is, *lets the cat out of the bag,* without intending it. In a broadside which he published against the author of the "Political Register," he says with infinite *naiveté*:—"Mr. Cobbett had been sentenced to two years' imprisonment for a libel; and during the time that he was in Newgate, it was discovered that he had been secretly in treaty with Government to avoid the sentence passed upon him; and that he had proposed to certain of the Agents of Ministers, that if they would let him off, they might make what future use they pleased of him: *he would entirely betray the cause of the people:* he would either write or not write, or *write against them,* as he had once done before, just as Ministers thought proper. To this, however, it was replied, that '*Cobbett had written on too many sides already to be worth a groat for the service of Government,' and he accordingly suffered his confinement.*"

This passage is at least worth a groat: it lets us into the Editor's real opinion of what it is that alone makes any writer "worth a groat for the service of Government," viz. his being able and willing *entirely to betray the cause of the people;* and, we should hope, may operate as an antidote to any future cant about sheep and shepherds!

The same consistent patriot and loyalist, the Sir Robert Filmer of the day, asked some time ago—"Where is the madman that believes the doctrine of Divine Right? Where is the madman that asserts that doctrine?" As no one else was found to do it, he himself, the other day, took up his own challenge, and affirmed, with a resolute air, that—"Louis XVIII. had the same right to the throne of France, independently of his merits or conduct, that Mr. Coke, of Norfolk, had to his estate at Holkham." He did not say whether James II. had the same right to the throne of England, independently of his conduct or merits, that Louis XVIII. has to the throne of France: but the inference of course is that the people of France belong to Louis XVIII. just as the live stock on a farm belongs to the owner of it, or as the slaves in the West Indies belong to the owners of the plantation, and that mankind are neither more nor less than a herd of slaves, the property of kings. This is at least as good a thing as the doctrine of divine right. We do not wonder that the writer, after this "delicious declaration," thought it proper to apologize to his court-readers for expressing his approbation of the abolition of the Slave Trade, as indirectly compromising those principles of legitimacy, which make one part of the species the property of another, and which we have seen so successfully established in Europe as the basis of liberty, humanity, and social order!

July 19, 1817.

THE Opposition, it seems, with Mr. Brougham at their head, "attack all that is valuable in our institutions." So says Lord Castlereagh; and, to make the thing the more incredible, so says *The Courier!* They attack Sir Judkin Fitzgerald and the use of the torture; and *therefore* they attack all that is valuable in our institutions. They attack the system of spies and informers; and therefore they attack all that is valuable in our institutions. They object to the moral characters of such men as Castles and Oliver; and therefore they attack all that is most respectable in the country. They consider Lord Sidmouth, who is "to acquaint us with the perfect spy o' th' time," as no conjurer, treat his circular letters and itinerant incendiaries with as little ceremony as respect; and therefore they are hostile to all that is venerable in our constituted authorities. They do not approve of the Suspension of the Habeas Corpus, of Standing Armies, and Rotten Boroughs; and therefore they would overturn all that is most valuable in the Constitution. They say that Lord Castlereagh was connected with the measures of the Irish government in the year 1798; and they are said to hold a language "grossly libellous." They say that they do not wish the same system to be introduced by his Lordship in this country; and their principles are denounced as "of a decidedly revolutionary character."

They think of the present administration as Mr. Canning formerly thought of it, and they think of Mr. Canning as all the world think. Is that all? Oh no! They speak against the renewal of the Income Tax; and this, in the opinion of some persons, is attacking what is more valuable than all our other institutions put together! For our own parts, our political confession of faith on this subject is short: we neither consider Lord Castlereagh as the Constitution, nor *The Courier* as the Country.

But if, after all, and in spite of our teeth, we should be forced to acknowledge that Sir Judkin Fitzgerald and the use of the torture, that the system of spies and informers, that Lord Sidmouth's sagacity, circulars, and travelling delegates, that arbitrary imprisonment and solitary confinement, the Suspension of the Habeas Corpus, Standing Armies, and Rotten Boroughs, Lord Castlereagh's past measures or future designs, Mr. Canning's love of liberty, and Mr. Vansittart's hankerings after the Income Tax, are all that is left *valuable in our institutions, or respectable in the country,* then we must say, that the more effectually the Opposition "attack all that is valuable in such institutions," the more we shall thank them; and that the sooner we can get rid of all that is "most respectable" in such a system, the less occasion we shall have to blush for the Country.

ENGLAND in 1798.

By S. T. Coleridge.

August 2, 1817.

"The Monthly Magazine tells us that this country has occasioned the death of 5,800,000 persons in Calabria, Russia, Poland, Germany, France, Spain, and Portugal. This country, reader, England! our country, our great, our glorious, our beloved country, according to this Magazine, has been the guilty cause of all this carnage!"—So says *Mr. Southey* apud *the Quarterly Review*, 1817. Thus sings Mr. Coleridge, in his "Fears in Solitude," 1798:—

"We have offended, oh! my countrymen!
We have offended very grievously,
And been most tyrannous.
——— Thankless too for peace;
(Peace long preserv'd by fleets and perilous seas)
Secure from actual warfare, we have lov'd
To swell the war-whoop, passionate for war!
Alas! for ages ignorant of all
Its ghastlier workings (famine or blue plague,
Battle, or siege, or flight through wintry snows),
We, this whole people, have been clamorous
For war and bloodshed; animating sports,
The which we pay for as a thing to talk of,
Spectators and not combatants! No guess
Anticipative of a wrong unfelt,
No speculation on contingency,
However dim and vague, too vague and dim
To yield a justifying cause; and forth
(Stuff'd out with big preamble, holy names,
And adjurations of the God in Heaven),
We send our mandates for the certain death
Of thousands and ten thousand! Boys and girls,
And women, that would groan to see a child
Pull off an insect's leg, all read of war,
The best amusement for our morning's meal!
The poor wretch, who has learnt his only prayers
For curses, who knows scarcely words enough
To ask a blessing from his Heavenly Father,
Becomes a fluent phraseman, absolute
And technical in victories and defeat,
And all our dainty terms for fratricide;
Terms which we trundle smoothly o'er our tongues,
Like mere abstractions, empty sounds to which

We join no feeling and attach no form!
As if the soldier died without a wound;
As if the fibres of this godlike frame
Were gored without a pang; as if the wretch
Who fell in battle, doing bloody deeds,
Pass'd off to heaven, translated, and not killed;
As though he had no wife to pine for him—
No God to judge him! Therefore, evil days
Are coming on us, O my countrymen!
And what if all-avenging Providence,
Strong and retributive, should make us know
The meaning of our words; force us to feel
The desolation and the agony
Of our fierce doings!

I have told,
O Britons! O my brethren! I have told
Most bitter truth, but without bitterness.
Nor deem my zeal or factious or mistimed:
For never can true courage dwell with them,
Who playing tricks with conscience, dare not look
At their own vices. We have been too long
Dupes of a deep delusion!—Others, meanwhile,
Dote with a mad idolatry; and all
Who will not fall before their images,
And yield them worship, they are enemies
Even of their country!

Such have I been deem'd." *—

S. T. C.

* That he might be deemed so no longer, Mr. COLERIDGE soon after became *passionate for war* himself; and "swell'd the war-whoop" in the Morning Post. "I am not indeed silly enough," he says, "to take as any thing more than a violent hyperbole of party debate, Mr. Fox's assertion that *the late war* (1802) *was a war produced by the* MORNING POST; or I should be proud to have the words inscribed on my tomb."—*Biographia Literaria,* vol. i. p. 212.

ON THE EFFECTS OF WAR AND TAXES.

> "Great princes have great playthings. Some have play'd
> At hewing mountains into men, and some
> At building human wonders mountain-high.
> But war's a game, which, were their subjects wise,
> Kings would not play at." COWPER.

August 31, 1817.

THE whole question of the effect of war and taxes, in an economical point of view, reduces itself to the distinction between *productive* and *unproductive labour.* It is a pity that some member of the House of Commons does not move a string of resolutions on this subject, as a comment on the measures of the present, and a guide to those of future reigns. A film appears to have been spread for some time over the eyes of the nation, as to the consequences of the course they were pursuing; and a good deal of pains has been taken, by sophistry, and false statements, to perplex a very plain question. But we are not without hopes, in the following observations, of putting the merits of our debt and taxes in so clear a light, that not even the Finance Committee shall be any longer blind to them.

Labour is of two kinds, productive and unproductive:—that which adds materially to the comforts and necessaries of life, or that which adds nothing to the common stock, or nothing in proportion to what it takes away from it in order to maintain itself. Money may be laid out, and people employed in either of these two kinds of labour equally, but not, we imagine, with equal benefit to the community.—[*See p.* 109, *&c. of this volume.*]

Suppose I employ a man in standing on his head, or running up and down a hill all day, and that I give him five shillings a day for his pains. He is equally employed, equally paid, and equally gains a subsistence in this way, as if he was employed, in his original trade of a shoemaker, in making a pair of shoes for a person who wants them. But in the one case he is employed in unproductive, in the other in productive labour. In the one, he is employed and paid and receives a subsistence for doing that which might as well be let alone; in the other, for doing that which is of use and importance, and which must either be done by him, or give some one else double trouble to do it. If I hire a livery-servant, and keep him fine and lazy and well-fed to stand behind my chair while I eat turtle or venison, this is another instance of unproductive labour. Now the person who is in real want of a pair of shoes, and who has by his own labour and skill raised money enough to pay for them, will not assuredly lay it out, in preference, in hiring the shoemaker to run up a hill for him, or to stand upon his head, or behind a chair for his amusement.* But if I have received this money from him in the shape of taxes, having already received enough in the same way to pay for my shoes, my stockings, my house, my furniture, &c. then it is very likely (as we see it constantly happen) that I shall lay out this last five shillings worth of taxes, which I probably get for doing nothing, in employing another person to do nothing, —or to run up a hill, or to stand upon his head, or wait behind me at dinner, while the poor man, who pays me the tax, goes without his shoes and his dinner. Is this clear? Or put it thus in two words. *That* is productive labour, for which a man will give the only money he has in the world, or a certain sum, having no more than other people: *that* is unproductive labour, for which a man will never give the only money he is worth, the money he has earned by his own labour, nor any money at all, unless he has ten times as much as he wants, or as other people

* We never knew but one instance to contradict this opinion. A person who had only fourpence left in the world, which his wife had put by to pay for the baking of some meat and a pudding, went and laid it out in purchasing a new string for a guitar. Some one on this occasion quoted the lines,

> "And ever against *eating* cares,
> Wrap me in soft Lydian airs."

have, to throw away in superfluities. A man who has only got money to buy a loaf will not lay it out in an ice. But he may lay it out in a dram! Yes; because to the wretched it is often more important to forget their future than even to supply their present wants. The extravagance and thoughtlessness of the poor arise, not from their having more than enough to satisfy their immediate necessities, but from their not having enough to ward off impending ones,—in a word, from *desperation*. This is the true answer to Mr. Malthus's politico-theological system of parish ethics, the only real clue to the causes and the cure of pauperism!

If the Board of Works were to have a canal made from London to the Land's End (as has been proposed) this, for aught we know, would be productive labour, and well paid for out of the public taxes; because the public might in the end reap the benefit of the money and the labour so employed. But if the Prince Regent were by the advice of some fantastical, purblind politician, to order this canal to be lined all the way with gold-leaf, which would be washed away as soon as the water came into the canal, this is what we should call unproductive labour. Such a project would indeed cost as much money, it would require the raising of as many taxes, it would keep as many men employed, it would maintain them while they were so employed, just as well as if they were employed in any other way; but when done, it would be of no use to Prince or people. We have heard of a patriotic nobleman, who had a brick-wall built round his estate, to give employment to the poor in his neighbourhood. If he had afterwards employed them to pull it down again, it would have given them twice the employment and done twice the good. But if the same persons had been employed in productive labour, in raising corn, in making furniture, in building or improving cottages, it would not have been equally adviseable to set them to work again to burn the corn, or destroy the furniture, or pull down the cottages. In spite then of the fashionable doctrines of political economy, so well suited to the extravagance of the times, there is something else to be considered in judging of the value of labour, besides what it costs, *viz.* what it *produces;* whether it is of use to any body, and to whom. All is not gain that goes out of the purse. The nobleman above mentioned did not take the money to pay for building the wall round his estate out of the pockets of the people; but suppose an equal sum to be taken yearly out of the Civil List or any other branch of public revenue, and employed in raising some huge heap of stones—not a monument, but a mausoleum of royal taste and magnificence—the question is, whether the money thus raised by taxes, and laid out in a job, is a saving or a loss to the public? And this question is, we conceive, answered by another, whether if the money had remained in the hands of the public, they would have agreed among themselves, to have laid it out in such a building for them to look at? It would hardly be thought wise to vote a sum of money, to build a *Cottage Ornée,* large enough to cover a whole county; though the expense (and, according to the theory we are combating, the benefit) would increase with the size of the building and the waste of work. The Pyramids of Egypt and the Pavilion at Brighton, are among the instances of unproductive labour.

We have been twenty years at war, and have laid out five hundred millions in war taxes; and what have we gained by it? Where are the *proceeds?* If it has not been thrown away in what produces no return, if it has not been sunk in the war, as much as if it had been sunk in the sea, if the government as good factors for the general weal have laid out all this enormous sum in useful works, in *productive labour,* let them give us back the principal and the interest, (which is just double) and keep the profits to themselves—instead of which, they have made away with the principal, and come to us to pay *them* the interest in taxes. They have nothing to shew for either, but spiked cannon, rotten ships, gunpowder blown into the air, heaps of dead men's sculls, the turned heads and coats of Poets Laureate, with the glories of Trafalgar and Waterloo, which however will pay no scores. Let them set them up at auction, and see what they will fetch. Not a *sous!* We have killed so many French, it is true. But we had better have spent powder and shot in shooting at crows. Though we have laid the ghost of the French Revolution, we cannot "go to supper" upon the carcase. If the present distress and difficulty arise merely from our no longer having a bug-bear to contend with, or because (as Mr. Southey says) the war is no longer a customer to the markets, to the amount of fifty millions a year, why not declare war upon the Man in the Moon to-morrow, and never leave off till we have sent him to keep Bonaparte company at St. Helena? Why, it is but ordering so many cannon and cutlasses, no matter for what purpose—and equipping, and fantastically accoutring so many loyal corps of *minions of the moon, Diana's foresters,* and "the manufactures of Birmingham and Sheffield would revive to-morrow." If we had howitzers before of a prodigious size, let us have bombs of a calibre that Lord Castlereagh never dreamt of; and instead of iron balls, golden ones. Why not? The expense would be the greater. If we made the earth ring before, let us now make the welkin roar. The absurdity would be as costly, and more bloodless. A voyage to the moon would take at least as much time, as many lives and millions to accomplish, as the march to Paris. But then our merchants would not meanwhile get a monopoly of the trade of Europe, to stimulate their laggard patriotism, nor would the sovereigns of Europe be able to plant the standard of Legitimacy on the horns of the moon!—But though we have nothing to shew for the money we have madly squandered in war, we have something to pay for it (rather more than we can afford) to contractors, monopolists, and sinecurists, to the great fundholders and borough-mongers, to those who have helped to carry on, and to those who have been paid for applauding this sport-royal, as the most patriotic and profitable employment of the wealth and resources of a country. These persons, the tax-receivers, have got a mortgage on the property, health, strength, and skill of the rest of the community, who pay the taxes, which bows their industry to the ground, and deprives them of the necessary means of subsistence. The principal of the debt which the nation has contracted, has been laid out in *unproductive labour*, in inflicting the mischiefs and miseries of war; and the interest is for the most part equally laid out in *unproductive labour*, in fomenting the pride and luxury of those who have made their fortunes by the war and taxes. In a word, the debt and taxes are a government machine, which diverts that portion of the wealth and industry of the people, which would otherwise be employed in supplying the wants and comforts (say) of a hundred persons, to pamper the extravagance, vices, and artificial appetites of a single individual; and so on in proportion to the whole country. Every tax laid on in this manner, unnerves the arm of industry, is wrung from the bowels of want, and breaks the spirit of a nation, lessens the number of hands which are employed in useful labour, to seduce them into artificial, dependent, and precarious modes of subsistence, while the rich themselves find their reward for the indulgence of their indolence and voluptuousness in " the gout, serpigo, and the rheum," so that " their proper loins do curse them." It has been said that the taxes taken from the people return to them again, like the vapours drawn up from the earth in clouds, that descend again in refreshing dews and fertilizing showers. On the contrary, they are like these dews and showers drawn off from the ground by artificial channels into private reservoirs and useless cisterns to stagnate and corrupt. The money which is paid in taxes is taken from the people; the labour for which it pays does not benefit the people. A tax which goes to pay for the feeding of a pair of curricle horses or favourite hunters, swallows up the subsistence of several poor families. We cannot for ourselves approve of the privations, of the hunger, cold, or nakedness, to which these poor families are exposed, to keep up the flesh and the spirit of the sleek and high-mettled inhabitants of the warm, well-littered stable, even though they were of the breed of Swift's Houyuhyms! But that is a different question. All that we mean to say here is, that the tax takes the corn out of the bellies of the one to put it into those of the other species. A tax which is laid on to pay for a dog-kennel or a stable, might have saved a whole village from going into ruin and decay: and the carriage that glitters like a meteor along the streets of the metropolis, often deprives the wretched inmate of the distant cottage of the chair he sits on, the table he eats on, the bed he lies on. A street lined with coaches and with beggars dying at the steps of the doors, gives a strong lesson to common sense and political foresight, if not to humanity. A nation cannot subsist on unproductive labour, on war and taxes, or be composed merely of parish and state paupers. All unproductive labour is supported by productive labour. All persons maintained by the taxes or employed by those who are maintained by them are a clog, a dead weight upon those who pay them, that consume the produce of the State, and add nothing to it—a dead carcase fastened to a living one, with this difference, that it still devours the food which it does not provide. Need we ask any farther, how war and taxes, sinecures and monopolies, by degrees, weaken, impoverish, and ruin a State? Or whether they can go on increasing for ever? There is an excess of inequality and oppression, of luxury and want, which no state can survive; as there is a point at which the palsied frame can no longer support itself, and at which the withered tree falls to the ground.

If the sovereign of a country were to employ the whole population in doing nothing but throwing stones into the sea, he would soon become the king of a desert island. If a sovereign exhausts the wealth and strength of a country in war, he will end in being a king of slaves and beggars. The national debt is just the measure, the check-account of the labour and resources of the country which have been so wasted—of the stones we have been throwing into the sea. This debt is in fact an obligation entered into by the government on the part of the tax-payers, to indemnify the tax-receivers for their sacrifices in enabling the government to carry on the war. It is a power of attorney, extorted from nine-tenths of the community, making over to the remaining tenth an unlimited command over the resources, the comforts, the labour, the happiness and liberty of the great mass of society, by which their resources, their comforts, their labour, their happiness, and their liberty, have been lost, and made away with in government knick-knacks, and the kick-shaws of legitimacy. Half the resources and productive labour of the country for the last twenty years, have been sunk in this debt, and we are now called upon to make good the deficiency—how we can!—It has been shrewdly asked, whether, if every one paid a hundred *per cent.* income tax, the nation could flourish? And when we are told that "the war has been a *customer* to the country for a length of time to the amount of fifty millions a year," that is, has drained that sum from the pockets of the nation to employ the hands of the nation in *producing nothing*—we are at no loss to account for the consequences. A writer, whose own fault it is that we do not feel all the respect for him we could wish, has ridiculed the idea of a nation being in debt to itself, "like a tradesman to his creditors," and contends that "a much fairer instance would be that of a husband and wife playing cards at the same table against each other, where what the one loses, the other gains." Now men and their wives do not usually pay one another the money they lose at cards; and most people will be ready enough to reduce this simile to practice, by not paying the taxes, whenever the author shall have convinced Mr. Vansittart, that it is no matter whether the money is in the hands of the people or the government, and that to save trouble it had better remain where it is. Mr. Southey, in his late pamphlet, has very emphatically described the different effects of money laid out in war and peace, "What bounds," he exclaims, "could imagination set to the welfare and glory of this island, if a tenth part, or even a twentieth of what the war expenditure has been, were annually applied in improving and creating harbours, in bringing roads to the best possible repair, in colonizing upon our waste lands, in reclaiming fens, and conquering tracts from the sea, in encouraging the liberal arts, endowing schools and churches," &c. This is a singular slip of the pen in so noisy and triumphant a war-monger as the Poet Laureate. But logical inconsistency seems to be a sort of poetical license. Even in contradicting himself, he is not right. For the money as he proposes to employ it, would only degenerate into so many government jobs, and the low-lived mummery of Bible Societies. The pinnacle of prosperity and glory to which he would by these means raise the country, does not seem quite so certain. The other extreme of distress and degradation, to which the war-system has reduced it, is deep and deplorable indeed.

CHARACTER OF MR. BURKE.

October 5, 1817.

It is not without reluctance that we speak of the vices and infirmities of such a mind as Burke's: but the poison of high example has by far the widest range of destruction: and, for the sake of public honour and individual integrity, we think it right to say, that however it may be defended upon other grounds, the political career of that eminent individual has no title to the praise of consistency. Mr. Burke, the opponent of the American war, and Mr. Burke, the opponent of the French Revolution, are not the same person, but opposite persons—not opposite persons only, but deadly enemies. In the latter period, he abandoned not only all his practical conclusions, but all the principles on which they were founded. He proscribed all his former sentiments, denounced all his former friends, rejected and reviled all the maxims to which he had formerly appealed as incontestable. In the American war, he constantly spoke of the rights of the people as inherent, and inalienable: after the French Revolution, he began by treating them with the chicanery of a sophist, and ended by raving at them with the fury of a maniac. In the former case, he held out the duty of resistance to oppression, as the palladium and only ultimate resource of natural liberty; in the latter, he scouted, prejudged, vilified and nicknamed, all resistance in the abstract, as a foul and unnatural union of rebellion and sacrilege. In the one case, to answer the purposes of faction, he made it out, that the people are always in the right; in the other, to answer different ends, he made it out that they are always in the wrong—lunatics in the hands of their royal keepers, patients in the sick-wards of an hospital, or felons in the condemned cells of a prison. In the one, he considered that there was a constant tendency on the part of the prerogative to encroach on the rights of the people, which ought always to be the object of the most watchful jealousy, and of resistance, when necessary: in the other, he pretended to regard it as the sole occupation and ruling passion of those in power, to watch over the liberties and happiness of their subjects. The burthen of all his speeches on the American war, was conciliation, concession, timely reform, as the only practicable or desirable alternative of rebellion: the object of all his writings on the French Revolution was, to deprecate and explode all concession and all reform, as encouraging rebellion, and as an irretrievable step to revolution and anarchy. In the one, he insulted kings personally, as among the lowest and worst of mankind; in the other, he held them up to the imagination of his readers, as sacred abstractions. In the one case, he was a partisan of the people, to court popularity; in the other, to gain the favour of the Court, he became the apologist of all courtly abuses. In the one case, he took part with those who were actually rebels against his Sovereign: in the other, he denounced as rebels and traitors, all those of his own countrymen who did not yield sympathetic allegiance to a foreign Sovereign, whom we had always been in the habit of treating as an arbitrary tyrant.

Nobody will accuse the principles of his present Majesty, or the general measures of his reign, of inconsistency. If they had no other merit, they have, at least, that of having been all along actuated by one uniform and constant spirit: yet Mr. Burke at one time vehemently opposed, and afterwards most intemperately extolled them: and it was for his recanting his opposition, not for his persevering in it, that he received his pension. He does not himself mention his flaming speeches in the American war, as among the public services which had entitled him to this remuneration.

The truth is, that Burke was a man of fine fancy and subtle reflection; but not of sound and practical judgment, nor of high or rigid principles.—As to his understanding, he certainly was not a great philosopher; for his works of mere abstract reasoning are shallow and inefficient:—nor was he a man of sense and business; for, both in counsel and in conduct, he alarmed his friends as much at least as his opponents:—but he was an acute and accomplished man of letters—an ingenious political essayist. He applied the habit of reflection, which he had borrowed from his metaphysical studies, but which was not competent to the discovery of any elementary truth in that department, with great facility and success, to the mixed mass of human affairs. He knew more of the political machine than a recluse philosopher; and he speculated more profoundly on its principles and general results than a mere politician. He saw a number of fine distinctions and changeable aspects of things, the good mixed with the ill, and the ill mixed with the good; and with a sceptical indifference, in which the exercise of his own ingenuity was obviously the governing principle, suggested various topics to qualify or assist the judgment of others. But for this very reason, he was little calculated to become a leader or a partizan in any important practical measure. For the habit of his mind would lead him to find out a reason for or against any thing: and it is not on speculative refinements, (which belong to *every* side of a question), but on a just estimate of the aggregate mass and extended combinations of objections and advantages, that we ought to decide or act. Burke had the power of throwing true or false weights into the scales of political casuistry, but not firmness of mind (or, shall we say, honesty enough) to hold the balance. When he took a side, his vanity or his spleen more frequently gave the casting vote than his judgment; and the fieriness of his zeal was in exact proportion to the levity of his understanding, and the want of conscious sincerity.

He was fitted by nature and habit for the studies and labours of the closet; and was generally mischievous when he came out; because the very subtlety of his reasoning, which, left to itself, would have counteracted its own activity, or found its level in the common sense of mankind, became a dangerous engine in the hands of power, which is always eager to make use of the most plausible pretexts to cover the most fatal designs. That which, if applied as a general observation on human affairs, is a valuable truth suggested to the mind, may, when forced into the interested defence of a particular measure or system, become the grossest and basest sophistry. Facts or consequences never stood in the way of this speculative politician. He fitted them to his preconceived theories, instead of conforming his theories to them. They were the playthings of his style, the sport of his fancy. They were the straws of which his imagination made a blaze, and were consumed, like straws, in the blaze they had served to kindle. The fine things he said about Liberty and Humanity, in his speech on the Begum's affairs, told equally well, whether Warren Hastings was a tyrant or not: nor did he care one jot who caused the famine he described, so that he described it in a way that no one else could. On the same principle, he represented the French priests and nobles under the old regime as excellent moral people, very charitable and very religious, in the teeth of notorious facts,—to answer to the handsome things he had to say in favour of priesthood and nobility in general; and, with similar views, he falsifies the records of our English Revolution, and puts an interpretation on the word *abdication*, of which a schoolboy would be ashamed. He constructed his whole theory of government, in short, not on rational, but on picturesque and fanciful principles; as if the king's crown were a painted gewgaw, to be looked at on gala-days; titles an empty sound to please the ear; and the whole order of society a theatrical procession. His lamentations over the age of chivalry, and his projected crusade to restore it, are about as wise as if any one, from reading the Beggar's Opera, should take to picking of pockets: or, from admiring the landscapes of Salvator Rosa, should wish to convert the abodes of civilized life into the haunts of wild beasts and banditti. On this principle of false refinement, there is no abuse, nor system of abuses, that does not admit of an easy and triumphant defence; for there is something which a merely speculative enquirer may always find out, good as well as bad, in every possible system, the best or the worst; and if we can once get rid of the restraints of common sense and honesty, we may easily prove, by plausible words, that liberty and slavery, peace and war, plenty and famine, are matters of perfect indifference. This is the school of politics, of which Mr. Burke was at the head; and it is perhaps to his example, in this respect, that we owe the prevailing tone of many of those newspaper paragraphs, which Mr. Coleridge thinks so invaluable an accession to our political philosophy.

Burke's literary talents were, after all, his chief excellence. His style has all the familiarity of conversation, and all the research of the most elaborate composition. He says what he wants to say, by any means, nearer or more remote, within his reach. He makes use of the most common or scientific terms, of the longest or shortest sentences, of the plainest and most downright, or of the most figurative modes of speech. He gives for the most part loose reins to his imagination, and follows it as far as the language will carry him. As long as the one or the other has any resources in store to make the reader feel and see the thing as he has conceived it, in its nicest shades of difference, in its utmost degree of force and splendour, he never disdains, and never fails to employ them. Yet, in the extremes of his mixed style, there is not much affectation, and but little either of pedantry or of coarseness. He everywhere gives the image he wishes to give, in its true and appropriate colouring: and it is the very crowd and variety of these images that have given to his language its peculiar tone of animation, and even of passion. It is his impatience to transfer his conceptions entire, living, in all their rapidity, strength, and glancing variety, to the minds of others, that constantly pushes him to the verge of extravagance, and yet supports him there in dignified security—

> "Never so sure our rapture to create,
> As when he treads the brink of all we hate."

He is the most poetical of our prose writers, and at the same time his prose never degenerates into the mere effeminacy of poetry; for he always aims at overpowering rather than at pleasing; and consequently sacrifices beauty and delicacy to force and vividness. He has invariably a task to perform, a positive purpose to execute, an effect to produce. His only object is therefore to strike hard, and in the right place; if he misses his mark, he repeats his blow; and does not care how ungraceful the action, or how clumsy the instrument, provided it brings down his antagonist.

ON COURT-INFLUENCE.

> "To be honest as this world goes, is to be one man picked out of ten thousand."

January 3, 1818.

It is not interest alone, but prejudice or fashion that sways mankind. Opinion governs opinion. It is not merely what we can get by a certain line of conduct that we have to consider, but what others will think of it. The possession of money is but one mode of recommending ourselves to the good opinion of the world, of securing distinction and respect. Except as a bribe to popularity, money is of very limited value. Avarice is (oftener than we might at first suspect) only vanity in disguise. We should not want fine clothes or fine houses, an equipage or livery-servants, but for what others will think of us for having or wanting them. The chief and most expensive commodity that money is laid out in purchasing, is respect. Money, like other things, is worth no more than it will fetch. It is a passport into society: but if other things will answer the same purpose, as beauty, birth, wit, learning, desert in art or arms, dress, behaviour, the want of wealth is not felt as a very severe privation. If a man, who, on whatever pretensions, is received into good company, behaves with propriety and converses rationally, it is not inquired after he is gone, nor once thought of while he is present, whether he is rich or poor. In the mixed intercourse of private society every one finds his level, in proportion as he can contribute to its amusement or information. It is even more so in the general intercourse of the world, where a poet and a man of genius (if extrinsic circumstances make any difference) is as much courted and run after for being a common ploughman, as for being a peer of the realm. Burns, had he been living, would have started fair with Lord Byron in the race of popularity, and would not have lost it.

The temptation to men in public life to swerve from the path of duty, less frequently arises from a sordid regard to their private interests, than from an undue deference to popular applause. A want of political principle is, in nine cases out of ten, a want of firmness of mind to differ with those around us, and to stand the brunt of their avowed hostility or secret calumnies.

But still the world and its dread laugh prevails!"

An honest man is one whose sense of right and wrong is stronger than his anxiety that others should think or speak well of him. A man in the same sense forfeits his character for political integrity, whose love of truth truckles to his false shame and cringing complaisance, and who tampers with his own convictions, that he may stand well with the world. A man who sells his opinion merely to gain by his profligacy, is not a man without public principle, but common honesty. He ranks in the same class with a highwayman or a pickpocket.—It is true, interest and opinion are in general linked together; but opinion flies before, and interest comes limping after. As a woman first loses her virtue through her heart, so the yielding patriot generally sacrifices his character to his love of reputation.

It is usually supposed by those who make no distinction between the highest point of integrity and the lowest mercenariness, that Mr. Burke changed his principles to gain a pension: and that this was the main-spring of his subsequent conduct. We do not think so; though this may have been one motive, and a strong one to a needy and extravagant man. But the pension which he received was something more than a mere grant of money—it was a mark of royal favour, it was a tax upon public opinion. If any thing were wanting to fix his veering loyalty, it was the circumstance of the king's having his "Reflections on the French Revolution" bound in morocco (not an unsuitable binding), and giving it to all his particular friends, saying, "It was a book which every gentleman ought to read!" This praise would go as far with a vain man as a pension with a needy one; and we may be sure, that if there were any lurking seeds of a leaning to the popular side remaining in the author's breast, he would after this lose no time in rooting them out of the soil, that his works might reflect the perfect image of his royal master's mind, and have no plebeian stains left to sully it. Kings are great critics: they are the fountain of honour; the judges of merit. After such an authority had pronounced it "a book which every gentleman ought to read," what gentleman could refuse to read, or dare to differ with it? With what feelings a privy-counsellor would open the leaves of a book, which the king had had richly bound, and presented with his own hand! How lords of the bed-chamber would wonder at the profound arguments! How peeresses in their own right must simper over the beautiful similes! How the judges must puzzle over it! How the bishops would bless themselves at the number of fine things; and our great classical scholars, Doctors Parr and Burney, sit down for the first time in their lives to learn English, to write themselves into a bishopric! Burke had long laboured hard to attain a doubtful pre-eminence. He had worked his way into public notice by talents which were thought specious rather than solid, and by sentiments which were obnoxious to some, suspected by others. His connexions and his views were ambiguous. He professedly espoused the cause of the people, and found it as hard to defend himself against popular jealousy as ministerial resentment. He saw court-lacqueys put over his head; and country squires elbowing him aside. He was neither understood by friends nor enemies. He was opposed, thwarted, cross-questioned, and obliged to present " a certificate of merit" (as he himself says) at every stage of his progress through life. But the king's having pronounced that " his book was one which every gentleman ought to read," floated him at once out of the flats and shallows in which his voyage of popularity had been bound, into the full tide of court-favour; settled all doubts; smoothed all difficulties; rubbed off old scores; made the crooked straight, and the rough plain;—what was obscure, became profound;—what was extravagant, lofty; every sentiment was liberality, every expression elegance; and from that time to this, Burke has been the oracle of every dull venal pretender to taste or wisdom. Those who had never heard of or despised him before, now joined in his praise. He became a fashion; he passed into a proverb; he was an idol in the eyes of his readers, as much as he could ever, in the days of his youthful vanity, have been in his own; he was dazzled with his own popularity; and all this was owing to the king. No wonder he was delighted with the change, infatuated with it, infuriated! It was better to him than four thousand pounds a-year for his own life, and fifteen hundred a-year to his widow during the joint-lives of four other persons. It was what all his life he had been aiming at.—" Thou hast it now, King, Cawdor, Glamis, all!" It was what the nurses had prophecied of him, and what the school-boy had dreamt; and that which is first, is also last in our thoughts. It was this that tickled his vanity more than his pension: it was this that raised his gratitude, that melted his obdurate pride, that opened the sluices of his heart to the poison of corruption, that exorcised the low, mechanic, vulgar, morose, sour principles of liberty clean out of him, left his mind "swept and garnished," parched and dry, fevered with revenge, bloated with adulation; and made him as shameless and abandoned in sacrificing every feeling of attachment or obligation to the people, as he had before been bold and prodigal in heaping insult and contumely upon the throne. He denounced his former principles, in the true spirit of an apostate, with a fury equal to the petulant and dogmatical tone in which he had asserted them; and then proceeded to abuse all those who doubted the honesty or wisdom of this change of opinion. He, in short, looked upon every man as his enemy who did not think "his book fit for a gentleman to read;" and would willingly have committed every such presumptuous sceptic to the flames for not bowing down in servile adoration before this idol of his vanity and reputation. Hence the frantic philippics in his latter revolutionary speeches and writings, and the alteration from a severe and stately style of eloquence and reasoning in his earlier compositions to the most laboured paradoxes and wildest declamation. We do not mean to say that his latest works did not display the greatest genius. His native talents blazed out, undisguised and unconfined in them. *Indignatio facit versus.* Burke's best Muse was his vanity or spleen. He felt quite at home in giving vent to his personal spite and venal malice. He pleaded his own cause and the cause of the passions better and with more eloquence, than he ever pleaded the cause of truth and justice. He felt the one rankling in his heart with all their heat and fury; he only conceived the other with his understanding coldly and circuitously.—The "Letters of William Burke" give one, however, a low idea of Burke's honesty, even in a pecuniary point of view.—(See Barry's "Life.") He constantly tells Barry, as a source of consolation to his friend, and a compliment to his brother, "that though his party had not hitherto been successful, or had not considered him as they ought, matters were not so bad with him but that he could still afford to be honest, and not desert the cause." This is very suspicious. This querulous tone of disappointment, and cockering up of his boasted integrity, must have come from Burke himself; who would hardly have expressed such a sentiment, if it had not been frequently in his thoughts; or if he had not made out a previous debtor and creditor account between preferment and honesty, as one of the regular principles of his political creed.

The same narrow view of the subject, drawn from a supposition that money, or interest in the grossest sense, is the only inducement to a dereliction of principle or sinister conduct, has been applied to shew the sincerity of the present laureate in his change of opinions; for it was said that the paltry salary of 100*l.* a-year was not a sufficient temptation to any man of common sense, and who had other means of gaining an ample livelihood honourably, to give up his principles and his party, unless he did so conscientiously. That is not the real alternative of the case. It is not the hundred pounds salary; it is the honour (some may think it a disgrace) conferred along with it, that enhances the prize. "And with it words of so sweet breath composed, as made the gift more rare"* It is the introduction to Carlton-House, the smile, the squeeze by the hand that awaits him there, "escap'd from Pyrrho's maze, and Epicurus' sty." The being presented at court is worth more than a hundred pounds a-year. A person with a hundred thousand pounds a-year can only be presented at court, and would consider it the greatest mortification to be shut out. It is the highest honour in the land; and Mr. Southey, by accepting his place and discarding his principles, receives that highest honour as a matter of course, in addition to his salary and his butt of sack. He is ushered into the royal presence as by a magic charm, the palace-gates fly open at the sight of his laurel-crown, and he stands in the midst of "Britain's warriors, her statesmen, and her fair," as if suddenly dropped from the clouds. Is this nothing to a vain man? Is it nothing to the author of "Wat Tyler" and "Joan of Arc" to have those errors of his youth veiled in the honours of his riper years? To fill the poetic

* We hope Mr. Southey has not found the truth of the latter part of the passage. "Rich gifts wax poor, when givers prove unkind."

throne of Dryden, of Shadwell, of Cibber, and of Pye? To receive distinctions which Spenser, Shakspeare, and Milton never received, and to chaunt to the unaverted ear of sovereignty strains such as they never sung? To be seen on each returning birth-day joining the bright throng, the lengthened procession, gay, gilt, painted, coronetted, garlanded, that as it passes to and from St. James's, all London, in sunshine or in shower, pours out to gaze at? We tremble for the consequences, should any thing happen to disturb the Laureate in his dream of perfect felicity. Racine died broken-hearted, because Louis XIV. frowned upon him as he passed; and yet Racine was as great a poet and as pious a man as Mr. Southey.

To move in the highest circles, to be in favour at courts, to be familiar with princes, is then an object of ambition, which may be supposed to fascinate a less romantic mind than Mr. Southey's, setting the lucrativeness of his conversion out of the question. Many persons have paid dear for this proud elevation, with bankrupt health and beggared fortunes. How many are ready to do so still! Mr. Southey only paid for it *with his opinion;* and some people think it as much as his opinion was worth. Are we to suppose Mr. Southey's vanity of so sordid a kind, that it must be bribed by his avarice? Might not the Poet-laureate be supposed to catch at a title or a blue ribbon, if it were offered him, without a round salary attached to it?

Why do country gentlemen wish to get into parliament, but to be seen there? Why do overgrown merchants and rich nabobs wish to sit there, like so many overgrown schoolboys? Look at the hundreds of thousands of pounds squandered in contested elections? It is not "gain but glory" that provokes the combatants. Do you suppose that these persons expect to repay themselves by making a market of their constituents, and selling their votes to the best bidder? No: but they wish to be thought to have the greatest influence, the greatest number of friends and adherents in their county; and they will pay any price for it. We put into the lottery, indeed, in hopes of what we can get, but in the lottery of life honour is the great prize. It is the opinion of the people for which the candidate at an election contends; and on the same principles he will barter the opinion of the people, their rights and liberty, and his own independence and character, not for gold, but for the friendship of a court-favourite. Not that gold has not its weight too, for the great and powerful have that also to bestow:—it is true, that

> —— "In their Livery
> Walk Crowns and Crownets, Realms and Islands
> As Plates drop from their Pockets."

But opinion is a still more insinuating and universal menstruum for dissolving honesty. *That sweet smile that hangs on princes' favours* is more effectual than even the favours themselves!

ON COURT INFLUENCE.

(CONCLUDED.)

> "To be honest as this world goes, is to be one man picked out of ten "thousand."

January 10, 1818.

WE are all of us more or less the slaves of opinion. There is no one, however mean or insignificant, whose approbation is altogether indifferent to us; whose flattery does not please, whose contempt does not mortify us. There is an atmosphere of this sort always about us, from which we can no more withdraw ourselves than from the air we breathe. But the air of a Court is the concentrated essence of the opinion of the world. The atmosphere there is mephitic. It is subtle poison, the least exhalation of which taints the vitals of its victims. It is made up of servile adulation, of sneering compliments, of broken promises, of smiling professions, of stifled opinions, of hollow thanks, of folly and lies—

> "Soul-killing lies, and truths that work small good."

It is infected with the breath of flatterers, and the thoughts of Kings! Let us see how its influence descends:—from the King to the people, to his Ministers first, from the Ministers to both Houses of Parliament, from Lords to Ladies, from the Clergy to the Laity, from the high to the low, from the rich to the poor, and "pierces through the body of the city, country, court"—it is beauty, birth, wit, learning, riches, numbers: it is fear and favour; it has all the splendour that can seduce, all the power that can intimidate, all the interest that can corrupt, on its side; so that the opinion of the King is the opinion of the nation; and if that opinion is not a wise one, hangs like a millstone round its neck, oppresses it like a night-mare, weighs upon it like lead, makes truth a lie, right wrong, converts liberty into slavery, peace into war, plenty to famine, turns the heads of a whole people, and bows their bodies to the earth. "Whosoever shall stumble against this stone, it shall bruise him: but whomsoever it falls upon, it shall grind him to powder." The whisper of a King rounded in the ear of a favourite is re-echoed back in speeches and votes of Parliament, in addresses and resolutions from associations in town and country, drawls from the pulpit, brawls from the bar, resounds like the thunder of a people's voice, roars in the cannon's mouth, and disturbs the peace of nations. The frown of monarchs is like the speck seen in the distant horizon, which soon spreads and darkens the whole hemisphere. Who is there in his senses that can withstand the gathering storm, or oppose himself to this torrent of opinion setting in upon him from the throne and absorbing by degrees every thing in its vortex—undermining every principle of independence, confounding every distinction of the understanding, and obliterating every trace of liberty? To argue against it, is like arguing against the motion of the world with which we are carried along: its influence is as powerful and as imperceptible. To question it, is folly; to resist it, madness. To differ with the opinion of a whole nation, seems as presumptuous as it is unwise: and yet the very circumstance which makes it so uniform, is that which makes it worth nothing. Authority is more absolute than reason. Truth curtesies to power. No arguments could persuade ten millions of men in one country to be all of one mind, and thirty millions in another country to be of just the contrary one; but the word of a King does it! We do not like to differ from the company we are in. How much more difficult is it to brave the opinion of the world! No man likes to be frowned out of society. No man likes to be without sympathy. He must be a proud man indeed who can do without it; and proud men do not like to be made a mark for "scorn to point his slow and moving finger at." No man likes to be thought the enemy of his king and country, without just cause. No man likes to be called a fool or a knave, merely because he is not a fool and a knave. It is not desirable to have to answer arguments backed with informations filed *ex officio;* it is not amusing to become a bye-word with the mob. A nickname is *the hardest stone that the devil can throw at a man.* It will knock down any man's resolution. It will stagger his reason. It will tame his pride. Fasten it upon any man, and he will try to shake it off, at any rate, though he should part with honour and honesty along with it. To be shut out from public praise or private friendship, to be lampooned in newspapers or Anti-Jacobin reviews, to be looked blank upon in company, is not "a consummation devoutly to be wished." The unfavourable opinion of others gives you a bad opinion of yourself or them: and neither of these conduces to persevering, high-minded integrity. To wish to serve mankind, we should think well of them. To be able to serve them, they should think well of us. To keep well with the public, is not more necessary to a man's private interest than to his general utility. It is a hopeless task to be always striving against the stream: it is a thankless one to be in a state of perpetual litigation with the community. The situation of a strange dog in a country town, barked at and worried by all the curs in the village, is about as enviable as that of a person who affects singularity in politics. What is a man to do who gets himself into this predicament, in an age when patriotism is a misnomer in language, and public principle a solecism in fact? If he cannot bring the world round to his opinion, he must as a forlorn hope go over to theirs, and be content to be knave— or nothing.

Such is the force of opinion, that we would undertake to drive a first Minister from his place and out of the country, by merely being allowed to hire a number of dirty boys to hoot him along the streets from his own house to the treasury and from the treasury back again. How would a certain distinguished character, remarkable for uniting the *suaviter in modo* with the *fortiter in re*, and who, with an invariable consistency in his political principles, carries the easiness of his temper to a degree of apparent *non-chalance*, bear to have a starling in his neighbourhood taught to repeat nothing but Walcheren, or to ring the changes in his ears upon the names of Castles, Oliver, and Reynolds? Can we wonder then at the feats which such Ministers have performed with the Attorney-General at their backs, and the country at their heels, in full cry against every one who was not a creature of the Ministers,—for whose morals they could not vouch as government-spies, or whose talents they did not reward as government-critics?—Mr. Coleridge, in his Literary Biography, lately published, complains with pathetic bitterness of the wanton and wilful slanders formerly circulated with so much zeal in the Anti-Jacobin against himself, Mr. Southey, and his other poetical friends, merely for a difference of political opinion; and he significantly assigns these slanders as the reason why himself and his friends remained so long adverse to the party who were the authors of them! We will venture to go a little further, and say, that they were not only the reason of their long estrangement from the Court-party, but of their final reconciliation to it. They had time to balance and reflect, and to make a choice of evils—they deliberated between the loss of principle and of character, and they were undone. They thought it better to be the accomplices of venality and corruption than the mark for them to shoot their arrows at: they took shelter from the abuse by joining in the cry. Mr. Southey says that he has not changed his principles, but that circumstances have changed, and that he has grown wiser from the events of five-and-twenty years. How is it that his present friend and associate in the Quarterly Review, who was formerly a contributor to the Beauties of the Anti-Jacobin, has not changed too? The world has gone round in his time too, but he remains firm to his first principles. He worships the sun wherever he sees it. Court-favour, "the cynosure of longing eyes," sheds a more steady influence on its votaries than vague popularity. The confined, artificial air of a Court has a wonderful effect in stopping that progress of the mind with the march of events, of which Mr. Southey boasts, and prematurely fixes the volatility of genius in a *caput mortuum* of prejudice and servility, in those who are admitted within the magic circle! The Anti-Jacobin poet and orator, Mr. Canning, has not become a renegado to the opinions of the Court: the Jacobin poet and prose-writer, Mr. Southey, has become a renegado to his own. —In an article in the Quarterly Review (some months back) there was an argument to shew that the late war against France was all along the undoubted result of popular opinion, "because from the first party-spirit ran so high upon this subject, that any one who expressed an opinion against it did so at the hazard of his reputation, fortune, or even life." The author of this singular argument, we believe, was one of those, who did not at the critical period here alluded to approve of it, and who has since become a convert to its justice and humanity. His own statement may account for his change of opinion. What a pity for a man to hazard his life and fortune in a cause by maintaining an opinion, and to lose his character afterwards by relinquishing it. The present Poet-laureate has missed indeed the crown of martyrdom, and has gained a crown of laurel in its stead!

The same consistent writers, and friends of civil and religious liberty, who are delighted with the restoration of the Bourbons, of the Pope, and the Inquisition, have lately made an attempt to run down the Dissenters in this country; and in this they are right. They dwell with fondness on "the single-heartedness of the Spanish nation," who are slaves and bigots to a man, and scoff at the Presbyterians and Independents of this country (who ousted Popery and slavery at the Revolution, and who had a main hand in placing and continuing the present family on the throne) as but half-Englishmen, and as equally disaffected to Church and State. There is some ground for the antipathy of our political changelings to a respectable, useful, and conscientious body of men: and we will here, in discharge of an old debt, say what this ground is. If it were only meant that the Dissenters are but half Englishmen, because they are not professed slaves—that they are disaffected to the Constitution in Church and State, because they are not prepared to go all the lengths of despotism and intolerance under a Protestant hierarchy and Constitutional King, which they resisted "at the peril of their characters, their fortunes, and their lives," under a persecuting priesthood and an hereditary Pretender, this would be well: but there is more in it than this. Our sciolists would persuade us that the different sects are hot-beds of sedition, because they are nurseries of public spirit, and independence, and sincerity of opinion in all other respects. They are so necessarily, and by the supposition. They are Dissenters from the Established Church: they submit voluntarily to certain privations, they incur a certain portion of obloquy and ill-will, for the sake of what they believe to be the truth: they are not time-servers on the face of the evidence, and that is sufficient to expose them to the instinctive hatred and ready ribaldry of those who think venality the first of virtues, and prostitution of principle the best sacrifice a man can make to the Graces or his Country. The Dissenter does not change his sentiments with the seasons: he does not suit his conscience to his convenience. This is enough to condemn him for a pestilent fellow. He will not give up his principles because they are unfashionable, therefore he is not to be trusted. He speaks his mind bluntly and honestly, therefore he is a secret disturber of the peace, a dark conspirator against the State. On the contrary, the different sects in this country are, or have been, the steadiest supporters of its liberties and laws: they are checks and barriers against the insidious or avowed encroachments of arbitrary power, as effectual and indispensable as any others in the Constitution: they are depositaries of a principle as sacred and somewhat rarer than a devotion to Court-influence—we mean the love of truth. It is hard for any one to be an honest politician who is not born and bred a Dissenter. Nothing else can sufficiently inure and steel a man against the prevailing prejudices of the world, but that habit of mind which arises from non-conformity to its decisions in matters of religion. There is a natural alliance between the love of civil and religious liberty, as much as between Church and State. Protestantism was the first school of political liberty in Europe: Presbyterianism has been one great support of it in England. The sectary in religion is taught to appeal to his own bosom for the truth and sincerity of his opinions, and to arm himself with stern indifference to what others think of them. This will no doubt often produce a certain hardness of manner and cold repulsiveness of feeling in trifling matters, but it is the only sound discipline of truth, or inflexible honesty in politics as well as in religion. The same principle of independent inquiry and unbiassed conviction which makes him reject all undue interference between his Maker and his conscience, will give a character of uprightness and disregard of personal consequences to his conduct and sentiments in what concerns the most important relations between man and man. He neither subscribes to the dogmas of priests, nor truckles to the mandates of Ministers. He has a rigid sense of duty which renders him superior to the caprice, the prejudices, and the injustice of the world; and the same habitual consciousness of rectitude of purpose, which leads him to rely for his self-respect on the testimony of his own heart, enables him to disregard the groundless malice and rash judgments of his opponents. It is in vain for him to pay his court to the world, to fawn upon power; he labours under certain insurmountable disabilities for becoming a candidate for its favour: he dares to contradict its opinion and to condemn its usages in the most important article of all. The world will always look cold and askance upon him; and therefore he may defy it with less fear of its censures. The Presbyterian is said to be sour: he is not therefore over-complaisant—

> "Or if severe in thought,
> "The love he bears to virtue is in fault."

Dissenters are the safest partizans, and the steadiest friends. Indeed they are almost the only people who have an idea of an abstract attachment to a cause or to individuals, from a sense of fidelity, independently of prosperous or adverse circumstances, and in spite of opposition. No patriotism, no public spirit, not reared in that inclement sky and harsh soil, in "the *hortus siccus* of dissent," will generally last: it will either bend in the storm or droop in the sunshine. *Non ex quovis ligno fit Mercurius.* You cannot engraft a medlar on a crab-apple. A thorough-bred Dissenter will never make an accomplished Courtier. The antithesis of a Presbyterian Divine of the old school is a Poet-laureate of the new. We have known instances of both; and give it decidedly in favour of old-fashioned honesty over new-fangled policy.

We have known instances of both. The one we would willingly forget; the others we hope never to forget, nor can we ever. A Poet-laureate is an excrescence even in a Court; he is doubly nugatory as a Courtier and a Poet; he is a refinement upon insignificance, and a superfluous piece of supererogation. But a Dissenting Minister is a character not so easily to be dispensed with, and whose place cannot well be supplied. It is the fault of sectarianism that it tends to scepticism; and so relaxes the springs of moral courage and patience into levity and indifference. The prospect of future rewards and punishments is a useful set-off against the immediate distribution of places and pensions; the anticipations of faith call off our attention from the grosser illusions of sense. It is a pity that this character has worn itself out; that that pulse of thought and feeling has ceased almost to beat in the heart of a nation, who, if not remarkable for sincerity and plain downright well-meaning, are remarkable for nothing. But we have known some such, in happier days; who had been brought up and lived from youth to age in the one constant belief of God and of his Christ, and who thought all other things but dross compared with the glory hereafter to be revealed. Their youthful hopes and vanity had been mortified in them, even in their boyish days, by the neglect and supercilious regards of the world; and they turned to look into their own minds for something else to build their hopes and confidence upon. They were true Priests. They set up an image in their own minds, it was truth: they worshipped an idol there, it was justice. They looked on man as their brother, and only bowed the knee to the Highest. Separate from the world, they walked humbly with their God, and lived in thought with those who had borne testimony of a good conscience, with the spirits of just men in all ages. They saw Moses when he slew the Egyptian, and the Prophets who overturned the brazen images; and those who were stoned and sawn asunder. They were with Daniel in the lions' den, and with the three children who passed through the fiery furnace, Meshech, Shadrach, and Abednego; they did not crucify Christ twice over, or deny him in their hearts, with St. Peter; the Book of Martyrs was open to them; they read the story of William Tell, of John Huss and Jerome of Prague, and the old one-eyed Zisca; they had Neale's History of the Puritans by heart, and Calamy's Account of the Two Thousand Ejected Ministers, and gave it to their children to read, with the pictures of the polemical Baxter, the silver-tongued Bates, the mild-looking Calamy, and old honest Howe; they believed in Lardner's Credibility of the Gospel History: they were deep-read in the works of the *Fratres Poloni*, Pripscovius, Crellius, Cracovius, who sought out truth in texts of Scripture, and grew blind over Hebrew points; their aspiration after liberty was a sigh uttered from the towers, "time-rent," of the Holy Inquisition; and their zeal for religious toleration was kindled at the fires of Smithfield. Their sympathy was not with the oppressors, but the oppressed. They cherished in their thoughts—and wished to transmit to their posterity—those rights and privileges for asserting which their ancestors had bled on scaffolds, or had pined in dungeons, or in foreign climes. Their creed too was "Glory to God, peace on earth, good will to man." This creed, since profaned and rendered vile, they kept fast through good report and evil report. This belief they had, that looks at something out of itself, fixed as the stars, deep as the firmament, that makes of its own heart an altar to truth, a place of worship for what is right, at which it does reverence with praise and prayer like a holy thing, apart and content: that feels that the greatest being in the universe is always near it, and that all things work together for the good of his creatures, under his guiding hand. This covenant they kept, as the stars keep their courses: this principle they stuck by, for want of knowing better, as it sticks by them to the last. It grew with their growth, it does not wither in their decay. It lives when the almond-tree flourishes, and is not bowed down with the tottering knees. It glimmers with the last feeble eyesight, smiles in the faded cheek like infancy, and lights a path before them to the grave!—This is better than the life of a whirligig Court poet.

ON THE CLERICAL CHARACTER.

———— "Now mark a spot or two,
Which so much virtue would do well to clear."——COWPER.

Jan. 24, 1818.

THE clerical character has, no doubt, its excellences, which have been often insisted on: it has also its faults, which cannot be corrected or guarded against, unless they are pointed out. The following are some of them.

The first, and most obvious objection we have to it, arises from the dress. All artificial distinctions of this kind have a tendency to warp the understanding and sophisticate the character. They create egotism. A man is led to think of himself more than he should, who by any outward marks of distinction invites others to fix their attention on him. They create affectation; for they make him study to be not like himself, but like his dress. They create hypocrisy; for as his thoughts and feelings cannot be as uniform and mechanical as his dress, he must be constantly tempted to make use of the one as a cloak to the other, and to conceal the defects or aberrations of his mind by a greater primness of professional costume, or a more mysterious carriage of his person—

——"And in Franciscan think to pass disguised.

No man of the ordinary stamp can retain a downright unaffected simplicity of character who is always reminding others, and reminded himself, of his pretensions to superior piety and virtue by a conventional badge, which implies neither one nor the other, and which must gradually accustom the mind to compromise appearances for reality, the form for the power of godliness. We do not care to meet the Lawyers fluttering about Chancery-lane in their full-bottomed wigs and loose silk gowns: their dress seems to sit as loose upon them as their opinions, and they wear their own hair under the well-powdered dangling curls, as they bury the sense of right and wrong under the intricate and circuitous forms of law: but we hate much more to meet a three-cornered well-pinched clerical hat on a prim expectant pair of shoulders, that seems to announce to half a street before it, that sees the theological puppet coming, with a mingled air of humility and self-conceit—"Stand off, for I am holier than you." We are not disposed to submit to this pharisaical appeal; we are more inclined to resent than to sympathise with the claims to our respect, which are thus mechanically perked in our faces. The dress of the bar merely implies a professional indifference to truth or falsehood in those who wear it, and they seldom carry it out of Court: the dress of the pulpit implies a greater gravity of pretension; and they therefore stick to it as closely as to a doublet and hose of religion and morality. If the reverend persons who are thus clothed with righteousness as with a garment, are sincere in their professions, it is well: if they are hypocrites, it is also well. It is no wonder that the class of persons so privileged are tenacious of the respect that is paid to the cloth; that their tenderness on this subject is strengthened by all the incentives of self-love; by the *esprit de corps;* by the indirect implication of religion itself in any slight put upon its authorised Ministers; and that the deliberate refusal to acknowledge the gratuitous claims which are thus set up to our blind homage, is treated as a high offence against the good order of society in the present world, and threatened with exemplary punishment in the next. There is nothing fair or manly in all this. It is levying a tax on our respect under fraudulent, or at best, equivocal pretences. There is no manner of connexion between the thing and the symbol of it, to which public opinion is expected to bow. The whole is an affair of dress—a dull masquerade. There is no proof of the doctrine of the Trinity in a three-cornered hat, nor does a black coat without a cape imply sincerity and candour. A man who wishes to pass for a saint or a philosopher on the strength of a button in his hat or a buckle in his shoes, is not very likely to be either; as the button in the hat or the buckle in the shoes will answer all the same purpose with the vulgar, and save time and trouble. Those who make their dress a principal part of themselves, will, in general, become of no more value than their dress. Their understandings will receive a costume. Their notions will be as stiff and starched as their bands; their morals strait-laced and ricketty; their pretended creed formal and out of date; and they themselves a sort of demure lay-figures, sombre Jacks-of-the Green, to carry about the tattered fragments and hoarded relics of bigotry and superstition, which, when they no longer awe the imagination or impose on credulity, only insult the understanding and excite contempt.—No one who expects you to pay the same regard to the cut or colour of his coat as to what he says or does, will be anxious to set an exclusive value on what can alone entitle him to respect. You are to take his merit for granted on the score of civility, and he will take it for granted himself on the score of convenience. He will do all he can to keep up the farce. These gentlemen find it no hardship

> "To counterfeiten chere
> Of court, and ben estatelich of manere,
> And to ben holden digne of reverence."

On the contrary, if you offer to withhold it from them,

> "Certain so wroth are they,
> That they are out of all charity."

This canonical standard of moral estimation is too flattering to their pride and indolence to be parted with in a hurry; and nothing will try their patience or provoke their humility so much as to suppose that there is any truer stamp of merit than the badge of their profession. It has been contended, that more is made here of the clerical dress than it is meant to imply; that it is simply a mark of distinction, to know the individuals of that particular class of society from others, and that they ought to be charged with affectation, or an assumption of self-importance for wearing it, no more than a waterman, a fireman, or a chimney-sweeper, for appearing in the streets in their appropriate costume. We do not think "the collusion holds in the exchange." If a chimney-sweeper were to jostle a spruce divine in the street, which of them would ejaculate the word "Fellow?" The humility of the churchman would induce him to lift up his cane at the sooty professor, but the latter would hardly take his revenge by raising his brush and shovel, as equally respectable insignia of office. As to the watermen and firemen, they do not, by the badges of their trade, claim any particular precedence in moral accomplishments, nor are their jacket and trowsers hieroglyphics of any particular creed, which others are bound to believe on pain of damnation. It is there the shoe pinches. Where external dress really denotes distinction of rank in other cases, as in the dress of officers in the army, those who might avail themselves of this distinction lay it aside as soon as possible; and, unless very silly fellows or very great coxcombs, do not choose to be made a gazing-stock to women and children. But there is in the clerical habit something too sacred to be lightly put on or off: *once a priest, and always a priest:* it adheres to them as a part of their function; it is the outward and visible sign of an inward and invisible grace; it is a light that must not be hid; it is a symbol of godliness, an edifying spectacle, an incentive to good morals, a discipline of humanity, and a *memento mori*, which cannot be too often before us. To lay aside their habit, would be an unworthy compromise of the interests of both worlds. It would be a sort of denying Christ. They therefore venture out into the streets with this gratuitous obtrusion of opinion and unwarrantable assumption of character wrapped about them, ticketted and labelled with the Thirty-nine Articles, St. Athanasius's Creed, and the Ten Commandments,—with the Cardinal Virtues and the Apostolic Faith sticking out of every corner of their dress, and angling for the applause or contempt of the multitude. A full-dressed ecclesiastic is a sort of go-cart of divinity; an ethical automaton. A clerical prig is, in general, a very dangerous as well as contemptible character. The utmost that those who thus habitually confound their opinions and sentiments with the outside coverings of their bodies can aspire to, is a negative and neutral character, like wax-work figures, where the dress is done as much to the life as the man, and where both are respectable pieces of pasteboard, or harmless compositions of fleecy hosiery.

The bane of all religions has been the necessity (real or supposed) of keeping up an attention and attaching a value to external forms and ceremonies. It was, of course, much easier to conform to these, or to manifest a reverence for them, than to practise the virtues or understand the doctrines of true religion, of which they were merely the outward types and symbols. The consequence has been, that the greatest stress has been perpetually laid on what was of the least value, and most easily professed. The form of religion has superseded the substance; the means have supplanted the end; and the sterling coin of charity and good works has been driven out of the currency, for the base counterfeits of superstition and intolerance, by all the money-changers and dealers in the temples established to religion throughout the world. Vestments and chalices have been multiplied for the reception of the Holy Spirit; the tagged points of controversy and lackered varnish of hypocrisy have eaten into the solid substance and texture of piety; "and all the inward acts of worship, issuing from the native strength of the soul, run out (as Milton expresses it) lavishly to the upper skin, and there harden into the crust of formality." Hence we have had such shoals of

> "Eremites and friars,
> White, black, and grey, with all their trumpery"—

who have foisted their "idiot and embryo" inventions upon us for truth, and who have fomented all the bad passions of the heart, and let loose all the mischiefs of war, of fire, and famine, to avenge the slightest difference of opinion on any one iota of their lying creeds, or the slightest disrespect to any one of those mummeries and idle pageants which they had set up as sacred idols for the world to wonder at. We do not forget, in making these remarks, that there was a time when the persons who will be most annoyed and scandalized at them, would have taken a more effectual mode of shewing their zeal and indignation; when to have expressed a free opinion on a Monk's cowl or a Cardinal's hat, would have exposed the writer who had been guilty of such sacrilege, to the pains and penalties of excommunication: to be burnt at an *auto da fe;* to be consigned to the dungeons of the Inquisition, or doomed to the mines of Spanish America; to have his nose slit, or his ears cut off, or his hand reduced to a stump. Such were the considerate and humane proceedings by which the Priests of former times vindicated their own honour, which they pretended to be the honour of God. Such was their humility, when they had the power. Will they complain now, if we only criticise the colour of a coat, or smile at the circumference of a Doctor of Divinity's wig, since we can do it with impunity? We cry them mercy!

ON THE CLERICAL CHARACTER.

———— "Now mark a spot or two,
Which so much virtue would do well to clear."—COWPER.

(CONTINUED.)

Jan. 31, 1818.

MANY people seem to think, that the restraints imposed on the Clergy by the nature of their profession, take away from them, by degrees, all temptation to violate the limits of duty, and that the character grows to the cloth. We are afraid that this is not altogether the case.

How little can be done in the way of extracting virtues or intellect from a piece of broad-cloth or a beaver hat, we have an instance in the Quakers, who are the most remarkable, and the most unexceptionable class of professors in this kind. They bear the same relation to genuine characters, not brought up in the trammels of dress and custom, that a clipped yew-tree, cut into the form of a peacock or an arm-chair, does to the natural growth of a tree in the forest, left to its own energies and luxuriance. The Quakers are docked into form, but they have no spirit left. They are without ideas, except in trade; without vices or virtues, unless we admit among the latter those which we give as a character to servants when we turn them away, viz. "that they are cleanly, sober, and honest." The Quaker is, in short, a negative character, but it is the best that can be formed in this mechanical way. The Priest is not a negative character; he is something positive and disagreeable. He is not, like the Quaker, distinguished from others merely by singularity of dress and manner, but he is distinguished from others by pretensions to superiority over them. His faults arise from his boasted exemption from the opposite vices; and he has one vice running through all his others—hypocrisy. He is proud, with an affectation of humility; bigotted, from a pretended zeal for truth; greedy, with an ostentation of entire contempt for the things of this world; professing self-denial, and always thinking of self-gratification; censorious, and blind to his own faults; intolerant, unrelenting, impatient of opposition, insolent to those below, and cringing to those above him, with nothing but Christian meekness and brotherly love in his mouth. He thinks more of external appearances than of his internal convictions. He is tied down to the opinions and prejudices of the world in every way. The motives of the heart are clogged and checked at the outset, by the fear of idle censure; his understanding is the slave of established creeds and formulas of faith. He can neither act, feel, or think for himself, or from genuine impulse. He plays a part through life. He is an actor upon a stage. The public are a spy upon him, and he wears a mask the better to deceive them. If in this sort of theatrical assumption of character he makes one false step, it may be fatal to him, and he is induced to have recourse to the most unmanly arts to conceal it, if possible. As he cannot be armed at all points against the flesh and the devil, he takes refuge in self-delusion and mental imposture; learns to play at fast and loose with his own conscience, and to baffle the vigilance of the public by dexterous equivocations; sails as near the wind as he can, shuffles with principle, is punctilious in matters of form, and tries to reconcile the greatest strictness of decorum and regularity of demeanour with the least possible sacrifice of his own interest or appetites. Parsons are not drunkards, because it is a vice that is easily detected and immediately offensive; but they are great eaters, which is no less injurious to the health and intellect. They indulge in all the sensuality that is not prohibited in the Decalogue: they monopolize every convenience they can lay lawful hands on: and consider themselves as the peculiar favourites of

Heaven, and the rightful inheritors of the earth. They are on a short allowance of sin; and are only the more eager to catch at all the stray bits and nice morsels they can meet. They are always considering how they shall indemnify themselves in smaller things, for their grudging self-denial in greater ones. Satan lies in wait for them in a pinch of snuff, in a plate of buttered toast, or the kidney end of a loin of veal. They lead their cooks the devil of a life. Their dinner is the principal event of the day. They say a long grace over it, partly to prolong the pleasure of expectation, and to keep others waiting. They are appealed to as the most competent judges, as arbiters *deliciarum* in all questions of the palate. Their whole thoughts are taken up in pampering the flesh, and comforting the spirit with all the little debasing luxuries which do not come under the sentence of damnation, or breed scandal in the parish. You find out their true character in those of them who have quitted the cloth, and think it no longer necessary to practise the same caution or disguise. You there find the dogmatism of the divine ingrafted on the most lax speculations of the philosophical freethinker, and the most romantic professions of universal benevolence made a cover to the most unfeeling and unblushing spirit of selfishness. The mask is taken off, but the character was the same under a more jealous attention to appearances. With respect to one vice from which the Clergy are bound to keep themselves clear, St. Paul has observed, that *it is better to marry than burn*. "Continents," says Hobbes, "have more of what they contain than other things." The Clergy are men: and many of them, who keep a sufficient guard over their conduct, are too apt, from a common law of our nature, to let their thoughts and desires wander to forbidden ground. This is not so well. It is not so well to be always thinking of the peccadillos they cannot commit: to be hankering after the fleshpots of Egypt: to have the charms of illicit gratification enhanced by privations, to which others are not liable; to have the fancy always prurient, and the imagination always taking a direction which they themselves cannot follow.

> "Where's that palace, whereunto foul things
> Sometimes intrude not? Who has that breast so pure,
> But some uncleanly apprehensions
> Keep leets and law-days, and in Sessions sit
> With meditations lawful?"

But the mind of the Divine and Moralist by profession is a sort of sanctuary for such thoughts. He is bound by his office to be always detecting and pointing out abuses, to describe and conceive of them in the strongest colours, to denounce and to abhor vice in others, to be familiar with the diseases of the mind, as the physician is with those of the body. But that this sort of speculative familiarity with vice leads to a proportionable disgust at it, may be made a question. The virtue of prudes has been thought doubtful: the morality of priests, even of those who lead the most regular lives, is not, perhaps, always "pure in the last recesses of the mind." They are obliged, as it were, to have the odious nature of sin habitually in their thoughts, and in their mouths; to wink, to make wry faces at it, to keep themselves in a state of incessant indignation against it. It is like living next door to a brothel, a situation which produces a great degree of irritation against vice, and an eloquent abuse of those who are known to practise it, but is not equally favourable to the growth and cultivation of sentiments of virtue. To keep theoretical watch and ward over vice, to be systematic spies and informers against immorality, "while *they* the supervisors grossly gape on," is hardly decent. It is almost as bad as belonging to the Society for the Suppression of Vice—a Society which appears to have had its origin in much the same feeling as the monkish practice of auricular confession in former times.—Persons who undertake to pry into, or cleanse out all the filth of a common sewer, either cannot have very nice noses, or will soon lose them. Swift used to say, that people of the nicest imaginations have the dirtiest ideas. The virtues of the priesthood are not the virtues of humanity. They are not honest, cordial, unaffected, and sincere. They are *the mask*, not the man. There is always the feeling of something hollow, assuming, and disagreeable, in them. There is something in the profession that does not sit easy on the imagination. You are not at home with it. Do you, or do you not, seek the society of a man for being a Parson? You would as soon think of marrying a woman for being an old maid!

To proceed to what we at first proposed, which was a consideration of the Clerical Character, less in connexion with private morality than with public principle. We have already spoken of the Dissenting Clergy as, in this respect, an honest and exemplary body of men. They are so by the supposition, in what relates to matters of opinion. The Established Clergy of any religion certainly are not so, by the same self-evident rule; on the contrary, they are bound to conform their professions of religious belief to a certain popular and lucrative standard, and bound over to keep the peace by certain articles of faith. It is a rare felicity in any one who gives his attention fairly and freely to the subject, and has read the Scriptures, the Misnah, and the Talmud—the Fathers, the Schoolmen, the Socinian Divines, the Lutheran and Calvinistic controversy, with innumerable volumes appertaining thereto and illustrative thereof, to believe all the Thirty-nine Articles, "except one." If those who are destined for the episcopal office exercise their understandings honestly and openly upon every one of these questions, how little chance is there that they should come to the same conclusion upon them all? If they do not inquire, what becomes of their independence of understanding? If they conform to what they do not believe, what becomes of their honesty? Their estimation in the world, as well as their livelihood, depends on their tamely submitting their understanding to authority at first, and on their not seeing reason to alter their opinion afterwards. Is it likely that a man will intrepidly open his eyes to conviction, when he sees poverty and disgrace staring him in the face as the inevitable consequence? Is it likely, after the labours of a whole life of servility and cowardice—after repeating daily what he does not understand, and what those who require him to repeat it do not believe, or pretend to believe, and impose on others only as a ready test of insincerity, and a compendious shibboleth of want of principle: after doing morning and evening service to the God of this world—after keeping his lips sealed against the indiscreet mention of the plainest truths, and opening them only to utter mental reservations—after breakfasting, dining, and supping, waking and sleeping, being clothed and fed, upon a collusion,—after saying a double grace and washing his hands after dinner, and preparing for a course of smutty jests to make himself good company,—after nodding to Deans, bowing to Bishops, waiting upon Lords, following in the train of Heads of Colleges, watching the gracious eye of those who have presentations in their gift, and the lank cheek of those who are their present incumbents,—after finding favour, patronage, promotion, prizes, praise, promises, smiles, squeezes of the hand, invitations to tea and cards with the ladies, the epithets, " a charming man" " an agreeable creature," " a most respectable character," the certainty of reward, and the hopes of glory, always proportioned to the systematic baseness of his compliance with the will of his superiors, and the sacrifice of every particle of independence, or pretence to manly spirit and honesty of character,—is it likely, that a man so tutored and trammelled, and inured to be his own dupe, and the tool of others, will ever, in one instance out of thousands, attempt to burst the cobweb fetters which bind him in the magic circle of contradictions and enigmas, or risk the independence of his fortune for the independence of his mind? *Principle* is a word that is not to be found in the Young Clergyman's Best Companion: it is a thing he has no idea of, except as something pragmatical, sour, puritanical, and Presbyterian. To oblige is his object, not to offend. He wishes " to be conformed to this world, rather than transformed." He expects one day to be a Court-divine, a dignitary of the Church, an ornament to the State; and he knows all the texts of Scripture, which, tacked to a visitation, an assize, or corporation-dinner sermon, will float him gently, " like little wanton boys that swim on bladders," up to the palace at Lambeth. A hungry poet, gaping for solid pudding or empty praise, may easily be supposed to set about a conscientious revision and change of his unpopular opinions, from the reasonable prospect of a place or pension, and to eat his words the less scrupulously, the longer he has had nothing else to eat. A snug, promising, soft, smiling, orthodox Divine, who has a living attached to the cure of souls, and whose sentiments are beneficed, who has a critical *bonus* for finding out that all the books he cannot understand are written against the Christian Religion, and founds the doctrine of the Trinity, and his hopes of a Bishopric, on the ignorant construction of a Greek particle, cannot be expected to change the opinions to which he has formerly subscribed his belief, with the revolutions of the sun or the changes of the moon. His political, as well as religious creed, is installed in hopes, pampered in expectations; and the longer he winks and shuts his eyes and holds them close, catching only under their drooping lids " glimpses that may make him less forlorn," day-dreams of lawn-sleeves, and nightly beatific visions of episcopal mitres, the less disposed will he be to open them to the broad light of reason, or to forsake the primrose path of preferment, to tear and mangle his sleek tender-skinned conscience, dipped and softened in the milk-bath of clerical complaisance, among the thorns and briars of controversial divinity, or to get out on the other side upon a dark and dreary waste, amidst a crew of hereticks and schismatics, and Unitarian dealers in " potential infidelity"—

> " Who far from steeples and their sacred sound,
> In fields their sullen conventicles found."

This were too much to expect from the chaplain of an Archbishop.

Take one illustration of the truth of all that has been here said, and of more that might be said upon the subject. It is related in that valuable comment on the present reign and the existing order of things, Bishop Watson's Life, that the late Dr. Paley having at one time to maintain a thesis in the University, proposed to the Bishop, for his approbation, the following:—"That the eternity of Hell torments is contradictory to the goodness of God." The Bishop observed, that he thought this a bold doctrine to maintain in the face of the Church; but Paley persisted in his determination. Soon after, however, having sounded the opinions of certain persons, high in authority, and well read in the orthodoxy of preferment, he came back in great alarm, said he found the thing would not do, and begged, instead of his first thesis, to have the reverse one substituted in its stead, *viz.*—"That the Eternity of Hell torments is *not* contradictory to the goodness of God."—What burning daylight is here thrown on clerical discipline, and the bias of a University education! This passage is worth all Mosheim's Ecclesiastical History, Wood's Athenæ Oxonienses, and Mr. Coleridge's two Lay Sermons. This same shuffling Divine is the same Dr. Paley, who afterwards employed the whole of his life, and his moderate second-hand abilities, in tampering with religion, morality, and politics,—in trimming between his convenience and his conscience,—in crawling between heaven and earth, and trying to cajole both. His celebrated and popular work on Moral Philosophy, is celebrated and popular for no other reason, than that it is a somewhat ingenious and amusing apology for existing abuses of every description, by which any thing is to be got. It is a very elaborate and consolatory elucidation of the text, *that men should not quarrel with their bread and butter*. It is not an attempt to show what is right, but to palliate and find out plausible excuses for what is wrong. It is a work without the least value, except as a convenient common-place book or *vade mecum*, for tyro politicians and young divines, to smooth their progress in the Church or the State. This work is a text-book in the University: its morality is the acknowledged morality of the House of Commons. The Lords are above it. They do not affect that sort of casuistry, by which the country gentlemen contrive to oblige the Ministers, and to reconcile themselves to their constituents.

ON THE CLERICAL CHARACTER.

"Priests were the first deluders of mankind,
Who with vain faith made all their reason blind;
Not Lucifer himself more proud than they,
And yet persuade the world they must obey;
Of avarice and luxury complain,
And practise all the vices they arraign.
Riches and honour they from laymen reap,
And with dull *crambe* feed the silly sheep.
As Killigrew buffoons his master, they
Droll on their god, but a much duller way.
With hocus pocus, and their heavenly light,
They gain on tender consciences at night.
Whoever has an over zealous wife,
Becomes the priest's Amphitrio during life."

Marvel's State Poems.

(CONCLUDED.)

February 7, 1818.

THIS then is the secret of the alliance between Church and State—make a man a tool and a hypocrite in one respect, and he will make himself a slave and a pander in every other, that you can make it worth his while. Those who make a regular traffic of their belief in religion, will not be backward to compromise their sentiments in what relates to the concerns between man and man. He who is in the habit of affronting his Maker with solemn mockeries of faith, as the means of a creditable livelihood, will not bear the testimony of a good conscience before men, if he finds it a losing concern. The principle of integrity is gone; the patriotism of the religious sycophant is rotten at the core. Hence we find that the Established Clergy of all religions have been the most devoted tools of power. Priestcraft and Despotism have gone hand in hand—have stood and fallen together. It is this that makes them so fond and loving; so pious and so loyal; so ready to play the Court-game into one another's hands, and so firmly knit and leagued together against the rights and liberties of mankind. Thus Mr. Southey sings in laureat strains:—

"One fate attends the altar and the throne."

Yet the same peremptory versifier qualifies the Church of Rome with the epithets of "that Harlot old,—

"The same that is, that was, and is to be,"—

without giving us to understand whether in Popish countries, the best and most "single-hearted" portion of Europe, the same lofty and abstracted doctrine holds good. This uncivil laureat has indeed gone so far in one of his "songs of delight and rustical roundelays," as to give the Princess Charlotte the following critical advice:—

"Bear thou that great Eliza in thy mind,
Who from a wreck this fabric edified,
AND HER WHO, TO A NATION'S VOICE RESIGNED,
WHEN ROME IN HOPE HER WILIEST ENGINES PLIED,
BY HER OWN HEART AND RIGHTEOUS HEAV'N APPROVED,
STOOD UP AGAINST THE FATHER WHOM SHE LOV'D."

These lines seem to glance at contingent rebellion, at speculative treason; they have a squint, a strong cast of the eye, that way. But it is neither our business nor inclination to point out passages in prose or verse, for the animadversion of the Attorney-General. Mr. Croker, we fear, however, must have been greatly scandalised at this specimen of his friend's original mode of thinking for himself in such delicate matters as the cashiering of Kings and encouraging their daughters, as in duty bound, to stand up against them whenever Mr. Southey pleases. *Launce* could not have been more put to it when his dog misbehaved "among the gentlemanlike dogs at the Duke's table." than the Admiralty Secretary at this faux-pas of Mr. Southey's reformed Jacobin Muse. It was shewing the lady's breeding to some purpose. This gratuitous piece of advice to a Protestant Princess is, however, just the reverse of that which Cardinal Wolsey gave to a Popish ruler of these realms, Henry VIII., before that Monarch saw reason to change his religious principles for a wife, as Mr. Southey has changed his political ones for a pension. The Cardinal was almost as wise a man in his generation as Mr. Southey is in his; saw as far into reasons of state, and charged by anticipation all the evils of anarchy and rebellion since his time on that very Protestant religion, which the modern courtier under the Protestant succession considers as the only support of passive obedience and non-resistance. Cavendish, in his Memoirs, in the Harleian Miscellany, makes Wolsey on his death-bed give this testamentary advice to his Sovereign:—"And, Master Kingston, I desire you further to request his Grace, in God's name, that he have a vigilant eye to suppress the hellish Lutherans, that they increase not through his great negligence, in such a sort as to be compelled to take up arms to subdue them, as the King of Bohemia was; whose commons being infected with Wickliff's heresies, the King was forced to take that course. Let him consider the story of King Richard the Second, the second son of his progenitor, who lived in the time of Wickliff's seditions and heresies: did not the commons, I pray you, in his time, rise against the nobility and chief governors of this realm; and at the last, some of them were put to death without justice or mercy? And, under pretence of having all things common, did they not fall to spoiling and robbing, and at last took the King's person, and carried him about the city, making him obedient to their proclamations?"—[The author of *Wat Tyler* has given a very different version of this story.]—"Did not also the traitorous heretick, Sir John Oldcastle, Lord Cobham, pitch a field with hereticks against King Henry the Fourth, where the King was in person, and fought against them, to whom God gave the victory? Alas! if these be not plain precedents and sufficient persuasions to admonish a Prince, then God will take away from us our present rulers, and leave us to the hands of our enemies. And then will ensue mischief upon mischief, inconveniences, barrenness, and scarcity, for want of good orders in the commonwealth, from which God of his tender mercy defend us."—*Harleian Miscell.* vol. iv. p. 556.

The dying Cardinal might here be supposed to have foreseen the grand Rebellion, the glorious Revolution of 1688, the expulsion of the Stuarts, and the Protestant ascendancy, the American and the French Revolutions—as all growing out of Wickliff's heresy, and the doctrines of the hellish Lutherans. Our laurel-honouring laureat cannot see all this after it has happened. Wolsey was a prophet; he is only a poet. Wolsey knew (and so would any man but a poet), that to allow men freedom of opinion in matters of religion, was to make them free in all other things. Mr. Southey, who raves in favour of the Bourbons and against the Pope, is "blind with double darkness." He will assuredly never find that "single-heartedness" which he seeks, but in the bosom of the Church of Rome.

One mischief of this alliance between Church and State (which the old-fashioned Statesman understood so thoroughly and the modern sciolist only by halves) is, that it is tacit and covert. The Church does not profess to take any active share in affairs of State, and by this means is able to forward all the designs of indirect and crooked policy more effectually and without suspicion. The garb of religion is the best cloak for power. There is nothing so much to be guarded against as the wolf in sheep's clothing. The Clergy pretend to be neutral in all such matters, not to meddle with politics. But that is, and always must be, a false pretence. *Those that are not with us, are against us,* is a maxim that always holds true. These pious pastors of the people and accomplices of the government make use of their heavenly calling and demure professions of meekness and humility, as an excuse for never committing themselves on the side of the people: but the same sacred and spiritual character, not to be sullied by mixing with worldly concerns, does not hinder them from employing all their arts and influence on the side of power and of their own interest. Their religion is incompatible with a common regard to justice or humanity; but it is compatible with an excess of courtly zeal. The officiating Clergyman at Derby the other day pestered Brandreth to death with importunities to inform against his associates, but put his hand before his mouth when he offered to say what he knew of Oliver, the Government-spy. This is not exactly as it should be; but it cannot be otherwise than it is. Priests are naturally favourers of power, inasmuch as they are dependent on it.—Their power over the mind is hardly sufficient of itself to insure absolute obedience to their authority, without a reinforcement of power over the body. The secular arm must come in aid of the spiritual. The law is necessary to compel the payment of tythes. Kings and conquerors make laws, parcel out lands, and erect churches and palaces for the priests and dignitaries of religion: "they will have them to shew their mitred fronts in Courts and Parliaments;" and in return, Priests anoint Kings with holy oil, hedge them round with inviolability, spread over them the mysterious sanctity of religion, and, with very little ceremony, make over the whole species as slaves to these Gods upon earth by virtue of divine right! This is no losing trade. It aggrandizes those who are concerned in it, and is death to the rest of the world. It is a solemn league and covenant fully ratified and strictly carried into effect, to the very letter, in all countries, Pagan, Mahommedan, and Christian,—except this. It is time to put an end to it every where. But those who are pledged to its support, and "by this craft have their wealth," have unfortunately remained of one opinion, quite "single-hearted" from the beginning of the world: those who, like Mr. Southey, are for separating the Man of Sin from the Scarlet Whore, change their opinions once every five and twenty years. Need we wonder at the final results? Kings and priests are not such coxcombs or triflers as poets and philosophers. The two last are always squabbling about their share of reputation; the two first amicably divide the spoil. It is the opinion, we understand, of an eminent poet and a minute philosopher of the present day, that the press ought to be shackled,—severely shackled; and particularly that the *Edinburgh Review*, the *Examiner*, and the *Yellow Dwarf*, as full of *Examinerisms*, ought to be instantly put down. Another poet or philosopher, who has not been so severely handled in these works, thinks differently; and so do we. Nay, Mr. ——, himself has been a long time in coming to this opinion; and no wonder, for he had a long way to come in order to arrive at it. But all the Kings that ever were, and ninety-nine out of a hundred of all the Priests that surround them, jump at this conclusion concerning the fatal consequences of the Liberty of the Press—by instinct. We have never yet seen that greatest calamity that can befal mankind, deprecated by Mr. Burke, namely, literary men acting in *corps*, and making common cause for the benefit of mankind, as another description of persons act in concert and make common cause against them. He himself was an instance how little need be dreaded in this way. If the National Assembly had sent for Burke over, to assist in framing a Constitution for them, this traitor to liberty and apostate from principle, instead of loading the French Revolution with every epithet of obloquy and execration which his irritable vanity and mercenary malice could invent, would have extolled it to the skies, as the highest monument of human happiness and wisdom. But the genius of philosophy, as he said, is not yet known. It is a subject which we shall shortly endeavour to make clear.

——— "At this day
When a Tartarean darkness overspreads
The groaning nations; when the impious rule,
By will or by established ordinance,
Their own dire agents, and constrain the good
To acts which they abhor; though I bewail
This triumph, yet the pity of my heart
Prevents me not from owning that the law,
By which mankind now suffers, is most just.

FOR BY SUPERIOR ENERGIES; MORE STRICT
AFFIANCE WITH EACH OTHER; FAITH MORE FIRM
IN THEIR UNHALLOWED PRINCIPLES; THE BAD
HAVE FAIRLY EARNED A VICTORY O'ER THE WEAK,
THE VACILLATING, INCONSISTENT GOOD"

WORDSWORTH.

In another point of view, Priests are a sort of women in the State, and naturally subject to the higher powers. The Church has no means of temporal advancement but through the interest and countenance of the State. It receives what the other is pleased to allow it as a mark of friendship, out of the public purse. The Clergy do not engage in active or lucrative professions: they are occupied with praise and prayer, and the salvation of souls—with heaping up for themselves treasures in heaven, and wrath upon their enemies' heads against the day of judgment. The candidate for Church preferment must therefore look for it as a free gift at the hands of the great and powerful; he must win his way to wealth and honours by "the sufferance of supernal power." The Church can only hope for a comfortable establishment in the world by finding favour, as a handmaid, in the eye of the State: the Church must wed the State, both for protection and a maintenance. The preacher of God's word looks for his reward in heaven, but he must live in the mean time. But he is precluded by his cloth and his spiritual avocations from getting on in the world by the usual means of interest or ambition. His only hope of advancement lies in the Bishop's blessing and his patron's smile. These may in time translate him to a vacant diocese of 10,000*l.* a year. His labours in the cure of souls, or the settling the most difficult point of controversial divinity, would not, on an average calculation, bring him in a 100*l.* Parson Adams could not dispose of his manuscript sermons to the booksellers; and he ruined his hopes of preferment with Lady Booby, by refusing to turn pimp. Finally, the Clergy are lovers of abstract power, for they are themselves the representatives of almighty power: they are ambassadors of religion, delegates of heaven. The authority under which they act is not always respected so readily, cordially, and implicitly, as it ought to be, and they are indignant at the neglect. They become tetchy and imperious, and mingle the irritability of self-love with their zeal for the honour of God. They are not backward to call for fire from heaven, and to put down the Atheist and the Schismatic by the strong hand of power. *Fear God and honour the King*, is the motto of priestcraft; but it is not a sound logical dilemma, for this reason, that God is always the same; but Kings are of all sorts, good, bad, or indifferent—wise, or mad, or foolish—arbitrary tyrants, or constitutional Monarchs, like our own. The rule is absolute in the first case, not in the second. But the Clergy, by a natural infirmity, are disposed to force the two into a common analogy. They are servants of God by profession, and sycophants of power from necessity. They delight to look up with awe to Kings, as to another Providence. It was a Bishop, in the reign of James I. who drew a parallel between "their divine and sacred Majesties," meaning the pitiful tyrant whom he served, and God Almighty: yet the Attorney-General of that day did not prosecute him for blasphemy. The Clergy fear God more than they love him. They think more of his power than of his wisdom or goodness. They would make Kings Gods upon earth; and as they cannot clothe them with the wisdom or beneficence of the Deity, would arm them with his power at any rate.*

* "And for the Bishops (in Edward VI.'s days), they were so far from any such worthy attempts, as that they suffered themselves to be the common stales to countenance, with their prostituted gravities, every politick fetch that was then on foot, as oft as the potent Statists pleased to employ them. Never do we read that they made use of their authority, and high place of access, to bring the jarring nobility to Christian peace, or to withstand their disloyal projects: but if a toleration for Mass were to be begged of the King for his sister Mary, lest Charles the Fifth should be angry, who but the grave prelates, *Cranmer* and *Ridley*, must be sent to extort it from the young King! But out of the mouth of that godly and royal child, Christ himself

WHAT IS THE PEOPLE?

March 7, 1818.

—And who are you that ask the question? One of the people. And yet you would be something! Then you would not have the People nothing. For what is the People? Millions of men, like you, with hearts beating in their bosoms, with thoughts stirring in their minds, with the blood circulating in their veins, with wants and appetites, and passions and anxious cares, and busy purposes and affections for others and a respect for themselves, and a desire of happiness, and a right to freedom, and a will to be free. And yet you would tear out this mighty heart of a nation, and lay it bare and bleeding at the foot of despotism: you would slay the mind of a country to fill up the dreary aching void with the old, obscene, drivelling prejudices of superstition and tyranny: you would tread out the eye of Liberty (the light of nations) like "a vile jelly," that mankind may be led about darkling to its endless drudgery, like the Hebrew Sampson (shorn of his strength and blind), by his insulting taskmasters: you would make the throne every thing, and the people nothing, to be yourself less than nothing, a very slave, a reptile, a creeping, cringing sycophant, a court favourite, a pander to Legitimacy—that detestable fiction, which would make you and me and all mankind its slaves or victims; which would, of right and with all the sanctions of religion and morality, sacrifice the lives of millions to the least of its caprices; which subjects the rights, the happiness, and liberty of nations, to the will of some of the lowest of the species; which rears its bloated hideous form to brave the will of a whole people; that claims mankind as its property, and allows human nature to exist only upon sufferance; that haunts the understanding like a frightful spectre,

returned such an awful repulse to those halting and time-serving Prelates, that, after much importunity they went their way, not without shame and tears."——*Milton—Of Reformation in England, and the Causes that have hitherto hindered it.*

and oppresses the very air with a weight that is not to be borne; that like a witch's spell covers the earth with a dim and envious mist, and makes us turn our eyes from the light of heaven, which we have no right to look at without its leave: robs us of "the unbought grace of life," the pure delight and conscious pride in works of art or nature; leaves us no thought or feeling that we dare call our own; makes genius its lacquey, and virtue its easy prey; sports with human happiness, and mocks at human misery; suspends the breath of liberty, and almost of life; exenterates us of our affections, blinds our understandings, debases our imaginations, converts the very hope of emancipation from its yoke into sacrilege, binds the successive countless generations of men together in its chains like a string of felons or galley-slaves, lest they should "resemble the flies of a summer," considers any remission of its absolute claims as a gracious boon, an act of royal clemency and favour, and confounds all sense of justice, reason, truth, liberty, humanity, in one low servile deathlike dread of power without limit and without remorse! *

Such is the old doctrine of Divine Right, new-vamped up under the style and title of Legitimacy. "Fine word, Legitimate!" We wonder where our English politicians picked it up. Is it an echo from the tomb of the martyred monarch, Charles the First? Or was it the last word which his son, James the Second, left behind him in his flight, and bequeathed with his *abdication*, to his legitimate successors? It is not written in our annals in the years 1688, in 1715, or 1745. It was not sterling then, which was only fifteen years before his present Majesty's accession to the throne. Has it become so since? Is the Revolution of 1688 at length acknowledged to be a blot in the family escutcheon of the Prince of Orange or the Elector of Hanover? Is the choice of the people, which raised them to the throne, found to be the only flaw in their title to the suc-

* This passage is nearly a repetition of what was said before; but as it contains the sum and substance of all I have ever said on such subjects, I have let it stand.

cession; the weight of royal gratitude growing more uneasy with the distance of the obligation? Is the alloy of liberty, mixed up with it, thought to debase that *fine carat*, which should compose the regal diadem? Are the fire-new specimens of the principles of the Right-Liners, and of Sir Robert Filmer's patriarchal scheme, to be met with in *The Courier*, *The Day*, *The Sun*, and some time back, in *The Times*, handed about to be admired in the highest circle, like the new gold coinage of sovereigns and half-sovereigns? We do not know. It may seem to be *Latter Lammas* with the doctrine at this time of day; but better late than never. By taking root in the soil of France, from which it was expelled (not quite so long as from our own), it may in time stretch out its feelers and strong suckers to this country; and present an altogether curious and novel aspect, by ingrafting the principles of the House of Stuart on the illustrious stock of the House of Brunswick,

"Miraturque novas frondes, et non sua poma."

What then is the People? We will answer first, by saying what it is not; and this we cannot do better than in the words of a certain author, whose testimony on the subject is too important not to avail ourselves of it again in this place. That infatuated drudge of despotism, who at one moment asks, "Where is the madman that maintains the doctrine of divine right?" and the next affirms, that "Louis XVIII. has the same right to the throne of France, independently of his merits or conduct, that Mr. Coke of Norfolk has to his estate at Holkham,"* has given us a tolerable clue to what we have to

* What is the amount of this right of Mr. Coke's? It is not greater than that of the Lords Balmerino and Lovatt to their estates in Scotland, or to the heads upon their shoulders, the one of which however were forfeited, and the other stuck upon Temple Bar, for maintaining, in theory and practice, that James II. had the same right to the throne of these realms, independently of his merits or conduct, that Mr. Coke has to his estate at Holkham. So thought they. So did not think George II.

expect from that mild paternal sway to which he would so kindly make us and the rest of the world over, in hopeless perpetuity. In a violent philippic against the author of the *Political Register*, he thus inadvertently expresses himself:—" Mr. Cobbett had been sentenced to two years imprisonment for a libel, and during the time that he was in Newgate, it was discovered that he had been in treaty with Government to avoid the sentence passed upon him; and that he had proposed to certain of the agents of Ministers, that if they would let him off, they might make what future use they pleased of him; *he would entirely betray the cause of the people*; he would either write or not write, or *write against them*, as he had once done before, just as Ministers thought proper. To this, however, it was replied, that " Cobbett had written on too many sides already *to be worth a groat for the service of Government*;" and he accordingly suffered his confinement!"—We here then see plainly enough what it is that, in the opinion of this very competent judge, alone renders any writer " worth a groat for the service of Government," *viz.* that he shall be able and willing entirely to betray the cause of the people. It follows from this principle (by which he seems to estimate the value of his lucubrations in the service of Government—we do not know whether the Government judge of them in the same way), that the cause of the people and the cause of the Government, who are represented as thus anxious to suborn their creatures to write against the people, are not the same but the reverse of one another. This slip of the pen in our professional retainer of legitimacy, though a libel on our own Government, is, notwithstanding, a general philosophic truth (the only one he ever hit upon), and an axiom in political mechanics, which we shall make the text of the following commentary.

What are the interests of the people? Not the interests of those who would betray them. Who is to judge of those interests? Not those who would suborn others to betray them. That Government is instituted for the benefit of the governed, there can be little doubt; but the interests of the Government (when once it becomes absolute and independent of the people) must be directly at variance with those of the governed. The interests of the one are common and equal rights: of the other, exclusive and invidious privileges. The essence of the first is to be shared alike by all, and to benefit the community in proportion as they are spread: the essence of the last is to be destroyed by communication, and to subsist only—in wrong of the people. Rights and privileges are a contradiction in terms: for if one has more than his right, others must have less. The latter are the deadly nightshade of the commonwealth, near which no wholesome plant can thrive,—the ivy clinging round the trunk of the British oak, blighting its verdure, drying up its sap, and oppressing its stately growth. The insufficient checks and balances opposed to the overbearing influence of hereditary rank and power in our own Constitution, and in every Government which retains the least trace of freedom, are so many illustrations of this principle, if it needed any. The tendency in arbitrary power to encroach upon the liberties and comforts of the people, and to convert the public good into a stalking-horse to its own pride and avarice, has never (that we know) been denied by any one but "the professional gentleman," who writes in *The Day and New Times*. The great and powerful, in order to be what they aspire to be, and what this gentleman would have them, perfectly independent of the will of the people, ought also to be perfectly independent of the assistance of the people. To be formally invested with the attributes of Gods upon earth, they ought first to be raised above its petty wants and appetites: they ought to give proofs of the beneficence and wisdom of Gods, before they can be trusted with the power. When we find them seated above the world, sympathizing with the welfare, but not feeling the passions of men, receiving neither good nor hurt, neither tilth nor tythe from them, but bestowing their benefits as free gifts on all, they may then be expected, but not till then, to rule over us like another Providence. We may make them a present of all the taxes they do not apply to their own use: they are perfectly welcome to all the power, to the possession of which they are perfectly indifferent, and to the abuse of which they can have no possible temptation. But Legitimate Governments (flatter them as we will) are not another Heathen mythology. They are neither so cheap nor so splendid as the Delphin edition of Ovid's Metamorphoses. They are indeed "Gods to punish," but in other respects "men of our infirmity." They do not feed on ambrosia or drink nectar; but live on the common fruits of the earth, of which they get the largest share, and the best. The wine they drink is made of grapes: the blood they shed is that of their subjects: the laws they make are not against themselves: the taxes they vote, they afterwards devour. They have the same wants that we have: and having the option, very naturally help themselves first, out of the common stock, without thinking that others are to come after them. With the same natural necessities, they have a thousand artificial ones besides; and with a thousand times the means to gratify them, they are still voracious, importunate, unsatisfied. Our State-paupers have their hands in every man's dish, and fare sumptuously every day. They live in palaces, and loll in coaches. In spite of Mr. Malthus, their studs of horses consume the produce of our fields, their dog-kennels are glutted with the food which would maintain the children of the poor. They cost us so much a year in dress and furniture, so much in stars and garters, blue ribbons, and grand crosses,— so much in dinners, breakfasts, and suppers, and so much in suppers, breakfasts, and dinners.* These heroes of the Income-tax, Worthies of the Civil List, Saints of the Court-calendar *(compagnons du lys)*, have their naturals and non-naturals, like the rest of the world, but at a dearer rate. They are real *bona fide* personages, and do not live upon air. You will find it easier to keep them a week than a month; and at the end of that time, waking from the sweet dream of Legitimacy, you may say with

* See the description of Gargantua in Rabelais.

Caliban, "Why, what a fool was I to take this drunken monster for a God!" In fact, the case on the part of the people is so far self-evident. There is but a limited earth and a limited fertility to supply the demands both of Government and people; and what the one gains in the division of the spoil, beyond its average proportion, the other must needs go without. Do you suppose that our gentlemen-placemen and pensioners would suffer so many wretches to be perishing in our streets and highways, if they could relieve their extreme misery without parting with any of their own superfluities? If the Government take a fourth of the produce of the poor man's labour, they will be rich, and he will be in want. If they can contrive to take one half of it by legal means, or by a stretch of arbitrary power, they will be just twice as rich, twice as insolent and tyrannical, and he will be twice as poor, twice as miserable and oppressed, in a mathematical ratio to the end of the chapter, that is, till the one can extort and the other endure no more. It is the same with respect to power. The will and passions of the great are not exerted in regulating the seasons, or rolling the planets round their orbits for our good, without fee or reward, but in controling the will and passions of others, in making the follies and vices of mankind subservient to their own, and marring,

"Because men suffer it, their toy, the world."

This is self-evident, like the former. Their will cannot be paramount, while any one in the community, or the whole community together, has the power to thwart it. A King cannot attain absolute power, while the people remain perfectly free; yet what King would not attain absolute power? While any trace of liberty is left among a people, ambitious Princes will never be easy, never at peace, never of sound mind; nor will they ever rest or leave one stone unturned, till they have succeeded in destroying the very name of liberty, or making it into a by-word, and in rooting out the germs of every popular right and liberal principle from a soil once sacred to liberty. It is not enough that they have secured the whole power of the state in their hands,—that they carry every measure they please without the chance of an effectual opposition to it: but a word uttered against it is torture to their ears,—a thought that questions their wanton exercise of the royal prerogative rankles in their breasts like poison. Till all distinctions of right and wrong, liberty and slavery, happiness and misery, are looked upon as matters of indifference, or as saucy, insolent pretensions,—are sunk and merged in their idle caprice and pampered self-will, they will still feel themselves "cribbed, confined, and cabin'd in:" but if they can once more set up the doctrine of Legitimacy, "the right divine of Kings to govern wrong," and set mankind at defiance with impunity, they will then be "broad and casing as the general air, whole as the rock." This is the point from which they set out, and to which by the grace of God and the help of man they may return again. Liberty is short and fleeting, a transient grace that lights upon the earth by stealth and at long intervals—

> "Like the rainbow's lovely form,
> Evanishing amid the storm;
> Or like the Borealis race,
> That shift ere you can point their place;
> Or like the snow falls in the river,
> A moment white, then melts for ever."

But power is eternal; it is "enthroned in the hearts of Kings." If you want the proofs, look at history, look at geography, look abroad; but do not look at home!

The power of an arbitrary King or an aspiring Minister does not increase with the liberty of the subject, but must be circumscribed by it. It is aggrandized by perpetual, systematic, insidious, or violent encroachments on popular freedom and natural right, as the sea gains upon the land by swallowing it up.—What then can we expect from the mild paternal sway of absolute power, and its sleek minions? What the world has always received at its hands, an abuse of power as vexatious, cowardly, and unrelenting, as the power itself was unprincipled, preposterous, and unjust. They who get wealth and power from the people, who drive them like cattle to slaughter or to market, "and levy cruel wars, wasting the earth;" they who wallow in luxury, while the people are "steeped in poverty to the very lips," and bowed to the earth with unremitting labour, can have but little sympathy with those whose loss of liberty and property is their gain. What is it that the wealth of thousands is composed of? The tears, the sweat, and blood of millions. What is it that constitutes the glory of the Sovereigns of the earth? To have millions of men their slaves. Wherever the Government does not emanate (as in our own excellent Constitution) from the people, the principle of the Government, the *esprit de corps*, the point of honour, in all those connected with it, and raised by it to privileges above the law and above humanity, will be hatred to the people. Kings who would be thought to reign in contempt of the people, will shew their contempt of them in every act of their lives. Parliaments, not chosen by the people, will only be the instruments of Kings, who do not reign in the hearts of the people, "to betray the cause of the people." Ministers, not responsible to the people, will squeeze the last shilling out of them. *Charity begins at home*, is a maxim as true of Governments as of individuals. When the English Parliament insisted on its right of taxing the Americans without their consent, it was not from an apprehension that the Americans would, by being left to themselves, lay such heavy duties on their own produce and manufactures, as would afflict the generosity of the mother-country, and put the mild paternal sentiments of Lord North to the blush. If any future King of England should keep a wistful eye on the map of that country, it would rather be to hang it up as a trophy of legitimacy, and to "punish the last successful example of a democratic rebellion," than from any yearnings of fatherly goodwill to the American people, or from finding his "large heart" and capacity for good government, "confined in too narrow room" in the united kingdoms of Great Britain, Ireland, and Hanover. If Ferdinand VII. refuses the South

American patriots leave to plant the olive or the vine, throughout that vast continent, it is his pride, not his humanity, that steels his royal resolution.*

In 1781, the Controller-general of France, under Louis XVI. Monsieur Joli de Fleuri, defined the people of France to be *un peuple serf, corveable et baillable, a merci et misericorde*. When Louis XVIII. as the Count de Lille, protested against his brother's accepting the Constitution of 1792 (he has since become an accepter of Constitutions himself, if not an observer of them,) as compromising the rights and privileges of the noblesse and clergy as well as of the crown, he was right in considering the Bastile, or "King's castle," with the picturesque episode of the Man in the Iron Mask, the fifteen thousand *lettres de cachet*, issued in the mild reign of Louis XV., *corvees*, tythes, game-laws, holy water, the right of pillaging, imprisoning, massacring, persecuting, harassing, insulting, and ingeniously tormenting the minds and bodies of the whole French people at every moment of their lives, on every possible pretence, and without any check or control but their own mild paternal sentiments towards them, as among the *menus plaisirs*, the chief points of etiquette, the immemorial privileges, and favourite amusements of Kings, Priests, and Nobles, from the beginning to the end of time, without which the bare title of King, Priest, or Noble, would not have been worth a groat.

The breasts of Kings and Courtiers then are not the safest depository of the interests of the people. But they know best what is for their good! Yes—to prevent it! The people may indeed feel their grievance, but their betters, it is said, must apply the remedy—which they take good care never to do! If the people

* The Government of Ovando, a Spanish Grandee and Knight of Alcantara, who had been sent over to Mexico soon after its conquest, exceeded in treachery, cruelty, wanton bloodshed, and deliberate extortion, that of all those who had preceded him; and the complaints became so loud, that Queen Isabel on her death-bed requested that he might be recalled; but Ferdinand found that Ovando had sent home *much gold*, and he retained him in his situation.—*See Capt. Burney's History of the Buccaneers.*

want judgment in their own affairs (which is not certain, for they only meddle with their own affairs when they are forcibly brought home to them in a way which they can hardly misunderstand), this is at any rate better than the want of sincerity, which would constantly and systematically lead their superiors to betray those interests, from their having other ends of their own to serve. It is better to trust to ignorance than to malice—to run the risk of sometimes miscalculating the odds than to play against loaded dice. The people would in this way stand as little chance in defending their purses or their persons against Mr. C——— or Lord C————, as an honest country gentleman would have had in playing at put or hazard with Count Fathom or Jonathan Wild. A certain degree of folly, or rashness, or indecision, or even violence in attaining an object, is surely less to be dreaded than a malignant, deliberate, mercenary intention in others to deprive us of it. If the people must have attorneys, and the advice of counsel, let them have attorneys and counsel of their own chusing, not those who are employed by special retainer against them, or who regularly hire others *to betray their cause.*

————————" O silly sheep,
Come ye to seek the lamb here of the wolf?"

This then is the cause of the people, the good of the people, judged of by common feeling and public opinion. Mr. Burke contemptuously defines the people to be " any faction that at the time can get the power of the sword into its hands." No: that may be a description of the Government, but it is not of the people. The people is the hand, heart, and head of the whole community acting to one purpose, and with a mutual and thorough consent. The hand of the people so employed to execute what the heart feels, and the head thinks, must be employed more beneficially for the cause of the people, than in executing any measures which the cold hearts, and contriving heads of any faction, with distinct privileges and interests, may dictate to betray their cause. The will of the people necessarily tends to the general good as its end; and it must attain that end, and can only attain it, in proportion as it is guided—First, by popular feeling, as arising out of the immediate wants and wishes of the great mass of the people,—secondly, by public opinion, as arising out of the impartial reason and enlightened intellect of the community. What is it that determines the opinion of any number of persons in things they actually feel in their practical and home results? Their common interest. What is it that determines their opinion in things of general inquiry, beyond their immediate experience or interest? Abstract reason. In matters of feeling and common sense, of which each individual is the best judge, the majority are in the right; in things requiring a greater strength of mind to comprehend them, the greatest power of understanding will prevail, if it has but fair play. These two, taken together, as the test of the practical measures or general principles of Government, must be right, cannot be wrong. It is an absurdity to suppose that there can be any better criterion of national grievances, or the proper remedies for them, than the aggregate amount of the actual, dear-bought experience, the honest feelings, and heart-felt wishes of a whole people, informed and directed by the greatest power of understanding in the community, unbiassed by any sinister motive. Any other standard of public good or ill must, in proportion as it deviates from this, be vitiated in principle, and fatal in its effects. *Vox populi vox Dei*, is the rule of all good Government: for in that voice, truly collected and freely expressed (not when it is made the servile echo of a corrupt Court, or a designing Minister), we have all the sincerity and all the wisdom of the community. If we could suppose society to be transformed into one great animal (like Hobbes's Leviathan), each member of which had an intimate connexion with the head or Government, so that every want or intention of every individual in it could be made known and have its due weight, the State would have the same consciousness of its own wants and feelings, and the same interest in providing for them, as an individual has with respect to his own welfare. Can any one doubt that such a state of society in which the greatest knowledge of its interests was thus combined with the greatest sympathy with its wants, would realize the idea of a perfect Commonwealth? But such a Government would be the precise idea of a truly popular or *representative* Government. The opposite extreme is the purely hereditary and despotic form of Government, where the people are an inert, torpid mass, without the power, scarcely with the will, to make its wants or wishes known: and where the feelings of those who are at the head of the State, centre in their own exclusive interests, pride, passions, prejudices; and all their thoughts are employed in defeating the happiness and undermining the liberties of a country.

WHAT IS THE PEOPLE?

(CONCLUDED.)

March 14, 1818.

It is not denied that the people are best acquainted with their own wants, and most attached to their own interests. But then a question is started, as if the persons asking it were at a great loss for the answer,—Where are we to find the intellect of the people? Why, all the intellect that ever was is theirs. The public opinion expresses not only the collective sense of the whole people, but of all ages and nations, of all those minds that have devoted themselves to the love of truth and the good of mankind, —who have bequeathed their instructions, their hopes, and their example to posterity,—who have thought, spoke, written, acted, and suffered in the name and on the behalf of our common nature. All the greatest poets, sages, heroes, are ours originally, and by right. But surely Lord Bacon was a great man? Yes; but not because he was a lord. There is nothing of hereditary growth but pride and prejudice. That "fine word Legitimate" never produced any thing but bastard philosophy and patriotism! Even Burke was one of the people, and would have remained with the people to the last, if there had been no court-side for him to go over to. The King gave him his pension, not his understanding or his eloquence. It would have been better for him and for mankind if he had kept to his principles, and gone without his pension. It is thus that the tide of power constantly setting in against the people, swallows up natural genius and acquired knowledge in the vortex of corruption, and then they reproach us with our want of leaders of weight and influence, to stem the torrent. All that has ever been done for society, has, however, been done for it by this intellect, before it was cheapened to be a cat's-paw of divine right. All discoveries and all improvements in arts, in science, in legislation, in civilization, in every thing dear and valuable to the heart of man, have been made by this intellect—all the triumphs of human genius over the rudest barbarism, the darkest ignorance, the grossest and most inhuman superstition, the most unmitigated and remorseless tyranny, have been gained for themselves by the people. Great Kings, great law-givers, great founders, and great reformers of religion, have almost all arisen from among the people. What have hereditary Monarchs, or regular Governments, or established priesthoods, ever done for the people? Did the Pope and Cardinals first set on foot the Reformation? Did the Jesuits attempt to abolish the Inquisition? For what one measure of civil or religious liberty did our own Bench of Bishops ever put themselves forward? What judge ever proposed a reform in the laws! Have not the House of Commons, with all their "tried wisdom," voted for every measure of Ministers for the last twenty-five years, except the Income-tax? It is the press that has done every thing for the people, and even for Governments.—"If they had not ploughed with our heifer, they would not have found out our riddle." And it has done this by slow degrees, by repeated, incessant, and incredible struggles with the oldest, most inveterate, powerful, and active enemies of the freedom of the press and of the people, who wish, in spite of the nature of things and of society, to retain the idle and mischievous privileges they possess as the relics of barbarous and feudal times, who have an exclusive interest as a separate cast in the continuance of all existing abuses, and who plead a permanent *vested right* in the prevention of the progress of reason, liberty, and civilization. Yet they tax us with our want of intellect; and *we* ask them in return for their court-list of great names in arts or philosophy, for the coats of arms of their heroic vanquishers of error and intolerance, for their devout benefactors and royal martyrs of humanity. What are the claims of the people—the obvious, undoubted rights of common justice and humanity, forcibly withheld from them by pride, bigotry, and selfishness,—demanded for them, age after age, year after year, by the wisdom and virtue of the enlightened and disinterested part of mankind, and only grudgingly yielded up, with indecent, disgusting excuses, and sickening delays, when the burning shame of their refusal can be no longer concealed by fear of favour from the whole world. What did it not cost to abolish the Slave Trade? How long will the Catholic Claims be withheld by our State-jugglers? How long, and for what purpose? We may appeal, in behalf of the people, from the interested verdict of the worst and weakest men now living, to the disinterested reason of the best and wisest men among the living and the dead. We appeal from the corruption of Courts, the hypocrisy of zealots, and the dotage of hereditary imbecility, to the innate love of liberty in the human breast, and to the growing intellect of the world. We appeal to the pen, and they answer us with the point of the bayonet; and, at one time, when that had failed, they were for recommending the dagger.* They quote Burke, but rely on the Attorney-General. They hold Universal Suffrage to be the most dreadful of all things, and a Standing Army the best representatives of the people abroad and at home. They think Church-and-King mobs good things, for the same reason that they are alarmed at a meeting to petition for a Reform of Parliament. They consider the cry of "No Popery" a sound, excellent, and constitutional cry,—but the cry of a starving popu-

* See Coleridge's "Friend," No. 15.

lation for food, strange and unnatural. They exalt the war-whoop of the Stock Exchange into the voice of undissembled patriotism, while they set down the cry for peace as the work of the Jacobins, the ventriloquism of the secret enemies of their country. The writers on the popular side of the question are factious, designing demagogues, who delude the people to make tools of them: but the government-writers, who echo every calumny, and justify every encroachment on the people, are profound philosophers and very honest men. Thus when Mr. John Gifford, the Editor of the "Anti-Jacobin" (not Mr. William Gifford, who at present holds the same office under Government, as the Editor of the "Quarterly Review"), denounced Mr. Coleridge as a person, who had "left his wife destitute and his children fatherless," and proceeded to add—"*Ex hoc disce* his friends Lamb and Southey" —we are to suppose that he was influenced in this gratuitous statement purely by his love for his King and country. Loyalty, patriotism, and religion, are regarded as the natural virtues and plain unerring instincts of the common people: the mixture of ignorance or prejudice is never objected to in these: it is only their love of liberty or hatred of oppression that are discovered, by the same liberal-minded junto, to be proofs of a base and vulgar disposition. The Bourbons are set over the immense majority of the French people against their will, because a talent for governing does not go with numbers. This argument was not thought of when Bonaparte tried to shew his talent for governing the people of the Continent against their will, though he had quite as much talent as the Bourbons. Mr. Canning rejoiced that the first successful resistance to Bonaparte was made in Russia, a country of barbarians and slaves. The heroic struggles of "the universal Spanish nation" in the cause of freedom and independence, have ended in the destruction of the Cortes and the restoration of the Inquisition, but without making the Duke of Wellington look thoughtful:—not a single renegado poet has vented his indignation in a single ode, elegy, or sonnet; nor does Mr. Southey "make him a willow cabin at its gate, write loyal cantos of contemned love, and sing them loud even in the dead of the night!" He indeed assures us in the "Quarterly Review," that the Inquisition was restored by the voice of the Spanish people. He also asks, in the same place, "whether the voice of God was heard in the voice of the people at Jerusalem, when they cried, 'Crucify him, crucify him?'" We do not know; but we suppose, he would hardly go to the Chief Priests and Pharisees to find it. This great historian, politician, and logician, breaks out into a rhapsody against the old maxim, *vox populi vox Dei*, in the midst of an article of 55 pages, written expressly to prove that the last war was "the most popular, *because* the most just and necessary war that ever was carried on." He shrewdly asks, "Has the *vox populi* been the *vox Dei* in France for the last twenty-five years?" But, at least, according to his own shewing, it has been so in this country for all that period. We, however, do not think so. The voice of the country has been for war, because the voice of the King was for it, which was echoed by Parliament, both Lords and Commons, by Clergy and Gentry, and by the populace, till, as Mr. Southey himself states in the same connected chain of reasoning, the cry for war became *so* popular, that all those who did not join in it (of which number the Poet-laureate himself was one) were "persecuted, insulted, and injured in their persons, fame, and fortune." This is the true way of accounting for the fact, but it unfortunately knocks the Poet's inference on the head. Mr. Locke has observed, that there are not so many wrong opinions in the world as we are apt to believe, because most people take their opinions on trust from others. Neither are the opinions of the people their own, when they have been bribed or bullied into them by a mob of Lords and Gentlemen, following in full cry at the heels of the Court. The *vox populi* is the *vox Dei* only when it springs from the individual, unbiassed feelings, and unfettered, independent opinion of the people. Mr. Southey does not understand the terms of this good old adage, now that he is so furious against it: we fear, he understood them no better when he was as loudly in favour of it.

All the objections, indeed, to the voice of the people being the best rule for Government to attend to, arise from the stops and impediments to the expression of that voice, from the attempts to stifle or to give it a false bias, and to cut off its free and open communication with the head and heart of the people—by the Government itself. The sincere expression of the feelings of the people must be true; the full and free development of the public opinion must lead to truth, to the gradual discovery and diffusion of knowledge in this, as in all other departments of human inquiry. It is the interest of Governments in general to keep the people in a state of vassalage as long as they can—to prevent the expression of their sentiments, and the exercise and improvement of their understandings, by all the means in their power. They have a patent, and a monopoly, which they do not like to have looked into or to share with others. The argument for keeping the people in a state of lasting wardship, or for treating them as lunatics, incapable of self-government, wears a very suspicious aspect, as it comes from those who are trustees to the estate, or keepers of insane asylums. The long minority of the people would, at this rate, never expire, while those who had an interest had also the power to prevent them from arriving at years of discretion: their government-keepers have nothing to do but to drive the people mad by ill-treatment, and to keep them so by worse, in order to retain the pretence for applying the gag, the strait waistcoat, and the whip as long as they please. It is like the dispute between Mr. Epps, the angry shopkeeper in the Strand, and his journeyman, whom he would restrict from setting up for himself. Shall we never serve out our apprenticeship to liberty? Must our indentures to slavery bind us for life? It is well, it is perfectly well. You teach us nothing, and you will not let us learn. You deny us education, like Orlando's eldest brother, and then "stying us" in the den of legitimacy, you refuse to let us take the management of our own affairs into our own hands, or to seek our fortunes in the world ourselves. You found a right to treat us with indignity on the plea of your own neglect and injustice. You abuse a trust in order to make it perpetual. You profit of our ignorance and of your own wrong. You degrade, and then enslave us; and by enslaving, you degrade us more, to make us more and more incapable of ever escaping from your selfish, sordid yoke. There is no end of this. It is the fear of the progress of knowledge and a *Reading Public,* that has produced all the fuss and bustle and cant about Bell and Lancaster's plans, Bible and Missionary, and Auxiliary and Cheap Tract Societies, and that when it was impossible to prevent our reading something, made the Church and State so anxious to provide us with that sort of food for our stomachs, which they thought best. The Bible is an excellent book; and when it becomes the Statesman's Manual, in its precepts of charity—not of beggarly alms-giving, but of peace on earth and good will to man, the people may read nothing else. It reveals the glories of the world to come, and records the preternatural dispensations of Providence to mankind two thousand years ago. But it does not describe the present state of Europe, or give an account of the measures of the last or of the next reign, which yet it is important the people of England should look to. We cannot learn from Moses and the Prophets what Mr. Vansittart and the Jews are about in 'Change-alley. Those who prescribe us the study of the miracles and prophecies, themselves laugh to scorn the promised deliverance of Joanna Southcott and the Millennium. Yet they would have us learn patience and resignation from the miraculous interpositions of Providence recorded in the Scriptures. "*When the sky falls*"—the proverb is somewhat musty. The worst compliment ever paid to the Bible was the recommendation of it as a political palliative by the Lay Preachers of the day.

To put this question in a different light, we might ask, What is the public? and examine what would be the result of depriving the people of the use of their understandings in other matters as well as government—to subject them to the trammels of prescriptive prejudice and hereditary pretension. Take the stage as an example. Suppose Mr. Kean should have a son, a little crook-kneed, raven-voiced, disagreeable, mischievous, stupid urchin, with the faults of his father's acting exaggerated tenfold, and none of his fine qualities,—what if Mr. Kean should take it into his head to get out letters-patent to empower him and his heirs for ever, with this hopeful commencement, to play all the chief parts in tragedy, by the grace of God and the favour of the Prince Regent! What a precious race of tragedy kings and heroes we should have! They would not even play the villain with a good grace. The theatres would soon be deserted, and the race of the Keans would "hold a barren sceptre" over empty houses, to be "wrenched from them by an unlineal hand!"—But no! For it would be necessary to uphold theatrical order, the cause of the legitimate drama, and so to levy a tax on all those who staid away from the theatre, or to drag them into it by force. Every one seeing the bayonet at the door, would be compelled to applaud the hoarse tones and lengthened pauses of the illustrious house of Kean; the newspaper critics would grow wanton in their praise, and all those would be held as rancorous enemies of their country, and of the prosperity of the stage, who did not join in the praises of the best of actors. What a falling off would there be from the present system of universal suffrage and open competition among the candidates, the frequency of rows in the pit, the noise in the gallery, the whispers in the boxes, and the lashing in the newspapers the next day!

In fact, the argument drawn from the supposed incapacity of the people against a representative Government, comes with the worst grace in the world from the patrons and admirers of hereditary government. Surely, if government were a thing requiring the utmost stretch of genius, wisdom, and virtue, to carry it on, the office of King would never even have been dreamt of as hereditary, any more than that of poet, painter, or philosopher. It is easy here "for the Son to tread in the Sire's steady steps." It requires nothing but the will to do it. Extraordinary talents are not once looked for. Nay, a person, who would never have risen by natural abilities to the situation of churchwarden or parish beadle, succeeds by unquestionable right to the possession of a throne, and wields the energies of an empire, or decides the fate of the world, with the smallest possible share of human understanding. The line of distinction which separates the regal purple from the slabbering-bib, is sometimes fine indeed; as we see in the case of the two Ferdinands. Any one above the rank of an ideot is supposed capable of exercising the highest functions of royal state. Yet these are the persons who talk of the people as a swinish multitude, and taunt them with their want of refinement and philosophy. *

* * * * * * * * * * *

* * * * * * * * * * *

The great problem of political science is not of so profoundly metaphysical or highly poetical a cast as Mr. Burke represents it. It is simply a question on the one part, with how little expense of liberty and property the Government, "that complex constable," as it has been quaintly called, can keep the peace; and on the other part, for how great a sacrifice of both, the splendour of the throne and the safety of the state can be made a pretext. Kings and their Ministers generally strive to get their hands in our pockets, and their feet on our necks; the people and their representatives will be wise enough, if they can only contrive to prevent them; but this, it must be confessed, they do not always succeed in. For a people to be free, it is sufficient that they will to be free. But the love of liberty is less strong than the love of power, and is guided by a less sure instinct in attaining its object. Milton only spoke the sentiments of the English people of his day (sentiments too which they had acted upon), in strong language, when he said, in answer to a foreign pedant:—"*Liceat, quæso, populo qui servitutis jugum in cervicibus grave sentit, tam sapienti esse, tam docto, tamque nobili, ut sciat quid tyranno suo faciendum sit; etiamsi neque exteros neque grammaticos sciscitatum mittat.*"—(*Defensio pro populo Anglicano.*) Happily the whole of the passage is not applicable to their descendants in the present day; but at all times a people may be allowed to know when they are oppressed, enslaved, and miserable, to feel their wrongs and to demand a remedy—from the superior knowledge and humanity of Ministers, who, if they cannot cure the State-malady, ought in decency, like other doctors, to resign their authority over the patient. The people are not subject to fanciful wants, speculative longings, or hypochondriacal complaints. Their disorders are real, their complaints substantial and well-founded. Their grumblings are in general seditions of the belly. They do not cry out till they are hurt. They do not stand upon nice questions, or trouble themselves with Mr. Burke's Sublime and Beautiful; but when they find the money conjured clean out of their pockets, and the Constitution suspended over their heads, they think it time to look about them. For example, poor Evans, that amateur of music and politics (strange combination of tastes), thought it hard, no doubt, to be sent to prison and deprived of his flute by a State-warrant, because there was no ground for doing it by law; and Mr. Hiley Addington, being himself a flute-player, thought so too: though, in spite of this romantic sympathy, the Minister prevailed over the musician, and Mr. Evans has, we believe, never got back his flute. For an act of injustice, by the new system, if complained of "forsooth," becomes justifiable by the very resistance to it: if not complained of, nobody knows any thing about it, and so it goes equally unredressed in either way. Or to take another obvious instance and sign of the times: a tenant or small farmer who has been distrained upon and sent to gaol or to the workhouse, probably thinks, and with some appearance of reason, that he was better off before this change of circumstances; and Mr. Cobbett, in his twopenny Registers, proves to him so clearly, that this change for the worse is owing to the war and taxes, which have driven him out of his house and home, that Mr. Cobbett himself has been forced to quit the country to argue the question, whether two and two make four, with Mr. Vansittart, upon safer ground to himself, and more equal ground to the Chancellor of the Exchequer. Such questions as these are, one would think, within the verge of common sense and reason. For any thing we could ever find, the people have as much common sense and sound judgment as any other class of the community. Their folly is second-hand, derived from their being the dupe of the passions, interests, and prejudices of their superiors. When they judge for themselves, they in general judge right. At any rate, the way to improve their judgment in their own concerns (and if they do not judge for themselves, they will infallibly be cheated both of liberty and property, by those who kindly insist on relieving them of that trouble) is not to deny them the use and exercise of their judgment altogether. Nothing can be pleasanter than one of the impositions of late attempted to be put upon the people, by persuading them that economy is no part of a wise Government. The people must be pretty competent judges of the cheapness of a Government. But it is pretended by our high-flying sinecurists and pensioners, that this is a low and vulgar view of the subject, taken up by interested knaves, like Paine and Cobbett, to delude, and, in the end, make their market of the people. With all the writers and orators who compose the band of gentlemen pensioners and their patrons, politics is entirely a thing of sentiment and imagination. To speak of the expenses of Government, as if it were a little paltry huckstering calculation of profit and loss, quite shocks their lofty, liberal, and disinterested notions. They have no patience with the people if they are not ready to sacrifice their all for the public good! This is something like a little recruiting cavalry-lieutenant we once met with, who, sorely annoyed at being so often dunned for the arrears of board and lodging by the people where he took up his quarters, exclaimed with the true broad Irish accent and emphasis—"*Vulgar ideas! These wretches always expect one to pay for what one has of them!*" Our modest lieutenant thought, that while he was employed on his Majesty's service, he had a right to pick the pockets of his subjects, and that if they complained of being fobbed of what was their own, they were blackguards and *no gentlemen!* Mr. Canning hit upon nothing so good as this, in his luminous defence of his Lisbon Job!

But allow the people to be as gross and ignorant as you please, as base and stupid as you can make them or keep them, "duller than the fat weed that roots itself at ease on Lethe's wharf,"—is nothing ever to rouse them? Grant that they are slow of apprehension—that they do not see till they feel. Is that a reason that they are not to feel then, neither? Would you blindfold them with the double bandages of bigotry, or quench their understandings with "the dim suffusion," "the drop serene," of Legitimacy, that "they may roll in vain and find no dawn" of liberty, no ray of hope? Because they do not see tyranny till it is mountain high, "making Ossa like a wart," are they not to feel its weight when it is heaped upon them, or to throw it off with giant strength and a convulsive effort? If they do not see the evil till it has grown enormous, palpable, and undeniable, is that a reason why others should then deny that it exists, or why it should not be removed? They do not snuff arbitrary power a century off: they are not shocked at it on the other side of the globe, or of the Channel: are they not therefore to see it, could it in time be supposed to stalk over their heads, to trample and grind them to the earth? If in their uncertainty how to deal with it, they sometimes strike random blows, if their despair makes them dangerous, why do not they, who, from their elevated situation, see so much farther and deeper into the principles and consequences of things—in their boasted wisdom prevent the causes of complaint in the people before they accumulate to a terrific height, and burst upon the heads of their oppressors? The higher classes, who would disqualify the people from taking the cure of their disorders into their own hands, might do this very effectually, by preventing the first symptoms of their disorders. They would do well, instead of abusing the blunders and brutishness of the multitude, to shew their superior penetration and zeal in detecting the first approaches of mischief, in withstanding *every* encroachment on the comforts and rights of the people, in guarding every bulwark against the influence and machinations of arbitrary power, as a precious, inviolable, sacred trust. Instead of this, they are the first to be lulled into security, a security "as gross as ignorance made drunk"—the last to believe the consequences, because they are the last to feel them. Instead of this, the patience of the lower classes, in submitting to privations and insults, is only surpassed by the callousness of their betters in witnessing them. The one never set about the redress of grievances or the reform of abuses, till they are no longer to be borne; the others will not hear of it even then. It is for this reason, among others, that the *vox populi* is the *vox Dei*, that it is the agonizing cry of human nature raised, and only raised, against intolerable oppression and the utmost extremity of human suffering. The people do not rise up till they are trod down. They do not turn upon their tormentors till they are goaded to madness. They do not complain till the thumbscrews have been applied, and have been strained to the last turn. Nothing can ever wean the affections or confidence of a people from a Government (to which habit, prejudice, natural pride, perhaps old benefits and joint struggles for liberty have attached them) but an excessive degree of irritation and disgust, occasioned either by a sudden and violent stretch of power, contrary to the spirit and forms of the established Government, or by a blind and wilful adherence to old abuses and established forms, when the changes in the state of manners and opinion have rendered them as odious as they are ridiculous. The Revolutions of Switzerland, the Low Countries, and of America, are examples of the former—the French Revolution of the latter: our own Revolution of 1688 was a mixture of the two. As a general rule, it might be laid down, that for every instance of national resistance to tyranny, there ought to have been hundreds, and that all those which have been attempted ought to have succeeded. In the case of Wat Tyler, for instance, which has been so naturally dramatised by the poet-laureate, the rebellion was crushed, and the ringleaders hanged by the treachery of the Government; but the grievances of which they had complained were removed a few years after, and the rights they had claimed granted to the people, from the necessary progress of civilization and knowledge. Did not Mr. Southey know, when he applied for an injunction against Wat Tyler, that the feudal system had been abolished long ago?—Again, as nothing rouses the people to resistance but extreme and aggravated injustice, so nothing can make them persevere in it, or push their efforts to a successful and triumphant issue, but the most open and unequivocal determination to brave their cries and insult their misery. They have no principle of union in themselves, and nothing brings or holds them together but the strong pressure of want, the stern hand of necessity—" a necessity that is not chosen, but chuses,—a necessity paramount to deliberation, that admits of no discussion and demands no evidence, that can alone, (according to Mr. Burke's theory) justify a resort to anarchy," and that alone ever did or can produce it. In fine, there are but two things in the world, might and right. Whenever one of these is overcome, it is by the other. The triumphs of the people, or the stand which they at any time make against arbitrary sway, are the triumphs of reason and justice over the insolence of individual power and authority, which, unless as it is restrained, curbed, and corrected by popular feeling or public opinion, can be guided only by its own drunken, besotted, mad pride, selfishness and caprice, and must be productive of all the mischief, which it can wantonly or deliberately commit with impunity.

The people are not apt, like a fine lady, to affect the vapours of discontent; nor to volunteer a rebellion for the theatrical eclat of the thing. But the least plausible excuse, one kind word, one squeeze of the hand, one hollow profession of good will, subdues the soft heart of rebellion, (which is " too foolish fond and pitiful" to be a match for the callous hypocrisy opposed to it) dissolves and melts the whole fabric of popular innovation like butter in the sun. Wat Tyler is a case in point again. The instant the effeminate king and his unprincipled courtiers gave them fair words, they dispersed, relying in their infatuation on the word of the King as binding, on the oath of his officers as sincere; and no sooner were they dispersed than they cut off their leaders' heads, and poor John Ball's along with them, in spite of all his texts of Scripture. The story is to be seen in all the shop-windows, *written in very choice blank verse!*—That the people are rash in trusting to the promises of their friends, is true; they are more rash in believing their enemies. If they are led to expect too much in theory, they are satisfied with too little in reality. Their anger is sometimes fatal while it lasts, but it is not roused very soon, nor does it last very long. Of all dynasties, anarchy is the shortest lived. They are violent in their revenge, no doubt; but it is because justice has been long denied them, and they have to pay off a very long score at a very short notice. What Cæsar says of himself, might be applied well enough to the people, that they "did never wrong but with just cause." The errors of the people are the crimes of Governments. They apply sharp remedies to lingering diseases, and when they get sudden power in their hands, frighten their enemies, and wound themselves with it. They rely on brute force and the fury of despair, in proportion to the treachery which surrounds them, and to the degradation, the want of general information and mutual co-operation, in which they have been kept, on purpose to prevent them from ever acting in concert, with wisdom, energy, confidence, and calmness, for the public good. The American Revolution produced no horrors, because its enemies could not succeed in sowing the seeds of terror, hatred, mutual treachery, and universal dismay in the hearts of the people. The French Revolution, under the auspices of Mr. Burke, and other friends of social order, was tolerably prolific of these horrors. But that should not be charged as the fault of the Revolution or of the people. Timely Reforms are the best preventives of violent Revolutions. If Governments are determined that the people shall have no redress, no remedies for their acknowledged grievances, but violent and desperate ones, they may thank themselves for the obvious consequences. Despotism must always have the most to fear from the re-action of popular fury, where it has been guilty of the greatest abuses of power, and where it has shewn the greatest tenaciousness of those abuses; putting an end to all prospect of amicable arrangement, and provoking the utmost vengeance of its oppressed and insulted victims. This tenaciousness of power is the chief obstacle to improvement, and the cause of the revulsions which follow the attempts at it. In America, a free Government was easy of accomplishment, because it was not necessary, in building up, to pull down: there were no nuisances to abate. The thing is plain. Reform in old Governments is just like the new improvements in the front of Carlton House, that would go on fast enough but for the vile, old, dark, dirty, crooked streets, which cannot be removed without giving the inhabitants notice to quit. Mr. Burke, in regretting these old institutions as the result of the wisdom of ages, and not the remains of Gothic ignorance and barbarism, played the part of *Crockery*, in the farce of *Exit by Mistake*, who sheds tears of affection over the loss of the old windows and buttresses of the houses that no longer jut out to meet one another, and stop up the way.

There is one other consideration which may induce hereditary Sovereigns to allow some weight to the arguments in favour of popular feeling and public opinion. They are the only security which they themselves possess individually for the continuance of their splendour and power. Absolute monarchs have nothing to fear from the people, but they have every thing to fear from their slaves and one another. Where power is lifted beyond the reach of the law or of public opinion, there is no principle to oppose it, and he who can obtain possession of the throne (by whatever means) is always the rightful possessor of it, till he is supplanted by a more fortunate or artful successor, and so on in a perpetual round of treasons, conspiracies, murders, usurpations, regicides, and rebellions, with which the people have nothing to do, but as passive, unconcerned spectators.—Where the son succeeds to the father's throne by assassination, without being amenable to public justice, he is liable to be cut off himself by the same means, and with the same impunity. The only thing that can give stability or confidence to power, is that very will of the people, and public censure exercised upon public acts, of which legitimate Sovereigns are so disproportionately apprehensive. For one regicide committed by the people, there have been thousands committed by Kings themselves. A Constitutional King of England reigns in greater security than the Persian Sophi, or the Great Mogul; and the Emperor of Turkey, or the Autocrat of all the Russias, has much more to fear from a cup of coffee or the bowstring, than the Prince Regent from the speeches and writings of all the Revolutionists in Europe. By removing the barrier of public opinion, which interferes with their own lawless acts, despotic Kings lay themselves open to the hand of the assassin,—and while they reign in contempt of the will, the voice, the heart and mind of a whole people, hold their crowns, and every moment of their lives at the mercy of the meanest of their slaves.

ON THE REGAL CHARACTER.

May 16, 1818.

THIS is a subject exceedingly curious, and worth explaining. In writing a criticism, we hope we shall not be accused of intending a libel.

Kings are remarkable for long memories, in the merest trifles. They never forget a face or person they have once seen, nor an anecdote they have been told of any one they know. Whatever differences of character or understanding they manifest in other respects, they all possess what Dr. Spurzheim would call the *organ of individuality*, or the power of recollecting particular local circumstances, nearly in the same degree; though we shall attempt to account for it without recurring to his system. This kind of personal memory is the natural effect of that self-importance which makes them attach a corresponding importance to all that comes in contact with themselves. Nothing can be a matter of indifference to a King, that happens to a King. That intense consciousness of their personal identity, which never quits them, extends to whatever falls under their immediate cognisance. It is the glare of Majesty reflected from their own persons on the persons of those about them that fixes their attention; and it is the same false glare that makes them blind and insensible to all that lies beyond that narrow sphere. "My Lord," said an English King to one of his courtiers, "I have seen you in that coat before with different buttons"—to the astonishment of the Noble Peer. There was nothing wonderful in it. It was the habitual jealousy of the Sovereign of the respect due to him, that made him regard with lynx-eyed watchfulness even the accidental change of dress in one of his favourites. The least diminution of glossy splendour in a birth-day suit, considered as a mark of slackened duty, or waning loyalty, would expose it, tarnished and thread-bare, to the keen glance of dormant pride, waked to suspicion. A God does not penetrate into the hearts of his worshippers with surer insight, than a King, fond of the attributes of awe and sovereignty, detects the different degrees of hollow adulation in those around him. Every thing relating to external appearance and deportment is scanned with the utmost nicety, as compromising the dignity of the royal presence. Involuntary gestures become overt acts; a look is construed into high treason; an inconsiderate word is magnified into a crime against the State. To suggest advice, or offer information unasked, is to arraign the fallibility of the throne: to hint a difference of opinion to a King, would create as great a shock, as if you were to present a pistol to the breast of any other man. "Never touch a King," was the answer of an infirm Monarch to one who had saved him from a dangerous fall. When a glass of wine was presented to the Emperor Alexander by a servant in livery, he started, as if he had trod upon a serpent. Such is their respect for themselves:

Such is their contempt for human nature!—"There's a divinity doth hedge a King," that keeps their bodies and their minds sacred within the magic circle of a name; and it is their fear lest this circle should be violated or approached without sufficient awe, that makes them observe and remember the countenances and demeanour of others with such infinite circumspection and exactness.

As Kings have the sagacity of pride, courtiers have the cunning of fear. They watch their own behaviour and that of others with breathless apprehension, and move amidst the artificial forms of court-etiquette, as if the least error must be fatal to them. Their sense of personal propriety is heightened by servility: every faculty is wound up to flatter the vanity and prejudices of their superiors. When Coates painted a portrait in crayons of the Queen, on her first arrival in this country, the King, followed by a train of attendants, went to look at it. The trembling artist stood by. "Well, what do you think?" said the King to those in waiting. Not a word in reply. "Do you think it like?" Still all was hushed as death. "Why, yes, I think it is like, very like." A buzz of admiration instantly filled the room; and the old Duchess of Northumberland, going up to the artist, and tapping him familiarly on the shoulder, said, "Remember, Mr. Coates, I am to have the first copy." On another occasion, when the Queen had sat for her portrait, one of the Maids of Honour coming into the room, curtesied to the reflection in the glass, affecting to mistake it for the Queen. The picture was, you may be sure, a flattering likeness. In the "Memoirs of Count Grammont," it is related of Louis XIV. that having a dispute at chess with one of his courtiers, no one present would give an opinion. "Oh!" said he, "here comes Count Hamilton, he shall decide which of us is in the right." "Your Majesty is in the wrong," replied the Count, without looking at the board. On which, the King remonstrating with him on the impossibility of his judging till he saw the state of the game, he answered, "Does your Majesty suppose that if you were in the right, all these noblemen would stand by and say nothing?" A

King was once curious to know, which was the tallest, himself or a certain courtier. "Let us measure," said the King. The King stood up to be measured first; but when the person who was fixed upon to take their height came to measure the Nobleman, he found it quite impossible, as he first rose on tip-toe, then crouched down, now shrugged up his shoulders to the right, then twisted his body to the left. Afterwards his friend asking him the reason of these unaccountable gesticulations, he replied, "I could not tell whether the King wished me to be taller or shorter than himself; and all the time I was making those odd movements, I was watching his countenance to see what I ought to do." If such is the exquisite pliability of the inmates of a court in trifles like these, what must be their independence of spirit and disinterested integrity in questions of peace and war, that involve the rights of Sovereigns or the liberties of the people! It has been suggested (and not without reason), that the difficulty of trusting to the professions of those who surround them, is one circumstance that renders Kings such expert physiognomists, the language of the countenance being the only one they have left to decypher the thoughts of others; and the very disguises which are practised to prevent the emotions of the mind from appearing in the face, only rendering them more acute and discriminating observers. It is the same insincerity and fear of giving offence by candour and plain-speaking in their immediate dependents, that makes Kings gossips and inquisitive. They have no way of ascertaining the opinions of others, but by getting them up into a corner, and extorting the commonest information from them, piecemeal, by endless teasing tiresome questions, and cross-examination. The walls of a palace, like those of a nunnery, are the favoured abode of scandal and tittle-tattle. The inhabitants of both are equally shut out from the common privileges and common incidents of humanity, and whatever relates to the every-day world about us, has to them the air of a romance. The desire which the most meritorious Princes have shewn to acquire information on matters of fact rather than of opinion, is partly because their prejudices will not suffer them to exercise their understandings freely on the most important speculative questions, partly from their jealousy of being dictated to on any point that admits of a question;—as, on the other hand, the desire which the Sovereigns of northern and uncultivated kingdoms have shewn to become acquainted with the arts and elegances of life in southern nations, is evidently owing to their natural jealousy of the advantages of civilization over barbarism. From the principle last stated, Peter the Great visited this country, and worked in our dock-yards as a common shipwright. To the same source may be traced the curiosity of the Duchess of Oldenburgh to see a beef-steak cooked, to take a peep into Mr. Meux's great brewing-vat, and to hear Mr. Whitbread speak!

The common regal character is then the reverse of what it ought to be. It is the purely *personal*, occupied with its own petty feelings, prejudices, and pursuits; whereas it ought to be the purely philosophical, exempt from all personal considerations, and contemplating itself only in its general and paramount relation to the State. This is the reason why there have been so few great Kings. They want the power of abstraction: and their situations are necessarily at variance with their duties, in this respect; for every thing forces them to concentrate their attention upon themselves, and to consider their rank and privileges in connexion with their private advantage, rather than with public good. This is but natural. It is easier to employ the power they possess in pampering their own appetites and passions, than to wield it for the benefit of a great empire. They see well enough how the community is made for them, not so well how they are made for the community. Not knowing how to act as stewards for their trust, they set up for heirs to the estate, and waste it at their pleasure:—without aspiring to reign as Kings, they are contented to live as *spunges* upon royalty. A great King ought to be the greatest philosopher and the truest patriot in his dominions: hereditary Kings can be but common mortals. It is not that they are not equal to other men, but to be equal to their rank as

Kings, they ought to be more than men. Their power is equal to that of the whole community: their wisdom and virtue ought to keep pace with their power. But in ordinary cases, the height to which they are raised, instead of enlarging their views or ennobling their sentiments, makes them giddy with vanity, and ready to look down on the world which is subjected to their power, as the plaything of their will. They regard men crawling on the face of the earth, as we do insects that cross our path, and survey the common drama of human life, as a fantoccini exhibition got up for their amusement. There is no sympathy between Kings and their subjects—except in a constitutional monarchy like ours, through the medium of Lords and Commons! Take away that check upon their ambition and rapacity, and their pretensions become as monstrous as they are ridiculous. Without the common feelings of humanity in their own breasts, they have no regard for them in their aggregate amount and accumulating force. Reigning in contempt of the people, they would crush and trample upon all power but their own. They consider the claims of justice and compassion as so many impertinent interferences with the royal prerogative. They despise the millions of slaves whom they see linked to the foot of the throne; and they soon hate what they despise. They will sacrifice a kingdom for a caprice, and mankind for a bauble. Weighed in the scales of their pride, the meanest things become of the greatest importance: weighed in the balance of reason, the universe is nothing to them. It is this overweening, aggravated, intolerable sense of swelling pride and ungovernable self-will, that so often drives them mad; as it is their blind fatuity and insensibility to all beyond themselves, that, transmitted through successive generations and confirmed by regal intermarriages, in time makes them idiots. When we see a poor creature like Ferdinand VII., who can hardly gabble out his words like a human being, more imbecile than a woman, more hypocritical than a priest, decked and dandled in the long robes and swaddling-clothes of legitimacy, lullabied to rest with the dreams of superstition, drunk with the patriot blood of his country, and launching the thunders of his coward-arm against the rising liberties of a new world, while he claims the style and title of Image of the Divinity, we may laugh or weep, but there is nothing to wonder at. Tyrants lose all respect for humanity in proportion as they are sunk beneath it;—taught to believe themselves of a different species, they really become so; lose their participation with their kind; and, in mimicking the God, dwindle into the brute! Blind with prejudices as a mole, stung with truth as with scorpions, sore all over with wounded pride like a boil, their minds a heap of morbid proud flesh and bloated humours, a disease and gangrene in the State, instead of its life-blood and vital principle;—foreign despots claim mankind as their property, "independently of their conduct or merits," and there is one Englishman found base enough to echo the foul calumny against his country and his kind.

We might, in the same manner, account for the disparity between the public and private character of Kings. It is the misfortune of most Kings (not their fault) to be born to thrones, a situation which ordinary talents or virtue cannot fill with impunity. We often find a very respectable man make but a very sorry figure as a Sovereign. Nay, a Prince may be possessed of extraordinary virtues and accomplishments, and not be the more thought of for them. He may, for instance, be a man of good nature and good manners, graceful in his person, the idol of the other sex, the model of his own; every word or look may be marked with the utmost sense of propriety and delicate attention to the feelings of others; he may be a good classic, well versed in history,—may speak Italian, French, Spanish, and German fluently; he may be an excellent mimic; he may say good things, and do friendly ones; he may be able to join in a catch, or utter a repartee, or dictate a billet-doux; he may be master of Hoyle, and deep in the rules of the Jockey club; he may have an equal taste in ragouts and poetry, in dancing and in dress; he may adjust a toupee with the dexterity of a friseur, or tie a cravat with the hand and eye of a man-milliner: he may have all these graces and accomplishments, and as many more, and yet he may be nothing; as without any one of them he may be a great Prince. They are not the graces and accomplishments of a Sovereign, but of a lord of the bedchamber. They do not shew a great mind, bent on great objects, and swayed by lofty views. They are rather foibles and blemishes in the character of a ruler, for they imply that his attention has been turned as much upon adorning his own person as upon advancing the State. Charles II. was a King, such as we have here described; amiable, witty, and accomplished, and yet his memory is equally despised and detested. Charles was without strength of mind, or public principle. He could not arrive at the comprehension of that mixed mass of thought and feeling, a *kingdom*—he thought merely of the *throne*. He was as unlike Cromwell in the manner in which he came by the sovereignty of the realm as in the use he made of it. He saw himself, not in the glass of history, but in the glass on his toilette; not in the eyes of posterity, but in those of his courtiers and mistresses. Instead of regulating his conduct by public opinion and abstract reason, he did every thing from a feeling of personal vanity. Charles would have been more annoyed with the rejection of a licentious overture than with the rebellion of a province; and poured out the blood of his subjects with the same gaiety and indifference as he did a glass of wine. He had no idea of his obligations to the State, and only laid aside the private gentleman, to become the tyrant of his people. Charles was popular in his life-time, Cibber tells us, because he used to walk out with his spaniels and feed his ducks in St. James's park. History has consigned his name to infamy for the executions under Jefferies, and for his league with a legitimate despot (Louis XIV.), to undermine the liberties of his country.

What is it, then, that makes a great Prince? Not the understanding Purcell or Mozart, but the having an ear open to the voice of truth and justice! Not a taste in made dishes, or French wines, or court-dresses, but a fellow-feeling with the calamities of hunger, of cold, of disease, and nakedness! Not a knowledge of the elegances of fashionable life, but a heart that feels for the millions of its fellow-beings in want of the common necessaries of life! Not a set of brilliant frivolous accomplishments, but a manly strength of character, proof against the seductions of a throne! He, in short, is a patriot King, who without any other faculty usually possessed by Sovereigns, has one which they seldom possess,—the power in imagination of changing places with his people. Such a King may indeed aspire to the character of a ruling providence over a nation; any other is but the head-cypher of a court.

THE FUDGE FAMILY IN PARIS.

Edited by Thomas Brown, *the younger, Author of the "Twopenny Post-bag."*—Longmans.

April 25, 1818.

THE spirit of poetry in Mr. Moore is not a lying spirit. "Set it down, my tables"—we have still, in the year 1818, three years after the date of Mr. Southey's laureateship, one poet, who is an honest man. We are glad of it: nor does it spoil our theory, for the exception proves the rule. Mr. Moore unites in himself two names that were sacred, till they were prostituted by our modern mountebanks, the Poet and the Patriot. He is neither a coxcomb nor a catspaw,—a whiffling turncoat, nor a thorough-paced tool, a mouthing sycophant, "a full solempne man," like Mr. Wordsworth,—a whining monk, like Mr. Southey,—a maudlin Methodistical lay-preacher, like Mr. Coleridge,—a merry Andrew, like the fellow that plays on the salt-box at Bartlemy Fair,—or the more pitiful jack-pudding, that makes a jest of humanity in St. Stephen's Chapel. Thank God, he is like none of these—he is not one of the Fudge Family. He is neither a bubble nor a cheat. He makes it his business neither to hoodwink his own understanding, nor to blind or gag others. He is a man of wit and fancy, but he does not sharpen his wit on the edge of human agony, like the House of Commons' jester, nor strew the flowers of fancy, like the Jesuit Burke, over the carcase of corruption, for he is a man not only of wit and fancy, but of common sense and common humanity. He sees for himself, and he feels for others. He employs the arts of fiction, not to adorn the deformed, or disguise the false, but to make truth shine out the clearer, and beauty look more beautiful. He does not make verse, "immortal verse," the vehicle of lies, the bawd of Legitimacy, the pander of antiquated prejudices, and of vamped-up sophistry; but of truths, of home, heartfelt truths, as old as human nature and its wrongs. Mr. Moore calls things by their right names: he shews us kings as kings, priests as priests, knaves as knaves, and fools as fools. He makes us laugh at the ridiculous, and hate the odious. He also speaks with authority, and not as certain scribes that we could mention. He has been at Court, and has seen what passes there.

"Tam knew what's what full brawly."

But he was a man before he became a courtier, and has continued to be one afterwards; nor has he forgotten what passes in the human heart. From what he says of the Prince, it is evident that he speaks from habits of personal intimacy: he speaks of Lord Castlereagh as his countryman. In the Epistles of the Fudge Family, we see, as in a glass without a wrinkle, the mind and person of Royalty in full dress, up to the very throat, and we have a whole-length figure of his Lordship, in the sweeping, serpentine line of beauty, down to his very feet.*—We have heard it said of our poet, by a late celebrated wit and orator, that "there was no man who put so much of his heart into his fancy as Tom Moore; that his soul seemed as if it were a particle of fire separated from the sun, and were always fluttering to get back to that source of light and heat." We think this

* "I look down towards his feet;
But that's a fable."—OTHELLO.

criticism as happy as it is just: but it will be evident to the readers of the *Fudge Family*, that the soul of "a certain little gentleman" is not attracted with the same lively or kindly symptoms to the Bourbons, or to their benefactors and restorers "under Providence!" The title of this delightful little collection of sweets and bitters, of honey and gall, is, we suppose, an allusion to the short ejaculation which honest Burchell, in the "Vicar of Wakefield," uttered at the end of every sentence, in the conversation of Miss Amelia Carolina Wilhelmina Skeggs and her friend, on the Court and Fashionables; and which word, "Fudge," our malicious Editor thinks equally applicable to the cant upon the same subjects at the present day,—to the *fade politesse* of the *ancient regime*,—to "the damnable face-making" of Holy Alliances, and "the *flocci-nauci-pili-nihili-fication*" of Legitimacy. He may be wrong in this; but if so, we are most assuredly in the wrong with him: and we confess, it gives us as much pleasure to agree with this writer, as it does to differ with some others that we could mention, but that they are not worth mentioning.—The Correspondents of the Fudge Family in Paris are much of the same stamp (with one exception) as the Correspondents of Dr. S———, in his work of that name, which was lately put a stop to by that sort of censorship of the press which is exercised by the reading public; only the Correspondents in the present volume have a very different Editor from him of "*The Day and New Times*," or, as it is at present called, *The New Times* alone, the *Day* having been left out as an anomaly, "*ut lucus a non lucendo*:" for the readers of that paper roll their eyes in vain, and "find no dawn; but, in its stead, total eclipse and ever-during dark surrounds them."—But to return from "the professional *gentleman*," as he calls himself, his scavenger's bell, his mud-cart of liberal phraseologies, and go-cart of slavery and superstition, to something as different as genius from dulness, as wit from malice, as sense from moon-struck madness, as independence from servility, as the belles-lettres from law-stationery, as Parnassus from Grub-street, or as the grub from the butterfly,—as the man who winged his airy way from a Court which was unworthy of him, and which would have made him unworthy of himself, "as light as bird from brake," is from the man (if so he can be called) who would grope his way there on all fours, bringing, as the sacrifice best worthy of himself and of the place, his own dignity of spirit and the rights of his fellow-creatures, to be trampled down by the obscene hoofs of a base oligarchy. But we have already in another place spoken our minds of that person, in a way to cut off the communication between his "blind mouth" and the Midas ears of the Stock Exchange; and we do not wish to deprive him of a livelihood. He may receive his Treasury wages for us, so that he no longer levies them on public credulity, and we no longer confound "his sweet voice" with that of the country or city, though it may echo the Court. The *New Times* is a nuisance; but it is not one that requires to be abated. It speaks a plain, intelligible language. Its principles are as palpable as they are base. Its pettifogging pedantry and its Billingsgate slang can deceive nobody that is worth undeceiving. It is the avowed organ of the deliberate, detestable system which has long been covertly pursued in a certain quarter. This paper raves aloud, under the ambiguous garb of phrenzy, what its patrons think in secret. It proclaims on the house-tops what is whispered in the high places. It soothes the ears of flatterers, of tyrants, and of slaves,—but it sounds the alarm to free men. It is so far a great public good. It tells the people of England what is prepared for them, and what they have to expect. "Nothing is sacred in its pages but tyranny." It links this country in chains of vassalage to the legitimate despotisms of the Continent, which have been a bye-word with us for ages. It binds this nation, hand and foot, in the trammels of lasting servitude,—it puts the yoke upon our necks as we put pack-saddles upon asses,—marks the brand upon our foreheads as we ruddle over sheep,—binds us in "with shame, with rotten parchments, and vile inky blots,"—makes England, that threw off the yoke of a race of hereditary pretenders, shew "like a rebel's whore," and every morning illegitimates the House of Brunswick, and strikes at the title of the Prince Regent to the succession of the Crown, to which his ancestors had no just claim but the choice of the people. It is not a paper for a free people to endure, if a people that has oppressed the struggling liberties of another nation can dare to call itself free; or for the Sovereign of a free people to look at, if a Prince who had restored a despot to a throne, in contempt of the voice of the people, could be supposed to respect the rights of human nature more than his own power. It reverses the Revolution of 1688, by justifying the claims of the Bourbons,—brings back Popery and slavery here, by parity of reasoning,—and sends the illustrious members of the present Royal Family a packing, as vagabonds and outlaws—by RIGHT DIVINE. If this is not a legitimate conclusion from the Doctor's reasoning,—from his "brangle and brave-all, discord and debate,"—why then

> "The pillar'd firmament is rottenness,
> And earth's base built on stubble."

The chief *Dramatis Personæ* in the *Fudge Family* are,—Comic Personages, Miss Biddy Fudge and Mr. Bob Fudge, her brother: Mr. Philip Fudge, their father, and a friend of Lord Castlereagh, a grave gentleman; and a Mr. Phelim Connor, who is a patriotic, or, which is the same thing, a tragic writer. Miss Biddy Fudge takes the account of poke-bonnets and love-adventures upon herself; Mr. Bob, the *patés*, jockey-boots, and high collars: Mr. Phil. Fudge addresses himself to the Lord Viscount Castlereagh; and Mr. Phelim, "the sad historian of pensive Europe," appeals, we confess, more effectually to us, in words

> "As precious as the ruddy drops
> That visit our sad hearts."

Take for example the following magnanimous and most heroical Epistle:—

FROM PHELIM CONNOR TO ———

" Return!"—no never, while the withering hand
Of bigot power is on that helpless land;
While, for the faith my fathers held to God,
Ev'n in the fields where free those fathers trod,
I am proscrib'd, and—like the spot left bare
In Israel's halls, to tell the proud and fair
Amidst their mirth, that Slavery had been there
On all I love, home, parents, friends, I trace
The mournful mark of bondage and disgrace!
No!—let *them* stay, who in their country's pangs
See nought but food for factions and harangues;
Who yearly kneel before their masters' doors,
And hawk their wrongs, as beggars do their sores:
* Still let your * * * * *
* * * * * * * *
Still hope and suffer, all who can!—but I,
Who durst not hope, and cannot bear, must fly.

But whither?—every-where the scourge pursues—
Turn where he will, the wretched wanderer views,
In the bright, broken hopes of all his race,
Countless reflections of th' Oppressor's face!
Every-where gallant hearts, and spirits true,
Are serv'd up victims to the vile and few;
While E******, every-where—the general foe
Of Truth and Freedom, wheresoe'er they glow—
Is first, when tyrants strike, to aid the blow!

I have thought it prudent to omit some parts of Mr. Phelim Connor's letter. He is evidently an intemperate young man, and has associated with his cousins, the Fudges, to very little purpose.

Oh, E****** ! could such poor revenge atone
For wrongs, that well might claim the deadliest one ;
Were it a vengeance, sweet enough to sate
The wretch who flies from thy intolerant hate,
To hear his curses on such barbarous sway
Echoed, where'er he bends his cheerless way ;
Could *this* content him, every lip he meets
Teems for his vengeance with such poisonous sweets ;
Were *this* his luxury, never is thy name
Pronounc'd, but he doth banquet on thy shame ;
Hears maledictions ring from every side
Upon that grasping power, that selfish pride,
Which vaunts its own, and scorns all rights beside ;
That low and desperate envy, which to blast
A neighbour's blessings, risks the few thou hast ;—
That monster, Self, too gross to be conceal'd
Which ever lurks behind thy proffer'd shield ;—
That faithless craft, which in thy hour of need,
Can court the slave, can swear he shall be freed,
Yet basely spurns him, when thy point is gain'd,
Back to his masters, ready gagg'd and chain'd !
Worthy associate of that band of Kings,
That royal, rav'ning flock, whose vampire wings
O'er sleeping Europe treacherously brood,
And fan her into dreams of promis'd good,
Of hope, of freedom—but to drain her blood !

If *thus* to hear thee branded be a bliss
That Vengeance loves, there's yet more sweet than this,—
That 'twas an Irish head, an Irish heart,
Made thee the fall'n and tarnish'd thing thou art ;
That, as the Centaur gave th' infected vest
In which he died, to rack his conqueror's breast,
We sent thee C————gh :—as heaps of dead
Have slain their slayers by the pest they spread,
So hath our land breath'd out—thy fame to dim,
Thy strength to waste, and rot thee, soul and limb—

Her worst infections all condens'd in him!

* * * * * * *

When will the world shake off such yokes? Oh, when
Will that redeeming day shine out on men,
That shall behold them rise, erect and free
As Heav'n and Nature meant mankind should be?
When Reason shall no longer blindly bow
To the vile pagod things, that o'er her brow,
Like him of Jaghernaut, drive trampling now;
Nor conquest dare to desolate God's earth;
Nor drunken Victory, with a Nero's mirth,
Strike her lewd harp amidst a people's groans;—
But, built on love, the world's exalted thrones
Shall to the virtuous and the wise be given—
Those bright, those sole Legitimates of Heaven!

When will this be?—or, oh! is it, in truth,
But one of those sweet, day-break dreams of youth,
In which the Soul, as round her morning springs,
'Twixt sleep and waking, sees such dazzling things!
And must the hope, as vain as it is bright,
Be all giv'n up?—and are *they* only right,
Who say this world of thinking souls was made
To be by Kings partition'd, truck'd, and weigh'd
In scales that, ever since the world begun,
Have counted millions but as dust to one?
Are *they* the only wise, who laugh to scorn
The rights, the freedom to which man was born;
Who * * * * * *
* * * * * * *

Who, proud to kiss each separate rod of power,
Bless, while he reigns, the minion of the hour;
Worship each would-be God, that o'er them moves,
And take the thundering of his brass for Jove's!
If *this* be wisdom, then farewell my books,
Farewell ye shrines of old, ye classic brooks,

Which fed my soul with currents, pure and fair,
Of living truth, that now must stagnate there!—
Instead of themes that touch the lyre with light,—
Instead of Greece, and her immortal fight
For Liberty, which once awak'd my strings,
Welcome the Grand Conspiracy of Kings,
The High Legitimates, the Holy Band,
Who, bolder ev'n than He of Sparta's land,
Against whole millions, panting to be free,
Would guard the pass of right-line tyranny!
Instead of him, th' Athenian bard, whose blade
Had stood the onset which his pen pourtray'd,
Welcome * * * * * *
* * * * * * * *

And, 'stead of Aristides—woe the day
Such names should mingle!—welcome C————gh!

Here break we off, at this unhallow'd name,
Like priests of old, when words ill-omen'd came.
My next shall tell thee, bitterly shall tell,
Thoughts that * * * * *
* * * * * * * *

Thoughts that—could patience hold—'twere wiser far
To leave still hid and burning where they are!

Indignatio facit versus. Mr. Moore's better genius is here his spleen. The politician sharpens the poet's pen. Poor Phelim resumes this subject twice afterwards, and the last time with such force and spirit, that he is compelled to break off in the middle, for fear of consequences. But as far as he goes, we will accompany him.

Yes—'twas a cause, as noble and as great
As ever hero died to vindicate—
A Nation's right to speak a Nation's voice,
And own no power but of the Nation's choice!

Such was the grand, the glorious cause that now
Hung trembling on Napoleon's single brow;
Such the sublime arbitrement, that pour'd,
In patriot eyes, a light around his sword,
A glory then, which never, since the day
Of his young victories, had illum'd its way!
Oh, 'twas not then the time for tame debates,
Ye men of Gaul, when chains were at your gates;
When he, who fled before your Chieftain's eye,
As geese from eagles on Mount Taurus fly,
Denounc'd against the land, that spurn'd his chain,
Myriads of swords to bind it fast again—
Myriads of fierce invading swords, to track
Through your best blood his path of vengeance back;
When Europe's Kings, that never yet combin'd
But (like those upper Stars, that, when conjoin'd,
Shed woe and pestilence) to scourge mankind,
Gather'd around, with hosts from every shore,
Hating Napoleon much, but Freedom more;
And, in that coming strife, appall'd to see
The world yet left one chance for liberty!—
No, 'twas not then the time to weave a net
Of bondage round your Chief; to curb and fret
Your veteran war-horse, pawing for the fight,
When every hope was in his speed and might—
To waste the hour of action in dispute,
And coolly plan how Freedom's *boughs* should shoot,
When your invader's axe was at the *root!*
No, sacred Liberty! that God, who throws
Thy light around, like his own sunshine, knows
How well I love thee, and how deeply hate
All tyrants, upstart and Legitimate—
Yet, in that hour, were France my native land,
I would have followed, with quick heart and hand,
Napoleon, Nero—ay, no matter whom—
To snatch my country from that damning doom,—

That deadliest curse that on the conquered waits
A Conqueror's satrap, thron'd within her gates!
True, he was false, despotic—all you please—
Had trampled down man's holiest liberties—
Had, by a genius form'd for nobler things
Than lie within the grasp of *vulgar* Kings,
But rais'd the hopes of men—as eaglets fly
With tortoises aloft into the sky
To dash them down again more shatteringly!
*All this I own—but still * * *
* * * * * * * * *

All is not in this high-wrought strain, which we like as well as the War Eclogues of Tyrtæus, or the Birth-day Odes (which seem also to have broke off in the middle) of Mr. Southey. Mr. Thomas Brown the Younger, is a man of humanity, as Mr. Southey formerly was: he is also a man of wit, which Mr. Southey is not. For instance, Miss Biddy Fudge, in her first letter, writes as follows:—

By the bye though at Calais, Papa had a touch
Of romance on the pier, which affected me much.
At the sight of that spot, where our darling Dixhuit,
Set the first of his own dear legitimate feet,†
(Modell'd out so exactly, and—God bless the mark!
'Tis a foot, Dolly, worthy so *Grand* a *Monarque*)
He exclaim'd, "Oh mon Roi!" and, with tear-dropping eye,
Stood to gaze on the spot—while some Jacobin nigh,
Mutter'd out with a shrug (what an insolent thing!)
"Ma foi, he be right—'tis de Englishman's King;

* Somebody (Fontenelle, I believe) has said, that if he had his hand full of truths, he would open but one finger at a time; and I find it necessary to use the same sort of reserve with respect to Mr. Phelim Connor's very plain-spoken letters. The remainder of this Epistle is so full of unsafe matter of fact, that it must, for the present at least, be withheld from the public.

† To commemorate the landing of Louis le Desiré from England, the impression of his foot is marked out upon the pier at Calais, and a pillar with an inscription raised opposite to the spot."

And dat *gros pied de cochon*—begar, me vil say
Dat de foot look mosh better, if turn'd toder way."

Mr. Phil. Fudge, in his dreams, thinks of a plan for changing heads.

Good Viscount S—dm—th, too, instead
Of his own grave, respected head,
Might wear (for aught I see that bars)
  Old Lady Wilhelmina Frump's—
So while the hand sign'd *Circulars*,
  The head might lisp out, "What is trumps?"
The R—g—t's brains could we transfer
To some robust man-milliner,
The shop, the shears, the lace, and ribbon,
Would go, I doubt not, quite as glib on;
And, *vice versâ*, take the pains
To give the P—ce the shopman's brains,
The only change from thence would flow,
Ribbons would not be wasted so!

Or here is another proposal for weighing the head of the State;

Suppose, my Lord,—and far from me
To treat such things with levity—
But just suppose the R—g—t's weight
Were made thus an affair of state;
And, ev'ry sessions, at the close,
  'Stead of a speech, which, all can see, is
Heavy and dull enough, God knows
  We were to try how heavy *he* is.
Much would it glad all hearts to hear
  That, while the Nation's Revenue
Loses so many pounds a year,
  The P——e, God bless him! *gains* a few.

With bales of muslin, chintzes, spices,
  I see the Easterns weigh their Kings;—

But, for the R—g—t, my advice is,
  We should throw in much *heavier* things:
For instance, ———'s quarto volumes,
  Which, though not spices, serve to wrap them;
Dominic St—dd—t's Daily columns,
  " Prodigious!"—in, of course we'd clap them—
Letters, that C—rtw—t's pen indites,
  In which, with logical confusion,
The *Major* like a *Minor* writes,
  And never comes to a *conclusion:*
Lord S—m—rs' pamphlet, or his head—
(Ah, *that* were worth its weight in lead!)
Along with which we *in* may whip, sly,
The Speeches of Sir John C—x H—pp—sly;
That Baronet of many words,
Who loves so, in the House of Lords,
To whisper Bishops—and so nigh
  Unto their wigs in whisp'ring goes,
That you may always know him by
  A patch of powder on his nose!—
If this won't do, we must in cram
The " Reasons" of Lord B—ck—gh—m;
(A book his Lordship means to write,
  Entitled, " Reasons for my Ratting:"
Or, should these prove too small and light,
  His ——'s a host, we'll bundle *that* in!
And, *still* should all these masses fail
To stir the R—g—t's ponderous scale,
Why then, my Lord, in heaven's name,
  Pitch in, without reserve or stint,
The whole of R—g—ly's beauteous dame—
  If that won't raise him, devil's in't.

But we stop here, or we shall quote the whole work. We like the political part of this *jeu d'esprit* better, on the whole, than the merely comic and familiar. Bob Fudge is almost too suffocating a coxcomb, even in description, with his stays and *patés;* and Miss Biddy Fudge, with her *poke* bonnet and her princely lover, who turned out to be no better than a man-milliner, is not half so interesting as a certain Marchioness in the Twopenny Post Bag, with curls "in the manner of Ackermann's dresses for May, and her yellow charioteer." Besides, Miss Biddy's amour ends in nothing. In short, the Fudges abroad are not such fat subjects for ridicule as the Fudges at home. "They do not cut up so well in the cawl; they do not tallow so in the kidneys:" but as far as they go, Mr. Brown, Junior, uses the dissecting knife with equal dexterity, and equally to the delight and edification of the byestanders.

CHARACTER OF LORD CHATHAM.

1807.

Lord Chatham's genius burnt brightest at the last. The spark of liberty, which had lain concealed and dormant, buried under the dirt and rubbish of state intrigue and vulgar faction, now met with congenial matter, and kindled up "a flame of sacred vehemence" in his breast. It burst forth with a fury and a splendour that might have awed the world, and made kings tremble. He spoke as a man should speak, because he felt as a man should feel, in such circumstances. He came forward as the advocate of liberty, as the defender of the rights of his fellow-citizens, as the enemy of tyranny, as the friend of his country, and of mankind. He did not stand up to make a vain display of his talents, but to discharge a duty, to maintain that cause which lay nearest to his heart, to preserve the ark of the British constitution from every sacrilegious touch, as the high-priest of his calling, with a pious zeal. The feelings and the rights of Englishmen were enshrined in his heart; and with their united force braced every nerve, possessed every faculty, and communicated warmth and vital energy to every part of his being. The whole man moved under this impulse. He felt the cause of liberty as his own. He resented every injury done to her as an injury to himself, and every attempt to defend it as an insult upon his understanding. He did not stay to dispute about words, about nice distinctions, about trifling forms. He laughed at the little attempts of little retailers of logic to entangle him in senseless argument. He did not come there as to a debating club, or law court, to start questions and hunt them down; to wind and unwind the web of sophistry; to pick out the threads, and untie every knot with scrupulous exactness; to bandy logic with every pretender to a paradox; to examine, to sift evidence; to dissect a doubt and halve a scruple; to weigh folly and knavery in scales together, and see on which side the balance preponderated; to prove that liberty, truth, virtue, and justice were good things, or that slavery and corruption were bad things. He did not try to prove those truths which did not require any proof, but to make others feel them with the same force that he did; and to tear off the flimsy disguises with which the sycophants of power attempted to cover them.—The business of an orator is not to convince, but persuade; not to inform, but to rouse the mind; to build upon the habitual prejudices of mankind, (for reason of itself will do nothing,) and to add feeling to prejudice, and action to feeling. There is nothing new or curious or profound in Lord Chatham's speeches. All is obvious and common; there is nothing but what we already knew, or might have found out for ourselves. We see nothing but the familiar every-day face of nature. We are always in broad day-light. But then there is the same difference between our own conceptions of things and his representation of them, as there is between the same objects seen on a dull cloudy day, or in the blaze of sunshine. His common sense has the effect of inspiration. He electrifies his hearers, not by the novelty of his ideas, but by their force and intensity. He has the same ideas as other men, but he has them in a thousand times greater clearness and strength and vividness. Perhaps there is no man so poorly furnished with thoughts and feelings but that if he could recollect all that he knew, and had all his ideas at perfect command, he would be able to confound the puny arts of the most dexterous sophist that pretended to make a dupe of his understanding. But in the mind of Chatham, the great substantial truths of common sense, the leading maxims of the Constitution, the real interests and general feelings of mankind, were in a manner embodied. He comprehended the whole of his subject at a single glance—every thing was firmly rivetted to its place; there was no feebleness, no forgetfulness, no pause, no distraction; the ardour of his mind overcame every obstacle, and he crushed the objections of his adversaries as we crush an insect under our feet.—His imagination was of the same character with his understanding, and was under the same guidance. Whenever he gave way to it, it "flew an eagle flight, forth and right on;" but it did not become enamoured of its own motion, wantoning in giddy circles, or "sailing with supreme dominion through the azure deep of air." It never forgot its errand, but went strait forward, like an arrow to its mark, with an unerring aim. It was his servant, not his master.

To be a great orator does not require the highest faculties of the human mind, but it requires the highest exertion of the common faculties of our nature. He has no occasion to dive into the depths of science, or to soar aloft on angels' wings. He keeps upon the surface, he stands firm upon the ground, but his form is majestic, and his eye sees far and near: he moves among his fellows, but he moves among them as a giant among common men. He has no need to read the heavens, to unfold the system of the universe, or create new worlds for the delighted fancy to dwell in; it is enough that he sees things as they are; that he knows and feels and remembers the common circumstances and daily transactions that are passing in the world around him. He is not raised above others by being superior to the common interests, prejudices, and passions of mankind, but by feeling them in a more intense degree than they do. Force then is the sole characteristic excellence of an orator; it is almost the only one that can be of any service to him. Refinement, depth, elevation, delicacy, originality, ingenuity, invention, are not wanted: he must appeal to the sympathies of human nature, and whatever is not founded in these, is foreign to his purpose. He does not create, he can only imitate or echo back the public sentiment. His object is to call up the feelings of the human breast; but he cannot call up what is not already there. The first duty of an orator is to be understood by every one; but it is evident that what all can understand, is not in itself difficult of comprehension. He cannot add any thing to the materials afforded him by the knowledge and experience of others.

Lord Chatham, in his speeches, was neither philosopher nor poet. As to the latter, the difference between poetry and eloquence I take to be this: that the object of the one is to delight the imagination, that of the other to impel the will. The one ought to enrich and feed the mind itself with tenderness and beauty, the other furnishes it with motives of action. The one seeks to give immediate pleasure, to make the mind dwell with rapture on its own workings—it is to itself "both end and use:" the other endeavours to call up such images as will produce the strongest effect upon the mind, and makes use of the passions only as instruments to attain a particular purpose. The poet lulls and soothes the mind into a forgetfulness of itself, and "laps it in Elysium:" the orator strives to awaken it to a sense of its real interests, and to make it feel the necessity of taking the most effectual means for securing them. The one dwells in an ideal world; the other is only conversant about realities. Hence poetry must be more ornamented, must be richer and fuller and more delicate, because it is at liberty to select whatever images are naturally most beautiful, and likely to give most pleasure; whereas the orator is confined to particular facts, which he may adorn as well as he can, and make the most of, but which he cannot strain beyond a certain point without running into extravagance and affectation, and losing his end. However, from the very nature of the case, the orator is allowed a greater latitude, and is compelled to make use of harsher and more abrupt combinations in the decoration of his subject; for his art is an attempt to reconcile beauty and deformity together: on the contrary, the materials of poetry, which are chosen at pleasure, are in themselves beautiful, and naturally combine with whatever else is beautiful. Grace and harmony are therefore essential to poetry, because they naturally arise out of the subject; but whatever adds to the effect, whatever tends to strengthen the idea or give energy to the mind, is of the nature of eloquence. The orator is only concerned to give a tone of masculine firmness to the will, to brace the sinews and muscles of the mind; not to delight our nervous sensibilities, or soften the mind into voluptuous indolence. The flowery and sentimental style is of all others the most intolerable in a speaker.—I shall only add on this subject, that modesty, impartiality, and candour, are not the virtues of a public speaker. He must be confident, inflexible, uncontrolable, overcoming all opposition by his ardour and impetuosity. We do not *command* others by sympathy with them, but by power, by passion, by will. Calm inquiry, sober truth, and speculative indifference will never carry any point. The passions are contagious; and we cannot contend against opposite passions with nothing but naked reason. Concessions to an enemy are clear loss: he will take advantage of them, but make us none in return. He will magnify the weak sides of our argument, but will be blind to whatever makes against himself. The multitude will always be inclined to side with that party, whose passions are the most inflamed, and whose prejudices are the most inveterate. Passion should therefore never be sacrificed to punctilio. It should indeed be governed by prudence, but it should itself govern and lend its impulse and direction to abstract reason. Fox was a reasoner, Lord Chatham was an orator. Burke was both a reasoner and a poet; and was therefore still farther removed from that conformity with the vulgar notions and mechanical feelings of mankind, which will always be necessary to give a man the chief sway in a popular assembly.

CHARACTER OF MR. BURKE, 1807.*

The following speech is perhaps the fairest specimen I could give of Mr. Burke's various talents as a speaker. The subject itself is not the most interesting, nor does it admit of that weight and closeness of reasoning which he displayed on other occasions. But there is no single speech which can convey a satisfactory idea of his powers of mind: to do him justice, it would be necessary to quote all his works; the only specimen of Burke is, *all that he wrote.* With respect to most other speakers, a specimen is generally enough, or more than enough. When you are acquainted with their manner, and see what proficiency they have made in the mechanical exercise of their profession, with what facility they can borrow a simile, or round a period, how dexterously they can argue, and object, and rejoin, you are satisfied; there is no other difference in their speeches than what arises from the difference of the subjects. But this was not the case with Burke. He brought his subjects along with him; he drew his materials from himself. The only limits which circumscribed his variety were the stores of his own mind. His stock of ideas did not consist of a few meagre facts, meagrely stated, of half a dozen common-places tortured in a thousand different ways: but his mine of wealth was a profound understanding, inexhaustible as the human heart, and various as the sources of nature. He therefore enriched every subject to which he applied himself, and new subjects were only the occasions of calling forth fresh powers of mind which had not been before exerted. It would therefore be in vain to look for the proof of his powers in any one of his speeches or writings: they all contain some additional proof of power. In speaking of Burke, then, I shall speak of the whole compass and circuit of his mind—not of that small part or section of him which I have been able to give: to do otherwise would be like the story of the man who put the

* This character was written in a fit of extravagant candour, at a time when I thought I could do justice, or more than justice, to an enemy, without betraying a cause.

brick in his pocket, thinking to shew it as the model of a house. I have been able to manage pretty well with respect to all my other speakers, and curtailed them down without remorse. It was easy to reduce them within certain limits, to fix their spirit, and condense their variety; by having a certain quantity given, you might infer all the rest; it was only the same thing over again. But who can bind Proteus, or confine the roving flight of genius?

Burke's writings are better than his speeches, and indeed his speeches are writings. But he seemed to feel himself more at ease, to have a fuller possession of his faculties in addressing the public, than in addressing the House of Commons. Burke was *raised* into public life: and he seems to have been prouder of this new dignity than became so great a man. For this reason, most of his speeches have a sort of parliamentary preamble to them: there is an air of affected modesty, and ostentatious trifling in them: he seems fond of coqueting with the House of Commons, and is perpetually calling the Speaker out to dance a minuet with him, before he begins. There is also something like an attempt to stimulate the superficial dulness of his hearers by exciting their surprise, by running into extravagance: and he sometimes demeans himself by condescending to what may be considered as bordering too much upon buffoonery, for the amusement of the company. Those lines of Milton were admirably applied to him by some one—" The elephant to make them sport wreathed his proboscis lithe." The truth is, that he was out of his place in the House of Commons; he was eminently qualified to shine as a man of genius, as the instructor of mankind, as the brightest luminary of his age: but he had nothing in common with that motley crew of knights, citizens, and burgesses. He could not be said to be " native and endued unto that element." He was above it; and never appeared like himself, but when, forgetful of the idle clamours of party, and of the little views of little men, he appealed to his country, and the enlightened judgment of mankind.

I am not going to make an idle panegyric on Burke (he has no need of it); but I cannot help looking upon him as the chief boast and ornament of the English House of Commons. What has been said of him is, I think, strictly true, that "he was the most eloquent man of his time: his wisdom was greater than his eloquence." The only public man that in my opinion can be put in any competition with him, is Lord Chatham: and he moved in a sphere so very remote, that it is almost impossible to compare them. But though it would perhaps be difficult to determine which of them excelled most in his particular way, there is nothing in the world more easy than to point out in what their peculiar excellences consisted. They were in every respect the reverse of each other. Chatham's eloquence was popular: his wisdom was altogether plain and practical. Burke's eloquence was that of the poet; of the man of high and unbounded fancy: his wisdom was profound and contemplative. Chatham's eloquence was calculated to make men *act;* Burke's was calculated to make them *think.* Chatham could have roused the fury of a multitude, and wielded their physical energy as he pleased: Burke's eloquence carried conviction into the mind of the retired and lonely student, opened the recesses of the human breast, and lighted up the face of nature around him. Chatham supplied his hearers with motives to immediate action: Burke furnished them with *reasons* for action which might have little effect upon them at the time, but for which they would be the wiser and better all their lives after. In research, in originality, in variety of knowledge, in richness of invention, in depth and comprehension of mind, Burke had as much the advantage of Lord Chatham as he was excelled by him in plain common sense, in strong feeling, in steadiness of purpose, in vehemence, in warmth, in enthusiasm, and energy of mind. Burke was the man of genius, of fine sense, and subtle reasoning; Chatham was a man of clear understanding, of strong sense, and violent passions. Burke's mind was satisfied with speculation: Chatham's was essentially *active:* it could not rest without an object. The power which governed Burke's mind was his Imagination; that which gave its *impetus* to Chatham's was Will. The one was almost the creature of pure intellect, the other of physical temperament.

There are two very different ends which a man of genius may propose to himself either in writing or speaking, and which will accordingly give birth to very different styles. He can have but one of these two objects; either to enrich or strengthen the mind; either to furnish us with new ideas, to lead the mind into new trains of thought, to which it was before unused, and which it was incapable of striking out for itself; or else to collect and embody what we already knew, to rivet our old impressions more deeply; to make what was before plain still plainer, and to give to that which was familiar all the effect of novelty. In the one case we receive an accession to the stock of our ideas; in the other, an additional degree of life and energy is infused into them: our thoughts continue to flow in the same channels, but their pulse is quickened and invigorated. I do not know how to distinguish these different styles better than by calling them severally the inventive and refined, or the impressive and vigorous styles. It is only the subject-matter of eloquence, however, which is allowed to be remote or obscure. The things in themselves may be subtle and recondite, but they must be dragged out of their obscurity and brought struggling to the light; they must be rendered plain and palpable, (as far as it is in the wit of man to do so) or they are no longer eloquence. That which by its natural impenetrability, and in spite of every effort, remains dark and difficult, which is impervious to every ray, on which the imagination can shed no lustre, which can be clothed with no beauty, is not a subject for the orator or poet. At the same time it cannot be expected that abstract truths or profound observations should ever be placed in the same strong and dazzling points of view as natural objects and mere matters of fact. It is enough if they receive a reflex and borrowed lustre, like that which cheers the first dawn of morning, where the effect of surprise and novelty gilds every object, and the joy of beholding another world gradually emerging out of the gloom of night, "a new creation rescued from his reign," fills the mind with a sober rapture. Philosophical eloquence is in writing what *chiaro scuro* is in painting; he would be a fool who should object that the colours in the shaded part of a picture were not so bright as those on the opposite side; the eye of the connoisseur receives an equal delight from both, balancing the want of brilliancy and effect with the greater delicacy of the tints, and difficulty of the execution. In judging of Burke, therefore, we are to consider first the style of eloquence which he adopted, and secondly the effects which he produced with it. If he did not produce the same effects on vulgar minds, as some others have done, it was not for want of power, but from the turn and direction of his mind.* It was because his subjects, his ideas, his arguments, were less vulgar. The question is not whether he brought certain truths equally home to us, but how much nearer he brought them than they were before. In my opinion, he united the two extremes of refinement and strength in a higher degree than any other writer whatever.

The subtlety of his mind was undoubtedly that which rendered Burke a less popular writer and speaker than he otherwise would have been. It weakened the impression of his observations upon others, but I cannot admit that it weakened the observations themselves; that it took any thing from their real weight and solidity. Coarse minds think all that is subtle, futile: that because it is not gross and obvious and palpable to the senses, it is therefore light and frivolous, and of no importance in the real affairs of life; thus making their own confined understandings the measure of truth, and supposing that whatever they do not distinctly perceive, is nothing. Seneca, who was not one of the

* For instance: he produced less effect on the mob that compose the English House of Commons than Chatham or Fox, or even Pitt.

vulgar, also says, that subtle truths are those which have the least substance in them, and consequently approach nearest to non-entity. But for my own part I cannot help thinking that the most important truths must be the most refined and subtle; for that very reason, that they must comprehend a great number of particulars, and instead of referring to any distinct or positive fact, must point out the combined effects of an extensive chain of causes, operating gradually, remotely, and collectively, and therefore imperceptibly. General principles are not the less true or important because from their nature they elude immediate observation; they are like the air, which is not the less necessary because we neither see nor feel it, or like that secret influence which binds the world together, and holds the planets in their orbits. The very same persons who are the most forward to laugh at all systematic reasoning as idle and impertinent, you will the next moment hear exclaiming bitterly against the baleful effects of new-fangled systems of philosophy, or gravely descanting on the immense importance of instilling sound principles of morality into the mind. It would not be a bold conjecture, but an obvious truism to say, that all the great changes which have been brought about in the moral world, either for the better or worse, have been introduced not by the bare statement of facts, which are things already known, and which must always operate nearly in the same manner, but by the development of certain opinions and abstract principles of reasoning on life and manners, on the origin of society and man's nature in general, which being obscure and uncertain, vary from time to time, and produce correspondent changes in the human mind. They are the wholesome dew and rain, or the mildew and pestilence that silently destroy. To this principle of generalization all religious creeds, the institutions of wise lawgivers, and the systems of philosophers, owe their influence.

It has always been with me a test of the sense and candour of any one belonging to the opposite party, whether he allowed Burke to be a great man. Of all the persons of this description that I have ever known, I never met with above one or two who would make this concession; whether it was that party feelings ran too high to admit of any real candour, or whether it was owing to an essential vulgarity in their habits of thinking, they all seemed to be of opinion that he was a wild enthusiast, or a hollow sophist, who was to be answered by bits of facts, by smart logic, by shrewd questions, and idle songs. They looked upon him as a man of disordered intellects, because he reasoned in a style to which they had not been used and which confounded their dim perceptions. If you said that though you differed with him in sentiment, yet you thought him an admirable reasoner, and a close observer of human nature, you were answered with a loud laugh, and some hackneyed quotation. "Alas! Leviathan was not so tamed!" They did not know whom they had to contend with. The corner stone, which the builders rejected, became the head-corner, though to the Jews a stumbling block, and to the Greeks foolishness; for indeed I cannot discover that he was much better understood by those of his own party, if we may judge from the little affinity there is between his mode of reasoning and theirs.—The simple clue to all his reasonings on politics is, I think, as follows. He did not agree with some writers, that that mode of government is necessarily the best which is the cheapest. He saw in the construction of society other principles at work, and other capacities of fulfilling the desires, and perfecting the nature of man, besides those of securing the equal enjoyment of the means of animal life, and doing this at as little expense as possible. He thought that the wants and happiness of men were not to be provided for, as we provide for those of a herd of cattle, merely by attending to their physical necessities. He thought more nobly of his fellows. He knew that man had affections and passions and powers of imagination, as well as hunger and thirst and the sense of heat and cold. He took his idea of political society from the pattern of private life, wishing, as he himself expresses it, to incorporate the domestic charities with the orders of the state, and to blend them together. He strove to establish an analogy between the compact that binds together the community at large, and that which binds together the several families that compose it. He knew that the rules that form the basis of private morality are not founded in reason, that is, in the abstract properties of those things which are the subjects of them, but in the nature of man, and his capacity of being affected by certain things from habit, from imagination, and sentiment, as well as from reason

Thus, the reason why a man ought to be attached to his wife and children is not, surely, that they are better than others, (for in this case every one else ought to be of the same opinion) but because he must be chiefly interested in those things which are nearest to him, and with which he is best acquainted, since his understanding cannot reach equally to every thing; because he must be most attached to those objects which he has known the longest, and which by their situation have actually affected him the most, not those which in themselves are the most affecting, whether they have ever made any impression on him or no; that is, because he is by his nature the creature of habit and feeling, and because it is reasonable that he should act in conformity to his nature. Burke was so far right in saying that it is no objection to an institution, that it is founded in *prejudice*, but the contrary, if that prejudice is natural and right; that is, if it arises from those circumstances which are properly subjects of feeling and association, not from any defect or perversion of the understanding in those things which fall strictly under its jurisdiction. On this profound maxim he took his stand. Thus he contended, that the prejudice in favour of nobility was natural and proper, and fit to be encouraged by the positive institutions of society; not on account of the real or personal merit of the individuals, but because such an institution has a tendency to enlarge and raise the mind, to keep alive the memory of past greatness, to connect the different ages of the world together, to carry back the imagination over a long tract of time, and feed it with the contemplation of remote events: because it is natural to think highly of that which inspires us with high thoughts, which has been connected for many generations with splendour, and affluence, and dignity, and power, and privilege. He also conceived, that by transferring the respect from the person to the thing, and thus rendering it steady and permanent, the mind would be habitually formed to sentiments of deference, attachment, and fealty, to whatever else demanded its respect: that it would be led to fix its view on what was elevated and lofty, and be weaned from that low and narrow jealousy which never willingly or heartily admits of any superiority in others, and is glad of every opportunity to bring down all excellence to a level with its own miserable standard. Nobility did not therefore exist to the prejudice of the other orders of the state, but by, and for them. The inequality of the different orders of society did not destroy the unity and harmony of the whole. The health and well-being of the moral world was to be promoted by the same means as the beauty of the natural world; by contrast, by change, by light and shade, by variety of parts, by order and proportion. To think of reducing all mankind to the same insipid level, seemed to him the same absurdity as to destroy the inequalities of surface in a country, for the benefit of agriculture and commerce. In short, he believed that the interests of men in society should be consulted, and their several stations and employments assigned, with a view to their nature, not as physical, but as moral beings, so as to nourish their hopes, to lift their imagination, to enliven their fancy, to rouse their activity, to strengthen their virtue, and to furnish the greatest number of objects of pursuit and means of enjoyment to beings constituted as man is, consistently with the order and stability of the whole.

The same reasoning might be extended farther. I do not say that his arguments are conclusive: but they are profound and *true*, as far as they go. There may be disadvantages and abuses necessarily interwoven with his scheme, or opposite advantages of infinitely greater value, to be derived from another order of things and state of society. This however does not invalidate either the truth or importance of Burke's reasoning; since the advantages he points out as connected with the mixed form of government are really and necessarily inherent in it: since they are compatible in the same degree with no other; since the principle itself on which he rests his argument (whatever we may think of the application) is of the utmost weight and moment; and since on whichever side the truth lies, it is impossible to make a fair decision without having the opposite side of the question clearly and fully stated to us. This Burke has done in a masterly manner. He presents to you one view or face of society. Let him, who thinks he can, give the reverse side with equal force, beauty, and clearness. It is said, I know, that truth is *one*; but to this I cannot subscribe, for it appears to me that truth is *many*. There are as many truths as there are things and causes of action and contradictory principles at work in society. In making up the account of good and evil, indeed, the final result must be one way or the other; but the particulars on which that result depends are infinite and various.

It will be seen from what I have said, that I am very far from agreeing with those who think that Burke was a man without understanding, and a merely florid writer. There are two causes which have given rise to this calumny; namely, that narrowness of mind which leads men to suppose that the truth lies entirely on the side of their own opinions, and that whatever does not make for them is absurd and irrational; secondly, a trick we have of confounding reason with judgment, and supposing that it is merely the province of the understanding to pronounce sentence, and not to give in evidence, or argue the case; in short, that it is a passive, not an active faculty. Thus there are persons who never run into any extravagance, because they are so buttressed up with the opinions of others on all sides, that they cannot lean much to one side or the other; they are so little moved with any kind of reasoning, that they remain at an equal distance from every extreme, and are never very far from the truth, because the slowness of their faculties will not suffer them to make much progress in error. These are persons of great judgment. The scales of the mind are pretty sure to remain even, when there is nothing in them. In this sense of the word, Burke must be allowed to have wanted judgment, by all those who think that he was wrong in his conclusions. The accusation of want of judgment, in fact, only means that you yourself are of a different opinion. But if in arriving at one error he discovered a hundred truths, I should consider myself a hundred times more indebted to him than if, stumbling on that which I consider as the right side of the question, he had committed a hundred absurdities in striving to establish his point. I speak of him now merely as an author, or as far as I and other readers are concerned with him; at the same time, I should not differ from any one who may be disposed to contend that the consequences of his writings as instruments of political power have been tremendous, fatal, such as no exertion of wit or knowledge or genius can ever counteract or atone for.

Burke also gave a hold to his antagonists by mixing up sentiment and imagery with his reasoning; so that being unused to such a sight in the region of politics, they were deceived, and could not discern the fruit from the flowers. Gravity is the cloke of wisdom; and those who have nothing else think it an insult to affect the one without the other, because it destroys the only foundation on which their pretensions are built. The easiest part of reason is dulness; the generality of the world are therefore concerned in discouraging any example of unnecessary brilliancy that might tend to shew that the two things do not always go together. Burke in some measure dissolved the spell. It was discovered, that his gold was not the less valuable for being wrought into elegant shapes, and richly embossed with curious figures; that the solidity of a building is not destroyed by adding to it beauty and ornament; and that the strength of a man's understanding is not always to be estimated in exact proportion to his want of imagination. His understanding was not the less real, because it was not the only faculty he possessed. He justified the description of the poet,—

> "How charming is divine philosophy!
> Not harsh and crabbed as dull fools suppose,
> But musical as is Apollo's lute!"

Those who object to this union of grace and beauty with reason, are in fact weak-sighted people, who cannot distinguish the noble and majestic form of Truth from that of her sister Folly, if they are dressed both alike! But there is always a difference even in the adventitious ornaments they wear, which is sufficient to distinguish them.

Burke was so far from being a gaudy or flowery writer, that he was one of the severest writers we have. His words are the most like things; his style is the most strictly suited to the subject. He unites every extreme and every variety of composition; the lowest and the meanest words and descriptions with the highest. He exults in the display of power, in shewing the extent, the force, and intensity of his ideas; he is led on by the mere impulse and vehemence of his fancy, not by the affectation of dazzling his readers by gaudy conceits or pompous images. He was completely carried away by his subject. He had no other object but to produce the strongest impression on his reader, by giving the truest, the most characteristic, the fullest, and most forcible description of things, trusting to the power of his own mind to mould them into grace and beauty. He did not produce a splendid effect by setting fire to the light vapours that float in the regions of fancy, as the chemists make fine colours with phosphorus, but by the eagerness of his blows struck fire from the flint, and melted the hardest substances in the furnace of his imagination. The wheels of his imagination did not catch fire from the rottenness of the materials, but from the rapidity of their motion. One would suppose, to hear people talk of Burke, that his style was such as would have suited the "Lady's Magazine;" soft, smooth, showy, tender, insipid, full of fine words, without any meaning. The essence of the gaudy or glittering style consists in producing a momentary effect by fine words and images brought together, without order or connexion. Burke most frequently produced an effect by the remoteness and novelty of his combinations, by the force of contrast, by the striking manner in which the most opposite and unpromising materials were harmoniously blended together; not by laying his hands on all the fine things he could think of, but by bringing together those things which he knew would blaze out into glorious light by their collision. The florid style is a mixture of affectation and common-place. Burke's was an union of untameable vigour and originality.

Burke was not a verbose writer. If he sometimes multiplies words, it is not for want of ideas, but because there are no words that fully express his ideas, and he tries to do it as well as he can by different ones. He had nothing of the *set* or formal style, the measured cadence, and stately phraseology of Johnson, and most of our modern writers. This style, which is what we understand by the *artificial*, is all in one key. It selects a certain set of words to represent all ideas whatever, as the most dignified and elegant, and excludes all others as low and vulgar. The words are not fitted to the things, but the things to the words. Every thing is seen through a false medium. It is putting a mask on the face of nature, which may indeed hide some specks and blemishes, but takes away all beauty, delicacy, and variety. It destroys all dignity or elevation, because nothing can be raised where all is on a level, and completely destroys all force, expression, truth, and character, by arbitrarily confounding the differences of things, and reducing every thing to the same insipid standard. To suppose that this stiff uniformity can add any thing to real grace or dignity, is like supposing that the human body in order to be perfectly graceful, should never deviate from its upright posture. Another mischief of this method is, that it confounds all ranks in literature. Where there is no room for variety, no discrimination, no nicety to be shewn in matching the idea with its proper word, there can be no room for taste or elegance. A man must easily learn the art of writing, when every sentence is to be cast in the same mould: where he is only allowed the use of one word, he cannot choose wrong, nor will he be in much danger of making himself ridiculous by affectation or false glitter, when, whatever subject he treats of, he must treat of it in the same way. This indeed is to wear golden chains for the sake of ornament.

Burke was altogether free from the pedantry which I have here endeavoured to expose. His style was as original, as expressive, as rich and varied, as it was possible; his combinations were as exquisite, as playful, as happy, as unexpected, as bold and daring, as his fancy. If any thing, he ran into the opposite extreme of too great an inequality, if truth and nature could ever be carried to an extreme.

Those who are best acquainted with the writings and speeches of Burke will not think the praise I have here bestowed on them exaggerated. Some proof will be found of this in the following extracts. But the full proof must be sought in his works at large, and particularly in the "Thoughts on the Discontents;" in his "Reflections on the French Revolution;" in his "Letter to the Duke of Bedford;" and in the "Regicide Peace." The two last of these are perhaps the most remarkable of all his writings, from the contrast they afford to each other. The one is the most delightful exhibition of wild and brilliant fancy, that is to be found in English prose, but it is too much like a beautiful picture painted upon gauze; it wants something to support it: the other is without ornament, but it has all the solidity, the weight, the gravity of a judicial record. It seems to have been written with a certain constraint upon himself, and to shew those who said he could not *reason,* that his arguments might be stripped of their ornaments without losing any thing of their force. It is certainly, of all his works, that in which he has shewn most power of logical deduction, and the only one in which he has made any important use of facts. In general he certainly paid little attention to them: they were the playthings of his mind. He saw them as he pleased, not as they were; with the eye of the philosopher or the poet, regarding them only in their general principle, or as they might serve to decorate his subject. This is the natural consequence of much imagination: things that are probable are elevated into the rank of realities. To those who can reason on the essences of things, or who can invent according to nature, the experimental proof is of little value. This was the case with Burke. In the present instance, however, he seems to have forced his mind into the service of facts: and he succeeded completely. His comparison between our connexion with France or Algiers, and his account of the conduct of the war, are as clear, as convincing, as forcible examples of this kind of reasoning, as are any where to be met with. Indeed I do not think there is any thing in Fox, (whose mind was purely historical) or in Chatham, (who attended to feelings more than facts) that will bear a comparison with them.

Burke has been compared to Cicero—I do not know for what reason. Their excellences are as different, and indeed as opposite, as they well can be. Burke had not the polished elegance; the glossy neatness, the artful regularity, the exquisite modulation of Cicero: he had a thousand times more richness and originality of mind, more strength and pomp of diction.

It has been well observed, that the ancients had no word that properly expresses what we mean by the word *genius*. They perhaps had not the thing. Their minds appear to have been too exact, too retentive, too minute and subtle, too sensible to the external differences of things, too passive under their impressions, to admit of those bold and rapid combinations, those lofty flights of fancy, which, glancing from heaven to earth, unite the most opposite extremes, and draw the happiest illustrations from things the most remote. Their ideas were kept too confined and distinct by the material form or vehicle in which they were conveyed, to unite cordially together, or be melted down in the imagination. Their metaphors are taken from things of the same class, not from things of different classes; the general analogy, not the individual feeling, directs them in their choice. Hence, as Dr. Johnson observed, their similes are either repetitions of the same idea, or so obvious and general as not to lend any additional force to it; as when a huntress is compared to Diana, or a warrior rushing into battle to a lion rushing on his prey. Their *forte* was exquisite art and perfect imitation. Witness their statues and other things of the same kind. But they had not that high and enthusiastic fancy which some of our own writers have shewn. For the proof of this, let any one compare Milton and Shakspeare with Homer and Sophocles, or Burke with Cicero.

It may be asked whether Burke was a poet. He was so only in the general vividness of his fancy, and in richness of invention. There may be poetical passages in his works, but I certainly think that his writings in general are quite distinct from poetry; and that for the reason before given, namely, that the subject-matter of them is not poetical. The finest parts of them are illustrations or personifications of dry abstract ideas;* and the union between the idea and the illustration is not of that perfect and pleasing kind as to constitute poetry, or indeed to be admissible, but for the effect intended to be produced by it; that is, by every means in our power to give animation and attraction to subjects in themselves barren of ornament, but which at the same time are pregnant with the most important consequences, and in which the understanding and the passions are equally interested.

I have heard it remarked by a person, to whose opinion I would sooner submit than to a general council of critics, that the sound of Burke's prose is not musical; that it wants cadence; and that instead of being so lavish of his imagery as is generally supposed, he seemed to him to be rather parsimonious in the use of it, always expanding and making the most of his ideas. This may be true if we compare him with some of our poets, or perhaps with some of our early prose writers, but not if we compare him with any of our political writers or parliamentary speakers.

* As in the comparison of the British Constitution to the "proud keep of Windsor," &c. the most splendid passage in his works.

There are some very fine things of Lord Bolingbroke's on the same subjects, but not equal to Burke's. As for Junius, he is at the head of his class; but that class is not the highest. He has been said to have more dignity than Burke. Yes—if the stalk of a giant is less dignified than the strut of a *petit-maître.* I do not mean to speak disrespectfully of Junius, but grandeur is not the character of his composition; and if it is not to be found in Burke, it is to be found nowhere.

CHARACTER OF MR. FOX, 1807.*

I SHALL begin with observing generally, that Mr. Fox excelled all his contemporaries in the extent of his knowledge, in the clearness and distinctness of his views, in quickness of apprehension, in plain, practical common sense, in the full, strong, and absolute possession of his subject. A measure was no sooner proposed than he seemed to have an instantaneous and intuitive perception of its various bearings and consequences; of the manner in which it would operate on the different classes of society, on commerce or agriculture, on our domestic or foreign policy; of the difficulties attending its execution; in a word, of all its practical results, and the comparative advantages to be gained either by adopting or rejecting it. He was intimately acquainted with the interests of the different parts of the community, with the minute and complicated details of political economy, with our external relations, with the views, the resources, and the maxims of other states. He was master of all those facts and circumstances which it was necessary to know in order to judge fairly and determine wisely; and he knew them not loosely or lightly, but in number, weight, and measure. He had also

* If I had to write a character of Mr. Fox at present, the praise here bestowed on him would be "craftily qualified." His life was deficient in the three principal points, the beginning, the middle, and the end. He began a violent Tory, and became a flaming patriot out of private picque; he afterwards coalesced with Lord North, and died an accomplice with Lord Grenville. But—*what I have written, I have written.* So let it pass.

stored his memory by reading and general study, and improved his understanding by the lamp of history. He was well acquainted with the opinions and sentiments of the best authors, with the maxims of the most profound politicians, with the causes of the rise and fall of states, with the general passions of men, with the characters of different nations, and the laws and constitution of his own country. He was a man of a large, capacious, powerful, and highly cultivated intellect. No man could know more than he knew; no man's knowledge could be more sound, more plain and useful; no man's knowledge could lie in more connected and tangible masses; no man could be more perfectly master of his ideas, could reason upon them more closely, or decide upon them more impartially. His mind was full, even to overflowing. He was so habitually conversant with the most intricate and comprehensive trains of thought, or such was the natural vigour and exuberance of his mind, that he seemed to recal them without any effort. His ideas quarrelled for utterance. So far from ever being at a loss for them, he was obliged rather to repress and rein them in, lest they should overwhelm and confound, instead of informing the understandings of his hearers.

If to this we add the ardour and natural impetuosity of his mind, his quick sensibility, his eagerness in the defence of truth, and his impatience of every thing that looked like trick or artifice or affectation, we shall be able in some measure to account for the character of his eloquence. His thoughts came crowding in too fast for the slow and mechanical process of speech. What he saw in an instant, he could only express imperfectly, word by word, and sentence after sentence. He would, if he could, "have bared his swelling heart," and laid open at once the rich treasures of knowledge with which his bosom was fraught. It is no wonder that this difference between the rapidity of his feelings, and the formal round-about method of communicating them, should produce some disorder in his frame; that the throng of his ideas should try to overleap the narrow boundaries which confined them, and tumultuously break down their prison-doors, instead of waiting to be let out one by one, and following patiently at due intervals and with mock dignity, like poor dependents, in the train of words:—that he should express himself in hurried sentences, in involuntary exclamations, by vehement gestures, by sudden starts and bursts of passion. Every thing shewed the agitation of his mind. His tongue faltered, his voice became almost suffocated, and his face was bathed in tears. He was lost in the magnitude of his subject. He reeled and staggered under the load of feeling which oppressed him. He rolled like the sea beaten by a tempest.* Whoever, having the feelings of a man, compared him at these times with his boasted rival,—his stiff, straight, upright figure, his gradual contortions, turning round as if moved by a pivot, his solemn pauses, his deep tones, "whose sound reverbed their own hollowness," must have said, This is a man; that is an automaton. If Fox had needed grace, he would have had it; but it was not the character of his mind, nor would it have suited with the style of his eloquence. It was Pitt's object to smooth over the abruptness and intricacies of his argument by the gracefulness of his manner, and to fix the attention of his hearers on the pomp and sound of his words. Lord Chatham, again, strove to *command* others; he did not try to convince them, but to overpower their understandings by the greater strength and vehemence of his own; to awe them by a sense of personal superiority: and he therefore was obliged to assume a lofty and dignified manner. It was to him they bowed, not to truth; and whatever related to *himself*, must therefore have a tendency to inspire respect and admiration. Indeed, he would never have attempted to gain that ascendant over men's minds that he did, if either his mind or body had been different from what they were; if his temper had not urged him to control and command others, or if his personal advantages had not enabled him to secure that kind of authority which he coveted. But it would have been ridiculous in Fox to have affected either the

* See an excellent character of Fox by a celebrated and admirable writer, which appeared in the *Morning Chronicle*, November, 1806, from which this passage is taken as nearly as I could recollect it.

smooth plausibility, the stately gravity of the one, or the proud, domineering, imposing dignity of the other; or even if he could have succeeded, it would only have injured the effect of his speeches.* What he had to rely on was the strength, the solidity of his ideas, his complete and thorough knowledge of his subject. It was his business therefore to fix the attention of his hearers, not on himself, but on his subject; to rivet it there, to hurry it on from words to things:—the only circumstance of which they required to be convinced with respect to himself, was the sincerity of his opinions; and this would be best done by the earnestness of his manner, by giving a loose to his feelings, and by shewing the most perfect forgetfulness of himself, and of what others thought of him. The moment a man shews you either by affected words or looks or gestures, that he is thinking of himself, and you, that he is trying either to please or terrify you into compliance, there is an end at once to that kind of eloquence which owes its effect to the force of truth, and to your confidence in the sincerity of the speaker. It was, however, to the confidence inspired by the earnestness and simplicity of his manner, that Mr. Fox was indebted for more than half the effect of his speeches. Some others (as Lord Lansdown for instance) might possess nearly as much information, as exact a knowledge of the situation and interests of the country; but they wanted that zeal, that animation, that enthusiasm, that deep sense of the importance of the subject, which removes all doubt or suspicion from the minds of the hearers and communicates its own warmth to every breast. We may convince by argument alone; but it is by the interest we discover in the success of our reasonings, that we persuade others to feel and act with us. There are two circumstances which Fox's

* There is an admirable, judicious, and truly useful remark in the preface to Spenser, (not by Dr. Johnson, for he left Spenser out of his poets, but by *one* Upton,) that the question was not whether a better poem might not have been written on a different plan, but whether Spenser would have written a better one on a different plan. I wish to apply this to Fox's *ungainly* manner. I do not mean to say, that his manner was the best possible, (for that would be to say that he was the greatest man conceivable,) but that it was the best for him.

speeches and Lord Chatham's had in common: they are alike distinguished by a kind of plain downright common sense, and by the vehemence of their manner. But still there is a great difference between them, in both these respects. Fox in his opinions was governed by facts—Chatham was more influenced by the feelings of others respecting those facts. Fox endeavoured to find out what the consequences of any measure would be; Chatham attended more to what people would think of it. Fox appealed to the practical reason of mankind; Chatham to popular prejudice. The one repelled the encroachments of power by supplying his hearers with arguments against it; the other by rousing their passions and arming their resentment against those who would rob them of their birthright. Their vehemence and impetuosity arose also from very different feelings. In Chatham it was pride, passion, self-will, impatience of control, a determination to have his own way, to carry every thing before him;* in Fox it was pure good nature, a sincere love of truth, an ardent attachment to what he conceived to be right; an anxious concern for the welfare and liberties of mankind. Or if we suppose that ambition had taken a strong hold of both their minds, yet their ambition was of a very different kind: in the one it was the love of power, in the other it was the love of fame. Nothing can be more opposite than these two principles, both in their origin and tendency. The one originates in a selfish, haughty, domineering spirit; the other in a social and generous sensibility, desirous of the love and esteem of others, and anxiously bent upon gaining merited applause. The one grasps at immediate power by any means within its reach; the other, if it does not square its actions by the rules of virtue, at least refers them to a standard which comes the nearest to it—the disinterested applause of our country, and the enlightened judgment of posterity. The love of

* This may seem to contradict what I have before said of Chatham—that he spoke like a man who was discharging a duty, &c. but I there spoke of the tone he assumed, or his immediate feelings at the time, rather than of the real motives by which he was actuated.

fame is consistent with the steadiest attachment to principle, and indeed strengthens and supports it; whereas the love of power, where this is the ruling passion, requires the sacrifice of principle at every turn, and is inconsistent even with the shadow of it. I do not mean to say that Fox had no love of power, or Chatham no love of fame, (this would be reversing all we know of human nature,) but that the one principle predominated in the one, and the other in the other. My reader will do me great injustice if he supposes that in attempting to describe the characters of different speakers by contrasting their general qualities, I mean any thing beyond the *more* or *less*: but it is necessary to describe those qualities simply and in the abstract, in order to make the distinction intelligible. Chatham resented any attack made upon the cause of liberty, of which he was the avowed champion, as an indignity offered to himself. Fox felt it as a stain upon the honour of his country, and as an injury to the rights of his fellow citizens. The one was swayed by his own passions and purposes, with very little regard to the consequences; the sensibility of the other was roused, and his passions kindled into a generous flame, by a real interest in whatever related to the welfare of mankind, and by an intense and earnest contemplation of the consequences of the measures he opposed. It was this union of the zeal of the patriot with the enlightened knowledge of the statesman, that gave to the eloquence of Fox its more than mortal energy; that warmed, expanded, penetrated every bosom. He relied on the force of truth and nature alone; the refinements of philosophy, the pomp and pageantry of the imagination were forgotten, or seemed light and frivolous; the fate of nations, the welfare of millions, hung suspended as he spoke; a torrent of manly eloquence poured from his heart, bore down every thing in its course, and surprised into a momentary sense of human feeling the breathing corpses, the wire-moved puppets, the stuffed figures, the flexible machinery, the "deaf and dumb things" of a court.

I find (I do not know how the reader feels) that it is difficult *to write* a character of Fox without running into insipidity or extravagance. And the reason of this is, there are no splendid contrasts, no striking irregularities, no curious distinctions to work upon; no "jutting frieze, buttress, nor coigne of 'vantage," for the imagination to take hold of. It was a plain marble slab, inscribed in plain legible characters, without either hieroglyphics or carving. There was the same directness and manly simplicity in every thing that he did. The whole of his character may indeed be summed up in two words—strength and simplicity. Fox was in the class of common men, but he was the first in that class. Though it is easy to describe the differences of things, nothing is more difficult than to describe their degrees or quantities. In what I am going to say, I hope I shall not be suspected of a design to under-rate his powers of mind, when in fact I am only trying to ascertain their nature and direction. The degree and extent to which he possessed them can only be known by reading, or indeed by having heard his speeches.

His mind, as I have already said, was, I conceive, purely *historical:* and having said this, I have I believe said all. But perhaps it will be necessary to explain a little farther what I mean. I mean, then, that his memory was in an extraordinary degree tenacious of facts; that they were crowded together in his mind without the least perplexity or confusion; that there was no chain of consequences too vast for his powers of comprehension; that the different parts and ramifications of his subject were never so involved and intricate but that they were easily disentangled in the clear prism of his understanding. The basis of his wisdom was experience: however, he not only knew what had happened; but by an exact knowledge of the real state of things, he could always tell what in the common course of events would happen in future. The force of his mind was exerted upon facts: as long as he could lean directly upon these, as long as he had the actual objects to refer to, to steady himself by, he could analyse, he could combine, he could compare and reason upon them, with the utmost exactness; but he could not reason *out of* them. He was what is understood by a *matter-of-fact* reasoner. He was better acquainted with the concrete masses of things, their substantial forms, and practical connexions, than with their abstract nature or general definitions. He was a man of extensive information, of sound knowledge, and clear understanding, rather than the acute observer or profound thinker. He was the man of business, the accomplished statesman, rather than the philosopher. His reasonings were, generally speaking, calculations of certain positive results, which, the *data* being given, must follow as matters of course, rather than unexpected and remote truths drawn from a deep insight into human nature, and the subtle application of general principles to particular cases. They consisted chiefly in the detail and combination of a vast number of items in an account, worked by the known rules of political arithmetic; not in the discovery of bold, comprehensive, and original theorems in the science. They were rather acts of memory, of continued attention, of a power of bringing all his ideas to bear at once upon a single point, than of reason or invention. He was the attentive observer who watches the various effects and successive movements of a machine already constructed, and can tell how to manage it while it goes on as it has always done; but who knows little or nothing of the principles on which it is constructed, nor how to set it right, if it becomes disordered, except by the most common and obvious expedients. Burke was to Fox what the geometrician is to the mechanic. Much has been said of the "prophetic mind" of Mr. Fox. The same epithet has been applied to Mr. Burke, till it has become proverbial. It has, I think, been applied without much reason to either. Fox wanted the scientific part, Burke wanted the practical. Fox had too little imagination, Burke had too much: that is, he was careless of facts, and was led away by his passions to look at one side of a question only. He had not that fine sensibility to outward impressions, that nice *tact* of circumstances, which is necessary to the consummate politician. Indeed, his wisdom was more that of the legislator than of the active statesman. They both *tried* their strength in the Ulysses' bow of politicians, the French

Revolution: and they were both foiled. Fox indeed foretold the success of the French in combating with foreign powers. But this was no more than what every friend of the liberty of France foresaw or foretold as well as he. All those on the same side of the question were inspired with the same sagacity on the subject. Burke, on the other hand, seems to have been before-hand with the public in foreboding the internal disorders that would attend the Revolution, and its ultimate failure; but then it is at least a question whether he did not make good his own predictions: and certainly he saw into the causes and connexion of events much more clearly after they had happened than before. He was however undoubtedly a profound commentator on that apocalyptical chapter in the history of human nature, which I do not think Fox was. Whether led to it by the events or not, he saw thoroughly into the principles that operated to produce them; and he pointed them out to others in a manner which could not be mistaken. I can conceive of Burke, as the genius of the storm, perched over Paris, the centre and focus of anarchy, (so he would have us believe) hovering "with mighty wings outspread over the abyss, and rendering it pregnant," watching the passions of men gradually unfolding themselves in new situations, penetrating those hidden motives which hurried them from one extreme into another, arranging and analysing the principles that alternately pervaded the vast chaotic mass, and extracting the elements of order and the cement of social life from the decomposition of all society: while Charles Fox in the meantime dogged the heels of the Allies, (all the way calling out to them to stop) with his sutler's bag, his muster-roll, and army estimates at his back. He said, You have only fifty thousand troops, the enemy have a hundred thousand: this place is dismantled, it can make no resistance: your troops were beaten last year, they must therefore be disheartened this. This is excellent sense and sound reasoning, but I do not see what it has to do with philosophy. But why was it necessary that Fox should be a philosopher? Why, in the first place, Burke was a philosopher, and Fox, to keep up with him, must be so too. In the second place, it was necessary, in order that his indiscreet admirers, who have no idea of greatness but as it consists in certain names and pompous titles, might be able to talk big about their patron. It is a bad compliment we pay to our idol when we endeavour to make him out something different from himself; it shews that we are not satisfied with what he was. I have heard it said that he had as much imagination as Burke. To this extravagant assertion I shall make what I conceive to be a very cautious and moderate answer: that Burke was as superior to Fox in this respect as Fox perhaps was to the first person you would meet in the street. There is in fact hardly an instance of imagination to be met with in any of his speeches; what there is, is of the rhetorical kind. I may, however, be wrong. He might excel as much in profound thought, and richness of fancy, as he did in other things; though I cannot perceive it. However, when any one publishes a book called The Beauties of Fox, containing the original reflections, brilliant passages, lofty metaphors, &c. to be found in his speeches, without the detail or connexion, I shall be very ready to give the point up.

In logic Fox was inferior to Pitt—indeed, in all the formalities of eloquence, in which the latter excelled as much as he was deficient in the soul or substance. When I say that Pitt was superior to Fox in logic, I mean that he excelled him in the formal division of the subject, in always keeping it in view, as far as he chose; in being able to detect any deviation from it in others; in the management of his general topics; in being aware of the mood and figure in which the argument must move, with all its nonessentials, dilemmas, and alternatives; in never committing himself, nor ever suffering his antagonist to occupy an inch of the plainest ground, but under cover of a syllogism. He had more of "the dazzling fence of argument," as it has been called. He was, in short, better at his weapon. But then, unfortunately, it was only a dagger of lath that the wind could turn aside; whereas Fox wore a good trusty blade, of solid metal, and real execution.

I shall not trouble myself to inquire whether Fox was a man of strict virtue and principle; or in other words, how far he was one of those who screw themselves up to a certain pitch of ideal perfection, who, as it were, set themselves in the stocks of morality, and make mouths at their own situation. He was not one of that tribe, and shall not be tried by their self-denying ordinances. But he was endowed with one of the most excellent natures that ever fell to the lot of any of God's creatures. It has been said, that "an honest man's the noblest work of God." There is indeed a purity, a rectitude, an integrity of heart, a freedom from every selfish bias, and sinister motive, a manly simplicity and noble disinterestedness of feeling, which is in my opinion to be preferred before every other gift of nature or art. There is a greatness of soul that is superior to all the brilliancy of the understanding. This strength of moral character, which is not only a more valuable but a rarer quality than strength of understanding (as we are oftener led astray by the narrowness of our feelings, than want of knowledge) Fox possessed in the highest degree. He was superior to every kind of jealousy, of suspicion, of malevolence; to every narrow and sordid motive. He was perfectly above every species of duplicity, of low art and cunning. He judged of every thing in the downright sincerity of his nature, without being able to impose upon himself by any hollow disguise, or to lend his support to any thing unfair or dishonourable. He had an innate love of truth, of justice, of probity, of whatever was generous or liberal. Neither his education, nor his connexions, nor his situation in life, nor the low intrigues and virulence of party, could ever alter the simplicity of his taste, nor the candid openness of his nature. There was an elastic force about his heart, a freshness of social feeling, a warm glowing humanity, which remained unimpaired to the last. He was by nature a gentleman. By this I mean that he felt a certain deference and respect for the person of every man; he had an unaffected frankness and benignity in his behaviour to others, the utmost liberality in judging of their conduct and motives. A refined humanity constitutes the character of a gentleman.* He was the true friend of his country, as far as it is possible for a statesman to be so. But his love of his country did not consist in his hatred of the rest of mankind. I shall conclude this account by repeating what Burke said of him at a time when his testimony was of the most value. "To his great and masterly understanding he joined the utmost possible degree of moderation: he was of the most artless, candid, open, and benevolent disposition; disinterested in the extreme; of a temper mild and placable, even to a fault; and without one drop of gall in his constitution."

CHARACTER OF MR. PITT, 1806.

The character of Mr. Pitt was, perhaps, one of the most singular that ever existed. With few talents, and fewer virtues, he acquired and preserved in one of the most trying situations, and in spite of all opposition, the highest reputation for the possession of every moral excellence, and as having carried the attainments of eloquence and wisdom as far as human abilities could go. This he did (strange as it appears) by a negation (together with the common virtues) of the common vices of human nature, and by the complete negation of every other talent that might interfere with the only one which he possessed in a supreme degree, and which indeed may be made to include the appearance of all others—an artful use of words, and a certain dexterity of logical arrangement. In these alone his power consisted; and the defect of all other qualities, which usually constitute greatness, contributed to the more complete success of these. Having no strong feelings, no distinct perceptions, his mind

* To this character none of those who could be compared with him in talents had the least pretensions, as Chatham, Burke, Pitt, &c. They would *blackguard* and bully any man upon the slightest provocation, or difference of *opinion*.

having no link, as it were, to connect it with the world of external nature, every subject presented to him nothing more than a *tabula rasa*, on which he was at liberty to lay whatever colouring of language he pleased; having no general principles, no comprehensive views of things, no moral habits of thinking, no system of action, there was nothing to hinder him from pursuing any particular purpose, by any means that offered; having never any plan, he could not be convicted of inconsistency, and his own pride and obstinacy were the only rules of his conduct. Having no insight into human nature, no sympathy with the passions of men, or apprehension of their real designs, he seemed perfectly insensible to the consequences of things, and would believe nothing till it actually happened. The fog and haze in which he saw every thing communicated itself to others; and the total indistinctness and uncertainty of his own ideas tended to confound the perceptions of his hearers more effectually than the most ingenious misrepresentation could have done. Indeed, in defending his conduct he never seemed to consider himself as at all responsible for the success of his measures, or to suppose that future events were in our own power; but that as the best-laid schemes might fail, and there was no providing against all possible contingencies, this was a sufficient excuse for our plunging at once into any dangerous or absurd enterprize, without the least regard to consequences. His reserved logic confined itself solely to the *possible* and the *impossible;* and he appeared to regard the *probable* and *improbable,* the only foundation of moral prudence or political wisdom, as beneath the notice of a profound statesman; as if the pride of the human intellect were concerned in never entrusting itself with subjects, where it may be compelled to acknowledge its weakness.*

* One instance may serve as an example for all the rest:—When Mr. Fox last summer (1805) predicted the failure of the new confederacy against France, from a consideration of the circumstances and relative situation of both parties, that is, from an exact knowledge of the actual state of things, Mr. Pitt contented himself with answering—and, as in the blindness of his infatuation, he seemed to think quite satisfactorily,—" That he could not assent to the

From his manner of reasoning, he seemed not to have believed that the truth of his statements depended on the reality of the facts, but that the things depended on the order in which he arranged them in words: you would not suppose him to be agitating a serious question which had real grounds to go upon, but to be declaiming upon an imaginary thesis, proposed as an exercise in the schools. He never set himself to examine the force of the objections that were brought against his measures, or attempted to establish them upon clear, solid grounds of his own; but constantly contented himself with first gravely stating the logical form, or dilemma, to which the question reduced itself, and then, after having declared his opinion, proceeded to amuse his hearers by a series of rhetorical common places, connected together in grave, sonorous, and elaborately constructed periods, without ever shewing their real application to the subject in dispute. Thus, if any member of the Opposition disapproved of any measure, and enforced his objections by pointing out the many evils with which it was fraught, or the difficulties attending its execution, his only answer was, "that it was true there might be inconveniences attending the measure proposed, but we were to

honourable gentleman's reasoning, for that it went to this, that we were never to attempt to mend the situation of our affairs, because in so doing we might possibly make them worse." No; it was not on account of this abstract possibility in human affairs, or because we were not absolutely sure of succeeding (for that any child might know), but because it was in the highest degree probable, or *morally* certain, that the scheme would fail, and leave us in a worse situation than we were before, that Mr. Fox disapproved of the attempt. There is in this a degree of weakness and imbecility, a defect of understanding bordering on idiotism, a fundamental ignorance of the first principles of human reason and prudence, that in a great minister is utterly astonishing, and almost incredible. Nothing could ever drive him out of his dull forms, and naked generalities; which, as they are susceptible neither of degree nor variation, are therefore equally applicable to every emergency that can happen: and in the most critical aspect of affairs, he saw nothing but the same flimsy web of remote possibilities and metaphysical uncertainty. In his mind the wholesome pulp of practical wisdom and salutary advice was immediately converted into the dry chaff and husks of a miserable logic.

remember, that every expedient that could be devised might be said to be nothing more than a choice of difficulties, and that all that human prudence could do was to consider on which side the advantages lay; that for his part, he conceived that the present measure was attended with more advantages and fewer disadvantages than any other that could be adopted; that if we were diverted from our object by every appearance of difficulty, the wheels of government would be clogged by endless delays and imaginary grievances; that most of the objections made to the measure appeared to him to be trivial, others of them unfounded and improbable; or that if a scheme free from all these objections could be proposed, it might after all prove inefficient; while, in the mean time, a material object remained unprovided for, or the opportunity of action was lost." This mode of reasoning is admirably described by Hobbes, in speaking of the writings of some of the Schoolmen, of whom he says, that "they had learned the trick of imposing what they list upon their readers, and declining the force of true reason by verbal forks; that is, distinctions which signify nothing, but serve only to astonish the multitude of ignorant men." That what I have here stated comprehends the whole force of his mind, which consisted solely in this evasive dexterity and perplexing formality, assisted by a copiousness of words and common-place topics, will, I think, be evident to any one who carefully looks over his speeches, undazzled by the reputation or personal influence of the speaker. It will be in vain to look in them for any of the common proofs of human genius or wisdom. He has not left behind him a single memorable saying—not one profound maxim—one solid observation—one forcible description—one beautiful thought—one humorous picture—one affecting sentiment.* He has made

* I do remember one passage which has some meaning in it. At the time of the Regency Bill, speaking of the proposal to take the King's servants from him, he says, "What must that great personage feel when he waked from the trance of his faculties, and asked for his attendants, if he were told that his subjects had taken advantage of his momentary absence of mind, and stripped

no addition whatever to the stock of human knowledge. He did not possess any one of those faculties which contribute to the instruction and delight of mankind—depth of understanding, imagination, sensibility, wit, vivacity, clear and solid judgment. But it may be asked, If these qualities are not to be found in him, where are we to look for them? And I may be required to point out instances of them. I shall answer then, that he had none of the profound legislative wisdom, piercing sagacity, or rich, impetuous, high-wrought imagination of Burke; the manly eloquence, strong sense, exact knowledge, vehemence and natural simplicity of Fox; the ease, brilliancy, and acuteness of Sheridan. It is not merely that he had not all these qualities in the degree that they were severally possessed by his rivals, but he had not any of them in any striking degree. His reasoning is a technical arrangement of unmeaning common-places; his eloquence merely rhetorical; his style monotonous and artificial. If he could pretend to any one excellence in an eminent degree, it was to taste in composition. There is certainly nothing low, nothing puerile, nothing far-fetched or abrupt in his speeches; there is a kind of faultless regularity pervading them throughout; but in the confined, mechanical, passive mode of eloquence which he adopted, it seemed rather more difficult to commit errors than to avoid them. A man who is determined never to move out of the beaten road, cannot lose his way. However, habit, joined to the peculiar mechanical memory which he possessed, carried this correctness to a degree which, in an extemporaneous speaker, was almost miraculous; he perhaps hardly ever uttered a sentence that was not perfectly regular and connected. In this respect, he not only had the advantage over his own contemporaries, but perhaps no one that ever lived equalled him in this singular faculty. But for this, he would always have passed for a common man; and to

him of the symbols of his personal elevation." There is some grandeur in this. His admirers should have it inscribed in letters of gold; for they will not find another instance of the same kind.

this the constant sameness, and, if I may so say, vulgarity of his ideas, must have contributed not a little, as there was nothing to distract his mind from this one object of his unintermitted attention; and as even in his choice of words he never aimed at any thing more than a certain general propriety, and stately uniformity of style. His talents were exactly fitted for the situation in which he was placed; where it was his business, not to overcome others, but to avoid being overcome. He was able to baffle opposition, not from strength or firmness, but from the evasive ambiguity and impalpable nature of his resistance, which gave no hold to the rude grasp of his opponents: no force could bind the loose phantom, and his mind (though " not matchless, and his pride humbled by such rebuke,") soon rose from defeat unhurt,

> " And in its liquid texture mortal wound
> " Receiv'd no more than can the fluid air." *

* I would recommend to the reader a masterly and unanswerable essay on this subject, in the Morning Post, by Mr. Coleridge, (see following page) from which most of the above remarks are taken. See also Dr. Beddoes's Letter on the public merits of Mr. Pitt. I will only add, that it is the property of true genius, to force the admiration even of enemies. No one was ever hated or envied for his powers of mind, if others were convinced of their real excellence. The jealousy and uneasiness produced in the mind by the display of superior talents almost always arises from a suspicion that there is some trick or deception in the case, and that we are imposed on by an appearance of what is not really there. True warmth and vigour communicate warmth and vigour; and we are no longer inclined to dispute the inspiration of the oracle, when we feel the "*presens Divus*" in our own bosoms. But when, without gaining any new light or heat, we only find our ideas thrown into perplexity and confusion by an art that we cannot comprehend, this is a kind of superiority which must always be painful, and can never be cordially admitted. For this reason the extraordinary talents of Mr. Pitt were always viewed, except by those of his own party, with a sort of jealousy, and *grudgingly* acknowledged; while those of his rivals were admitted by all parties in the most unreserved manner, and carried by acclamation.

PITT AND BUONAPARTE.

From the Morning Post, March 19, 1800.

" PLUTARCH, in his comparative biography of Rome and Greece, has generally chosen for each pair of Lives the two contemporaries who most nearly resemble each other. His work would, perhaps, have been more interesting, if he had adopted the contrary arrangement, and selected those rather, who had attained to the possession of similar influence, or similar fame, by means, actions, and talents the most dissimilar. For power is the sole object of philosophical attention in man, as in inanimate nature; and in the one equally as in the other, we understand it more intimately, the more diverse the circumstances are with which we have observed it to exist. In our days, the two persons who appear to have influenced the interests and actions of men the most deeply and the most diffusively, are, beyond doubt, the Chief Consul of France, and the Prime Minister of Great Britain: and in these two, are presented to us similar situations, with the greatest dissimilitude of characters.

William Pitt was the younger son of Lord Chatham; a fact of no ordinary importance in the solution of his character, of no mean significance in the heraldry of morals and intellect. His father's rank, fame, political connexions, and parental ambition, were his mould: he was cast, rather than grew. A palpable election, a conscious predestination controlled the free agency, and transfigured the individuality of his mind, and that, which he might have been, was compelled into that, which he was to be. From his early childhood it was his father's custom to make him stand upon a chair, and declaim before a large company; by which exercise, practised so frequently, and continued for so many years, he acquired a premature and unnatural dexterity in the combination of words, which must of necessity have diverted his attention from present objects, obscured his impressions, and deadened his genuine feelings. Not the thing on which he was speaking, but the praises to be gained by the speech, were present to his intuition; hence he associated all the operations of his faculties with words, and his pleasures with the surprise excited by them. But an inconceivably large portion of human knowledge and human power is involved in the science and management of words; and an education of words, though it destroys genius, will often create and always foster, talent. The young Pitt was conspicuous far beyond his fellows, both at school and at college. He was always full-grown: he had neither the promise nor the awkwardness of a growing intellect. Vanity, early satiated, formed, and elevated itself into a love of power; and in losing this colloquial vanity, he lost one of the prime links that connect the individual with the species, too early for the affections, though not too early for the understanding. At College he was a severe student; his mind was founded and elemented in words and generalities, and these too formed all the superstructure. That revelry and that debauchery, which are so often fatal to the powers of intellect, would probably have been serviceable to him; they would have given him a closer communion with realities, they would have induced a greater presentness to present objects. But Mr. Pitt's conduct was correct, unimpressibly correct. His after-discipline in the special pleader's office, and at the Bar, carried on the scheme of his education with unbroken uniformity. His first political connexions were with the Reformers; but those who accuse him of sympathising or coalescing with their intemperate or visionary plans, misunderstand his character, and are ignorant of the historical facts. Imaginary situations in an imaginary state of things, rise up in minds that possess a power and facility in combining images. Mr. Pitt's ambition was conversant with old situations in the old state of things, which furnish nothing to the imagination, though much to the wishes. In his endeavours to realize his father's plan of reform, he was probably as sincere as a being, who had derived so little knowledge from actual impressions, could be. But his sincerity had no living root of affection: while it was propped up by his love of praise and immediate power, so long it stood erect, and no longer. He became a member of the Parliament, supported the popular opinions, and in a few years, by the influence of the popular party, was placed in that high and awful rank in which he now is. The fortunes of his country, we had almost said the fates of the world, were placed in his wardship—we sink in prostration before the inscrutable dispensations of Providence, when we reflect in whose wardship the fates of the world were placed.

The influencer of his country and of his species was a young man, the creature of another's predetermination, sheltered and weatherfended from all the elements of experience; a young man, whose feet had never wandered, whose very eye had never turned to the right or to the left, whose whole track had been as curveless as the motions of a fascinated reptile! It was a young man, whose heart was solitary, because he had existed always amid objects of futurity, and whose imagination too was unpopulous, because those objects of hope, to which his habitual wishes had transferred, and as it were, projected his existence, were all familiar and long established objects. A plant sown and reared in a hot-house, for whom the very air that surrounded him, had been regulated by the thermometer of previous purpose; to whom the light of nature had penetrated only through glasses and covers, who had had the sun without the breeze; whom no storm had shaken; on whom no rain had pattered; on whom the dews of Heaven had not fallen! A being, who had had no feelings connected with man or nature; no spontaneous impulses; no unbiassed and desultory studies; no genuine science; nothing that constitutes individuality in intellect; nothing that teaches brotherhood in affection. Such was the man, such, and so denaturalized the spirit, on whose wisdom and philanthropy the lives and living enjoyments of so many millions of human beings were made unavoidably dependent. From this time a real enlargement of mind became almost impossible. Pre-occupations, intrigue, the undue *passion* and anxiety, with which all facts must be surveyed; the crowd and confusion of these facts, none of them seen, but all communicated, and by that very circumstance, and by the necessity of perpetually classifying them, transmuted into words and generalities; pride, flattery, irritation, artificial power; these, and circumstances resembling these, necessarily render the heights of office barren heights, which command indeed a vast and extensive prospect, but attract so many clouds and vapours, that, most often, all prospect is precluded. Still, however, Mr. Pitt's situation, however inauspicious for his real being, was favourable to his fame. He heaped period on period; persuaded himself and the nation, that extemporaneous arrangement of sentences was eloquence; and that eloquence implied wisdom. His father's struggles for freedom, and his own attempts, gave him an almost unexampled popularity; and his office necessarily associated with his name all the great events, that happened during his administration. There were not, however, wanting men, who saw through the delusion: and refusing to attribute the industry, integrity, and enterprising spirit of our merchants, the agricultural improvements of our landholders, the great inventions of our manufacturers, or the valor and skilfulness of our sailors, to the merits of a Minister: they have continued to decide on his character from those acts and those merits which belong to him, and to him alone. Judging him by this standard, they have been able to discover in him no one proof or symptom of a commanding genius. They have discovered him never controlling, never creating, events, but always yielding to them with rapid change, and sheltering himself from inconsistency by perpetual indefiniteness. In the Russian War, they saw him abandoning meanly what he had planned weakly, and threatened insolently. In the debates on the Regency, they detected the laxity of his constitutional principles, and received proofs that his eloquence consisted not in the ready application of a general system to particular questions, but in the facility of arguing for or against any question by specious generalities, without reference to any system. In these debates, he combined what is most dangerous in democracy, with all that is most degrading in the old superstitions of Monarchy, and taught an inherency of the office in the person of the King, which made the office itself a nullity, and the Premiership, with its accompanying majority, the sole and permanent power of the State. And now came the French Revolution. This was a new event; the old routine of reasoning, the common trade of politics, were to become obsolete. He appeared wholly unprepared for it. Half favouring, half condemning, ignorant of what he favoured, and why he condemned; he neither displayed the honest enthusiasm and fixed principle of Mr. Fox, nor the intimate acquaintance with the general nature of man, and the consequent prescience of Mr. Burke. After the declaration of war, long did he continue in the common cant of office, in declamation about the Scheld, and Holland, and all the vulgar causes of common contests, and when at last the immense genius of his new supporter had beat him out of these words (words signifying places and dead objects, and signifying nothing more) he adopted other words in their places, other generalities—Atheism and Jacobinism, phrases, which he had learnt from Mr. Burke, but without learning the philosophical definitions and involved consequences, with which that great man accompanied those words. Since the death of Mr. Burke, the forms and the sentiments, and the tone of the French, have undergone many and important changes: how indeed is it possible, that it should be otherwise, while man is the creature of experience? But still Mr. Pitt proceeds in an endless repetition of the same general phrases. This is his element; deprive him of general and abstract phrases, and you reduce him to silence. But you cannot deprive him of them. Press him to specify an individual fact of advantage to be derived from a war, and he answers, Security. Call upon him to particularise a crime, and he exclaims, Jacobinism. Abstractions defined by abstractions—generalities defined by generalities! As a minister of France, he is still, as ever, the man of words and abstractions, figures, Custom-house reports, imports and exports, commerce and revenue all flourishing, all splendid. Never was such a prosperous country as England under his administration. *Let it be* objected, that the agriculture of the country is, by the overbalance of commerce, and by various and complex causes, in such a state, that the country hangs as a pensioner for bread on its neighbours, and a bad season uniformly threatens us with famine, this (it is replied) is owing to our prosperity—all prosperous nations are in great distress for food. Still prosperity, still general phrases, uninforced by one single image, one single fact of real national amelioration, of any one comfort enjoyed, where it was not before enjoyed, of any one class of society becoming healthier, or wiser, or happier. These are things, these are realities; and these Mr. Pitt has neither the imagination to body forth, or the sensibility to feel for. Once, indeed, in an evil hour intriguing for popularity, he suffered himself to be persuaded to evince a talent for the real, the individual: and he brought in his Poor Bill. When we hear the Minister's talents for finance so loudly trumpeted, we turn involuntarily to his Poor Bill, to that acknowledged abortion, that unanswerable evidence of his ignorance respecting all the fundamental relations and actions of property, and of the social union.

As his reasonings, even so is his eloquence. One character pervades his whole being. Words on words finely arranged, and so dexterously consequent, that the whole bears the semblance of argument, and still keeps awake a sense of surprise; but when all is done, nothing rememberable has been said; no one philosophical remark, no one image, not even a pointed aphorism. Not a sentence of Mr. Pitt's has ever been quoted, or formed the favourite phrase of the day, a thing unexampled in any man of equal reputation. But while he speaks, the effect varies according to the character of his auditor. The man of no talent is swallowed up in surprise: and when the speech is ended, he remembers his feelings, but nothing distinct of that which produced them; (how opposite an effect to that of nature and genius, from whose works the idea still remains, when the feeling is passed away, remains to connect itself with other feelings, and combine with new impressions!) The mere man of talent hears him with admiration, the mere man of genius with contempt; the philosopher neither admires nor contemns, but listens to him with a deep and solemn interest, tracing in the effects of his eloquence the power of words and phrases, and that peculiar constitution of human affairs in their present state, which so eminently favours this power.

Such appears to us to be the Prime Minister of Great Britain, whether we consider him a statesman or an orator. The same character betrays itself in his private life, the same coldness to realities, to images of realities, and to all whose excellence relates to reality.

He has patronised no science, he has raised no man of genius from obscurity; he counts no one prime work of God among his friends. From the same source he has no attachment to female society, no fondness for children, no perceptions of beauty in natural scenery; but he is fond of convivial indulgences, of that stimulation, which, keeping up the glow of self-importance and the sense of internal power, gives feelings without the mediation of ideas.

These are the elements of his mind; the accidents of his fortune, the circumstances that enabled such a mind to acquire and retain such a power, would form the subject of a philosophical history, and that too of no scanty size. We scarcely furnish the chapter of contents to a work which would comprise subjects so important and delicate, as the causes of the diffusion and intensity of secret influence, the machinery and state intrigue of marriages, the overbalance of the commercial interest; the panic of property struck by the late Revolution, the short-sightedness of the careful, the carelessness of the far-sighted; and all those many and various events which have given to a decorous profession of religion, and a seemliness of private morals, such an unwonted weight in the attainment and preservation of public power. We are unable to determine whether it be more consolatory or humiliating to human nature, that so many complexities of event, situation, character, age, and country, should be necessary in order to the production of a Mr. Pitt."

AN EXAMINATION OF MR. MALTHUS'S DOCTRINES.

1. OF THE GEOMETRICAL AND ARITHMETICAL SERIES.

WALLACE, the author of "*Various Prospects of Mankind, Nature, and Providence,*" was the first person, we believe, who applied the principle of the superior power of increase in population over the means of subsistence, as an insuperable objection to the arguments for the perfectibility of man, for which, in other respects, this author was an advocate. He has devoted a long and elaborate Essay to prove these two points:—1. That there is a natural and necessary inability in the means of subsistence to go on increasing always in the same ratio as the population, the limits of the earth necessarily limiting the actual increase of the one, and there being no limits to the tendency to increase in the other; 2. That the checks which have hitherto, and which always *must* keep population down to the level of the means of subsistence, are *vice* and *misery*; and consequently, that in a state of perfectibility, as it is called, viz. in a state of perfect wisdom, virtue, and happiness, where these indispensable checks to population, vice and misery, were entirely removed, population would go on increasing to an alarming and most excessive degree, and unavoidably end in the utmost disorder, confusion, vice and misery.—(See *Various Prospects, &c.* p. 113-123.)

The principle laid down by this author, that population could not go on for ever increasing at its natural rate, or free from every restraint, either moral or physical, without ultimately outstripping the utmost possible increase of the means of subsistence, we hold to be unquestionable, if not self-evident: the other principle assumed by the original author, viz. that vice and misery are the only possible checks to population, we hold to be false as a matter of fact, and peculiarly absurd and contradictory, when applied to that state of society contemplated by the author, that is to say, one in which abstract reason and pure virtue, or a regard to the general good, should have got the better of every animal instinct and selfish passion. Of this, perhaps, a word hereafter. But be this as it may, both the principle of the necessary increase of the population beyond the means of subsistence, and the application of that principle as a final obstacle to all Utopian perfectibility schemes, are borrowed (whole) by Mr. Malthus from Wallace's work. This is not very stoutly denied by his admirers; but, say they, Mr. Malthus was the first to reduce the inequality between the possible increase of food and population to a mathematical certainty, to the arithmetical and geometrical ratios. In answer to which, we say, that those ratios are, in a strict and scientific view of the subject, entirely fallacious—a pure fiction. For a grain of corn or of mustard-seed has the same or a greater power of propagating its species than a man, till it has overspread the whole earth, till there is no longer any room for it to grow or to spread farther. A bushel of wheat will sow a whole field: the produce of that field will sow twenty fields, and produce twenty harvests. Till there are no longer fields to sow, that is, till a country or the earth is exhausted, the means of subsistence will go on increasing in more than a geometrical ratio; will more than double itself in every generation or season, and will more than keep pace with the progress of population; for this is supposed only to double itself, where it is unchecked, every twenty years. Therefore it is not true as an abstract proposition, that of itself, or in the nature of the growth of the produce of the earth, food can only increase in the snail-pace progress of an arithmetical ratio, while population goes on at a swinging geometrical rate: for the food keeps pace, or more than keeps pace, with the population, while there is room to grow it in, and after that room is filled up, it does not go on, even in that arithmetical ratio—it does not increase at all, or very little. That is, the ratio, instead of being always true, is never true at all: neither before the soil is fully cultivated, nor afterwards. Food does not increase in an arithmetical series in China, or even in England: it increases in a geometrical series, or as fast as the population, in America. The rates at which one or the other increase naturally, or can be made to increase, have no relation to an arithmetical and geometrical series. They are co-ordinate till the earth, or any given portion of it, is occupied and cultivated, and, after that, they are quite disproportionate: or rather, both stop practically at the same instant; the means of subsistence with the limits of the soil, and the population with the limits of the means of subsistence. All that is true of Mr. Malthus's doctrine, then, is this, that the tendency of population to increase remains after the power of the earth to produce more food is gone; that the one is limited, the other unlimited. This is enough for the morality of the question: his mathematics are altogether spurious. Entirely groundless as they are, they have still been of the greatest use to Mr. Malthus, in alarming the imaginations and confounding the understandings of his readers. For, if the case had been represented as it stands, the increase of population would have seemed, till the limits of the earth were full, a great moral good; and after they were passed, a physical impossibility, the state of society remaining the same. But, by means of the arithmetical and geometrical series, ever present to the mental eye, and overlaying the whole question, whether applicable to it or not, it seems, first, as if this inordinate and unequal pressure of population on the means of subsistence was, at all times, and in all circumstances, equally to be dreaded, and equally inevitable; and again, as if, the more that population advanced, the greater the evil became, the actual excess as well as the tendency to excess. For it appears by looking at the scale, at the "stop-watch" of the new system of morals and legislation, as if, when the population is at 4, the means of subsistence is at 3; so that there is here only a deficit of 1 in the latter, and a small corresponding quantity of *vice* and *misery;* but that when it gets on to 32, the means of subsistence being only 6, here is a necessary deficiency of food, and all the comforts of life, to 26 persons out of 32, so that life becomes an evil, and the world a wretched lazar-house, a monstrous sink of misery and famine, one foul abortion, in proportion as it is full of human beings enjoying the comforts and necessaries of life. It consequently follows, that the more we can, by the wholesome *preventive* checks of vice and misery, keep back the principle of population to its first stages, and the means of subsistence to as low a level as possible, we keep these two mechanical, and otherwise unmanageable principles, in closer harmony,—hinder the one from pressing excessively on the other, and by producing the least possible quantity of good, prevent the greatest possible quantity of evil. This doctrine is false in fact and theory. Its advocates do not understand it, nor is it intelligible. The actual existence of 26 persons in want, when there is only food for six out of 32, is a chimera which never entered the brains of any one not an adept in Mr. Malthus's mathematical series; the population confessedly never can or does exceed the means of subsistence in a literal sense; and the tendency to exceed it in a moral sense, that is, so as to destroy the comforts and happiness of society, and occasion vice and misery, does not depend on the actual population supported by actual means of subsistence, but solely on the greater or less degree of *moral restraint*, in any number of individuals (ten hundred or ten millions), inducing them to go beyond or stop short of impending vice and misery in the career of population. The instant, however, any increase in population, with or without an increase in the means of subsistence, is hinted, the disciples of Mr. Malthus are struck with horror at the vice and misery which must ensue to keep this double population down; nay, mention any improvement, any reform, any addition to the comforts or necessaries of life, any diminution of vice and misery, and the infallible result in their apprehensive imaginations is only an incalculable increase of vice and misery, from the increased means of subsistence, and the increased population that would follow. They have but this one idea in their heads; it comes in at every turn, and nothing can drive it out. Twice last year did Major Torrens go down to the City Meeting with Mr. Malthus's arithmetical and geometrical ratios in his pocket, as a double and effectual bar to Mr. Owen's plan, or, indeed, if he is consistent, to any other plan of reform. He appeared to consider these ratios as decisive against any philosophical scheme of *perfectibility*, and as proportionably inimical to any subordinate approximation to any such ultimate visionary perfection. He argued that Mr. Owen's "projected villages," if realised in all their pauper splendour, and to the projector's heart's content, would, by providing for the support and increased comforts of an additional population, only (by that very means) give a double impetus to the mechanical operation of the ratios in question, and produce a double quantity of crime and misery, by making the principle of population press with extended force on the means of subsistence. This is what we cannot comprehend. Suppose Mr. Owen's plan, or any other, would afford double employment, double comfort and subsistence to the poor throughout the country, where would be the harm of this, where the objection, near or remote, except on the false principles laid down or insinuated in Mr. Malthus's work? For instance, if another island such as England could by an enchanter be conjured up in the middle of the sea, with all the same means of subsistence, arts, trades, agriculture, manufactures, institutions, laws, &c. as this country, we ask whether this new country would not be a good in proportion to the number of beings maintained in such a state of comfort: or, if these gentlemen will have it so, in proportion to the increase of population pressing on the means of subsistence? We say it would be a good, just in the same sense and proportion that it would be an evil, if England as it is, with all its inhabitants, means of subsistence, arts, trades, manufactures, agriculture, institutions, laws, King, Lords and Commons, were sunk in the sea? Who would not weep for England so sunk,—who would not rejoice to see another England so rising up out of the same element? The good would be immense, and the evil would be none: for it is evident, that though the population of both islands would be double that of either singly, it is the height of absurdity to suppose this would increase the tendency of the population to press more upon the means of subsistence, or to produce a greater quantity of vice and misery in either, than if the one or the other did not exist. But the case is precisely the same if we suppose England itself, *our* England, to be doubled in population and the means of subsistence:—if we suppose such an improvement in our arts, trade, manufactures, agriculture, institutions, laws, every thing, possible, as to maintain double the same number of Englishmen, in the same or in a greater degree of comfort and enjoyment, of liberty, virtue, knowledge, happiness, and independence. The population being doubled would not press more unequally on double the means of subsistence, than half that population would press on half those means of subsistence. If this increase would be an evil, the destroying half the present population, and half the present means of subsistence, the laying waste more lands, the destroying arts and the implements of husbandry, the re-barbarising and the re-enslaving the country, would be a good. The sinking the maritime counties with all their inhabitants in the Channel, instead of "redeeming tracts from the sea," would be a great good to the community and the State; the flooding the fen districts would do something, in like manner, to prevent the pressure of the principle of population on the level of the means of subsistence; and if thirty-nine out of forty of the counties could be struck off the list of shires, and the whole island reduced to a sand-bank, the King of England would reign, according to these speculatists, over forty or forty thousand times the quantity of liberty, happiness, wisdom, and virtue, that he now does, having no subjects, or only a select few, for the principle of population to commit its ravages upon, by overstepping the means of subsistence. The condition of New Zealand must approach nearer to the *beau ideal* of political philosophy contemplated by these persons, than the state of Great Britain in the reign of George III. Such is the logical result of their mode of reasoning, though they do not push it to this length;—they only apply it to the defence of all existing abuses, and the prevention of all timely reform! Its advocates are contented to make use of it as a lucky diversion against all Utopian projects of perfectibility, and against every practical advance in human improvement. But they cannot consistently stop here, for it requires not only a shrinking back from every progressive refinement, but a perpetual deterioration and retrograde movement from the positive advances we have made in civilization, comfort, and population, to the lowest state of barbarism, ignorance, and depopulation—till we come back to the age of acorns and pig-nuts, and reduce this once flourishing, populous, free, industrious, independent, and contented people, to a horde of wandering savages, housing in thickets, and living on dewberries, shell-fish, and crab-apples. *This will never do.*

ON THE

ORIGINALITY OF MR. MALTHUS'S ESSAY.

WE asserted in a former article, upon what we thought sufficient and mature grounds, that the author of the "Essay on Population" had taken the leading principle of that essay, and the general inference built on it, from Wallace's work, entitled, "Various Prospects of Mankind, Nature and Providence." We here repeat that assertion; and to enable our readers to judge for themselves, shall give the passage in Wallace on which it is founded. It is as follows:—

"But without entering further into these abstracted and uncertain speculations, it deserves our particular attention that as no Government which hath hitherto been established is free from all seeds of corruption, or can be expected to be eternal; so if we suppose a Government to be perfect in its original frame, and to be administered in the most perfect manner, after whatever model we suppose it to have been framed, such a perfect form would be so far from lasting for ever, that it must come to an end so much the sooner on account of its perfection. For, though happily such Governments should be firmly established—though they should be found consistent with the reigning passions of human nature, though they should spread far and wide—nay, though they should prevail universally, they must at last involve mankind in the deepest perplexity, and in universal confusion. For how excellent soever they may be in their own nature, they are altogether inconsistent with the present frame of nature, and with a limited extent of earth.

" Under a perfect Government, the inconveniences of having a family would be so entirely removed, children would be so well taken care of, and every thing become so favourable to populousness, that though some sickly seasons or dreadful plagues in particular climates might cut off multitudes, yet in general, mankind would increase so prodigiously, that the earth would at last be overstocked, and become unable to support its numerous inhabitants.

" How long the earth, with the best culture of which it is capable from human genius and industry, might be able to nourish its perpetually increasing inhabitants, is as impossible as it is unnecessary to be determined. It is not probable that it could have supported them during so long a period as since the creation of Adam. But whatever mav be supposed of the length of this period, of necessity it must be granted, that the earth could not nourish them for ever, unless either its fertility could be continually augmented, or by some secret in nature, like what certain enthusiasts have expected from the philosopher's stone, some wise adept in the occult sciences should invent a method of supporting mankind quite different from any thing known at present. Nay, though some extraordinary method of supporting them might possibly be found out, yet if there was no bound to the increase of mankind, which would be the case under a perfect

Government, there would not even be sufficient room for containing their bodies upon the surface of the earth, or upon any limited surface whatsoever. It would be necessary, therefore, in order to find room for such multitudes of men, that the earth should be continually enlarging in bulk, as an animal or vegetable body.

" Now since philosophers may as soon attempt to make mankind immortal, as to support the animal frame without food, it is equally certain that limits are set to the fertility of the earth; and that its bulk, so far as is hitherto known, hath continued always the same, and probably could not be much altered without making considerable changes in the solar system. It would be impossible, therefore, to support the great numbers of men who would be raised up under a perfect government; the earth would be overstocked at last, and the greatest admirers of such fanciful schemes must foresee the fatal period when they would come to an end, as they are altogether inconsistent with the limits of that earth in which they must exist.

" What a miserable catastrophe of the most generous of all human systems of Government! How dreadfully would the Magistrates of such commonwealths find themselves disconcerted at that fatal period, when there was no longer any room for new colonies, and when the earth could produce no farther supplies! During all the preceding ages, while there was room for increase, mankind must have been happy; the earth must have been a paradise in the literal sense, as the greatest part of it must have been turned into delightful and fruitful gardens. But when the dreadful time should at last come, when our globe, by the most diligent culture, could not produce what was sufficient to nourish its numerous inhabitants, what happy expedient could then be found out to remedy so great an evil?

" In such a cruel necessity, must there be a law to restrain marriage? Must multitudes of women be shut up in cloisters, like the ancient vestals or modern nuns? To keep a balance between the two sexes, must a proportionable number of men be debarred from marriage? Shall the Utopians, following the wicked policy of superstition, forbid their priests to marry; or shall they rather sacrifice men of some other profession for the good of the state? Or shall they appoint the sons of certain families to be maimed at their birth, and give a sanction to the unnatural institution of eunuchs? If none of these expedients can be thought proper, shall they appoint a certain number of infants to be exposed to death as soon as they are born, determining the proportion according to the exigencies of the state; and pointing out the particular victims by lot, or according to some established rule? Or, must they shorten the period of human life by a law, and condemn all to die after they had completed a certain age, which might be shorter or longer, as provisions were either more scanty or plentiful? Or, what other method should they devise (for an expedient would be absolutely necessary) to restrain the number of citizens within reasonable bounds?

"Alas! how unnatural and inhuman must every such expedient be accounted! The natural passions and appetites of mankind are planted in our frame, to answer the best ends for the happiness both of the individuals and of the species. Shall we be obliged to contradict such a wise order? Shall we be laid under the necessity of acting barbarously and inhumanly? Sad and fatal necessity! And which, after all, could never answer the end, but would give rise to violence and war. For mankind would never agree about such regulations. Force, and arms, must at last decide their quarrels, and the deaths of such as fell in battle, leave sufficient provisions for the survivors, and make room for others to be born.

"Thus the tranquillity and numerous blessings of the Utopian governments would come to an end; war, or cruel and unnatural customs, be introduced, and a stop put to the increase of mankind, to the advancement of knowledge, and to the culture of the earth, in spite of the most excellent laws and wisest precautions. The more excellent the laws had been, and the more strictly they had been observed, mankind must have sooner become miserable. The remembrance of former times, the greatness of their wisdom and virtue, would conspire to heighten their distress; and the world, instead of remaining the mansion of wisdom and happiness, become the scene of vice and confusion. Force and fraud must prevail, and mankind be reduced to the same calamitous condition as at present.

"Such a melancholy situation, in consequence merely of the want of provisions, is, in truth, more unnatural than all their present calamities. Supposing men to have abused their liberty, by which abuse vice has once been introduced into the world; and that wrong notions, a bad taste, and vicious habits have been strengthened by the defects of education and government, our present distresses may be easily explained. They may even be called natural, being the natural consequences of our depravity. They may be supposed to be the means by which Providence punishes vice; and by setting bounds to the increase of mankind, prevents the earth's being overstocked, and men being laid under the cruel necessity of killing one another. But to suppose that, in the course of a favourable Providence, a perfect government had been established, under which the disorders of human passions had been powerfully corrected and restrained; poverty, idleness, and war banished; the earth made a paradise; universal friendship and concord established, and human society rendered flourishing in all respects; and that such a lovely Constitution should be overturned, not by the vices of men, or their abuse of liberty, but by the order of nature itself, seems wholly unnatural, and altogether disagreeable to the methods of Providence.

"By reasoning in this manner, it is not pretended that 'tis unnatural to set bounds to human knowledge and happiness, or to the grandeur of society, and to confine what is finite to proper limits. It is certainly fit to set just bounds to every thing according to its nature, and to adjust all things in due proportion to one another. Undoubtedly, such an excellent order is actually established throughout all the works of God, in his wide dominions. But there are certain primary determinations in nature, to which all other things of a subordinate kind must be adjusted. A limited earth, a limited degree of fertility, and the continual increase of mankind, are three of these original constitutions. To these determinations, human affairs, and the circumstance of all other animals, must be adapted. In which view, it is unsuitable to our ideas of order, that while the earth is only capable of maintaining a determined number, the human race should increase without end. This would be the necessary consequence of a perfect government and education. On which account it is more contrary to just proportion, to suppose that such a perfect government should be established, in such circumstances, than that by permitting vice, or the abuse of liberty, in the wisdom of Providence, mankind should never be able to multiply so as to be able to overstock the earth

" From this view of the circumstances of the world, notwithstanding the high opinion we have of the merits of Sir Thomas More, and other admired projectors of perfect governments in ancient or modern times, we may discern how little can be expected from their most perfect systems.

" As for those worthy philosophers, patriots, and law-givers, who have employed their talents in framing such excellent models, we ought to do justice to their characters, and gratefully to acknowledge their generous efforts to rescue the world out of that distress into which it has fallen, through the imperfection of government. Sincere, and ardent in their love of virtue, enamoured of its lovely form, deeply interested for the happiness of mankind, to the best of their skill, and with hearts full of zeal, they have strenuously endeavoured to advance human society to perfection. For this, their memory ought to be sacred to posterity. But if they expected their beautiful systems actually to take place, their hopes were ill founded, and they were not sufficiently aware of the consequences.

" The speculations of such ingenious authors enlarge our views, and amuse our fancies. They are useful for directing us to correct certain errors at particular times. Able legislators ought to consider them as models, and honest patriots ought never to lose sight of them, or any proper opportunity of transplanting the wisest of their maxims into their own governments, as far as they are adapted to their particular circumstances, and will give no occasion to dangerous convulsions. But this is all that can be expected. Though such ingenious romances should chance to be read and admired, jealous and selfish politicians need not be alarmed. Such statesmen need not fear that ever such airy systems shall be able to destroy their craft, or disappoint them of their intention to sacrifice the interests of mankind to their own avarice or ambition. There is too powerful a charm, which works secretly in favour of such politicians, which will for ever defeat all attempts to establish a perfect government. There is no need of miracles for this purpose. The vices of mankind are sufficient. And we need not doubt but Providence will make use of them, for preventing the establishment of governments which are by no means suitable to the present circumstances of the earth."—See "Various Prospects of Mankind, Nature, and Providence," chap. 4. p. 113. 1761.

Here then we have not only the same argument stated, but stated in the same connexion, and brought to bear on the very same subject to which it is applied by the author of the Essay on Population. The principle, and the consequences deduced from it, are exactly the same. It may happen (and often does) that one man is the first to make a particular discovery or observation, and that another draws from it an important inference of which the former was not at all aware. But this is not the case in the present instance. As far as general reasoning will go, it is impossible that any thing should be stated more clearly, more fully and explicitly, than Wallace has here stated the argument against the progressive and ultimate amelioration of human society, from the sole principle of population. We have already seen that the addition which Mr. Malthus has made to the argument, from the geometrical and arithmetical series, is a fallacy, and not an improvement. The conclusion itself insisted on in the above passage, by Wallace, appears to us no better than a contradiction in terms. Of the possibility of realising such a Utopian system as he first supposes, that is, of making every motive and principle of action in the human mind absolutely and completely subservient to the dictates of reason and the calculation of consequences, we do not say a word; but we *do* say, that if such a system is possible, and if it were realised, it would not be destroyed by the principle of population, that is, by the unrestrained propagation of the species from a blind, headlong, instinctive, irrational impulse, and with a total and sovereign disregard of the fatal and overwhelming consequences which would ensue. The argument is a solecism; but if Wallace shewed his ingenuity in inventing it, Mr. Malthus has not shown his judgment in adopting it. Through the whole of the first edition of the Essay on Population, the author assumed the impulse to propagate the species as a law, and a physical necessity of the same force as that of preserving the individual, or, in other words, he sets down, 1st, hunger, 2d, the sexual appetite, as two co-ordinate, and equally irresistible principles of action. It was necessary that he should do this, in order to bear out his conclusion against the Utopian systems of his antagonists; for, in order to maintain that this principle of population would be proof against the highest possible degree of reason, we must suppose it to be an absolute physical necessity. If reason has any practical power over it, the highest reason must be able to attain an habitual power over it. Mr. Malthus, however, having by the rigid interpretation which he gave to his favourite principle, or by what he called the *iron law of necessity*, succeeded in laying the bugbear of the modern philosophy, relaxed considerably in the second and following editions of his book, in which he introduced *moral restraint* as a third check upon the principle of population, in addition to the two only ones of vice and misery, with which he before combated the Utopian philosophers; and *though he* does not lay an exaggerated or consistent stress on this third check, yet he thinks something may be done to lighten the intolerable pressure, the heavy hand of vice and misery, by flattering old maids, and frightening the poor into the practice of moral restraint! It will be recollected by those who are familiar with the history of Mr. Malthus's writings, that his first and grand effort was directed against the modern philosophy. The use which this author has since made of his principle, and of the arithmetical and geometrical ratios to shut up the workhouse, to *snub* the poor, to stint them in their wages, to deny them relief from the parish, and preach lectures to them on the new invented crime of matrimony, was an after-thought; of the merit of which we shall speak in another article.

ON THE PRINCIPLE OF POPULATION AS AFFECTING THE SCHEMES OF UTOPIAN IMPROVEMENT.

"A swaggering paradox, when once explained, soon sinks into an unmeaning common-place."

THIS excellent saying of a great man was never more strictly applicable to any system than it is to Mr. Malthus's paradox, and his explanation of it. It seemed, on the first publication of the Essay on Population, as if the whole world was going to be turned topsy-turvy, all our ideas of moral good and evil, were in a manner confounded, we scarcely knew whether we stood on our head or our heels: but after exciting considerable expectation, giving us a good shake, and making us a little dizzy, Mr. Malthus does as we do when we shew the children *London*,—sets us on our feet again, and every thing goes on as before. The common notions that prevailed on this subject, till our author's first population-scheme tended to weaken them, were that life is a blessing, and that the more people could be maintained in any state in a tolerable degree of health, comfort and decency, the better: that want and misery are not desirable in themselves, that famine is not to be courted for its own sake, that wars, disease and pestilence are not what every friend of his country or his species should pray *for* in the first place: that vice in its different shapes is a thing that the world could do very well without, and that if it could be got rid of altogether, it would be a great gain. In short, that the object both of the moralist and politician was to diminish as much as possible the quantity of vice and misery existing in the world: without apprehending that by thus effectually introducing more virtue and happiness, more reason and good sense, that by improving the manners of a people, removing pernicious habits and principles of acting, or securing greater plenty, and a greater number of mouths to partake of it, they were doing a disservice to humanity. Then comes Mr. Malthus with his octavo book, and tells us there is another great evil, which had never been found out, or at least not sufficiently attended to till his time, namely, excessive population: that this evil was infinitely greater and more to be dreaded than all others put together; and that its approach could only be checked by vice and misery: that any increase of virtue or happiness was the direct way to hasten it on; and that in proportion as we attempted to improve the condition of mankind, and lessened the restraints of vice and misery, we threw down the only barriers that could protect us from this most formidable scourge of the species, population. Vice and misery were indeed evils, but they were absolutely necessary evils; necessary to prevent the introduction of others of an incalculably and inconceivably greater magnitude; and that every proposal to lessen their actual quantity, on which the measure of our safety depended, might be attended with the most ruinous consequences, and ought to be looked upon with horror. I think that this description of the tendency and complexion of Mr. Malthus's first essay is not in the least exaggerated, but an exact and faithful picture of the impression, which it made on every one's mind.

After taking some time to recover from the surprise and hurry into which so great a discovery would naturally throw him, he comes forward again with a large quarto, in which he is at great pains both to say and unsay all that he has said in his former volume; and upon the whole concludes, that population is in itself a good thing, that it is never likely to do much harm, that virtue and happiness ought to be promoted by every practicable means, and that the most effectual as well as desirable check to excessive population is *moral restraint*. The mighty discovery thus reduced to, and pieced out by common sense, the wonder vanishes, and we breathe a little freely again. Mr. Malthus is, however, by no means willing to give up his old doctrine, or *eat his own words*: he stickles stoutly for it at times. He has his fits of reason and his fits of extravagance, his yielding and his obstinate moments, fluctuating between the two, and vibrating backwards and forwards with a dexterity of self-contradiction which it is wonderful to behold. The following passage is so curious in this respect that I cannot help quoting it in this place. Speaking of the Reply of the author of the Political Justice to his former work, he observes, " But Mr. Godwin says, that if he looks into the past history of the world, he does not see that increasing population has been controlled and confined by vice and misery *alone*. *In this observation I cannot agree with him.* I will thank Mr. Godwin to name to me any check, that in past ages has contributed to keep down the population to the level of the means of subsistence, that does not fairly come under some form of vice or misery; except indeed the check of *moral restraint, which I have mentioned in the course of this work*; and which to say the truth, whatever hopes we may entertain of its prevalence in future, has undoubtedly in past ages operated with very inconsiderable force."* When I assure the reader that I give him this passage fairly and fully, I think he will be of opinion with me, that it would be difficult to produce an

* The prevalence of this check may be estimated *by the general proportion* of virtue and happiness in the world, for if there were no such check, there could be nothing but vice and misery.

instance of a more miserable attempt to reconcile a contradiction by childish evasion, to insist upon an argument, and give it up in the same breath. Does Mr. Malthus really think that he has such an absolute right and authority over this subject of population, that provided he mentions a principle, or shews that he is not ignorant of it, and cannot be caught *napping* by the critics, he is at liberty to say that it has or has not had any operation, just as he pleases, and that the state of the fact is a matter of perfect indifference? He contradicts the opinion of Mr. Godwin that vice and misery are not the only checks to population, and gives as a proof of his assertion, that he himself truly has mentioned another check. Thus after flatly denying that moral restraint has any effect at all, he modestly concludes by saying that it has had some, no doubt, but promises that it will never have a great deal. Yet in the very next page, he says, "On this sentiment, whether virtue, prudence or pride, which I have already noticed under the name of moral restraint, or of the more comprehensive title, the *preventive* check, it will appear, that in the sequel of this work, I shall lay considerable stress." p. 385. This kind of reasoning is enough to give one the headache.

The most singular thing in this singular performance of our author is, that it should have been originally ushered into the world as the most complete and only satisfactory answer to the speculations of Godwin, Condorcet and others, or to what has been called the modern philosophy. A more complete piece of wrong-headedness, a more strange perversion of reason could hardly be devised by the wit of man. Whatever we may think of the doctrine of the progressive improvement of the human mind, or of a state of society in which every thing will be subject to the absolute control of reason, however absurd, unnatural, or impracticable we may conceive such a system to be, certainly it cannot without the grossest inconsistency be objected to it, that such a system would necessarily be rendered abortive, because if *reason* should ever get the mastery over all our actions, we shall then be governed entirely by our physical appetites and passions, without the least regard to consequences. This appears to me a refinement on absurdity. Several philosophers and speculatists had supposed that a certain state of society very different from any that has hitherto existed was in itself practicable; and that if it were realised, it would be productive of a far greater degree of human happiness than is compatible with the present institutions of society. I have nothing to do with either of these points. I will allow to any one who pleases that all such schemes are "false, sophistical, unfounded in the extreme." But I cannot agree with Mr. Malthus that they would be *bad,* in proportion as they were *good;* that their excellence would be their ruin; or that the true and only unanswerable objection against all such schemes is that very degree of happiness, virtue, and improvement, to which they are supposed to give rise. And I cannot agree with him in this, because it is contrary to common sense, and leads to the subversion of every principle of moral reasoning. Without perplexing himself with the subtle arguments of his opponents, Mr. Malthus comes boldly forward, and says, "Gentlemen, I am willing to make you large concessions, I am ready to allow the practicability and the desirableness of your schemes; the more happiness, the more virtue, the more refinement they are productive of, the better; all these will only add to the 'exuberant strength of my argument;' I have a short answer to all objections, to be sure I found it in an old political receipt-book, called Prospects, &c. by one Wallace, a man not much known, but no matter for that, *finding is keeping,* you know:" and with one smart stroke of his wand, on which are inscribed certain mystical characters, and algebraic proportions, he levels the fairy enchantment with the ground. For, says Mr. Malthus, though this improved state of society were actually realised, it could not possibly continue, but must soon terminate in a state of things pregnant with evils far more insupportable than any we at present endure, in consequence of the excessive population which would follow, and the impossibility of providing for its support.

This is what I do not understand. It is, in other words, to assert that the doubling the population of a country, for example, after a certain period, will be attended with the most pernicious effects, by want, famine, bloodshed, and a state of general violence and confusion; this will afterwards lead to vices and practices still worse than the physical evils they are designed to prevent, &c. and yet that at this period those who will be the most interested in preventing these consequences, and the best acquainted with the circumstances that lead to them, will neither have the understanding to foresee, nor the heart to feel, nor the will to prevent the sure evils to which they expose themselves and others, though this advanced state of population, which does not admit of any addition without danger is supposed to be the immediate result of a more general diffusion of the comforts and conveniences of life, of more enlarged and liberal views, of a more refined and comprehensive regard to our own permanent interests, as well as those of others, of correspondent habits and manners, and of a state of things, in which our gross animal appetites will be subjected to the practical control of reason. The influence of rational motives, of refined and long-sighted views of things is supposed to have taken place of narrow, selfish, and merely sensual motives: this is implied in the very statement of the question "What conjuration and what mighty magic" should thus blind our philosophical descendants on this single subject in which they are more interested than in all the rest, so that they should stand with their eyes open on the edge of a precipice, and instead of retreating from it, should throw themselves down headlong, I cannot comprehend; unless indeed we suppose that the impulse to propagate the species is so strong and uncontrolable, that reason has no power over it. This is what Mr. Malthus was at one time strongly disposed to assert, and what he is at present half inclined to retract. Without this foundation to rest on, the whole of his reasoning is unintelligible. It seems to me a most childish way of answering any one, who *chooses to* assert that mankind are capable of being governed entirely by their reason, and that it would be better for them if they were, to say, No, for if they were governed entirely by it, they would be much less able to attend to its dictates than they are at present: and the evils, which would thus follow from the unrestrained increase of population, would be excessive.—Almost every little Miss, who has had the advantage of a boarding-school education, or been properly tutored by her mamma, whose hair is not of an absolute flame-colour, and who has hopes in time, if she behaves prettily, of getting a good husband, waits patiently year after year, looks about her, rejects or trifles with half a dozen lovers, favouring one, laughing at another, chusing among them "as one picks pears, saying, this I like, that I loathe," with the greatest indifference, as if it were no such very pressing affair, and *all the while behaves very prettily*:—why, what an idea does Mr. Malthus give us of the grave, masculine genius of our Utopian philosophers, their sublime attainments and gigantic energy, that they will not be able to manage these matters as decently and cleverly as the silliest woman can do at present! Mr. Malthus indeed endeavours to soften the absurdity by saying that moral restraint at present owes its strength to selfish motives: what is that to the purpose? If Mr. Malthus chooses to say, that men will always be governed by the same gross mechanical motives that they are at present, I have no objection to make to it; but it is shifting the question: it is not arguing against the state of society we are considering from the consequences to which it would give rise, but against the possibility of its ever existing. It is absurd to object to a system on account of the consequences which would follow if we once suppose men to be actuated by entirely different motives and principles from what they are at present, and then to say, that those consequences would necessarily follow, because men would never be what we suppose them. It is very idle to alarm the imagination by deprecating the evils that must follow from the practical adoption of a particular scheme, yet to allow that we have no reason to dread those consequences, but because the scheme itself is impracticable.—

But I am ashamed of wasting the reader's time and my own in thus beating the air. It is not however my fault that Mr. Malthus has written nonsense, or that others have admired it. It is not Mr. Malthus's nonsense, but the opinion of the world respecting it, that I would be thought to compliment by this serious refutation of what in itself neither deserves nor admits of any reasoning upon it. If, however, we recollect the source from whence Mr. Malthus borrowed his principle and the application of it to improvements in political philosophy, we must allow that he is merely passive in error. The principle itself would not have been worth a farthing to him without the application, and accordingly he took them as he found them lying snug together; and as Trim having converted the old jack-boots into a pair of new mortars immediately planted them against whichever of my uncle Toby's garrisons the allies were then busy in besieging, so the public-spirited gallantry of our modern engineer directed him to bend the whole force of his clumsy discovery against that system of philosophy which was the most talked of at the time, but to which it was the least applicable of all others. Wallace, I have no doubt, took up his idea either as a paradox, or a *jeu d'esprit*, or because any thing, he thought, was of weight enough to overturn what had never existed any where but in the imagination; or he was led into a piece of false logic by an error we are very apt to fall into, of supposing because he had never been struck himself by the difficulty of population in such a state of society, that therefore the people themselves would not find it out, nor make any provision against it. But though I can in some measure excuse a lively paradox, I do not think the same favour is to be shewn to the dull, dogged, voluminous repetition of an absurdity.

I cannot help thinking that our author has been too much influenced in his different feelings on this subject, by the particular purpose he had in view at the time. Mr. Malthus might not improperly have taken for the motto of his first edition,—"These three bear record on earth, vice, misery, and population." In his answer to Mr. Godwin, this principle was represented as an evil, for which no remedy could be found but in evil;—that its operation was mechanical, unceasing, necessary; that it went straight forward to its end, unchecked by fear, or reason, or remorse; that the evils, which it drew after it, could only be avoided by other evils, by actual vice and misery. Population was, in fact, the great Devil, the untamed Beelzebub that was only kept chained down by vice and misery, and which, if it were once let loose from these restraints, would go forth, and ravage the earth. That they were, of course, the two main props and pillars of society, and that the lower and weaker they kept this principle, the better able they were to contend with it: that therefore any diminution of that degree of them, which at present prevails, and is found sufficient to keep the world in order, was of all things chiefly to be dreaded.—Mr. Malthus seems fully aware of the importance of the stage-maxim, To elevate and surprise. Having once heated the imaginations of his readers, he knows that he can afterwards mould them into whatever shape he pleases. All this bustle and terror, and stage-effect, and theatrical mummery was only to serve a temporary purpose, for all of a sudden the scene is shifted, and the storm subsides. Having frighted away the boldest champions of modern philosophy, this monstrous appearance, full of strange and inexplicable horrors, is suffered quietly to shrink back to its natural dimensions, and we find it to be nothing more than a common-sized tame looking animal, which however requires a chain and the whip of its keeper to prevent it from becoming mischievous. Mr. Malthus then steps forward and says, "The evil we were all in danger of was not population,—but philosophy. Nothing is to be done with the latter by mere reasoning. I, therefore, thought it right to make use of a little terror to accomplish the end. As to the principle of population you need be under no alarm; only leave it to me, and I shall be able to manage it very well. All its dreadful consequences may be easily prevented by a proper application of the motives of common prudence and common decency." If, however, any one should be at a loss to know how it is possible to reconcile such contradictions, I would suggest to Mr. Malthus the answer which Hamlet makes to his friend Guildenstern, "'Tis as easy as lying: govern these ventiges (the poor-rates and private charity) with your fingers and thumb, and this same instrument will discourse most excellent music; look you, here are the stops," (namely, Mr. Malthus's Essay and Mr. Whitbread's Poor Bill).*

ON THE APPLICATION OF MR. MALTHUS'S PRINCIPLE TO THE POOR LAWS.

In speaking of the abolition of the Poor Laws, Mr. Malthus says;—

"To this end, I should propose a regulation to be made, declaring, that no child born from any marriage, taking place after the expiration of a year from the date of the law, and no illegitimate child born two years from the same date, should ever be entitled to parish assistance. And to give a more general knowledge of this law, and to enforce it more strongly on the minds of the lower classes of people, the clergyman of each parish should, after the publication of banns, read a short address, stating the strong obligation on every man to support his own children; the impropriety, and even immorality, of marrying without a prospect of being able to do this; the evils which had resulted to the poor themselves from the attempt which had been made to assist by public institutions in a duty which ought to be exclusively appropriated to parents; and the absolute necessity which had at length appeared of abandoning all such institutions,

* Written in 1807, at a time when Mr. Whitbread's scheme was in agitation in the House of Commons, and Mr. Malthus used to wait in the lobbies with his essay in his hand, for the instruction and compliments of Honourable Members. The above article is taken from a Reply to Mr. Malthus, one of my very early Essays, the style of which is, I confess, a little exuberant, but of the arguments I see no reason to be ashamed.

on account of their producing effects totally opposite to those which were intended.

"This would operate as a fair, distinct, and precise notice, which no man could well mistake, and, without pressing hard on any particular individuals, would at once throw off the rising generation from that miserable and helpless dependence upon the government and the rich, the moral as well as physical consequences of which are almost incalculable.

"After the public notice which I have proposed had been given, and the system of poor-laws had ceased with regard to the rising generation, if any man chose to marry, without a prospect of being able to support a family, he should have the most perfect liberty so to do. Though to marry, in this case, is, in my opinion, clearly an immoral act, yet it is not one which society can justly take upon itself to prevent or punish; because the punishment provided for it by the laws of nature falls directly and most severely upon the individual who commits the act, and through him, only more remotely and feebly, on the society. When Nature will govern and punish for us, it is a very miserable ambition to wish to snatch the rod from her hands, and draw upon ourselves the odium of executioner. To the punishment therefore of Nature he should be left, the punishment of want. He has erred in the face of a most clear and precise warning, and can have no just reason to complain of any persons but himself when he feels the consequences of his error. All parish assistance should be most rigidly denied him; and he should be left to the uncertain support of private charity. He should be taught to know, that the laws of Nature, which are the laws of God, had doomed him and his family to starve,* for disobeying their repeated admonitions; that he had no claim of *right* on society for the smallest portion of food, beyond that which his labour would fairly purchase; and that if he and his family were saved from feeling the natural consequences of his imprudence, he would owe it to the pity of some

* Altered in the last edition, to "suffer."

kind benefactor, to whom, therefore, he ought to be bound by the strongest ties of gratitude."

This passage has been well answered by Mr. Cobbett in one word, "Parson;"—the most expressive apostrophe that ever was made; and it might be answered as effectually by another word, which I shall omit. When Mr. Malthus asserts, that the poor man and his family have been doomed to starve by the laws of nature, which are the laws of God, he means by the laws of God and nature, the physical and necessary inability of the earth to supply food for more than a certain number of human beings; but if he means that the wants of the poor arise from the impossibility of procuring food for them, while the rich roll in abundance, or, we will say, maintain their dogs and horses, &c. out of their ostentatious superfluities, he asserts what he knows not to be true. Mr. Malthus wishes to confound the necessary limits of the produce of the earth with the arbitrary and artificial distribution of that produce according to the institutions of society, or the caprice of individuals, the laws of God and nature with the laws of man. And what proves the fallacy is, that the laws of man in the present case actually afford the relief, which he would *wilfully* deny; he proposes to repeal those laws, and then to tell the poor man impudently, that "the laws of God and nature have doomed him and his family to starve, for disobeying their repeated admonitions," stuck on the church-door for the last twelve months! 'Tis much.

I have in a separate work made the following remarks on the above proposal, which are a little cavalier, not too cavalier;—a little contemptuous, not too contemptuous;—a little gross, but not too gross for the subject.

"I am not sorry that I am at length come to this passage. It will I hope decide the reader's opinion of the benevolence, wisdom, piety, candour, and disinterested simplicity of Mr. Malthus's mind. Any comments that I might make upon it to strengthen this impression must be faint and feeble. I give up the task of doing justice to the moral beauties that pervade every line of it, in despair. There are some instances of an heroical contempt for the narrow prejudices of the world, of a perfect refinement from the vulgar feelings of human nature, that must only suffer by a comparison with any thing else.

I shall not myself be so uncandid as not to confess, that I think the poor laws bad things; and that it would be well, if they could be got rid of, consistently with humanity and justice. This I do not think they could in the present state of things, and other circumstances remaining as they are. The reason why I object to Mr. Malthus's plan is, that it does not go to the root of the evil, or attack it in its principle, but its effects. He confounds the cause with the effect. The wide spreading tyranny, dependence, indolence, and unhappiness, of which Mr. Malthus is so sensible, are not occasioned by the increase of the poor-rates, but these are the natural consequence of that increasing tyranny, dependence, indolence, and unhappiness occasioned by other causes.

Mr. Malthus desires his readers to look at the enormous proportion in which the poor-rates have increased within the last ten years. But have they increased in any greater proportion than the other taxes, which rendered them necessary, and, which I think, were employed for much more mischievous purposes? I would ask, what have the poor got by their encroachments for the last ten years? Do they work less hard? Are they better fed? Do they marry oftener, and with better prospects? Are they grown pampered and insolent? Have they changed places with the rich? Have they been cunning enough, by means of the poor-laws, to draw off all their wealth and superfluities from the men of property? Have they got so much as a quarter of an hour's leisure, a farthing candle, or a cheese-paring more than they had? Has not the price of provisions risen enormously? Has not the price of labour almost stood still? Have not the government and the rich had their way in every thing?

Have they not gratified their ambition, their pride, their obstinacy, their ruinous extravagance? Have they not squandered the resources of the country as they pleased? Have they not heaped up wealth on themselves, and their dependents? Have they not multiplied sinecures, places, and pensions? Have they not doubled the salaries of those that existed before? Has there been any want of new creations of peers, who would thus be impelled to beget heirs to their titles and estates, and saddle the younger branches of their rising families, by means of their new influence, on the country at large? Has there been any want of contracts, of loans, of monopolies of corn, of a good understanding between the rich and the powerful to assist one another, and to fleece the poor? Have the poor prospered? Have the rich declined? What then have they to complain of? What ground is there for the apprehension, that wealth is secretly changing hands, and that the whole property of the country will shortly be absorbed in the poor's fund? Do not the poor create their own fund? Is not the necessity for such a fund first occasioned by the unequal weight with which the rich press upon the poor; and has not the increase of that fund in the last ten years been occasioned by the additional exorbitant demands, which have been made upon the poor and industrious, which, without some assistance from the public, they could not possibly have answered? Whatever is the increase in the nominal amount of the poor's fund, will not the rich always be able ultimately to throw the burthen of it on the poor themselves? But Mr. Malthus is a man of general principles. He cares little about these circumstantial details, and petty objections. He takes higher ground. He deduces all his conclusions, by an infallible logic, from the laws of God and nature. When our Essayist shall prove to me, that by these paper bullets of the brain, by his ratios of the increase of food, and the increase of mankind, he has prevented one additional tax, or taken off one oppressive duty, that he has made a single rich man retrench one article at his table: that he has made him keep a dog or a horse the less, or part with a single vice, arguing from a mathematical admeasurement of the size of the earth, and the number of inhabitants it can contain, he shall have my perfect leave to disclaim the right of the poor to subsistence, and to tie them down by severe penalties to their good behaviour, on the same profound principles. But why does Mr. Malthus practise his demonstrations on the poor only? Why are they to have a perfect system of rights and duties prescribed to them? I do not see why they alone should be put to live on these metaphysical board-wages, why they should be forced to submit to a course of *abstraction*; or why it should be meat and drink to them, more than to others, to do the will of God. Mr. Malthus's gospel is preached only to the poor!—Even if I approved of our author's plan, I should object to the principle on which it is founded. The parson of the parish, when a poor man comes to be married—No, not so fast. The author does not say, whether the lecture he proposes is to be read to the poor only, or to all ranks of people. Would it not sound oddly, if when the squire, who is himself worth a hundred thousand pounds, is going to be married to the rector's daughter, who is to have fifty, the curate should read them a formal lecture on their obligation to maintain their own children, and not turn them on the parish? Would it be necessary to go through the form of the address, when an amorous couple of eighty presented themselves at the altar? If the admonition were left to the parson's own discretion, what affronts would he not subject himself to, from his neglect of old maids, and superannuated widows, and from his applying himself familiarly to the little shopkeeper, or thriving mechanic? Well, then, let us suppose that a very poor hard-working man comes to be married, and that the clergyman can take the liberty with him: he is to warn him first against fornication, and in the next place against matrimony. These are the two greatest sins which a poor man can commit, who can neither be supposed to keep his wife, nor his girl. Mr. Malthus, however, does not think them equal: for he objects strongly to a country fellow's marrying a girl whom he has debauched, or, as the phrase is, making an honest woman of her, as aggravating the crime; because, by this means, the parish will probably have three or four children to maintain instead of one. However, as it seems rather too late to give advice to a man who is actually come to be married, it is most natural to suppose that he would marry the young woman in spite of the lecture. Here then he errs in the face of a precise warning, and should be left to the punishment of *nature*, the punishment of severe want. When he begins to feel the consequences of his error, all parish assistance is to be rigidly denied him, and the interests of humanity imperiously require that all other assistance should be withheld from him, or most sparingly administered. In the mean time, to reconcile him to this treatment, and let him see that he has nobody to complain of but himself, the parson of the parish comes to him with the certificate of his marriage, and a copy of the warning he had given him at the time, by which he is taught to know that the laws of nature, which are the laws of God, had doomed him and his family to starve for disobeying their repeated admonitions; that he had no claim of right to the smallest portion of food beyond what his labour would actually purchase; and that he ought to kiss the feet and lick the dust off the shoes of him, who gave him a reprieve from the just sentence which the laws of God and nature had passed upon him. To make this clear to him, it would be necessary to put the Essay on Population into his hands, to instruct him in the nature of a geometrical and arithmetical series, in the necessary limits to population from the size of the earth; and here would come in Mr. Malthus's plan of education for the poor, writing, arithmetic, the use of the globes, &c. for the purpose of proving to them the necessity of their being starved. It cannot be supposed that the poor man (what with his poverty and what with being priest-ridden) should be able to resist this body of evidence, he would open his eyes to his error, and "would submit to the sufferings that were abso-"lutely irremediable, with the fortitude of a man, and the resig-"nation of a Christian." He and his family might then be sent round the parish in a starving condition, accompanied by the constables and *quondam* overseers of the poor, to see that no person, blind to "the interests of humanity," practised upon them the abominable deception of attempting to relieve their remediless sufferings; and by the parson of the parish, to point out to the spectators the inevitable consequences of sinning against the laws of God and man. By celebrating a number of these *Auto da fes* yearly in every parish, the greatest publicity would be given to the principle of population, "the strict line of duty would be pointed out to every man," enforced by the most powerful sanctions; justice and humanity would flourish, they would be understood to signify that the poor have no right to live by their labour, and that the feelings of compassion and benevolence are best shewn by denying them charity; the poor would no longer be dependent on the rich, the rich could no longer wish to reduce the poor into a more complete subjection to their will, all causes of contention, of jealousy, and of irritation would have ceased between them, the struggle would be over, each class would fulfil the task assigned by heaven; the rich would oppress the poor without remorse, the poor would submit to oppression with a pious gratitude and resignation; the greatest harmony would prevail between the government and the people; there would be no longer any seditions, tumults, complaints, petitions, partisans of liberty, or tools of power; no grumbling, no repining, no discontented men of talents proposing reforms, and frivolous remedies, but we should all have the same gaiety and lightness of heart, and the same happy spirit of resignation that a man feels when he is seized with the plague, who thinks no more of the physician, but knows that his disorder is without cure. The best-laid schemes are subject, however, to unlucky reverses. Some such seem to lie in the way of that pleasing Euthanasia, and contented submission to the grinding law of necessity, projected by Mr. Malthus. We might never reach the philosophic temper of the inhabitants of modern Greece and Turkey in this respect. Many little things might happen to interrupt our progress, if we were put into ever so fair a train. For instance, the men might perhaps be talked over by the parson, and their understandings being convinced by the geometrical and arithmetical ratios, or at least so far puzzled, that they would have nothing to say for themselves, they might prepare to submit to their fate with a tolerable grace. But I am afraid that the women might prove refractory. They never will hearken to reason, and are much more governed by their feelings than by calculations. While the husband was instructing his wife in the principles of population, she might probably answer that "she did not see why her children should starve, when the squire's lady, or the parson's lady kept half a dozen lap-dogs, and that it was but the other day, that being at the hall, or the parsonage-house, she heard Miss declare that not one of the brood that were just littered should be drowned—It was *so inhuman* to kill the poor little things—Surely the children of the poor are as good as puppy-dogs! Was it not a week ago that the rector had a new pack of terriers sent down, and did I not hear the squire swear a tremendous oath, that he would have Mr. Such-a-one's fine hunter, if it cost him a hundred guineas? Half that sum would save us from ruin."—After this curtain-lecture, I conceive that the husband might begin to doubt the force of the demonstrations he had read and heard, and the next time his clerical monitor came, might pluck up courage to question the matter with him; and as we of the male sex, though dull of apprehension, are not slow at taking a hint, and can draw tough inferences from it, it is not impossible but the parson might be *gravelled*. In consequence of these accidents happening more than once, it would be buzzed about that the laws of God and nature, on which so many families had been doomed to starve, were not so clear as had been pretended. This would soon get wind among the mob: and at the next grand procession of the Penitents of famine, headed by Mr. Malthus in person, some discontented man of talents, who could not bear the distresses of others with the fortitude of a man and the resignation of a Christian, might undertake to question

Mr. Malthus, whether the laws of nature or of God, to which he had piously sacrificed so many victims, signified any thing more than the limited extent of the earth, and the natural impossibility of providing for more than a limited number of human beings; and whether those laws could be justly put in force, to the very letter, while the actual produce of the earth, by being better husbanded, or more equally distributed, or given to men and not to beasts, might maintain in comfort double the number that actually existed, and who, not daring to demand a *fair* proportion of the produce of their labour, humbly crave charity, and are refused out of regard to the interests of justice and humanity. Our philosopher, at this critical juncture not being able to bring into the compass of a few words all the history, metaphysics, morality, and divinity, or all the intricacies, subtleties, and callous equivocations contained in his quarto volume, might hesitate and be confounded—his own feelings and prejudices might add to his perplexity—his interrogator might persist in his question—the mob might become impatient for an answer, and not finding one to their minds, might proceed to extremities. Our unfortunate Essayist (who by that time would have become a bishop) might be ordered to the lamp-post, and his book committed to the flames;—I tremble to think of what would follow:—the poor-laws would be again renewed, and the poor no longer doomed to starve by the laws of God and nature! Some such, I apprehend, might be the consequences of attempting to enforce the abolition of the poor-laws, the extinction of private charity, and of instructing the poor in their metaphysical rights."

QUERIES RELATING TO THE ESSAY ON POPULATION.

QUERY 1. Whether the real source of Mr. Malthus's Essay is not to be found in a work published in the year 1761, entitled, "Various Prospects of Mankind," by a Scotchman of the name of Wallace? Or whether this writer has not both stated the principle of the disproportion between the unlimited power of increase in population, and the limited power of increase in the means of subsistence, which principle is the corner-stone of the Essay; and whether he has not drawn the very same *inference* from it that Mr. Malthus has done, *viz.* that vice and misery are necessary to keep population down to the level of the means of subsistence?

2. Whether the chapter in Wallace, written expressly to prove these two points (or in other words, to shew that the principle of population is necessarily incompatible with any great degree of improvement in government or morals) does not completely anticipate Mr. Malthus's work, both in its principle and its conclusion?

3. Whether the idea of an arithmetical and geometrical series by which Mr. Malthus has been thought to have furnished the precise rule or *calculus* of the disproportion between food and population, is not, strictly speaking, inapplicable to the subject; inasmuch as in new and lately occupied countries, the quantity of food may be made to increase nearly in the same proportion as population, and in all old and well cultivated countries must be stationary, or nearly so? Whether, therefore, this mode of viewing the subject has not tended as much to embarrass as to illustrate the question, and to divert the mind from the real source of the only necessary distinction between food and population, namely, the want of sufficient room for the former to grow in; a grain of corn, as long as it has room to increase and multiply, in fact propagating its species much faster even than a man?

4. Whether the argument borrowed from Wallace, and constituting the chief scope and tenor of the first edition of the Essay, which professed to overturn all schemes of human perfectibility and Utopian forms of government from the sole principle of population, does not involve a plain contradiction;—both these authors, first of all, supposing or taking for granted a state of society in which the most perfect order, wisdom, virtue, and hap-

piness shall prevail, and then endeavouring to shew that all these advantages would only hasten their own ruin, and end in famine, confusion, and unexampled wretchedness, in consequence of taking away the only possible checks to population, *vice* and *misery*? Whether this objection does not suppose mankind in a state of the most perfect reason, to be utterly blind to the consequences of the unrestrained indulgence of their appetites, and with the most perfect wisdom and virtue regulating all their actions, not to have the slightest command over their animal passions? There is nothing in any of the visionary schemes of human perfection so idle as this objection brought against them, which has no more to do with the reasonings of Godwin, Condorcet, &c. (against which Mr. Malthus's first Essay was directed) than with the prophecies of the Millennium!

5. Whether, in order to give some colour of plausibility to his argument, and to prove that the highest conceivable degree of wisdom and virtue could be of no avail in keeping down the principle of population, Mr. Malthus did not at first set out with representing this principle, to wit, the impulse to propagate the species, as a law of the same order and cogency as that of satisfying the cravings of hunger; so that reason having no power over it, vice and misery must be the necessary consequences, and only possible checks to population?

6. Whether this original view of the subject did not unavoidably lead to the most extravagant conclusions, not only by representing the total removal of all vice and misery as the greatest evil that could happen to the world, but (what is of more consequence than this speculative paradox) by throwing a suspicion and a stigma on all subordinate improvements or plans of reform, as so many clauses or sections of the same general principle? Whether the quantity of vice and misery necessary to keep population down to the level of the means of subsistence, being left quite undetermined by the author, the old barriers between vice and virtue, good and evil, were not broken down, and a perfect latitude of choice allowed between forms of government and modes of so-

ciety, according to the temper of the times, or the taste of individuals; only that vice and misery being always the *safe side*, the presumption would naturally be in favour of the most barbarous, ignorant, enslaved, and profligate? Whether the stumbling-block thus thrown in the way of those who aimed at any amendment in social institutions, does not obviously account for the alarm and opposition which Mr. Malthus's work excited on the one hand, and for the cordiality and triumph with which it was hailed on the other?

7. Whether this view of the question, which is all in which the Essay differs fundamentally from the received and less startling notions on the subject, is not palpably, and by the author's subsequent confession, false, sophistical, and unfounded?

8. Whether the additional principle of *moral restraint*, inserted in the second and following editions of the Essay as one effectual, and as the only desirable means of checking population, does not at once overturn all the paradoxical conclusions of the author respecting the state of man in society, and whether nearly all these conclusions do not still stand in Mr. Malthus's work as they originally stood, as false in fact as they are inconsistent in reasoning? Whether, indeed, it was likely, that Mr. Malthus would give up the sweeping conclusions of his first Essay, the fruits of his industry and the pledges of his success, without great reluctance; or in such a manner as not to leave the general plan of his work full of contradictions and almost unintelligible?

9. Whether, for example, in treating of the durability of a perfect form of government, Mr. Malthus has not "sicklied over the subject with the same pale and jaundiced cast of thought," by supposing vice and misery to be the only effectual checks to population; and in his tenacity on this his old and favourite doctrine, whether he has not formally challenged his opponents to point out any other, "except indeed" (he adds, recollecting himself) "moral restraint," which however he considers as of no effect at all?

10. Whether, consistently with this verbal acknowledgement

and virtual rejection of the influence of moral causes, the general tendency of Mr. M.'s system is not to represent the actual state of man in society as nothing better than a blind struggle between vice, misery, and the principle of population, the effects of which are just as mechanical as the ebbing and flowing of the tide, and to bury all other principles, all knowledge, or virtue, or liberty, under a heap of misapplied facts?

11. Whether, instead of accounting for the different degrees of happiness, plenty, populousness, &c. in different countries, or in the same country at different periods, from good or bad government, from the vicissitudes of manners, civilization, and knowledge, according to the common prejudice, Mr. Malthus does not expressly and repeatedly declare that political institutions are but as the dust in the balance compared with the inevitable consequences of the principle of population; and whether he does not treat with the utmost contempt all those, who not being in the secret of "the grinding law of necessity," had before his time superficially concluded that moral, political, religious, and other positive causes were of considerable weight in determining the happiness or misery of mankind? It were to be wished that the author, instead of tampering with his subject, and alternately holding out concessions, and then recalling them, had made one bold and honest effort to get rid of the bewildering effects of his original system, by affording his readers some clue to determine, both in what manner and to what extent other causes, independent of the principle of population, actually combine with that principle (no longer pretended to be absolute and uncontroulable) to vary the face of nature and society, under the same general law, and had not left this most important *desideratum* in his work, to be apocryphally supplied by the ingenuity and zeal of his apologists?

12. Whether Mr. Malthus does not uniformly discourage every plan for extending the limits of population, and consequently the sphere of human enjoyment, either by cultivating new tracts of soil, or improving the old ones, by repeating on all occasions

the same stale, senseless objection, that, *after all*, the principle of population will press as much as ever on the means of subsistence; or in other words, that though the means of subsistence and comfort will be increased, there will be a proportionable increase in the number of those who are to partake of it? Or whether Mr. Malthus's panic fear on this subject has not subsided into an equally unphilosophical indifference?

13. Whether the principle of moral restraint, formally recognized in Mr. Malthus's latter writings, and in reality turning all his paradoxes into mere impertinence, does not remain a dead letter, which he never calls into action, except for the single purpose of torturing the poor under pretence of reforming their morals?

14. Whether the avowed basis of the author's system on the poor-laws, is not the following:—that by the laws of God and nature, the rich have a right to starve the poor whenever they (the poor) cannot maintain themselves; and whether the deliberate sophistry by which this right is attempted to be made out, is not as gross an insult on the understanding as on the feelings of the public? Or whether this reasoning does not consist in a trite truism and a wilful contradiction; the truism being, that whenever the earth cannot maintain all its inhabitants, that then, by the laws of God and nature, or the physical constitution of things, some of them must perish; and the contradiction being, that the right of the rich to withhold a morsel of bread from the poor, while they themselves roll in abundance, is a law of God and nature, founded on the same physical necessity or absolute deficiency in the means of subsistence?

15. Whether the commentators on the Essay have not fallen into the same unwarrantable mode of reasoning, by confounding the real funds for the maintenance of labour, *i. e.* the actual produce of the soil, with the scanty pittance allowed out of it for the maintenance of the labourer (after the demands of luxury and idleness are satisfied) by the positive, varying laws of every country, or by the caprice of individuals?

16. Whether these two things are not fundamentally distinct themselves, and ought not to be kept so, in a question of su importance, as the right of the rich to starve the poor by syste

17. Whether Mr. Malthus has not been too much disposed consider the rich as a sort of Gods upon earth, who were mer employed in distributing the goods of nature and fortune am the poor, who themselves neither ate nor drank, "neither mar nor were given in marriage;" and consequently were altog unconcerned in the limited extent of the means of subsisten and the unlimited increase of population?

18. Lastly, whether the whole of the reverend author's nagement of the principle of population and of the necessity moral restraint, does not seem to have been copied from prudent Friar's advice in Chaucer?

> "Beware therefore with lordes for to play,
> Singeth Placebo:—
> To a poor man men should his vices tell,
> But not to a lord, though he should go to hell."

THE END.

J. M'Creery, Printer,
Black-Horse-Court, London.

Lightning Source UK Ltd.
Milton Keynes UK
UKHW02f2231110618
324081UK00012B/882/P